Economics of Nuclear Power

This book is a unique introduction to the economics and economic uncertainties of nuclear electricity generation. It examines the complex relationships among the financial, operational and regulatory cost drivers of nuclear power. It does so as a research monograph and as a textbook, by modelling and explaining one of the world's most opaque industries using empirical microeconomics, statistics and cost engineering.

Economics of Nuclear Power examines the costs and cost uncertainties of some of nuclear power's controversial externalities (such as managing used nuclear fuel and potential accidents), and compares these with the costly and uncertain externalities of carbon-based generators (natural gas and coal). With around 100 tables and figures, this book details nuclear power production with an international perspective. It also includes an overview of the past 70 years of international nuclear power developments.

This book is essential reading for students, scholars and professionals interested in energy economics, energy policy and nuclear technology.

Geoffrey Rothwell was a Senior Lecturer (1986–2013) in the Department of Economics, Stanford University, Stanford, California, USA.

Economics of Nuclear Power

Geoffrey Rothwell

Routledge
Taylor & Francis Group
LONDON AND NEW YORK

First published 2016
by Routledge
2 Park Square, Milton Park, Abingdon, Oxon OX14 4RN

and by Routledge
711 Third Avenue, New York, NY 10017

Routledge is an imprint of the Taylor & Francis Group, an informa business

British Library Cataloguing in Publication Data
A catalogue record for this book is available from the British Library

Library of Congress Cataloging in Publication Data
Rothwell, Geoffrey S., author.
Economics of nuclear power / Geoffrey Rothwell.
Includes bibliographical references and index.
1. Nuclear industry. 2. Nuclear energy–Economic aspects. I. Title.
HD9698.A2R68 2015
333.792'4–dc23
2015025361

ISBN: 978-1-138-85840-4 (hbk)
ISBN: 978-1-138-85841-1 (pbk)
ISBN: 978-1-315-71803-3 (ebk)

Typeset in Bembo
by Sunrise Setting Ltd, Paignton, UK

To my father, Michael Olin Rothwell, who, in October 1963, dragged his family to Richland, WA, the residential community for the Hanford Atomic Reservation, to represent Bechtel Power as a prime contractor in the construction of the Fast Flux Test Facility (FFTF), enabling his eldest son to graduate from a high school that had an atomic bomb and mushroom cloud as its mascot

Contents

Figures

Tables

Foreword

Given the increasingly problematic impacts on the climate from burning fossil fuels to power the industrial and industrialising world's economies, the competitiveness of alternative, 'low-carbon' energy technologies – in particular, electricity-generating technologies – has become one of the focal points in current climate policy debates. To develop a rational policy toward deploying such alternatives, we all need access to, and there must be transparency in, computing the costs of energy inputs and the prices of energy outputs, for example the levelised cost of electricity (LCOE), as discussed in the University of Chicago's 2004 report, *The Economic Future of Nuclear Power*.

Yet the sobering fact is that gaining access to reliable cost estimates is extremely challenging. In part, this is because the details on how costs are computed are not generally publicly available; they are hidden in proprietary reports. This makes judging claims of the competitiveness of various low-carbon energy alternatives difficult: is there enough information on which to base rational choices to guide the development of energy policy and energy markets to socially optimal outcomes?

Why is this so? For widely deployed technologies – such as fossil-fuel electricity generators – one can usually point to the already-existing production infrastructure. Because these technologies have largely embodied their respective learning curves, significant changes are unlikely in the construction and operating costs that make up their LCOE. The primary remaining uncertainty is the cost of fuel. For example, in the absence of carbon emission pricing, the long-run price volatility of natural gas is the driving factor in forecasting the LCOE for combined-cycle (natural) gas turbine (CCGT) power plants.

For energy technologies that are still incorporating their respective learning curves – especially those of which the cost structure depends critically on technology developments (such as electricity generation using solar-powered technologies) or on uncertain future regulatory constraints (such as carbon-based fuel and nuclear energy technologies) – reliable cost estimates are far more difficult to compute.

Further, their costs depend crucially on a variety of assumptions that might be difficult to justify with precision and are often not made explicit in their analyses. For example, the future competitiveness of electricity production by CCGTs will depend critically on carbon emissions policies, via regulation (for example caps on total emissions) or with 'carbon pricing' (for example with 'carbon taxes', or 'cap-and-trade' arrangements).

In addition, there are uncertainties associated with electricity-generating technologies that are 'intermittent', such as 'variable renewables'. These cannot be called upon at specific times to provide power because their production is subject to unpredictable fluctuations. It remains a matter of policy debate how the costs of integrating variable renewables into electricity distribution grids should be allocated, and therefore who should pay these 'system costs' and how they might be incorporated into the relevant LCOE.

Assessment of the costs associated with nuclear power suffers from similar difficulties. Yet there are additional difficulties that are unique to assessing new nuclear power. New nuclear power costs associated with the nuclear regulatory regime have been driven by difficult-to-predict changes in regulatory demands. This issue has been recently illustrated by the imposition of new US Nuclear Regulatory Commission (US NRC) requirements following the 'lessons learned' from the Fukushima-Daiichi disaster. Furthermore, as new reactor technologies are developed and reach commercialisation – such as the so-called Generation III and III+ reactor designs – nuclear power is experiencing renewed learning after the decline in supply chain experience. This relates to the fact that the build rate of nuclear reactors over the past few decades has been low in North America and Europe; as a consequence, the requisite highly trained workforce for building reactors is no longer in place. This is a situation that leads to considerable risks in construction cost estimates – as the French nuclear power industry, led by Areva, has learned by direct experience in its efforts to build nuclear reactors in Finland and with EDF in France.

Further, there is uncertainty associated with the manufacture of some unique nuclear power plant (NPP) components, such as the large pressure vessels required to house the nuclear reactor core. These pressure vessels can be manufactured by only a small number of large industrial firms with limited production capacity – resulting in potential construction bottlenecks (and associated increases in cost and construction lead times). These uncertainties feed another cost uncertainty for new nuclear: the risk premium on the cost of capital required by the financial industry. These impacts are complex to analyse. In summary, calculating a reasonable LCOE for nuclear power is difficult.

Given this context, those of us with an interest in the competitive posture of the various energy technologies hunger for definitive expositions on how costs are calculated. In this context, the present book offers a much-needed guide on how to examine the economics of one of the competing 'low-carbon' energy alternatives: nuclear power. Dr Geoffrey Rothwell is one of the few reputable economists who have delved into the minutia of estimating costs (and estimation error) for NPPs.

What has emerged is a book that provides the details for which the energy analysts and energy decision maker communities have been looking. When reading, keep in mind the following questions.

- Why is 'new nuclear' in North America and Europe so expensive when compared to other energy technologies and to nuclear power in Asia?
- Why is the 'nuclear renaissance' in Asia?
- What are the cost implications of our current nuclear safety and environmental regulatory regimes and financial rating analysts?

As a physicist, I cannot resist mentioning the frustration that I regularly experience when looking at cost calculations: why is there never discussion of estimate error? Anyone looking for error bars in currently available energy cost calculations will rarely succeed in finding them. Here, you will encounter probabilistic cost estimates everywhere! Of course, given my earlier comments, one should not expect precision: forecasting precision is simply not possible. Nevertheless, it is at least useful to know whether cost estimates are good to one or two significant digits – and it is furthermore useful to appreciate the sources of uncertainties. It should be clear that if one sees cost estimates on academic, government, or other websites that show costs to four significant digits, these need to be regarded with considerable scepticism.

I highly recommend this book as a continuation of the economic analysis done at the University of Chicago a decade ago, *The Economic Future of Nuclear Power*, which would have been unlikely had physicists not created the first controlled nuclear chain reaction at the University of Chicago seven decades ago.

Professor Robert Rosner, USA
University of Chicago, Chicago, IL
29 May 2015

Preface

This book was originally written as *The Economics of Future Nuclear Power: Update of the 2004 University of Chicago's 'The Economic Future of Nuclear Power'* (March 2011), for the Energy Policy Institute at Chicago, Harris School of Public Policy, University of Chicago, under ANL Contract #0F–34781, with funding from the US Department of Energy (US DOE). It therefore takes its structure from that report. The first two chapters provide background information to readers who are not familiar with the last 70 years of international nuclear power developments, or the changes in the nuclear power industry in the twenty-first century. Chapters 3 and 4 develop a levelised cost model of future nuclear power. The appendices to each extend and complement the chapters. Chapter 5 applies these techniques to model natural gas and coal-fired electricity-generating alternatives to simulate (using Monte Carlo techniques) electricity costs with reasonable probability densities of the cost drivers. (About 50% of this book was written by March 2011, Chapters 1–4 were completed by February 2013, when I retired from Stanford, and the remaining 20% was completed on 'free' weekends for two years beginning May 2013.)

I have written this book for four audiences:

1 nuclear engineers and nuclear engineering students interested in understanding the economics and finance of nuclear power plants (NPPs);
2 economists and economics students interested in nuclear power, electricity, or energy modelling;
3 policymakers and their staffs, particularly in energy agencies, departments and ministries; and
4 the public, curious about nuclear power costs and markets.

Therefore some economists might think the discussion here too simplistic or that the data analysis lacks degrees of freedom, while some decision makers might think it is too complex, given the number of equations. I hope that members of the nuclear community, broadly speaking (including mathematically oriented proponents and opponents), think it just right. The purpose is to let readers know that energy cost estimation – in particular, electricity-generating cost estimation – does not yield a point value, but a probability distribution.

Hence I discuss probability densities and how economists suggest decision makers should respond to uncertainty in making choices among alternative generating technologies. Because the focus is on modelling error in estimation, the discussion does not attempt to make the model more 'precise' than other models (for example by introducing complicated formulas to address second- and third-order concerns). In fact, I attempt to simplify cost models where appropriate to make them more transparent, given the complications introduced by probability functions.

In the cost engineering literature on which electricity cost estimation has relied since the 1930s (at least in the United States, with the establishment of electricity rate regulation), uncertainty in cost estimation is incorporated by means of including a contingency on the estimate of the *construction cost* of power plants. Under electricity rate regulation, much of the risk in the cost of electricity was passed to the customer with the supervision of the rate regulator. At the same time, new generating technologies became cheaper, with ever-larger power plants taking advantage of scale economies. Under this arrangement, the electric utility industry focused on the 'levelised cost of electricity' (LCOE) – that is, the cost that would equate the present value of generating costs with the present value of revenues, while paying off the bankers and yielding a reasonable rate of return to the equity investors, including on funds provided by the owner-operator. Hence, for more than 50 years, cost engineers focused on levelised cost as the single metric with which to compare generating costs. (No contingency was added to levelised cost itself; only to plant construction costs.)

After the increase in the cost of fuels following the Organization of Petroleum Exporting Countries (OPEC) oil embargo of late 1972, increases in the cost of generation resulting from environmental regulation, and the exhaustion of scale economies in relatively small electricity systems, cost uncertainty became a concern for customers, utilities, regulators and politicians. New regulations were targeted towards giving electric utilities incentives to control costs. However, with ever-rising rates, economists proposed electricity markets to impose cost discipline, but with mixed success and an increase in the volatility of electricity prices.

The questions of how to address generating cost uncertainties, magnified by unknowns surrounding greenhouse gas emissions and climate change, have become paramount. Adding a contingency to the construction cost of a power plant does not address the issue of input cost uncertainty, particularly with the capital market constraints imposed on relatively small electric utilities (electric utilities have merged in recent years to take advantage of scale economies, but many small utility systems remain) that are facing multibillion-dollar power plant construction costs. In electricity generation, sizes (both of the power plant and of the utility) matter.

This analysis therefore extends the levelised cost methodology by showing (in Chapter 3, Appendix 3A) that commonly accepted cost engineering guidelines regarding contingencies can be interpreted such that (a) the contingency on power plant construction costs is approximately equal to the standard deviation of the cost estimate, and (b) the appropriate cost of capital should reflect the ratio of the size of the generation project to the size of the firm. This provides a method for estimating an appropriate contingency on levelised cost and a rationale for considering total capital construction costs as another metric, with levelised cost, in choosing between electricity-generating options.

This methodology is applied to the choice between advanced light water reactors (ALWRs) – now under construction in Asia, the Russian Federation (Russia), the United States, Europe and the Middle East – and small modular reactors (SMRs) – now under development. In this context, several questions must be addressed, as follows.

1 What are the appropriate contingencies on future NPP construction and levelised costs?
2 What are the appropriate costs of capital for large and small projects, given the size of the electric utilities involved?
3 How can nuclear power compete with historically low natural gas prices when, as the marginal producer, natural gas combined-cycle turbines set the price of electricity in the United States? Natural gas prices are much higher outside of North America: if natural gas can be exported from North America, and its prices rise there, how can consumers, including energy-intensive industries, be protected from rising and increasingly volatile natural gas prices?

Before discussing nuclear technologies and their costs, some definitions are required. Throughout the analysis, costs (the sum of the values of inputs) and prices (as determined by market forces) will be given in real 2013 US dollars. The difference between costs and prices (that is, profit), for example between long-run average costs and spot prices, is a function of the number of consumers and producers in a market (among other influences, such as collusive behaviour by producers, etc.: see the 'industrial organisation' literature in economics). Further, economic profits to induce entry into a market, or economic losses leading to market exit, are incorporated into prices, but not necessarily incorporated into costs. Although 2013 was chosen as a base year, this does not imply that the costs and prices of 2013 were used; costs and prices of later years have been deflated to 2013.

Nominal currency over many years is used in regulation and taxation because regulated tariffs are set, and income taxes are calculated, for particular years. Therefore some cost estimates in the relevant literature are given in nominal currency and some are given in real currency. To adjust nominal currency to real currency (for example in determining what historical costs might be in today's currency), currency of a particular year is inflated (or deflated) to a base year using a price index. The price index used throughout this book is the US Producer Price Index (PPI) (all commodities), which reflects prices facing new nuclear power and nuclear fuel cycle producers. The PPI has been available on a monthly basis since January 1913, from the Federal Reserve Bank (and elsewhere), and is updated within two months. Hence users can inflate mid-2013 dollars in this book to within two months of the current date and can use current exchange rates to convert these updated dollars to any currency.

The price index does not address the issue of cost escalation. Some analysts use a cost escalator to adjust prices to a base year, but this cost escalator is appropriate only for a particular product in a particular industry. For example, there are power plant construction cost escalators to adjust the cost of power plants, but these would be inappropriate for adjusting the cost of fuel. Therefore historic costs and prices are inflated to mid-2013 US dollars, and real escalation is calculated based on changes in real costs or prices over time.

In addition, real and nominal costs of capital must be distinguished. The analysis uses the real weighted average cost of capital (WACC) – a weighted average between inflation-adjusted interest rates on debt and rates of return on equity – to discount costs and revenues to the present, as in the calculation of levelised cost. The difference between real and nominal discount rates is the rate of inflation (not the rate of escalation), where (1 plus the nominal discount rate) is equal to (1 plus the real discount rate) multiplied by (1 plus the inflation rate). Generally, this is approximated as the real rate equal to the nominal rate minus the rate of inflation, ignoring the product of the real rate and the inflation rate. (For example, if the real rate is 5% and the rate of inflation is 3%, the nominal rate is usually given as 8%, ignoring 5% × 3% = 0.15%.) Although ignoring this term does not introduce a large error, large errors can be introduced in the calculation of the real WACC if there are tax differences between interest rates and rates of return on equity (an issue discussed in Chapter 2, Section 2.4, and Chapter 2, Appendix 2A, Section 2A.3). Throughout the text, variables are written in italic; single letters representing (exogenously determined) parameter rates are written in bold (see the 'List of abbreviations' in this frontmatter). (Greek symbols are avoided except where in common usage, such as for the standard deviation, σ, and beta, or β, as used in the capital asset pricing model, or CAPM.)

I hope that you find this book interesting and useful as a reference. I encourage you to email your comments to me. I will attempt to answer your questions, and I will try to incorporate your suggestions and make the proper extensions to omitted topics, such as co-generation and renewables, in the next edition. Should you prefer alternative assumptions to those made here, I hope that the model has been adequately documented to allow you to extend the analysis using your own preferred assumptions. (All analyses, tables and figures have been calculated in a single worksheet.)

Geoffrey Rothwell
geoffrey_rothwell@yahoo.com
Ile-de-France, France
31 May 2015

Acknowledgements

The US Department of Energy (US DOE), through Argonne National Laboratories (ANL) Contract #0F–34781, funded the first draft of this book as an update to the University of Chicago's 2004 report, *The Economic Future of Nuclear Power*. The US DOE (NE and NA) also funded this research through Idaho National Laboratory (INL), Oak Ridge National Laboratory (ORNL) and Pacific Northwest National Laboratory (PNNL). The National Energy Policy Institute (NEPI) funded earlier work, and later and related drafts.

Thanks are due, for their encouragement, references, data and comments, to: Kenneth Arrow, Evelyne Bertel, Brad Carson, Thomas Cochran, Michael Corradini, Matthew Crozat, William D'haeseleer, Charles Forsberg, Francesco Ganda, Robert Graber, Jaejoo Ha, Darwin Hall, T. J. Harrison, Donald Hoffman, Ronald Horst, Hill Huntington, Andrew Kadak, Tony Knowles, Jon Koomey, Manki Lee, François Lévêque, Peter Lyons, William Magwood IV, Warren (Pete) Miller, Ilchong Nam, Roger Noll, William Nuttall, Per Peterson, William Rasin, Victor Reis, Robert Rosner, Alexey Soldatov, James Sweeney, J'Tia Taylor, George Tolley, Robert Vance, John Weyant, Kent Williams and Thomas Wood; seminar participants at the University of Chicago's Harris School of Public Policy, at l'École des Mines (Paris), at l'Autorité de Sûreté Nucléaire (French), at the Korean Advanced Institute of Science and Technology (KAIST), at the Korean Atomic Energy Research Institute (KAERI), at the Korean Development Institute (KDI) and at the Korean Energy Economics Institute (KEEI); the members of the Economic Modelling Working Group (EMWG) of the Generation IV International Forum (GIF) and colleagues at the Nuclear Energy Agency (NEA) of the Organisation for Economic Co-operation and Development (OECD). Thanks are also due for the editorial and publishing assistance of George Lobell, Vanessa Plaister, Jessica Stock and Lisa Thomson. Please pardon me if I have forgotten to mention your contribution.

This book reflects the views of the author and not those of the OECD NEA, Stanford University, University of Chicago, NEPI, US DOE, ANL, INL, ORNL, or PNNL.

Abbreviations, acronyms, parameters and variables

Abbreviations and acronyms

(This list does not include all corporations, country abbreviations, or US state abbreviations.)

2SLS	two-stage least squares
3SLS	three-stage least squares (equivalent to GLS + 2SLS)
AACE	Association for the Advancement of Cost Engineering (now AACE International)
ABARES	Australian Bureau of Agricultural and Resource Economics and Sciences
ABB	merger of Sweden's ASEA and Switzerland's BBC
ABWR	advanced boiling water reactor (General Electric, 1,300–1,350 MW)
ABWRa	amended ABWR (amendment to standard design approved by the US NRC)
ABWR-DCR	ABWR, amended for Design Certification Rule by STP NOC
ACostE	Association of Cost Engineers (UK)
ACPR	advanced Chinese pressurised reactor (1,000 MW)
ACR700	advanced CANDU reactor (Canada, 700 MW)
AEC	US Atomic Energy Commission (precursor of US NRC and US DOE-NE and -NA)
AECL	Atomic Energy Canada Ltd
AEG	Allgemeine Elektrizitäts-Gesellschaft [General Electricity Company] (Germany)
AEO	*Annual Energy Outlook* (US EIA)
AFUDC	allowance for funds used during construction (regulatory allowance for IDC)
AGR	advanced gas-cooled reactor (UK, 550–625 MW)

ALWR	advanced light water reactor (e.g. ABWR and AP1000)
ANL	Argonne National Laboratory
ANSI	American National Standards Institute
AP1000	advanced passive pressurised water reactor (Westinghouse, 1,117 MW)
AP1000a	AP1000 with amended design certification
APR1400	advanced power reactor (Korean, 1,345 MW)
APWR	advanced power reactor (Mitsubishi, 1,700 MW, gross)
ARA	absolute risk aversion
ASE	AtomStroyExport (Russian Federation)
ASEA	Allmänna Svenska Elektriska Aktiebolaget [General Swedish Electric Company] (Sweden)
ASN	L'Autorité de sûreté nucléaire (France)
B&W	Babcock & Wilcox (US)
BNFL	British Nuclear Fuels Ltd
BOP	balance of plant
BRC	Blue Ribbon Commission on America's Nuclear Future
BTU	British thermal unit (equal to 0.948 giga-joules)
BWR	boiling water reactor (e.g. manufactured in the United States by GE and of many sizes)
CANDU	Canadian deuterium uranium reactor (a specific PHWR, various sizes)
CAP1400	Chinese advanced passive reactor (1,400 MW, gross)
CAPM	capital asset pricing model
CARA	constant absolute risk aversion
CBO	Congressional Budget Office (US)
CCGT	combined-cycle gas turbine (burning natural gas, primarily methane, CH_4)
C-E	Combustion Engineering (an NSSS manufacturer, purchased by ABB in 1990)
CEA	Commissariat à l'Énergie Atomique (French, full name changed in 2010)
CEGB	Central Electricity Generating Board (UK, defunct)
CEO	chief executive officer
CFD	contract for difference
CFR	Code of Federal Regulations (US)
CGN	China General Nuclear Power Group
CHF	Swiss franc
CNNC	China National Nuclear Corporation
CNP	Chinese nuclear plant (610 MW)
CNPEC	Chinese Nuclear Power Engineering Company

CO_2	carbon dioxide
COA	code of accounts
COAL	'scrubbed coal new' technology (defined by US EIA)
COL	combined construction and operating licence
COLA	COL application
COMECON	Council for Mutual Economic Assistance (USSR, plus Eastern European countries)
CPR	Chinese pressurised reactor (1,000 MW)
CRF	capital recovery factor (similar to FCR, not taking into account tax effects)
CRRA	constant relative risk aversion
CSS	Chicago spreadsheet
CTBT	Comprehensive Nuclear Test Ban Treaty
CWIP	construction work in progress (a regulatory compensation for IDC)
D	deuterium (an element like hydrogen, but with twice the mass)
D&D	decontamination and dismantlement
DAE	Department of Atomic Energy (India)
DCA	design certification application (UK)
DCF	discounted cash flow (analysis)
DOE	Department of Energy (US)
DOJ	Department of Justice (US)
DPRK	Democratic People's Republic of Korea (also known as 'North Korea')
EBR	experimental fast breeder reactor (at INL)
ECP	electricity capacity planning
EDF	Electricité de France (now simply 'EDF')
EEDB	Energy Economic Database
EIA	Energy Information Administration (US)
EIS	environmental impact statement
EMG	Evaluation Methodology Group (of Gen IV Roadmap Committee)
EMWG	Economic Modelling Working Group (of GIF)
E.ON	German investor-owned electric utility (name derived from Greek *aeon*, meaning 'eternity')
EPA	Environmental Protection Agency (US)
EPC	engineering, procurement and construction (contract)
EPR	European pressurised reactor (French, 1,630 MW); known as the evolutionary power reactor in the United States
EPRI	Electric Power Research Institute (Palo Alto, CA)
ERCOT	Electricity Reliability Council of Texas (now TRE)

ESBWR	economic simplified boiling water reactor (GE-Hitachi, 1,520 MW)
ESP	early site permit (issued by the US NRC)
EUCG	(formerly) Electric Utility Cost Group
EUI	European University Institute
Eurodif	European Diffusion Enrichment Facility (France, George Besse I)
FBR	fast breeder reactor; fast burner reactor (both types of LMR)
FEPC	Federation of Electric Power Companies (Japan)
FERC	Federal Energy Regulatory Commission (US)
FFTF	Fast Flux Test Facility (Richland, WA)
FOAK	first-of-a-kind (costs)
FPL	Florida Power and Light
FSU	Former Soviet Union
G&A	general and administrative expenses
GAO	General Accounting Office (US)
GBM	geometric Brownian motion
GCR	gas-cooled reactor
GDA	generic design assessment (UK)
GDF Suez	Gaz de France with Compagnie de Suez (operates reactors in Belgium)
GE	General Electric (an NSSS manufacturer, now aligned with Hitachi)
Gen IV	Generation IV (advanced reactors for future demonstration and deployment)
GFR	gas-cooled fast reactor (a Gen IV reactor)
GIF	Gen IV International Forum (coordinator of R&D on Gen IV reactors)
GLS	generalised least squares
GW	gigawatt of electric capacity (equal to 1,000 MW, or 1,000,000 kW)
GWd	gigawatt-days (per tonne of heavy metal, e.g. uranium, MOX, etc.)
GWh	gigawatt-hour (1,000 times MWh)
GWY	gigawatt-year (365.25 times GWd)
HEC	(École des) Hautes Études Commerciales
HEU	highly enriched uranium
HI-SMUR 160	Holtec's 160 MW inherently safe modular underground reactor
HSE	Health and Safety Executive (UK)
HTGR	high temperature gas reactor
HWGCR	heavy water moderated, gas-cooled reactor
HWLWR	heavy water moderated, boiling light water cooled reactor

HWR	heavy water reactor
I&C	instrumentation and control (system)
IAEA	International Atomic Energy Agency
IDC	interest during construction
IEA	International Energy Agency
IEEE	Institute of Electrical and Electronics Engineers
INL	Idaho National Laboratory
IRS	Internal Revenue Service (US)
ISFSI	interim spent fuel storage installation
ITC	investment tax credit
JAEC	Japanese Atomic Energy Commission
KA-CARE	King Abdullah City for Atomic and Renewable Energy
KAERI	Korean Atomic Energy Research Institute
KEPCO	Korea Electric Power Company
kgHM	kilogram of heavy metal (including uranium oxide)
kg-SWU	kilogram of SWU (in enriching uranium)
kgU	kilogram of uranium
KHI	Korean Heavy Industries Ltd
KHNP	Korean Hydro and Nuclear Power Company
kW	kilowatt (electric)
kWh	kilowatt hour
KWU	Kraftwerk Union (German)
LCOE	levelised cost of electricity (or energy)
LEU	low enriched uranium (with less than 20% enrichment)
LFR	lead-cooled fast reactor (a Gen IV liquid-metal fast reactor)
LGP	loan guarantee programme
LMGMR	liquid-metal cooled and graphite-moderated reactor (a type of LMR)
LMR	liquid-metal (fast) reactor
LRAC	long-run average cost (equal to levelised cost in microeconomics)
LT	lead time (see variable *lt*)
LWGR	light water cooled, graphite moderated reactor
LWR	light water reactor (e.g. BWR, PWR and VVER)
MACRS	modified accelerated cost recovery system
Magnox	magnesium-clad natural uranium oxide
MBTU	million BTUs
MDC	maximum dependable capacity
MEAG	Municipal Electric Authority of Georgia
MES	minimum efficient scale
MFFF	MOX fuel fabrication facility
MHR	modular helium reactor
MIT	Massachusetts Institute of Technology (Cambridge, MA)

MLE	maximum likelihood estimation
MOU	memorandum of understanding
MOX	mixed oxide (uranium oxide plus plutonium oxide) fuel
MSR	molten salt reactor (a Gen IV molten fluoride salt fast reactor)
MT	metric tonne
MTCR	Missile Technology Control Regime
MTHM	metric tonnes of heavy metal (including irradiated uranium oxide)
MW	megawatt (electric), also MWe
MWh	megawatt-hour (i.e. 1,000 kWh)
MWth	megawatt (thermal)
NA	not applicable; not available
NARUC	National Association of Regulatory Utility Commissioners (US)
NBER	National Bureau of Economic Research (US)
NEA	Nuclear Energy Agency (OECD)
NECDB	Nuclear Energy Cost Database
NEI	Nuclear Energy Institute (Washington, DC)
NEMS	National Energy Modelling System (US EIA)
NEPA	National Environmental Policy Act of 1969 (US)
NEPI	National Energy Policy Institute (US)
NIID	Nuclear Integrated Information Database
NOAK	nth-of-a-kind
NOC	nuclear operating company
NP2010	Nuclear Power 2010 (US DOE programme)
NPD	nuclear power demonstration (a Canadian HWR)
NPP	nuclear power plant
NPT	Treaty on the Non-Proliferation of Nuclear Weapons, or Non-Proliferation Treaty
NPV	net present value
NRC	Nuclear Regulatory Commission (US)
NSSS	nuclear steam supply system
NUREG	US NRC Regulation
NWPA	US Nuclear Waste Policy Act of 1982 (with amendments)
NYSE	New York Stock Exchange
O&M	operations and maintenance
OC	overnight cost (see variable *OC*)
OCMR	organic cooled and moderated reactor
OCRWM	Office of Civilian Radioactive Waste Management (US DOE)
OECD	Organisation for Economic Co-operation and Development
OLS	ordinary least squares

ONR	Office of Nuclear Regulation (UK)
OPEC	Organization of Petroleum Exporting Countries
ORNL	Oak Ridge National Laboratory
PAA	Price–Anderson Nuclear Industries Indemnity Act (US)
PG&E	Pacific Gas & Electric (owner of Diablo Canyon NPP)
PGE EJ1	Polska Grupa Energetyczna SA, Nuclear Station 1 (Poland)
PHWR	pressurised heavy water reactor
PJM	Pennsylvania, New Jersey, Maryland electricity market
PNNL	Pacific Northwest National Laboratory
PPI	Producer Price Index
PPL	Pennsylvania Power and Light (formerly PP&L)
PRIS	Power Reactor Information System (IAEA)
PSEG	Public Service Enterprise Group (based in Newark, NJ)
PTC	production tax credit
Pu	plutonium
PUREX	plutonium-uranium extraction (a used nuclear fuel reprocessing technology)
PWR	pressurised water reactor
R&D	research and development
RBMK	high power channel type reactor (a specific Soviet-designed LWGR, e.g. at Chernobyl; abbreviation from the Russian)
RICE	regional integrated climate economics model
RP	risk premium
RPV	reactor pressure vessel
RRA	relative risk aversion
RSCAS	Robert Schuman Centre for Advanced Studies (EUI)
SCE&G	South Carolina Electric & Gas (building twin AP1000s at Summer Units 2 and 3)
SCWR	super-critical water reactor (a Gen IV water-moderated, water-cooled reactor)
SD	standard deviation
SEC	Securities and Exchange Commission (US)
SEDS	State Energy Date System (US EIA)
SFR	sodium-cooled fast reactor (a Gen IV fast reactor)
SGHWR	steam-generating, heavy water moderated reactor
SMART	system-integrated modular advanced reactor (a type of PWR)
SMP	Sellafield MOX plant (UK)
SMR	small modular reactor (here, limited to LWR technology)
SMUR	small modular underground reactor (designed by Holtec)

SNF	spent nuclear fuel
SRS	Savannah River site (US)
SSP	standby support programme
STP	South Texas Project
Str8line	straight-line depreciation
SWU	separative work unit (of enrichment)
T&D	transmission and distribution (expenses)
tCO_2	metric tonnes of carbon dioxide
Th	thorium
THORP	Thermal Oxide Reprocessing Plant (at Sellafield in Cumbria, England)
TMI	Three Mile Island (usually refers to accident at Unit 2 on 28 March 1979)
TRE	Texas Reliability Entity
tU	metric tonnes of uranium
tUF_6	metric tonnes of uranium hexafluoride
TVA	Tennessee Valley Authority
U	uranium (usually U_3O_8 or UO_2)
U_3O_8	uranium oxide ('yellowcake')
UAE	United Arab Emirates
UMRO	Uranium Market Research Organization
UNDP	United Nations Development Programme
UNICEF	United Nations Children's Fund
UO_2	uranium dioxide (used to produce nuclear fuel rods)
UOX	uranium oxide
URENCO	Uranium Enrichment Company
USC	US Code
USSR	Union of Soviet Socialist Republics
VHGT	very high temperature gas reactor (a Gen IV HTGR)
VVER	water-moderated, water-cooled electricity reactor (LWR built by the Soviet Union and Russia; abbreviation from the Russian)
WACC	weighted average cost of capital (an average of rates on debt and equity)
WPPSS	Washington Public Power Supply System
WWER	*See* VVER

Parameters and variables

(Variables or parameters are defined in or near the equation number given. All values are in real currency unless labelled as 'nominal'. Definitions of each variable of parameter can be found in, above, or below the equation identified.)

		Equation
$\underline{A}$	annual payment to debt capital, nominal	2A.2.13
A_{MWh}	annual payment to capital per MWh	2A.1.6
a, b, c	parameter estimates (roman font)	(Throughout)
a, *b*, *c*	parameters (italic font)	(Throughout)
AF	availability factor	3.4.3
AH	available hours (to generate electricity)	3.4.3
ARA	absolute risk aversion	3A.2.4
B	burnup rate in thermal MW-days per kg of heavy metal, e.g. kgU	4.2.1
BASE	overnight construction costs without contingency	3.2.1
$\underline{BV_t}$	book value of construction investment through year *t*, nominal	2A.2.4
$\underline{BVD_t}$	book value of nominal debt to nominal total construction investment	2A.2.4
$\underline{BVE_t}$	book value of nominal equity to nominal total construction investment	2A.2.5
c	parameter measuring risk aversion, assuming CARA	3A.2.15
C_{ON}	contingency rate on overnight costs as a percentage mark-up on *OC*	3.2.2
CC	capital construction costs as a function of *CN*, CN_t and CX_t	2A.1.11
CF	capacity factor as the percentage of maximum output	3.4.2
*CF**	capacity factor for the first NOAK plant	3.6.9
$\underline{CFlow}$	cash flow per period, nominal	2A.2.14
CN	contingency on overnight costs, in millions	2A.1.11
CO_{2COAL}	CO_2 in metric tonnes per MWh produced by a COAL unit	5.4.2
CO_{2CCGT}	CO_2 in metric tonnes per MWh produced by a CCGT unit	5.3.2
Corr	correlation (between two random variables)	3A.3.5
Cov	covariance (between two random variables)	3A.3.4

		Equation
CRF	capital recovery factor	2A.1.4
CU	capacity utilisation rate	3.4.7
cx_t	construction expenditure as a percentage of overnight costs in period t	2A.2.2
CX_t	construction expenditures in period t, in millions	2A.1.11
$\underline{CXD}_t$	construction expenditures in period t financed by debt, nominal	2A.2.4
$\underline{CXE}_t$	construction expenditures in period t financed by equity, nominal	2A.2.5
d	derivative (the first derivative, unless specified)	3A.2.4
d	debt cost-of-capital, real, known as the 'real interest rate'	2.4.1
$\underline{\mathbf{d}}$	debt cost-of-capital, nominal, known as the 'nominal interest rate'	2A.2.3
DCF	discounted cash flow	2A.1.12
dd	rate of return on nuclear decommissioning funds	3.2.4
$\underline{DEP}_t$	depreciation in year t, nominal	2A.2.10
df	degrees of freedom	3A.4.13
DH	derating hours, hours of generation lost for non-technical reasons	3.4.4
DIR	direct construction costs	3.2.1
DIR^+	direct construction costs *plus* indirects on *DIR* *plus* supplemental costs	3.6.1
DIR_{SMR}	direct construction costs for SMRs	3.5.1
dR	debt ratio: debt/(debt + equity)	2.4.1
dT	payback period on debt, default dT = T	2A.2.13
DT	decommissioning period length	2A.1.1
e	equity cost of capital, real	2.4.1
$\underline{\mathbf{e}}$	equity cost of capital, nominal	2A.2.1
e	'residual' in an OLS model	3A.4.12
E	electricity produced, e.g. per year, in millions of MWh	3.4.1
$E(\tilde{u})$	expectations operator	3A.1.1
$E[W(\tilde{u})]$	expected welfare function	3A.2.2
EAF	equivalent availability factor (similar to energy availability factor)	3.4.4
$\underline{EBIT}$	earnings before interest and taxes per period, nominal	2A.2.10

		Equation
eff	efficiency of converting MWth to MWe	4.2.1
EXP	O&M expenses plus fuel expenses	2A.2.8
expo(b)	exponential density	4.1.3
EXPO(b)	exponential distribution	4.1.4
F	fuel expenses, e.g. per year, in millions	4.2.1
F_{CCGT}	natural gas expenses, annual, CCGT	5.3.2
$F_{\mathrm{CCGT/MWh}}$	cost per MWh of natural gas to generate electricity, CCGT	5.3.2
F_{COAL}	coal expenses, annual, COAL	5.4.2
$F_{\mathrm{COAL/MWh}}$	cost per MWh of coal-fired electricity, COAL	5.4.2
F_{MWh}	fuel expenses per megawatt-hour	2A.1.8
FC	fuel cost in currency per kilogram of heavy metal, e.g. kgU	4.2.2
FE	feed assay index in uranium enrichment equations (see X_{FE})	4.2.6
FH	forced outage hours	3.4.5
FOM_{CCGT}	fixed O&M for CCGT	5.3.1
FOM_{COAL}	fixed O&M for COAL	5.4.1
FR	forced outage rate	3.4.5
FX	fixed overnight costs without indirects	3.6.1
FX^{+}	fixed overnight costs plus indirects for the NOAK plant	3.6.1
FX^{*}_{i}	FOAK fixed capital construction costs for the '*i*th' unit	3.6.4
GWY	gigawatt-years of operating experience	3.6.8
H	hardware in LEU and MOX fuel fabrication	(Table 4A.6)
HH	hours generator in operation	3.4.9
HR	heat rate: BTU per kWh (can be adjusted to MBTU per MWh)	5.3.2
$\mathrm{HR}_{\mathrm{CCGT}}$	heat rate for CCGTs	5.3.2
$\mathrm{HR}_{\mathrm{COAL}}$	heat rate for COAL	5.4.2
h, i, j, k	index numbers	(Throughout)
i	inflation rate	2A.2.2
IDC	interest during construction, in millions	3.3.1
idc	interest during construction factor as a percentage mark-up on OC	3.3.8

		Equation
$INDIR$	indirect costs in construction	3.2.1
$\underline{INT}$	interest expenses, e.g. per year, nominal	2A.2.11
itc	investment tax credit factor	2A.2.12
KC	total capital investment cost in EMWG (2007) (see Chapter 3, Section 3.2)	3.2.3
KC_{MOX}	construction cost for a MOX fabrication facility, unadjusted by CF	4A.3.2
KC_{MOX^*}	construction cost for a MOX fabrication facility, adjusted by CF	4A.3.1
kW	kilowatts associated with $VK^+_{/\mathrm{kW}}$	3.6.4
l	learning rate (See l_{cf}, l_{pl}, l_{un}, l_{vc})	(Throughout)
l_{cf}	learning rate on capacity factor (increase) based on experience in GWY	3.6.9
l_{pl}	learning rate in plant construction, cost decline with each doubling	3.6.7
l_{un}	learning rate in unit construction, cost decline with each doubling	3.6.6
l_{vc}	learning rate on variable costs based on experience in GWY	3.6.8
L	labour, number of employees at a nuclear facility, full-time equivalent	4.3.10
L_{MOX}	labour, number of employees at a MOX plant of $SIZE_{\mathrm{MOX}}$	4A.3.3
LC	levelised cost	2A.1.1
$LCOE$	levelised cost of electricity per megawatt-hour	2A.1.12
$\underline{LCOE}$	levelised cost of electricity for equity investors	2A.2.1
LKC	levelised capital construction costs	3.2.4
LL	PAA liability limit	3B.1.4
logn(μ, σ)	Lognormal density function	3A.1.6
logs(*a*, *b*)	logistic density function	3A.1.3
LOGS(*a*, *b*)	logistic distribution function	3A.1.4
loss	potential off-site damages after a NPP accident	3B.1.1
lt	lead time from 'first concrete' to commercial operation	2A.1.1
$\mathrm{lt_F}$	carrying time from fuel fabrication to reactor loading, e.g. 0.25 years	4.2.2

		Equation
lt_S	carrying time from enrichment to reactor loading, e.g. 0.5 years	4.2.2
lt_U	carrying time from uranium purchase to reactor load, e.g. 1 year	4.2.2
m	monthly weighted average cost of capital	3.3.1
M	maintenance expenses per year, *O&M* minus labour expenses	4.3.1
maxv(*a*, *b*)	extreme value density, also **minv**(*a*, *b*) for extreme minimum value	4.1.5
MAXV(*a*, *b*)	extreme value distribution, also **MINV**(*a*, *b*) for extreme minimum value	4.1.6
MW	generating capacity in MW(electric), MW, 'fixed' after construction	4.3.1
MW*	MW for reference power unit	3.6.3
N	number of power production units in a standard configured plant	3.6.2
N_{FOAK}	number of plants in a FOAK set	3.6.6
n(μ, σ)	normal density function with mean μ and variance σ^2	3A.1.1
NU	ratio of kg of natural uranium input to 1 kg of enriched uranium output	4.2.2
O&M	operation and maintenance expenses, annual	4.3.1
$O\&M_f$	fixed O&M costs, annual	2A.1.7
$O\&M_{IN}$	insurance expenses, annual	2A.1.7
$O\&M_{MWh}$	O&M expenses per MWh	2A.1.7
$O\&M_v$	variable O&M costs, annual	2A.1.7
OC	total overnight construction costs, equal to *BASE* plus contingency	3.2.2
om	O&M mark-up on labour cost	4.3.14
$OM_{CCGT/MWh}$	O&M per MWh for CCGT	5.3.1
$OM_{COAL/MWh}$	O&M per MWh for COAL	5.4.1
OWN	owners' costs during construction	3.2.1
$\underline{OY_t}$	operating income, nominal	2A.2.9
P_{CO2}	price of CO_2 per tonne	5.3.2
P_{COAL}	price of coal per MBTU	5.4.2
P_F	price of nuclear fuel by weight, kilograms of uranium, kgU	4.1.1
P_{FAB}	price of converting enriched UF_6 to UO_2 fuel	4.2.2

		Equation
P_{IN}	premium for insurance per MWh to cover damages of an NPP accident	4.3.16
P_L	price of labour: wages and benefits	4.1.1
P_{NGAS}	price of natural gas per MBTU	5.3.2
P_{SWU}	price of an SWU of enriching UF_6	4.2.2
$P_{\text{U}*}$	breakeven price of U_3O_8 such that MOX is competitive	4A.4.1
P_{UF6}	price of uranium oxide plus conversion to hexafluoride, UF_6, per kg	4.2.2
PE	product assay index in uranium enrichment equations (see X_{PE})	4.2.6
PIN	premiums for insurance to cover potential damages of an NPP accident	4.3.16
ptc	production tax credit per MWh	2A.2.12
PV	present value, known, before undertaking a project	3A.2.22
PVC(**e**)	present value of equity construction expenditures	2A.2.6
r	cost of capital, annual, equal to the real WACC, if not specified	2.4.1
$\underline{\mathbf{r}}$	cost of capital, annual, nominal	(Section 2A.3)
R_j	return on asset *j*, nominal	3A.3.4
R^2	a measure of goodness of fit in OLS	3A.4.14
ra	risk aversion parameter	3A.2.24
rb	cost of capital on current obligations, before project construction	3A.2.22
RC	reprocessing costs	4A.4.1
RF	reliability factor	3.4.5
RP	risk premium	3A.2.13
RRA	relative risk aversion	3A.2.8
RSS	residual sum of squares	3A.4.14
$\underline{RV}$	revenues, annual, nominal	2A.2.7
S	scale parameter for cost declines with increases in reactor size	3.5.1
SA	scheduled availability rate	3.4.10
ser	serial economies of production factor	3.5.2
SF	service factor	3.4.10
SH	scheduled outage hours	3.4.6

		Equation
$SIZE_{MOX}$	size in MTHM per year at MOX fabrication plant unadjusted by CF	4A.3.2
$SIZE_{MOX*}$	size in MTHM per year at MOX fabrication plant adjusted by CF	4A.3.1
SUPP	supplementary construction costs, e.g. first reactor fuel core	3.2.1
SWU	SWU required for a specific level of enrichment	4.2.5
t	time subscript	(Throughout)
T	economic life of the project	2A.1.1
$\underline{TAX_t}$	taxes in period *t*, nominal	2A.2.12
TC	total cost, annual, real	4.1.1
TE	tail assay index in uranium enrichment equations (see X_{TE})	4.2.6
tr	tax rate, corporate	2A.2.12
TSS	total sum of squares	3A.4.14
TT	total hours in an average year, equal to 365.25 × 24 hours = 8,766	3.4.1
$\underline{TX}$	total expenses, annual, nominal	2A.2.14
$\tilde{u}_t$, u_t	random shock $\tilde{u}_t$, and residual, u_t	3A.4.12
u_0	the initial value of random variable, e.g., initial wealth	3A.2.10
UP	unpaid premium (implicit) owing to the PAA liability limit	3B.1.4
$V(X_i)$	value function in calculating the optimal tails assay	4.2.6
Var	variance	3A.3.3
VC^*	variable costs of the first NOAK plant, annual	3.6.8
VK	variable overnight costs without indirects	3.6.1
VK^*	variable overnight cost in $/kW for the reference power unit	3.6.3
VK^+	variable overnight costs without indirects	3.6.1
$VK^+_{/kW}$	variable capital construction costs plus indirects in $/kW	3.6.2
VOM_{CCGT}	variable O&M for CCGT	5.3.1
VOM_{COAL}	variable O&M for COAL	5.4.1
W	wealth	3A.3.10
$W(\cdot)$	welfare function for wealth and changes in wealth	3A.2.1

		Equation
W'	first derivative of the welfare function with respect to $\tilde{u}$	3A.2.4
W''	second derivative of the welfare function with respect to $\tilde{u}$	3A.2.4
W'''	third derivative of the welfare function with respect to $\tilde{u}$	3A.2.10
WACC	weighted average cost of capital, real	2.4.1
WASTE	interim used fuel storage, disposal and other effluent costs	4.2.1
x	portion of portfolio invested in one equity	3A.3.6
x, y	generic variables, e.g. Equation (3A.4.6)	(Throughout)
X_{FE}	percentage of U-235 of natural uranium in feed assay	4.2.3
X_{PE}	percentage of U-235 in the enriched uranium product assay	4.2.3
X_{TE}	percentage of U-235 in uranium tails assay	4.2.4
$\underline{Y}_t$	income in year t, nominal	2A.2.12

Greek symbols

		Equation
α, β, γ	used as parameter in OLS estimation, e.g. in the CAPM	3A.4.5
Γ	gamma function	(Section 3.3)
ϵ	'error' in an OLS model	4.3.3
μ	first moment of a distribution, e.g. the mean in a normal distribution	3A.1.1
σ	standard deviation, square root of the variance	3A.1.1
Σ	summation, usually over time, t: Σ_t	(Throughout)
$\Phi(\sigma)$	welfare function of the standard deviation of changes in wealth, $\tilde{u}$	3A.2.13
Ω	wealth or net present value, object of the welfare function: $W(\Omega)$	(Section 3A.2)

1 An introduction to the international nuclear power industry

The future of the nuclear power industry depends on an interrelated combination of technical, economic and political benefits, costs, risks and uncertainties. This book models these costs, risks and uncertainties with microeconomics, econometrics and cost engineering techniques that might be new to the non-economist. It explores an industry that might be unknown to economists and one in which information is sometimes closely guarded because it is either proprietary or classified. The book tries to present all of the best recipes for understanding the costs and uncertainties of the most complex industry in history. It follows the 'empirical microeconomics' methodology of the Department of Economics, Stanford University, as described in *The New York Times* (2015).

This chapter introduces nuclear power technologies and nuclear fuel cycles with a detailed description of uranium markets and country nuclear programmes. Chapter 2 discusses new nuclear power and the regulation of the new nuclear power industry at both the federal and state levels in the United States. Chapter 3 analyses the levelised capital costs of advanced light water reactors (ALWRs) and small modular light water reactors (known simply as 'small modular reactors', or SMRs). Appendix 3A proposes appropriate construction cost contingencies and risk premiums associated with the cost of capital. Appendix 3B examines expected losses from a nuclear power plant (NPP) accident and appropriate insurance premiums to cover such losses. Chapter 4 calculates the levelised cost of electricity (LCOE) of new nuclear by adding fuel, operations and maintenance costs to the levelised capital costs derived in Chapter 3. Appendix 4A explores the cost of recycling used nuclear fuel. Chapter 5 simulates levelised cost probability distributions for new NPPs, as well as for natural gas with combined-cycle gas turbine technology, and emissions-controlled, coal-fired, steam-turbine generating technology. The last chapter shows that, because of the low correlation between the distribution of nuclear power and fossil-fuel costs, a robust (through decades of operation) portfolio of these technologies includes both nuclear power and fossil (such as natural gas) power (for example as renewables are eased into the mix, which is not modelled here). There is no 'literature review' in this book (for such a review, see D'haeseleer, 2013).

Throughout this analysis, the focus is on defining appropriate probability density functions for uncertain variables in calculating LCOEs. Some of the analysis might therefore appear simplistic, because more complex methods for calculating LCOE would lead to intractable probability functions. For example, the distribution of construction expenditures over the time of construction can be done by assuming expenditure percentages in each period, by using an assumed cumulative distribution, or by showing that the assumption of uniform expenditures in each month leads to a close approximation of the interest during construction (IDC). This latter approach allows for the simulation of the construction lead time based on empirical observations. In addition, these probabilities are modelled using publicly available data. Therefore, in the case of estimating the costs of reprocessing used light water reactor (LWR) fuel, there is little available data, leading to a greater reliance on micro-economic theory and cost-engineering techniques. This analysis is meant to be illustrative rather than demonstrative. The results are presented as probability densities and distributions, not as deterministic point estimates. Detailed information is provided so that readers can test their own hypotheses regarding the costs and benefits of new nuclear power.

1.1 Commercial nuclear power reactor technologies

Figure 1.1 presents a generic nuclear power unit with five systems:

- System 1 is the balance of plant (BOP), which supports all other systems;
- System 2 is the nuclear steam supply system (NSSS), which generates steam (or another hot gas);
- System 3 transforms the steam (or other gas) into electric power;
- System 4 transmits the electric power to the transmission grid connection at the 'busbar'; and
- System 5 cools the NSSS.

Figure 1.1 shows the three primary inputs – operation and maintenance (O&M), fresh fuel and coolant – and outputs of a nuclear power unit: megawatt hours (MWh), used fuel and effluents. Operation and maintenance refers to the physical inputs, but is measured as the sum of expenditures to acquire these inputs. (All references to cost per kilowatt hour, or kWh, for example mills or cents per kWh, have been changed to cost per MWh, for example US$/MWh, £/MWh, or €/MWh, because this is now the standard for quoting prices in electricity markets.)

Nuclear power plants can be classified by means of a few characteristics, as in Figure 1.2. First, a reactor has either a 'fast' or 'slow' chain reaction. In fast reactors, energy released in the chain reaction is not slowed by intentionally capturing ('moderating') neutrons. Neutrons can be captured to convert more uranium to more plutonium than moderated reactors (as well as to produce other isotopes); hence these are sometimes known as 'fast breeder reactors'. Fast reactors are also known as 'liquid-metal reactors' (LMRs), because liquid

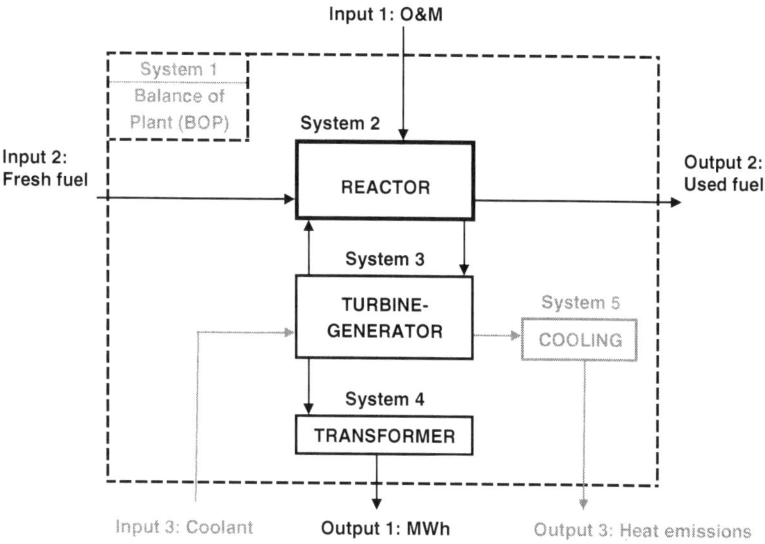

Figure 1.1 Systems diagram of a nuclear power plant.

Source: Author.

metals, such as sodium, are used to cool the reactor and transfer heat. There are several isotopes of plutonium (Pu), from Pu-238 to Pu-244.

Second, thermal reactor technologies (with 'slow' chain reactions) can be characterised along two dimensions: (a) the choice of nuclear reaction moderator, to capture nuclear particles; and (b) the choice of nuclear reactor coolant, to remove heat. To moderate and control the chain reaction, light water (H_2O), heavy water (D_2O, in which deuterium, D, has twice the mass of hydrogen), or graphite (carbon) are used. Coolants are either water (light or heavy) or gas (air, carbon dioxide, or helium). (For compatibility with IAEA, 2015a, two demonstration reactors are included in Figure 1.2: the organic [hydrocarbon] cooled and moderated reactor [OCMR] at Piqua, OH, which operated from 1963 to 1966; and the liquid-metal cooled and graphite-moderated reactor [LMGMR] at Hallam, NE, which operated in 1963 and 1964.)

Third, NPPs can be characterised by whether plants use a direct or an indirect cycle to transfer energy from the nuclear reactor to the turbine generator. The direct approach allows the reactor coolant to boil, changing from a liquid to a gas – that is, from water to steam – driving the turbine. (Hot helium can be used to drive turbines directly, similar to the operation of jet engines, as with some high temperature gas reactors, or HTGRs.) The indirect approach transfers the reactor's energy from a primary coolant circuit to a secondary circuit, through a steam generator, and the steam drives the turbine.

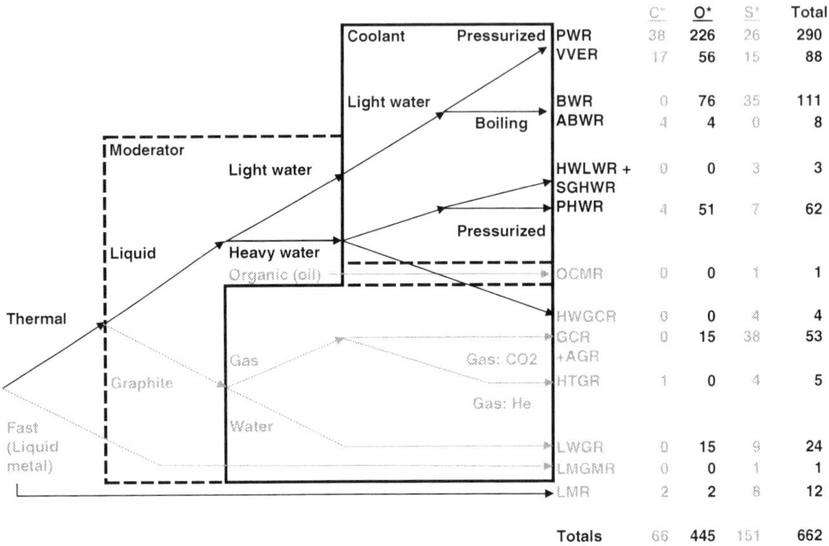

Figure 1.2 Commercial nuclear power reactor technologies, 2015.

* C = under construction; O = in operation; S = shut down (long-term or permanent).

Source: IAEA (2015b).

Fourth, NPPs can be categorised by 'generation':

- Generation I reactors were demonstration reactors that came into commercial operation before 1966;
- Generation II reactors were commercially deployed between 1966 and 1996;
- Generation III reactors have been commercially deployed since 1996, with the construction of the advanced boiling (light) water (moderated and cooled) reactor (ABWR) in Japan; and
- Generation IV reactors, some prototypes of which are under construction, but commercial deployment of these technologies is not expected until after 2030.

Although there have been many experimental reactors, there are only four commercially deployed types of Generation II commercial NPP using thermal reactors:

1 LWRs, including:

   a pressurised (light) water (moderated and cooled) reactors (PWRs) and water-moderated, water-cooled electricity reactors (WWERs, or VVERs from the Russian); and b boiling (light) water (moderated and cooled) reactors (BWRs) and ABWRs, which are considered the first Generation III nuclear power technology – see Chapter 2);

2 heavy water reactors (HWRs), including:

   a pressurised heavy water moderated and cooled reactors (PHWRs);
   b heavy water moderated, boiling light water cooled reactors (HWLWRs);
   c steam-generating (pressurised light water cooled) heavy-water moderated reactors (SGHWRs); and
   d heavy water moderated, gas-cooled reactors (HWGCRs);

3 gas-cooled (graphite moderated) reactors (GCRs), including:

   a the early British and French GCRs;
   b later British advanced GCRs (AGRs); and
   c high temperature gas-cooled (graphite moderated) reactors (HTGRs); and

4 light water cooled, graphite moderated reactors (LWGRs), including the USSR-designed high power channel type reactor (RBMK, from the Russian), for example at Chernobyl.

Many national programmes have foreseen three stages of NPP deployment:

1 GCRs and HWRs, using natural uranium;
2 LWRs and HTGRs, using enriched uranium, or a mixed oxide (uranium oxide and plutonium oxide) fuel, known as MOX (see Chapter 4, Appendix 4A); and
3 LMRs, using enriched uranium, MOX, thorium, or plutonium. (Thorium has several isotopes, from Th-228 to Th-234.)

Until the early 1970s, the GCR had the largest share of the NPP market. However, since the 1970s, the LWR has dominated the international nuclear power industry.

Section 1.4 discusses the history of nuclear power in six regions: the United States; the United Kingdom, with the Commonwealth of Nations; France and Western Europe; the former Soviet Union, with Eastern Europe and Central Asia; Latin America; and East Asia. Each region, except Latin America, has had a dominant technology: LWRs in the United States, the former Soviet Union/Eastern Europe, France, Western Europe and East Asia; GCRs in the United Kingdom; and HWRs in the Commonwealth of Nations. Heavy water reactors have been built in all regions and LMRs have been built in all regions except Latin America.

1.2 The nuclear fuel cycle

There are many ways of fuelling these various reactors. The reactor plus the fuel cycle constitute a 'nuclear energy system'. Figure 1.3 depicts many types of nuclear fuel cycle. The 'front end' involves steps leading to the delivery of nuclear fuel to the reactor: **(1) uranium mining, milling and conversion**; **(2) enrichment**; and **(3) (reconversion and) fuel fabrication**. The 'back end' involves steps after the used fuel is removed from the reactor: **(5) used fuel storage**; **(6) optional reprocessing** (Chapter 4, Appendix 4A discusses the cost of reprocessing and the fabrication of fuel with the resulting reactor-grade plutonium); and **(9) radioactive waste management**. The 'military' sector involves the production and dismantling of nuclear weapons using highly enriched uranium (HEU) or plutonium.

Natural uranium (U) consists of three primary isotopes: 99.275% U-238; 0.711% U-235; and 0.005% U-234. (There are also trace amounts of U-232, U-233, U-236, U-237 and U-239.) Uranium was mined early in the twentieth century as a source of radium, for example for the manufacture of luminous paint. Mining for the production of nuclear weapons started in the 1940s. Since the creation of a commercial market in the late 1960s, uranium exploration and production have been a function of uranium market prices (most uranium is traded in long-term contracts, but these contract prices are not publicly known; only spot-market prices are known). Uranium is primarily extracted through in-situ leaching, open pit and underground mining. Uranium ore is crushed and leached with acids to produce a uranium oxide powder, U_3O_8, known as

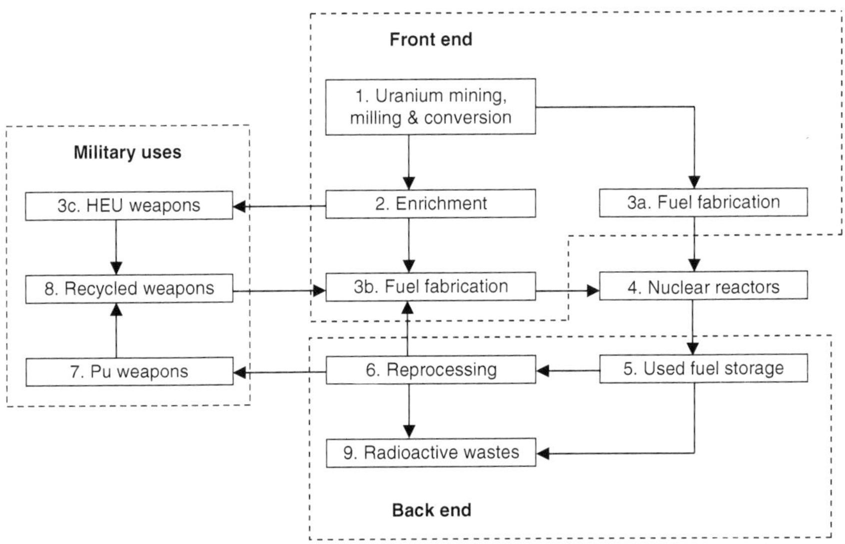

Figure 1.3 Nuclear fuel cycles.

Source: Author.

'yellowcake'. The U_3O_8 is converted into uranium hexafluoride (UF_6, a gas) for **(2) uranium enrichment**. Uranium production declined after the dissolution of the USSR, with lower quantities demanded and HEU being recycled. The Commonwealth of Nations (formerly the 'British Commonwealth') countries of Australia, Canada and Namibia are responsible for 35% of global production, while Kazakhstan produces nearly 37% (and the United States produces only about 3%) (WNA, 2015a). Section 1.3 discusses uranium quantities mined and prices paid since 1948.

Second, natural uranium can be manufactured directly into fuel through **(3a) fuel fabrication** for some reactor technologies, such as the HWR, or natural uranium can be enriched in U-235, by decreasing the percentage of the U-238, as shown in Figure 1.4:

> 171 metric tonnes of uranium (tU), with a 'feed assay' of 0.711% of natural U-235, and
> 100,000 separative work units (SWU), a measure of work per kilogram, yielding
> 152 tonnes of depleted uranium, with a 'tails assay' of 0.3% U-235, and
> 19 tonnes of uranium for fuel, with a 'product assay' of 4.0% U-235.

This is approximately the annual requirement of a 1,000 MW NPP. (Optimal product and tails assays are discussed in Chapter 4, Section 4.2.)

Uranium enrichment has been achieved commercially using two methods – diffusion and centrifuge – with laser enrichment under commercialisation (US NRC, 2014). In diffusion plants, the uranium gas is forced through a series of porous barriers that allow the smaller U-235 to penetrate more easily than the slightly larger U-238. This process requires pumping uranium gas through dozens of barriers for a 1–5% enrichment of nuclear reactor fuel. In centrifuge plants, the uranium gas is spun, with the lighter U-235 separating from the

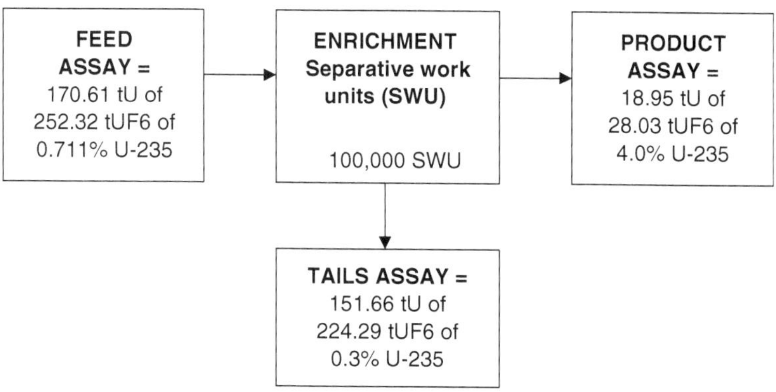

Figure 1.4 Low enriched uranium at 4% U-235 product assay.

Source: Calculated with WISE (2015a).

heavier U-238; uranium isotopes less than U-238 are also concentrated during the enrichment process. Highly enriched uranium can be diverted to the production of **(3c) HEU weapons**, raising proliferation concerns. Section 1.4 discusses the Non-Proliferation Treaty (NPT).

Through the 1970s, the United States dominated the Western enrichment market with its diffusion technology and the USSR monopolised Eastern markets with its diffusion, then centrifuge, technologies. However, with the opening of commercial centrifuge facilities in France, Germany, the Netherlands and the United Kingdom, and the opening of Russian output to international markets, there is no longer a single dominant provider of enrichment services. Figure 1.5 presents a supply curve for the international commercial enrichment market with the exit of the diffusion capacity (Rothwell, 2009). Demand requirements are approximately 51 million SWU per year (WNA, 2015b). Therefore the *marginal* producer has a production cost between US$75/kg-SWU and $84/kg-SWU. (Producers above these values are likely to be subsidised by their host governments for strategic reasons; below $75/kg-SWU, many non-Russian producers are not earning enough revenue to expand capacity.) Enrichment service prices should be lower over the next 50 years than they have been during the last 50 years.

Third, in **(3b) fuel fabrication**, the enriched uranium is converted to a metallic oxide and machined into fuel rods to be inserted into **(4) nuclear reactors**. From the analysis in Rothwell (2010), the fuel fabrication market can be seen to comprise four segments (the capacity amounts change from year to year, so they must be updated annually – for example see WISE, 2015b):

1 suppliers in Kazakhstan, Korea and Russia, with low labour and low (or depreciated) capital costs, with a combined capacity of about 5,400 tU

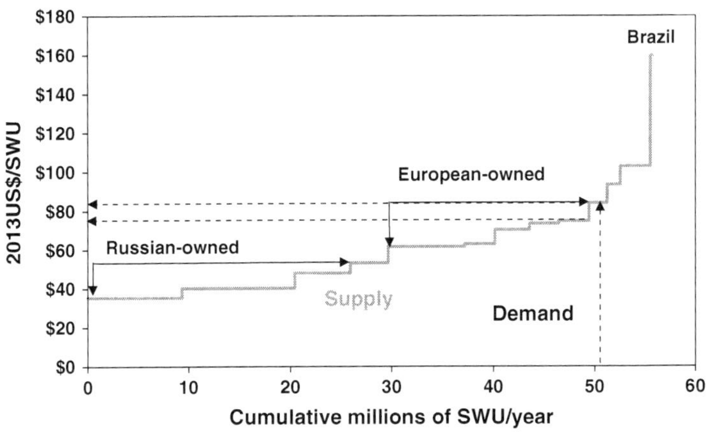

Figure 1.5 Enrichment services market with only centrifuge enrichers.

Source: Adapted and updated from Rothwell (2009), with WNA (2015b).

per year (the term 'Korea' is used in this book to refer to South Korea, or the Republic of Korea; when discussing the Democratic People's Republic of Korea, or DPRK, the term 'North Korea' is used);

2 large suppliers in Europe, Japan and the United States, with high labour and low (or depreciated) capital costs, with a combined capacity of about 8,100 tU per year; and
3 suppliers in the People's Republic of China (PRC, or simply 'China') and countries that do not enjoy scale economies, or which are new entrants, with a combined capacity of about 1250 tU per year for LWRs, for which the central government directly or indirectly subsidises production costs for economic development, energy security, or national security reasons.

The 'back end' of the nuclear fuel cycle includes **(5) used fuel storage**, **(6) reprocessing** (see Chapter 4, Appendix 4a), and **(9) radioactive waste** management and disposal. Because of the high radioactivity of used nuclear fuel and nuclear weapons proliferation concerns with the production of **(7) plutonium weapons**, the back end is the nuclear power industry's most controversial sector. There are two types of nuclear fuel cycle back ends: 'open' and 'closed'. Under the *open* fuel cycle, used fuel is cooled at the NPP, then stored and transported to a **(9) radioactive waste** repository. The United States buries radioactive military waste from military reprocessing in the Waste Isolation Pilot Project (WIPP), New Mexico. The history of Yucca Mountain, its cancellation, the Blue Ribbon Commission's findings and solutions to the 'waste confidence issue' are discussed in Chapter 2, Section 2.1.

A *closed* fuel cycle involves reprocessing used fuel to extract the uranium and plutonium, to be recycled as nuclear fuel (see Chapter 4, Appendix 4A). Although there are several reprocessing technologies, the plutonium-uranium extraction (PUREX) process has been the most successful: used fuel is dissolved in nitric acid and various elements are precipitated in nitrate forms, such as plutonium nitrate. These nitrates are converted to oxides, for example plutonium oxide, or metals, and fabricated into nuclear fuel – known as, MOX. Waste streams are contaminated by non-precipitated elements, yielding mixed radioactive and chemically hazardous waste (for example at Hanford near Richland, WA), included in these activities in the radioactive waste management sector. Current commercial nuclear fuel can be reprocessed only once and then must be disposed of, as in the open fuel cycle.

Finally, since the dissolution of the USSR, both HEU and plutonium weapons have been dismantled. Much of the HEU has been **(8) recycled**. This recycled HEU depressed uranium prices between November 1989 and December 2004.

Because of the importance of uranium in fuelling NPPs, the next section discusses the uranium market after the implementation of the US Atomic Energy Act of 1946 (the 'McMahon Act').

1.3 The uranium market, 1948–2014

Figure 1.6 presents spot prices of uranium (in 2013 US dollars per kilogram of uranium, or US$/kgU) and SWU prices in US$/kg-SWU. There have been five periods in the history of uranium prices, as follows.

- Period 1 began in the 1940s, with purchases by the US Atomic Energy Commission (US AEC).
- Period 2 began in 1968 with private ownership of uranium in the United States, but the US AEC maintaining a monopoly on uranium enrichment services. During this period, new private owners entered the market, with little supply of uranium, driving up its price.
- Period 3 began with the accident at Three Mile Island (TMI), in March 1979, after which NPPs under construction were cancelled and electric utilities left the uranium market. Uranium prices fell almost continuously throughout the period.
- Period 4 began with the end of the cold war, symbolically marked by the fall of the Berlin Wall in November 1989, and the entry of nuclear weapons HEU into the market. The price of uranium hit historic lows, before the possibility of a global nuclear renaissance pushed the price above its 1989 level in late 2003.

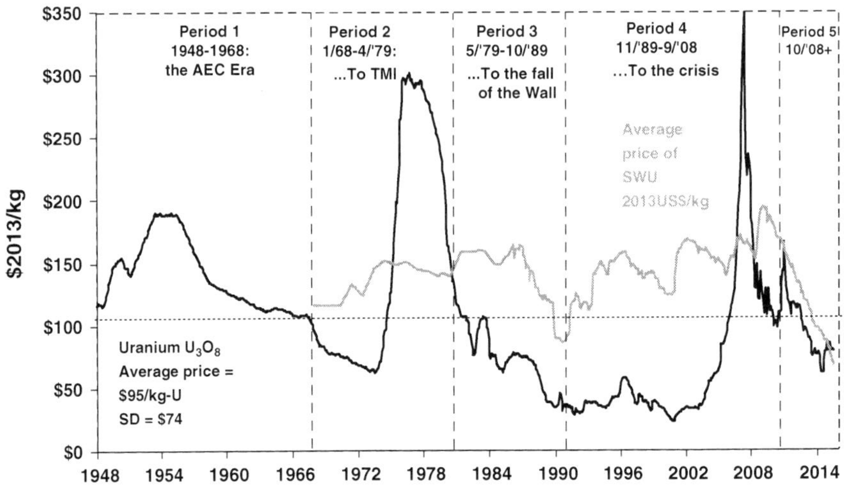

Figure 1.6 Natural uranium and SWU spot prices (2013 US$/kg).

Sources: Uranium prices, 1948–1972, are from US DOE (1981), converted to monthly prices by interpolation from mid-year to mid-year, and converted to 2013 dollars using the Producer Price Index (Federal Reserve Bank of St. Louis, 2015); prices January 1973–December 2006 are from ABARES (2008); prices since 2006 have been collected quarterly from the UxC website and converted to *approximate* monthly prices (UxC, 2015).

- Period 5 has been a time of price instability with the end of surplus stockpiles, the growth in nuclear power capacity in East Asia, and the halting of production at NPPs in Japan following the accident at Fukushima-Daiichi on 11 March 2011 and thereafter.

There have been two peaks in the spot price of uranium since 1968: \$301/kgU in the last quarter of 1976 (\$90/kgU in 1976 US dollars); and \$352/kgU in June 2007 (\$300/kgU in 2007 US dollars). Private parties, such as electric utilities, were allowed to buy uranium and enriching services from 1968. Because enriched uranium was being used to produce nuclear weapons, the US government was interested in maintaining stability in the price of uranium and enrichment. As a monopolist selling enrichment services to the private sector, the US AEC posted reasonable contract prices, but contract terms favoured the Commission. For example, in long-term US AEC contracts, customers were charged the price 'posted at the time of the sale' and the Commission could cancel the contract under force majeure:

> Applicable charges for enriching services and related services will be those in effect at the time of delivery of enriched uranium to the customer ... The contract may be terminated by AEC without cost to AEC upon reasonable notice.
>
> (US AEC, 1972: 46–47)

Following the US AEC's lead, the members of the Uranium Market Research Organization (UMRO), an international affiliation of uranium producers, adopted price 'in effect at the time of delivery'. The group met during the 1970s to divide markets and to set prices. For example, in October 1973, when the price was \$14.33/kgU (in 1973 US dollars), the group met to suggest that its members charge \$21.72/kgU for 1978 delivery to customers in Japan, Chinese Taipei and Korea, and only \$21.38/kgU to customers in Europe and the United States (Rothwell, 1980: 253). Following the dramatic rise in the price of oil, the price of uranium rose in January 1975 from \$14.33/kgU to \$35.27/kgU (in 1975 US dollars), thus eliminating the need to secure higher prices for uranium in a market in which the largest buyers were national governments.

Further, in July 1975, Westinghouse, the largest seller of NPPs, announced that it had sold short 40–60 million lbs of uranium for delivery to its NPPs between 1975 and 1985 – that is, it had contracted to sell 18,000–27,000 tU between 1975 and 1985 – but did not secure uranium to fulfil these contracts. In August 1975, the price hit \$57/kgU, and Westinghouse declared that it would be commercially impossible for it to honour its nuclear fuel contracts, claiming force majeure (Joskow, 1977). Prices increased to \$88/kgU in April 1976 (in 1976 US dollars) and remained above \$57/kgU until January 1981 (in 1981 US dollars).

These uranium price increases followed dramatic increases in the price of oil. In response to the Arab defeat in the Arab–Israeli War of October 1973, the embargo by the Organization of the Petroleum Exporting Countries (OPEC) of the supporters of Israel helped to more than double the price of oil from $17.92 per barrel to $40.66 per barrel in real terms (2013 US dollars) between mid-December 1973 and mid-January 1974. This price was maintained by a newly invigorated OPEC until the next oil price shock, which coincided with the Iranian Revolution in the first quarter of 1979. Following the collapse of the Persian Shah's regime in February 1979, the real price of oil rose from $40.62 per barrel in April 1979 to $85.59 per barrel by March 1980. The real price of oil fell slowly and did not rise above the March 1980 high until September 2007, when it reached $89.52 per barrel. During 2008, the price rose to a high of $146.71 per barrel in June 2008 – but then the bubble burst, with the financial collapse of Wall Street in September 2008, leading to a decline to $42.06 per barrel by February 2009. The price of oil then increased to a range of $75–$110 per barrel to the last week of November 2014, dropping below $50 per barrel in the first week of 2015.

A similar financial bubble developed in the uranium market, starting in December 2004. During each year, approximately 80,000 tU is purchased in the international uranium market to process into low enriched uranium (LEU) fuel. Most of this is acquired under long-term contracts. About 20% is traded on the spot market (at the prices in Figure 1.6). Therefore, at $100/kgU, 20% of the spot market could be purchased for $330 million, putting pressure on the market to raise spot prices. Apparently, this was happening in the mid-2000s, as explained in *The New York Times* (28 March 2007), which concluded: 'Some industry watchers fear the uranium market is entering the bust phase of another boom–bust cycle.' Three months after this article was published, the price of natural uranium rose to $300/kgU (in 2007 US dollars), then fell to $165/kgU (in 2008 US dollars) by March 2008 and to $99/kgU (in 2009 US dollars) by March 2009, at which point the price stagnated until August 2010, after which it again climbed, to reach almost $165/kgU in February 2011. During the last half of 2011 (that is, after the Fukushima-Daiichi accident), the price varied between $50 and $121/kgU, but fell from that plateau to about $62/kgU in July 2014, and fluctuated between $75/kgU and $88/kgU during 2015.

1.4 National nuclear power industries

Because some nuclear technologies can be used for both civilian and military purposes, as shown in Figure 1.3, the development of nuclear power has required international agreements to limit the proliferation of nuclear weapons, weapons-related materials and technologies. The primary mechanism to control the spread of nuclear weapons is the Treaty on the Non-Proliferation of Nuclear Weapons (the Non-Proliferation Treaty, or NPT, opened for signature in 1968), enforced by means of International Atomic Energy Agency (IAEA) inspections.

(The IAEA was established in 1957 and is associated with the United Nations.) At time of writing, all nations have signed the Treaty, except India, Israel, Pakistan and South Sudan. North Korea ratified the NPT in December 1985 and then withdrew from it in 2003. Further, an Additional Protocol allows the IAEA inspection authority to provide international assurance about both declared and possibly undeclared activities related to nuclear weapons.

The Treaty divides countries into 'nuclear-weapons states' and 'non-nuclear-weapons states'. The former, including (permanent members of the UN Security Council) China, France, Russia, the United Kingdom and the United States (and no others, even if they have such weapons), agree to reduce their stockpiles of nuclear weapons and not to transfer nuclear weapons, materials, or nuclear-weapons-related technologies to non-nuclear weapons states (Article I). These materials include HEU – that is, uranium that has been enriched above 20%.

In return, non-nuclear-weapons states agree not to develop nuclear weapons or explosive devices (Article II), provided that:

> Nothing in this Treaty shall be interpreted as affecting the inalienable right of the Parties to the Treaty to develop research, production and use of nuclear energy for peaceful purposes without discrimination and in conformity with Articles I and II of this Treaty.
>
> (Article IV)

Therefore the IAEA has the dual role of both preventing the spread of nuclear weapons technologies and facilitating the development of civilian nuclear power. It is in this context that commercial nuclear power has been developed in the United States, the United Kingdom and the Commonwealth of Nations, France and Western Europe, the former Soviet Union, Eastern Europe and Central Asia, Latin America and East Asia. (Much of the information in the following sections is from WNA, 2015c, which source should be consulted regularly, given the dynamic nature of the international commercial nuclear power industry.)

1.4.1 The United States

Research and development (R&D) on nuclear reactors began in the United States with the successful operation of an air-cooled, graphite-moderated, natural-uranium reactor (a GCR) at the University of Chicago in December 1942. Soon after the end of the Second World War, and the detonation of a uranium weapon in Hiroshima, Japan, and a plutonium weapon in Nagasaki, Japan, in August 1945, work began on nuclear reactors to generate useable energy. Nevertheless, the US Atomic Energy Act of 1946 restricted ownership of radioactive materials to the US government, restricted foreign access to nuclear R&D and established the US Atomic Energy Commission (US AEC). The US AEC directed R&D in the late 1940s and early 1950s. In December 1951, the

Experimental Fast Breeder Reactor (EBR-I) showed that electricity could be generated; the follow-on EBR-II operated from 1963 to 1994. In 1954, the *USS Nautilus* became the first nuclear-powered submarine.

The US Atomic Energy Act of 1954 allowed private ownership of nuclear reactors. Immediately, construction began on a 60 MW PWR prototype at Shippingport, PA. The Shippingport PWR achieved commercial operation in December 1958 (continuing to operate in various forms until 1982 and completely decommissioned by 1989). Next, several reactor types, including LWRs, HWRs, HTGRs and LMRs, were built under the US AEC's Power Demonstration Reactor Program, with contracts awarded between 1956 and 1965 (PNNL, 1968; US AEC and US DOJ, 1968). In 1960, Yankee-Rowe, a 175 MW PWR, and Dresden Unit 1, a 210 MW BWR, entered service. To encourage NPP orders, turnkey contracts for PWRs and BWRs were negotiated between 1965 and 1967 between electric utilities and four NSSS manufacturers: Westinghouse, General Electric (GE), Babcock & Wilcox (B&W), and Combustion Engineering (C-E). In 1966 and 1967, 50 units were ordered, signalling the commercial deployment of nuclear power in the United States. Orders continued until the accident in 1979 at TMI Unit 2, built by B&W. Babcock & Wilcox stopped producing PWRs, although it is, at time of writing, now trying to develop the mPower SMR, as discussed in Chapter 3, Section 3.5. Chapter 2 continues the history of the nuclear power industry in the United States since 1996.

1.4.2 The United Kingdom and the Commonwealth of Nations

Although the United Kingdom participated in the US nuclear weapons programme during the Second World War, the US Atomic Energy Act of 1946 restricted the United Kingdom's access to US R&D. In addition, while the United Kingdom participated in Canada's HWR R&D before the war's end, it began its indigenous nuclear programme in 1945 using GCR technology to develop nuclear devices. Its first graphite reactor and reprocessing facilities began operation in 1947. By 1951, it was operating two large-scale plutonium production reactors and reprocessing facilities at Windscale, and had tested its first nuclear device in 1952. (The graphite fire at Windscale in 1957 is considered to be the first major nuclear reactor accident.)

By 1953, the United Kingdom had developed a new fuel type, known as Magnox (an acronym for 'magnesium-clad natural uranium oxide'), which permitted sufficiently high temperatures in the reactor fuel core to produce electricity efficiently. In 1955, the United Kingdom started construction on eight 50 MW Magnox units at Calder Hall and Chapelcross to produce both plutonium and electricity. Construction started in 1960 on 18 Magnox units at nine plants, most rated near 220 MW. The United Kingdom followed this development with an AGR, using slightly enriched uranium from an enrichment facility at Capenhurst, completed in 1962. Fourteen AGRs at seven plants were built between 1965 and 1989, with capacities ranging from 550 MW to 625 MW. Only two GCRs were exported: to Italy in 1958; and to Japan in 1961. In an attempt to develop an internationally competitive technology, the United Kingdom built several reactor types: LMRs, SGHWRs and PWRs. The PWR was completed in 1995 and no NPPs have been built since then.

The Central Electricity Generating Board (CEGB) operated these NPPs until its privatisation in 1996, at which point (a) the GCRs were transferred to British Nuclear Fuels Ltd (BNFL), a government-owned company that participated in all aspects of the nuclear fuel cycle, including commercial reprocessing at Sellafield, situated next to Windscale, and (b) British Energy was formed to operate the AGRs and the PWR. All other reactor types were retired. British Energy was sold to Electricité de France (EDF) in 2008. Of the eight operating nuclear power stations that EDF Energy runs (comprising 14 AGRs and one PWR), all AGRs are scheduled to cease operation within the next decade (between 2016 and 2023), with Sizewell (a 1,196 MW PWR – the only PWR of the fleet) expected to retire in 2035.

Regarding the replacement of these plants, the United Kingdom has been active in encouraging the private development of new nuclear power since 2006 in terms of (a) reforming the licensing process by implementing a generic design assessment (GDA) to license standardised designs, and (b) providing government financial support similar to the support given to other low-carbon-generating alternatives.

There are three active GDAs under the Office of Nuclear Regulation (ONR), part of the UK Health and Safety Executive (HSE): the UK European pressurised reactor (EPR) approved in December 2012 submitted by Areva and EDF (joint-stock companies, in which the French government is the majority shareholder); the advanced passive pressurised water reactor (AP1000) submitted by Westinghouse with Toshiba with an interim approval; and the ABWR submitted by GE and Hitachi. (Rosatom has announced that it will submit the VVER-1200, also known as the AES-2006, for GDA in association with Rolls-Royce and Fortum.) Although not all designs have been certified, plans have been proposed:

1 by EDF Energy to build twin EPRs (1,670 MW, gross, units) at Hinkley Point Plant C, Units 1 and 2, and twin EPRs at Sizewell Plant C, Units 1 and 2;
2 by Horizon, a wholly owned subsidiary of Hitachi Ltd, to build twin ABWRs at Wylfa Newydd, Units 1 and 2, and twin ABWRs at Oldbury Plant B, Units 1 and 2; and
3 by NuGeneration, a joint venture of Toshiba (which has a 60% ownership share) and GDF Suez (with a 40% share) to build three AP1000s at Moorside.

To help to ensure the profitability of these projects, the UK government agreed in June 2013 (a) to guarantee loans of up to £10,000 million for the construction of Sizewell C and, in December 2013, agreed to consider a similar arrangement for Wylfa Newydd, and (b) to provide a contract for difference (CFD) for power produced at Hinkley Point C (under which contract if the market price is below an agreed 'strike' price, the guarantor pays the guaranteed the difference between the market price and the strike price, and if the market price is above the strike price, the guaranteed pays the guarantor the difference) (UK DECC, 2013).

The Commonwealth of Nations includes four nations outside the United Kingdom that have built commercial NPPs – Canada, India, Pakistan and South Africa – often helping one another.

As a part of the US and UK nuclear weapons development, in 1944 Canada began research on HWR technology and completed the world's first HWR in September 1945. Heavy water reactor technology was further demonstrated with a series of reactors in the 1950s built by Atomic Energy of Canada Ltd (AECL), owned by the Canadian government, culminating in the completion of the first Canadian deuterium uranium reactor (CANDU), a 25 MW nuclear power demonstration (NPD) reactor, in 1962. The NPP (a PHWR) used natural uranium with (non-pressurised) heavy water as a moderator and pressurised heavy water as a coolant. AECL scaled up the CANDU to 200 MW at Douglas Point, which began operating in 1966. Simultaneously, construction began on four more 515 MW units in Canada, two units in India, one unit in Pakistan and a HWLWR in Quebec, which was retired in 1977. During the 1970s, construction was completed on four units and started on nine more units in Canada, one unit in Argentina and one unit in Korea. Since then, AECL has completed additional construction on four units in Canada, two units in China, three units in Korea and two units in Romania. In 2014, memoranda of understanding (MOUs) with the China Nuclear Power Engineering Company (CNPEC) were signed to build CANDUs in Argentina and Romania, but construction has not yet started at time of writing.

After China tested its first nuclear device in 1964 (and after the Indo-Chinese war of 1962), India began its commercial nuclear power programme by importing two GE BWRs at Tarapur, completed in 1969 under turnkey contracts. In 1965, India began constructing a reprocessing facility and two CANDUs as a joint venture between AECL and the Indian Department of Atomic Energy (DAE). The Department completed the first 100 MW nuclear power unit in December 1973, with engineering and components supplied by AECL. After India's first 'peaceful nuclear device test' in 1974, Canada terminated cooperation with India, and the DAE completed the second unit, 200 MW, in 1980. Shortly thereafter, India's reprocessing plant began supplying MOX to its BWRs after its uranium supply was cut. As was exclaimed in the *Indian Express* (14 October 2000):

> With the loading of two more MOX fuel assemblies to the BWR at Tarapur, India has announced to the world that it can no longer be

> pressured with conditions in the matter of supply of enriched uranium … The BWRs were supplied by the U.S. in 1969. After the Pokharan–1 nuclear blast, India came under sanctions. Despite clear commitment, the U.S. reneged on supplying enriched uranium to Tarapur … With the perfection of MOX technology, India is sending out a strong signal to China, France, and the U.S., and indeed to the world, that any future negotiations in the nuclear reactor field would be on equal terms and would be free from any attendant compulsions like signing the CTBT (Comprehensive Test Ban Treaty) or the MTCR (Missile Technology Control Regime).

India has not signed the NPT nor has it joined the Missile Technology Control Regime (MTCR), and it continues to refuse to sign the Comprehensive Nuclear Test Ban Treaty (CTBT) until the United States eliminates its nuclear weapons stockpile. In the meantime, the Nuclear Power Corporation of India completed 18 PHWRs between 1984 and 2011. Four PHWRs, one VVER and a fast breeder reactor (FBR) are now under construction.

Soon after India started its nuclear programme, in 1966, construction began in Pakistan on a 125 MW CANDU. The unit was completed in 1972, after the war over Bangladesh's independence. Construction of a uranium enrichment facility at Kahuta (based on Urenco Group's centrifuge technology, obtained by scientist Abdul Qadeer Khan) began in 1975. A second NPP, a 300 MW Chinese PWR, was started in 1993 and completed in 2000. Pakistan conducted its first nuclear test in May 1998 and, as a result, Japan refused to supply a reactor pressure vessel to Pakistan, so China developed its industry to manufacture it.

Finally, South Africa started construction on two French 900 MW PWRs in 1976, bringing them into commercial operation in 1984 and 1985. While this plant was operating, the South African government (as described by its President de Klerk in a speech to the South African Parliament on 24 March 1993) secretly developed facilities to enrich uranium and test nuclear devices (De Villiers, Jardine and Reiss, 1993). South Africa abandoned these facilities by 1991 when it signed the NPT. South Africa was developing a 'pebble-bed' HTGR (based on a German design in which the uranium fuel spheres are coated with layers of graphite and ceramics) for international export, but could not sustain the R&D funding.

1.4.3 France and Western Europe

Without access to enrichment technologies, France began its nuclear programme in 1945, with the formation of the Commissariat à l'Énergie Atomique (CEA) to develop nuclear technology. Although the CEA conducted early research on HWRs, by the mid-1950s the CEA had focused its R&D on a dual-purpose GCR (producing both plutonium and electricity), moderated with graphite and cooled with pressurised CO_2. The first plant began operation in 1959 at Marcoule, with a reprocessing plant on site. France tested its first nuclear device in 1960. In addition, in 1967, France began operating uranium enrichment facilities.

Between 1960 and 1966, construction was completed on five GCRs, ranging in size from 38 MW to 480 MW. In addition, based on its experience with PWR technology for submarine propulsion, a 310 MW PWR was built with Westinghouse at Chooz and operated, beginning in 1966, in association with Belgium. In 1967 and 1968, construction started on eight more GCR units. However, with only one unit sold to Spain in 1968, it was apparent in the late 1960s that GCRs would be difficult to export. While President de Gaulle favoured continued investment in the French design, Pompidou, de Gaulle's successor, announced the end of the GCR programme in November 1969. To avoid the cost of developing another reactor, the French decided to build NPPs under licences from Westinghouse held by Framatome. In late 1970, construction began on two 900 MW PWRs. By April 1974, EDF had ordered 12 PWRs. By 1989, Framatome, later to become Areva, built 49 units and ten further units through the 1990s.

Throughout this period, France attempted to develop a large commercial LMR, starting with the Rapsodie demonstration project (which operated from 1967 to 1983), continuing with the 250 MW Phénix at Marcoule (which operated from 1974 to 2009), and concluding with the 1,200 MW Super Phénix (finished in 1985). Areva is, at time of writing, now building EPRs in China, Finland and France.

In 2004, EDF announced that it would build a first-of-its-kind Areva EPR at Flamanville on a site with two 1,400 MW class reactors. Concrete was poured in 2007 and construction was expected to take 54 months, with commercial operation to start in mid-2012. By mid-2010, the expected online date was extended to mid-2014. In mid-2011, the expected online date was extended to mid-2016 as a result of problems coordinating the work of the main subcontractors. By the end of 2015, EDF estimated that the total capital construction cost (overnight plus contingency and financing) would be €10,500 million helping to lead to a net loss of €4,830 million for 2014. In 2015, Areva informed the French nuclear regulator that 'anomalies' had been found in the carbon content of the reactor pressure vessel (RPV) (ASN, 2015), which would further delay operation to 2018. No other NPPs are under construction in France at time of writing and a new energy policy to reduce France's reliance on nuclear power is being considered. Further, it appears that Areva will be fragmented, resulting in 6,000 lost jobs and the selling of 'Areva NP' (Framatome) to EDF and China.

Unlike France and the United Kingdom, other Western European nations focused directly on building NPPs to generate electricity. Outside the United Kingdom, only LWRs are currently operating in Western Europe. These plants have been operating in Germany and Sweden, which developed their own reactor designs, and in other European nations, which imported their reactors.

West Germany began developing nuclear power technologies in the late 1950s. (East Germany is discussed along with Eastern Europe, in Section 1.4.4.) Like the United States, several reactor types were built before West Germany focused on BWRs and PWRs in the late 1970s. The first two BWRs were imported from GE in 1958 and 1962, and built with the German firm AEG. AEG built three more BWRs before forming a subsidiary, KWU, jointly owned with Siemens, in 1969. KWU completed six more BWRs by 1985. Brown-Boveri/Krupp began developing a 13 MW pebble-bed HTGR in 1961. High temperature gas reactor development continued with work on a high temperature thorium reactor in 1971. Brown-Boveri also built a 1,220 MW PWR, starting in 1975. Siemens initially focused on HWRs, building a 52 MW PHWR and a 100 MW HWGCR, but Siemens began building PWRs in 1965 and had completed 12 PWRs with KWU by 1989. In addition, a 20 MW LMR was built between 1974 and 1979. The only NPPs still operating in Germany are BWRs and PWRs built by KWU. In June 2000, Germany announced that it would phase out nuclear power. By the end of 2000, Siemens had merged its nuclear power division, AEG/KWU, with France's Framatome. After the Fukushima-Daiichi accident, all NPPs were scheduled for closure by 2022 and Siemens ended its partnership with Areva.

Sweden began its nuclear programme in 1957 when Swedish firm ASEA began building a 10 MW PHWR. After the plant was finished in 1964, ASEA switched to BWR technology, starting construction of its first BWR in 1966 and finishing its ninth unit in 1985. Westinghouse also started three PWRs between 1970 and 1973, and finished the last one in 1983. In 1980, a public referendum on nuclear power prompted the Swedish Parliament to stop constructing new NPPs and to attempt to retire all units. With the lack of nuclear construction after 1985, ASEA merged with Swiss Brown-Boveri to form ABB in 1988. In 1999, ABB sold its nuclear power division to BNFL. The two BWRs at Barsebäck were closed in 1999 and 2005. In 2010, the Swedish Parliament passed legislation to repeal the NPP closure policy and to allow the construction of new units to replace retiring units. However, the Swedish NPP operators have invested in life extensions, so that only three units are expected to be retired between 2020 and 2030. In 2012, the Swedish grid operator determined that the Ringhals site would be the most suitable for new units. In response, Vattenfall began investigating whether to replace the two older units at Ringhals by the mid-2020s, without any commitment to build new units.

Seven other Western European nations have imported NPPs. Finland imported two VVER-440s from the USSR in the early 1970s (later upgraded with Western control systems) and two BWRs from Sweden in the mid-1970s. France's Areva is, at time of writing, building an EPR at Olkiluoto. After receiving bids from three vendors, in late 2003, TVO signed a turnkey, fixed-price engineering, procurement and construction (EPC) contract with Areva to supply an EPR with a Siemens turbine generator for €3,200 million. Construction started in May 2005, with an anticipated online date of mid-2009. However, the project has experienced construction delays and cost overruns, and at the end of 2015 the expected commercial operation date was 2018, with a minimum construction cost of €8,500 million. This led to a delay (of up to five years) in the start of the construction of Olkiluoto 4. In May 2010, the Finnish government approved the building of Hanhikivi Unit 1, to be operated by Fennovoima Ltd. In December 2013, Fennovoima signed an EPC contract with the Russian supplier to build a VVER-1200 (AES-2006) with a minimum 34% Russian equity share (originally held by E.ON).

Regarding other countries in Western Europe that built NPPs, Belgium imported its PWRs from Westinghouse (five units starting in 1957) and Framatome (three units starting in 1975). In 2003, legislation was adopted to ban new construction of NPPs in Belgium, and all reactors will be retired by 2025.

Italy imported its BWRs from GE (two units starting in 1959), its GCR from the United Kingdom in 1958 and its PWR from Westinghouse in 1961. All units were retired by 1990. There are, at time of writing, no plans to build new nuclear in Italy.

The Netherlands imported its BWR from GE in 1965 (retired in 1997) and its PWR from KWU in 1969 at Borssele. There have been discussions about building a new unit to replace the ageing Borssele unit, but no plans have been finalised.

Spain imported its BWRs from GE (two units starting in 1966), its GCR from France in 1968 (retired in 1990), and its PWRs from Westinghouse (six units starting in 1964) and from KWU (one unit in 1979). In 1983, the Spanish government imposed a moratorium on building more NPPs. This was affirmed in 1994 and the NPPs under construction at that time were abandoned. No new nuclear is foreseen in Spain at time of writing.

Switzerland imported its BWRs from GE (two units starting in 1967), and its PWRs from Westinghouse (two units in 1965) and KWU (one unit in 1973). While Swiss NPPs are permitted to operate as long as they can show that they are safe to operate, there are no plans to replace these units once they have been retired.

Finally, Slovenia imported a 700 MW Westinghouse PWR in 1975, which began commercial operation in 1983, and it has been considering building a second unit at the same site, Krsko, for more than five years.

For more information on programmes in the European Union, see IEA (2014: ch. 10).

1.4.4 The former Soviet Union, Eastern Europe and Central Asia

The Union of Socialist Soviet Republics (USSR) and then former Soviet Union (FSU) commercially deployed two reactor types within its territory and in Eastern Europe: the RBMK (a LWGR) and the VVER (a LWR). In addition, it has commercialised fast reactor technology. Research on uranium began in the USSR in the early 1940s, allowing the construction of a uranium enrichment facility during the mid-1940s. This facilitated the testing of an HEU device in 1949.

To advance the development of a plutonium device, the first graphite reactor began operation in 1946. Based on this research, the USSR's first continuously operating NPP began producing electricity at 5 MW in 1954 in Obninsk. Construction on two prototype LWGRs using enriched uranium (one with 100 MW and another with 150 MW) began at Beloyarsky in the South Urals in 1958. The USSR scaled up this technology to 1,000 MW by 1970, and deployed the LWGR in the Russian Republic (11 units), Ukraine (four units at Chernobyl) and Lithuania (two units at 1,200 MW at Ignalina). No new RBMKs were constructed after the accident at Chernobyl on 26 April 1986.

Like the United States, the USSR developed PWR technology to power its ships. These were transformed into power reactors and, more recently, into SMRs.

1 In a first generation, two VVER prototypes (210 MW and 365 MW) were built, providing experience for a standardised VVER-440 (Model V230, with 440 MW), deployed starting in 1967 in the USSR (Russia) (six units), Bulgaria (four units), East Germany (four units) and the USSR (Armenia) (two units).
2 A second generation involved deployment of a VVER-440 (Model V213) with enhanced safety features, starting in 1970 in Finland (two units), the USSR (Ukraine) (two units), Hungary (four units), the USSR (Russia) (two units), East Germany (one unit) and Czechoslovakia (six units).
3 A third generation saw a VVER-1000 (1,000 MW) deployed starting in 1974 in the USSR (Russia) (11 units and where construction was restarted in June 2010 at Rostov 4, V-320), the USSR (Ukraine) (13 units) and Bulgaria (two units). Russia has built two VVER-1000s in China (Tianwan), a VVER in Iran (at Bushehr) and is, at time of writing, finishing two V-412 units at Kudankulam (India). Several VVERs are under construction in Russia and Ukraine, as well as two small floating PWRs (included with the VVERs in Figure 1.2).
4 'Generation III' VVER-1200s (AES-2006s), with a net generating capacity of about 1,100 MW, are under construction at Leningrad Plant 2, Units 1 and 2 (twin V-491), started in October 2008 and April 2010, and at Novovoronezh Plant 2, Units 1 and 2 (twin V-392M), started in June 2009 and in July 2009 (and similar to the design being discussed for construction in Turkey). Construction started on Belarusian Units 1 and 2 (twin V-491) in November 2013 and April 2014. Rosatom is also discussing the construction of VVER-1200s (AES-2006s) with Russian financing, for example in Finland (see Section 1.4.3) and in Hungary (see below).

The USSR's fast reactor development began in the mid-1950s with test reactors at Obninsk. In 1969, a demonstration fast reactor, BOR-60, began producing at 12 MW. This led to the design and construction between 1964 and 1973 of a 52 MW NPP that also desalinated water on the Caspian Sea in the USSR (Kazakhstan) (retired in 1999). This was scaled up to a 600 MW LMR at the Beloyarsky site, BN-600, which has been generating electricity since 1981. A larger unit, the BN-800, has, at time of writing, been under development and construction for some 20 years.

While most USSR plants were designed in Russian institutes, the Czech heavy equipment manufacturer Skoda, based on experience building a 110 MW HWGCR between 1958 and 1972, began supplying reactor components for the V213 units in the former Czechoslovakia. After the dissolution of the USSR, Skoda completed construction of two VVER-440s in the Slovak Republic and two VVER-1000s in the Czech Republic, with Western aid. Most NPPs in Eastern Europe outside the FSU have undergone safety upgrades since 1990.

New NPP development in Eastern Europe is being considered in Bulgaria, the Czech Republic, Hungary, Lithuania, Poland, Romania and the Slovak Republic. On 30 July 2014, the Bulgarian Council of Ministers approved an agreement between the Bulgarian utilities with Westinghouse and Toshiba to seek financing to build an AP1000 in Bulgaria. If financing can be found, an EPC contract will be tendered following European Union and Bulgarian procurement rules.

In the Czech Republic, negotiations regarding the building of two more units at Temelin have, at time of writing, been under way for several years. In June 2014, a Skoda–Russian consortium formed the Nuclear Power Alliance to consider the financing and building of Temelin Units 3 and 4 (twin VVER-1200s, or AES-2006s).

In March 2009, the Hungarian Parliament gave preliminary approval to building twin 1,000 MW NPPs at the Paks site, Units 5 and 6. In January 2014, the government signed an agreement with Rosatom to build two VVER-1200s (AES-2006s), with the first unit to be operating around 2023. In February 2014, Russia agreed to finance €10,000 million of the likely cost of €10,000–12,000 million, with Hungary repaying the loan over 21 years at interest rates under 5%. The Hungarian Parliament approved project financing before agreements on fuel provision and spent fuel were reached. However, the European Union has voiced objections to the proposed fuel agreements owing to energy security concerns.

In 2012, Lithuania signed an agreement with GE-Hitachi to build a single ABWR, with Hitachi as an investor holding 20% of the project, Latvia, another 20%, Estonia, 22%, and Lithuania, 38%. A combined construction and operating licence was expected to be issued in 2015, and a final investment decision and arrangements to be made soon after. Although a non-binding referendum rejected the construction of an NPP in Lithuania in October 2012, following the Russian annexation of the Crimea, representatives of the major Lithuanian parliamentary parties signed a resolution in March 2014 to build the Visaginas NPP for Lithuania's energy security.

Poland began building four VVER-440/V-213s in the 1980s at Zarnoweic, but cancelled these units in 1990 after the collapse of the USSR. In July 2014, Polish utility PGE EJ1 selected AMEC Nuclear UK to aid PGE EJ1 in choosing among four vendors: EDF and Areva, with the EPR; GE and Hitachi, with the ABWR; Westinghouse and Toshiba, with the AP1000; and a Korean consortium, with the APR1400. PGE EJ1 expects to choose a vendor by 2018 and begin construction in 2020, with Unit 1 to be completed by 2024, Unit 2, by 2025, and a second plant online by 2035.

Romania has been operating two CANDUs at the Cernavoda NPP through joint-stock company Nuclearelectrica, S.A. (Societatea Nationala): Unit 1, since 1996; and Unit 2, since 2007. In December 2010, the building of more nuclear units was approved. In November 2013, Nuclearelectrica and the China General Nuclear Power Group (CGN) signed a letter of intent to build Cernavoda Units 3 and 4 (both 720 MW PHWRs). In May 2014, negotiations began with the Industrial and Commercial Bank of China to finance the €6,500 million project, with CGN as the majority shareholder and Nuclearelectrica as a minority shareholder. In July 2014, CNPEC, a subsidiary of CGN, signed a cooperation agreement with Nuclearelectrica and CANDU Energy Inc. (a subsidiary of SNC-Lavalin Inc. of Montreal, sold by AECL in 2011) to construct the two units.

In the Slovak Republic, the construction of Mochovce Units 3 and 4 (VVER-440/V-213) was started in 1987, but was interrupted in 1992. Construction restarted in 2009 with the signing of contracts with Skoda (to supply steam turbines and other nuclear island equipment) and with Russia's AtomStroyExport (ASE) to supply the nuclear reactor. Since then, the completion has become more expensive than originally envisioned, leading to delays resulting from a lack of funds.

While it is difficult to place Iran in a particular nuclear industrial sphere, it has been pushed into that of Russia. Having ratified the NPT in 1970, Iran envisioned building up to two dozen NPPs. In 1975, it acquired Sweden's 10% share of France's European Diffusion Enrichment Facility (Eurodif), at a cost of approximately US$1,000 million. In 1976, Iran signed an MOU to buy and operate a PUREX reprocessing facility, to be built with US expertise. To prepare for this booming nuclear power industry, education and research facilities were constructed, and scientists and engineers educated and hired. From May 1975 to January 1978, KWU constructed two PWRs at Bushehr. By the time of the Iranian Revolution, Unit 1 was '85% complete' and Unit 2 was '50% complete', at a cost of approximately $2,500 million (Rothwell, 2012). After the Revolution, KWU stopped construction, France stopped sending LEU to Iran and the US reprocessing MOU evaporated. Bushehr was attacked several times during the Iran–Iraq war. After many years of international accusations and negotiations, Russia signed an agreement in January 1995 to complete Bushehr as a VVER-1000 with a net capacity of 915 MW, which was fuelled with Russian LEU and began commercial operation on 23 September 2013 (Khlopkov, 2010). Iran would like to complete the front end of the fuel cycle, given its history with international agreements, but this goal is problematic given Iran's history with the international community.

Finally, the Korean APR1400s being built in the United Arab Emirates (UAE) are discussed in association with Korea in Section 1.4.6.

1.4.5 Latin America

Three Latin American countries – Brazil, Argentina and Mexico – have small commercial nuclear programmes. Brazil began mining uranium in the 1940s, and attempted to develop a complete nuclear fuel cycle between the 1950s and the 1990s. Research reactors were built in the late 1950s and 1960s with US aid. In 1971, construction started on a 650 MW Westinghouse PWR, Angra 1, which was completed in 1984. Seeking nuclear fuel technologies (as Iran was during the 1970s – see Section 1.4.4), Brazil negotiated the purchase from German KWU of several NPPs, a commercial-scale uranium enrichment facility and a pilot reprocessing plant. Construction on Angra Unit 2 began in 1976 and continued for 24 years, until commercial operation in 2000. No other facilities were successfully completed. Brazil renounced nuclear weapons development in the 1990s and signed the NPT in 1998. To provide fuel for Angra and a nuclear submarine programme, Brazil began enriching uranium at a facility at Resende in 2006 with restricted IAEA inspections (Rothwell and Cabrera-Palmer, 2008). (Brazil negotiated these inspection restrictions to protect the intellectual property associated with its centrifuge design, which has magnetic bearings on both the top and bottom of the centrifuge.)

Argentina began its nuclear programme with the creation of the National Atomic Energy Commission in 1950 and started mining uranium in 1953. With US help, Argentina constructed its first research reactor in 1958 and built three more during the 1960s. In 1968, construction began on a Siemens 350 MW PHWR, which entered commercial operation in 1974. During the 1970s, an enrichment plant was built at Pilcaniyeu and a reprocessing facility at Ezeiza. A second NPP, a 600 MW CANDU, was started in 1974 and completed in 1984. In 1991, Argentina signed an agreement with Brazil to allow mutual inspections of each other's nuclear facilities and Argentina signed the NPT in 1995. Argentina started building an SMR, a 29 MW PWR with an integrated reactor and steam generator, in February 2014.

In addition, Mexico signed the NPT in 1969, and built two GE 700 MW BWRs between 1976 and 1995. Mexico is, at time of writing, now considering building two more NPPs (probably ABWRs) to achieve CO_2 reduction targets.

1.4.6 East Asia

The East Asian countries of China, Japan, Korea and Chinese Taipei lead the world in terms of NPPs currently under construction, and East Asia is likely to be the world leader in new nuclear power for the intermediate future.

During the 1950s, China worked with the USSR to develop nuclear devices. This led to the construction of a uranium enrichment facility and, eventually, to the testing of an HEU device in October 1964. By the end of 1968, China had developed facilities to fabricate, separate and assemble a plutonium device. The Cultural Revolution of the 1970s disrupted these activities. In the 1980s, China turned to commercial nuclear power development when it began constructing two PWRs: Qinshan Unit 1, on the central China coast; and Daya Bay Units 1 and 2, near Hong Kong. The China National Nuclear Corporation (CNNC) built Qinshan Unit 1, with a capacity of 300 MW, similar to the unit built in Pakistan. The two 944 MW units at Daya Bay were built with foreign equipment and engineering from France and the United Kingdom, with French and British financing. Both plants began operating in 1994. For a discussion of the emergence of the Chinese commercial nuclear programme, see Rothwell (2003).

China is, at time of writing, commercially operating or constructing 49 units (not including the 20 MW proto-FBRs): 32 are of Chinese design; six are of French and Chinese design (four older PWRs and two incomplete EPRs, expected to be completed in 2016 and 2017); four are Westinghouse/Toshiba AP1000s under construction; four are Russian VVERs (two are operating and two are under construction); and two are Canadian PHWRs (see Tables 1.1 and 1.2). These Chinese-designed plants are of five types:

- seven Chinese NPPs (CNPs) – one 300 MW unit and six 610 MW units;
- 22 1,000 MW Chinese pressurised reactors (CPRs);
- three 1,000 MW advanced Chinese pressurised reactors (ACPRs) under construction;
- a 1,400 MW Chinese advanced passive reactor (CAP1400), not yet under construction; and
- a 200 MW HTGR, under construction.

According to the IAEA (2015b), there are 38 more units planned for construction, including two LMRs. It is likely, with construction slowdowns and operating plant retirements elsewhere, that China will have the largest nuclear power programme globally by 2030.

The Japanese Atomic Energy Commission (JAEC) was established in 1956 to promote the peaceful uses of nuclear energy. After initial research, a prototype GE BWR (13 MW) was constructed between 1960 and 1965. GE completed two more BWRs (340 MW and 440 MW) between 1966 and 1971. GE began building BWRs with Toshiba in 1969 and Hitachi in 1970. Since then, Toshiba has completed 16 BWRs and Hitachi, eight BWRs. In the early 1990s, GE started building ABWRs with both Toshiba and Hitachi. Kashiwazki Kariwa Unit 3, an ABWR with Toshiba, was completed in 1996; Kashiwazki Kariwa Unit 4, an ABWR with Hitachi, was completed in 1997. Two more ABWRs are, at time of writing, under construction. The first PWR was ordered from Westinghouse (a 320 MW unit) in 1967.

Table 1.1 Nuclear power plants completed in East Asia, 2002–2015

	Country	*Name*	#	*Type*	*NSSS origin*	*Net MW*	*Thermal efficiency*	*Construction start*	*Operation start*	*Lead time*
1	China	Qinshan 2	1	CNP	China	610	32%	1996.417	2002.250	70
2	China	Qinshan 2	2	CNP	China	610	32%	1997.250	2004.333	85
3	China	Ling'ao-1	1	PWR	France	950	32%	1997.333	2002.333	60
4	Korea	Hanbit	5	OPR	Korea	950	35%	1997.417	2002.333	59
5	Korea	Hanbit	6	OPR	Korea	950	35%	1997.833	2002.916	61
6	China	Ling'ao-1	2	PWR	France	950	32%	1997.833	2003.000	62
7	Japan	Onagawa	3	BWR	Toshiba	796	33%	1998.000	2002.000	48
8	China	Qinshan 3	1	PHWR	Canada	677	31%	1998.417	2002.916	54
9	China	Qinshan 3	2	PHWR	Canada	677	31%	1998.667	2003.500	58
10	Korea	Hanul	5	OPR	Korea	950	35%	1999.750	2004.500	57
11	China	Tianwan	1	VVER	Russia	1,000	33%	1999.750	2006.333	79
12	Japan	Hamaoka	5	ABWR	Toshiba	1,325	34%	2000.500	2005.000	54
13	Korea	Hanul	6	OPR	Korea	950	35%	2000.667	2005.250	55
14	China	Tianwan	2	VVER	Russia	1,000	33%	2000.750	2007.333	79
15	Japan	Higachi Dori	1	BWR	Toshiba	1,067	32%	2000.833	2005.167	52
16	Japan	Shika	2	ABWR	Hitachi	1,304	33%	2001.583	2006.500	59
17	Japan	Tomari	3	PWR	Japan	866	33%	2004.833	2009.916	61
18	China	Ling'ao-2	1	CPR	China	1,000	34%	2005.916	2010.667	57

Table 1.1 (continued)

	Country	*Name*	*#*	*Type*	*NSSS origin*	*Net MW*	*Thermal efficiency*	*Construction start*	*Operation start*	*Lead time*
19	China	Qinshan 2	3	CNP	China	610	32%	2006.250	2010.750	54
20	Korea	Shin Kori	1	OPR	Korea	988	34%	2006.417	2011.083	56
21	China	Ling'ao-2	2	CPR	China	1,000	34%	2006.417	2010.667	51
22	China	Qinshan 2	4	CNP	China	610	32%	2007.000	2011.916	59
23	Korea	Shin Kori	2	OPR	Korea	995	34%	2007.417	2012.500	61
24	China	Hongyanhe	1	CPR	China	1,060	34%	2007.583	2013.333	69
25	Korea	Shin Wolsong	1	OPR	Korea	950	34%	2007.833	2012.500	56
26	China	Ningde	1	CPR	China	1,000	34%	2008.083	2013.250	62
27	China	Hongyanhe	2	CPR	China	1,000	34%	2008.250	2014.333	73
28	China	Ningde	2	CPR	China	1,000	34%	2008.833	2014.000	62
29	China	Fuqing	1	CPR	China	1,000	34%	2008.833	2014.833	72
30	China	Yangjiang	1	CPR	China	1,000	34%	2008.917	2014.167	63
31	China	Fangjiashan	1	CPR	China	1,000	34%	2008.917	2014.833	71
32	China	Fangjiashan	2	CPR	China	1,000	34%	2009.500	2015.000	66

Source: IAEA (2015b).

Note: Construction start and operation start were digitalised so that their difference multiplied by 12 is equal to the construction lead time in months.

Table 1.2 Nuclear power plants under construction in East Asia

Country	*Name*	*#*	*Type*	*NSSS*	*Net MW*	*Thermal efficiency*	*Construction start*	*Start month*
Japan	Shimane	3	ABWR	Japan	1,325	34%	2007	10
Korea	Shin Wolsong[a]	2	OPR	Korea	960	34%	2008	9
Korea	Shin Kori	3	APR	Korea	1,340	34%	2008	10
China	Hongyanhe[a]	3	CPR	China	1,000	34%	2009	3
China	Sanmen	1	AP1000	US	1,000	29%	2009	3
China	Fuqing[a]	2	CPR	China	1,000	34%	2009	6
China	Yangjiang[a]	2	CPR	China	1,000	34%	2009	6
China	Hongyanhe	4	CPR	China	1,000	34%	2009	8
China	Haiyang	1	AP1000	US	1,000	29%	2009	9
Korea	Shin Kori	4	APR	Korea	1,340	34%	2009	8
China	Taishan	1	EPR	France	1,660	36%	2009	11
China	Sanmen	2	AP1000	US	1,000	29%	2009	12
China	Ningde[a]	3	CPR	China	1,000	34%	2010	1
China	Changjiang	1	CNP	China	610	32%	2010	4
China	Taishan	2	EPR	France	1,660	36%	2010	4
Japan	Ohma	1	ABWR	Japan	1,343	34%	2010	5
China	Haiyang	2	AP1000	US	1,000	29%	2010	6

Table 1.2 (continued)

Country	*Name*	#	*Type*	*NSSS*	*Net MW*	*Thermal efficiency*	*Construction start*	*Start month*
China	Fangchenggang	1	CPR	China	1,000	34%	2010	7
China	Ningde	4	CPR	China	1,000	34%	2010	9
China	Changjiang	2	CNP	China	610	32%	2010	11
China	Yangjiang	3	CPR	China	1,000	34%	2010	11
China	Fangchenggang	2	CPR	China	1,000	34%	2010	12
China	Fuqing	3	CPR	China	1,000	34%	2010	12
Korea	Shin Hanul	1	APR	Korea	1,340	34%	2012	7
China	Yangjiang	4	CPR	China	1,000	34%	2012	11
China	Fuqing	4	CPR	China	1,000	34%	2012	11
China	Tianwan	3	VVER	Russia	990	33%	2012	12
China	Shidao Bay	1	HTGR	China	200	42%	2012	12
Korea	Shin Hanul	2	APR	Korea	1,340	34%	2013	6
China	Yangjiang	5	ACPR	China	1,000	34%	2013	8
China	Yangjiang	6	ACPR	China	1,000	34%	2013	12
China	Tianwan	4	VVER	Russia	990	33%	2013	9
China	Hongyanhe	5	ACPR	China	1,000	34%	2015	3

[a] Unit connected to the grid in early 2015.

Source: IAEA (2015b); WNA (2015c).

Westinghouse built two more PWRs, starting work with Mitsubishi in 1970. Since then, Mitsubishi has completed 19 PWRs.

Three other reactor types have been built: a 150 MW GCR was imported from the United Kingdom in 1961 (generating electricity between 1965 and 1976); Hitachi built a 150 MW HWLWR between 1972 and 1979; and a series of LMRs. An experimental LMR (Joyo) began operating in 1977, leading to the construction of a 250 MW unit at Monju in 1986. Monju was finished in 1994, but suffered a sodium fire in its cooling system in 1995 and has never been commercially operated.

To prepare for the deployment of LMRs, Japan began developing reprocessing facilities to recover plutonium for MOX and LMRs in 1968. A prototype reprocessing plant was completed in 1981 at Tokai, with a capacity of 3 tonnes per year. Construction on a full-scale reprocessing plant began in 1993 at Rokkasho; completion was expected in 2005, but at time of writing Rokkasho has yet to be completed. Until completion, Rokkasho serves as an away-from-reactor used fuel storage site. However, two accidents galvanised Japanese public opinion against reprocessing and LMR deployment: (a) a fire at Tokai in 1997; and (b) a criticality accident at Tokai in 1999, while preparing fuel for the Joyo experimental LMR. Since these accidents, orders for more LWRs have slowed: only two units are under construction at time of writing. The future of Japan's nuclear power industry is uncertain after the Fukushima-Daiichi accident (Aoki and Rothwell, 2013): operation at all plants ceased in 2011. Some nuclear units will be restarted (although it is uncertain when) and some will be retired (although, again, it is uncertain when).

Korea began its nuclear programme in 1972. The Korea Electric Power Company (KEPCO) ordered six Westinghouse PWRs between 1972 and 1981: two at 600 MW and four at 900 MW. This was followed by orders for two Framatome PWRs in 1983. These experiences led to the formation of the Korean Heavy Industries Ltd (KHI), in association with C-E, then owned by BNFL. KHI built four 950 MW NPPs between 1989 and 1999. Two pairs of twin units are under construction at time of writing. In addition, in 1977, KEPCO ordered a 650 MW CANDU from AECL. Between 1992 and 1999, AECL worked with KHI to complete three units. The Korea Hydro and Nuclear Power Company (KHNP) developed the advanced power reactor (APR1400, producing 1,345 MW net), and is building three units in Korea and four units (Barakah Units 1, 2, 3 and 4) in the UAE, construction started in July 2012, May 2013, September 2014 and September 2015. (For a description of the history of the development of the commercial nuclear power industry in Korea, see IAEA, 2009.) Further, Korea has licensed a small modular PWR, known as the system-integrated modular advanced reactor (SMART) (KEPCO, 2013), and has signed an MOU with Saudi Arabia to explore the manufacturing, construction and operation of SMARTs in Saudi Arabia.

Unlike South Korea, North Korea built two 5 MW graphite reactors with USSR aid in the 1970s. In the 1980s, North Korea began construction on a 200 MW graphite reactor and reprocessing facilities. After withdrawing from the NPT in 1993 and its system of international inspections by the IAEA, it began stockpiling used fuel for reprocessing. In response, the United States, with Japan and South Korea, negotiated an agreement to build two 1,000 MW LWRs, with KEPCO as the prime contractor, in exchange for dismantling North Korea's reactors and reprocessing facilities, and submitting to IAEA inspections. North Korea has delayed compliance. Construction of these LWRs never started. It is also likely that North Korea tested a nuclear device in February 2013.

Like India, Chinese Taipei started its nuclear programme after China conducted the first test of a nuclear device in 1964. A small Canadian HWR was built between 1969 and 1973, and retired in 1988. When Chinese Taipei began to make inquiries to purchase reprocessing technology in the early 1970s, the United States strongly discouraged it from doing so. Instead, Chinese Taipei started its commercial nuclear power programme in 1972 by ordering a Westinghouse PWR. Four PWRs were completed between 1978 and 1983. In 1978, GE began building two BWRs, completing them in 1984 and 1985. Later, in 1999, GE started construction of two ABWRs (Lungmen Units 1 and 2). However, as a result of political problems, at time of writing the plants have not yet been connected to the grid.

References

Aoki, M., and Rothwell, G. 2013. 'A comparative institutional analysis of the Fukushima nuclear disaster: Lessons and policy implications', *Energy Policy*, 53: 240–247.

Australian Bureau of Agricultural and Resource Economics and Sciences (ABARES). 2008. *Summary of Australian for Uranium: Worksheet 344 – Uranium prices*. Available from Department of Agriculture, Fisheries and Forestry, GPO Box 1563, Canberra, ACT 2601.

Autorité de Sûreté Nucléaire (ASN). 2015. 'Background to the discovery of the anomaly affecting the Flamanville EPR reactor vessel (excessively high carbon content in the vessel closure head and vessel bottom head)', 31 July. Available online at www.french-nuclear-safety.fr/recherche/resultat?SearchText=anomaly+Flamanville&SearchContentClassID=-1

D'haeseleer, W. 2013. *Synthesis on the Economics of Nuclear Energy: Final Report*. Study for the European Commission, DG Energy, 27 November. Available online at www.mech.kuleuven.be/en/tme/research/energy_environment/Pdf/wpen2013-14.pdf

De Villiers, J., Jardine, R., and Reiss, M. 1993. 'Why South Africa gave up the bomb', *Foreign Affairs*, 72(5): 199.

Federal Reserve Bank of St. Louis. 2015. *Producer Price Index: All Commodities*. Available online at http://research.stlouisfed.org/fred2/series/PPIACO/downloaddata?cid=31

Indian Express. 2000. 'India perfects MOX fuel N-tech Cocks a Snook at China, USA, and France', *Indian Express*, 14 October. Available online at www.wise-paris.org/index.html?/english/othersnews/year_2000/othersnews001017.html&/english/frame/menu.html&/english/frame/band.html

International Atomic Energy Agency (IAEA). 2009. *Nuclear Technology and Economic Development in the Republic of Korea*. Available online at www.iaea.org/sites/default/files/rok0809.pdf

International Atomic Energy Agency (IAEA). 2015a. *Nuclear Power Reactors in the World*. Available online at www-pub.iaea.org/MTCD/Publications/PDF/rds-2-34_web.pdf

International Atomic Energy Agency (IAEA). 2015b. *Power Reactor Information System*. Available online at www.iaea.org/pris/

International Energy Agency (IEA). 2014. *Energy Policies of IEA Countries: European Union*. Available online at www.iea.org/bookshop/486-Energy_Policies_of_IEA_Countries_-_The_European_Union

Joskow, P. 1977. 'Commercial impossibility, the uranium market, and the Westinghouse case', *Journal of Legal Studies*, 6(1): 119–176.

Khlopkov, A. 2010. 'Iran breakthrough for the Russian nuclear industry', *Moscow Defense Brief*, 1(19). Available online at http://mdb.cast.ru/mdb/1-2010/item6/

Korea Electric Power Company (KEPCO). 2013. 'Small and Modular reactor development, safety and licensing in Korea', paper presented at IAEA Technical Working Group on Advanced Technologies for LWRs, 18–20 June, Vienna. Available online at www.iaea.org/NuclearPower/Downloadable/Meetings/2013/2013-06-18-06-20-TWG-NPTD/35-korea-smr.pdf

New York Times, The. 2007. 'High price of uranium prods U.S. mines to life', 28 March. Available online at www.nytimes.com/2007/03/28/business/worldbusiness/28iht-uranium.1.5056467.html?_r=0

New York Times, The. 2015. 'How Stanford took on the giants of economics', 10 September. Available online at www.nytimes.com/2015/09/13/upshot/how-stanford-took-on-the-giants-of-economics.html

Pacific Northwest Laboratory (PNNL). 1968. *Fast Flux Test Facility Conceptual System Design Description for the Building Electrical Power System No. 12*. Available online at www.osti.gov/scitech/servlets/purl/1088249/

Rothwell, G. 1980. 'Market coordination in the uranium oxide industry', *The Antitrust Bulletin*, 25(1): 233–268.

Rothwell, G. 2003. 'Standardization, diversity, and learning in China's nuclear power program', in T. Guinnane, W. Sundstrom and W. Whatley (eds) *History Matters: Essays on Economic Growth, Technology, and Demographic Change*, Redwood City, CA: Stanford University Press, pp. 221–241.

Rothwell, G. 2009. 'Market power in uranium enrichment', *Science & Global Security*, 17(2–3): 132–154.

Rothwell, G. 2010. 'International nuclear fuel fabrication supply: Are fabrication services assured?', *Energy Economics*, 32(3): 538–544.

Rothwell, G. 2012. 'The levelised cost of generating electricity at Bushehr', PNNL Working Paper, 14 February.

Rothwell, G., and Cabrera-Palmer, B. 2008. 'Why is Brazil enriching uranium?', *Energy Policy*, 36(7): 2570–2577.

UK Department of Energy and Climate Change (DECC). 2013. 'Electricity Market Reform (EMR)', in DECC, *2010 to 2015 Government Policy: UK Energy Security*, Appendix 5. Available online at www.gov.uk/government/policies/maintaining-uk-energy-security–2/supporting-pages/electricity-market-reform

US Atomic Energy Commission (US AEC). 1972. *AEC Gaseous Diffusion Plant Operations*, ORO–684. Washington, DC: US AEC.

US Atomic Energy Commission (US AEC) and US Department of Justice (US DOJ). 1968. *Competition in the Nuclear Power Supply Industry*, NYO–3853–1. Washington, DC: US AEC.

US Department of Energy (US DOE). 1981. *Statistical Data of the Uranium Industry*, GJO–100(81). Available online at www.osti.gov/scitech/servlets/purl/6137459

US Nuclear Regulatory Commission (US NRC). 2014. *GE laser enrichment facility licensing*. Available online at www.nrc.gov/materials/fuel-cycle-fac/laser.html

Ux Consulting Company, LLC (UxC). 2015. *UxC nuclear fuel price indicators*. Available online at www.uxc.com/review/uxc_Prices.aspx

World Information Service on Energy (WISE). 2015a. 'Uranium enrichment calculator', *Uranium Project*. Available online at www.wise-uranium.org/nfcue.html

World Information Service on Energy (WISE). 2015b. 'Uranium enrichment and fuel fabrication', *WISE Uranium Project*. Available online at www.wise-uranium.org/indexe.html

World Nuclear Association (WNA). 2015a. *World uranium mining production*. Available online at www.world-nuclear.org/info/Nuclear-Fuel-Cycle/Mining-of-Uranium/World-Uranium-Mining-Production/

World Nuclear Association (WNA). 2015b. *Uranium enrichment*. Available online at www.world-nuclear.org/info/Nuclear-Fuel-Cycle/Conversion-Enrichment-and-Fabrication/Uranium-Enrichment/

World Nuclear Association (WNA). 2015c. *Country profiles*. Available online at www.world-nuclear.org/info/Country-Profiles/

2 Regulating light water reactors in the United States

The last nuclear power plant (NPP) to be ordered in the United States, and not cancelled later, was the Palo Verde nuclear generating station in Arizona, ordered in October 1973 and, at 4,200 megawatts (MW), the largest NPP in the United States. (Palo Verde is a three-unit 'System 80' pressurised water reactor, or PWR, made by the company Combustion Engineering and a precursor of the 'System 80+' standardised design that the US Nuclear Regulatory Commission, or NRC, approved in 1997 – see Table 2.1.) After the 1973–74 oil embargo and oil price spike, the growth in electricity use dropped from about 7% a year to about 3% a year throughout the 1970s among Organisation for Economic Co-operation and Development (OECD) member countries, leading to construction delays at many nuclear plants.

Later in the 1970s, with double-digit inflation and associated increases in the cost of capital of over 20% a year, capital-intensive nuclear plants were cancelled, as well as oil refineries and chemical plants. After the accident at Three Mile Island (TMI) on 28 March 1979, the time taken to license NPPs doubled, leading to even more nuclear plant cancellations. In 1983, the Washington Public Power Supply System (WPPSS, pronounced 'whoops'), defaulted on US$2,250 million in bonds ($4,500 million in 2013 US dollars) – something that Wall Street has neither forgotten nor forgiven. The last nuclear plant placed in service in the United States was that ordered by the Tennessee Valley Authority (TVA) at Watts Bar in 1996, on which construction began in 1973. (This one-unit reactor in Tennessee can be found on the map at US NRC, 2015b.) Watts Bar is also where nuclear construction restarted in the United States (in 2008), with TVA completing Watts Bar, Unit 2 (a Westinghouse PWR) under licensing and in compliance with the set of US NRC regulations that were in effect when the construction of the unit began, known as '10 CFR Part 50' ('CFR' referring to the US Code of Federal Regulations).

In response to the problems facing the nuclear power industry during the last three decades, successive congresses and presidential administrations have attempted to re-energise nuclear generation in the United States. This chapter summarises changes in legislation, regulation and administration to promote the building of advanced NPPs in the United States. These include, for example, the advanced passive(ly safe) PWR (AP1000) built by Westinghouse – also

Table 2.1 Standardised nuclear power plant design certification applications (DCAs)

System	*Applicant*	*Accepted*	*Approved*
System 80+	Westinghouse–Combustion Engineering	Sep-87	May-97
ABWR	General Electric, GE	Sep-87	Aug-97
AP600	Westinghouse	Jun-92	Dec-99
AP1000	Westinghouse–BNFL	Mar-02	Jan-06
AP1000a	Toshiba–Westinghouse–Shaw	May-07	Dec-11
ABWR-DRC	South Texas Project NOC	Jun-09	Dec-11
ESBWR	GE–Hitachi Nuclear Energy	Aug-05	Sep-14
US EPR	AREVA Consortium	Dec-07	2016+
US-APWR	Mitsubishi Heavy Industries	Dec-07	Deferred
ABWR: renew	Toshiba Corporation Power Systems Co.	Oct-10	2016+
ABWR: renew	GE–Hitachi Nuclear Energy	Dec-10	2016+
APR1400	KHNP–KEPCO	Mar-15	2016+

Sources: US DOE (2015); US NRC (2015d).

Note: ABWR = advanced boiling water reactor; ABWR-DCR = ABWR amended for Design Certification Rule; AP = advanced passive reactor; APR1400 = advanced power reactor; ESBWR= economic simplified boiling water reactor; US APWR = US advanced pressurised water reactor; US EPR = US evolutionary power reactor (US NRC, 2015c).

known as a 'Generation III' or 'III+' advanced light water reactor (ALWR) (see Table 2.1) – and proposed small modular reactors (SMRs), including small light water reactors (SLWRs).

This book refers to ALWRs and SMRs as 'new nuclear'; although it could also consider non-LWR SMRs, such as high temperature gas reactors (HTGRs), this book discusses only small LWRs. (On the economics of producing electricity and/or hydrogen with the modular helium reactor, or MHR, see Rothwell and Williams, 2006.)

2.1 Changes in US Nuclear Regulatory Commission licensing procedures

Delays in the operating licensing process were one of the key elements slowing nuclear plant completions after 1974, with the implementation of the US National Environmental Policy Act of 1969 (NEPA) requiring the approval of an environmental impact statement (EIS) before a construction licence could be granted for a nuclear facility. In response to these delays, the US NRC introduced (and incorporated into 10 CFR Part 52):

1 design certification of standardised nuclear designs, as in Table 2.1;
2 early site permits (ESPs) for standardised nuclear sites, as in Table 2.2; and
3 combined construction *and* operating licence (COL) applications (COLAs), as in Table 2.3.

Table 2.2 Early site permit applications

Reactor site	*County, State*	*Applied*	*Approved*
Clinton	DeWitt, IL	Sep-03	Mar-07
Grand Gulf	Claiborne, MS	Oct-03	Apr-07
North Anna	Louisa, VA	Sep-03	Nov-07
Vogtle	Burke, GA	Aug-06	Aug-09
PSEG site	Salem, NJ	May-10	2015+

Source: US NRC (2013).

Table 2.3 Combined construction and operating licence applications (COLAs)

Proposed new nuclear power plants	*#, State*	*Ref. design*	*Applied*
South Texas Project Units 3 & 4	2, TX	ABWR	Sep-07
North Anna Unit 3	1, VA	ESBWR	Nov-07
William Lee Units 1 & 2	2, SC	AP1000a	Dec-07
Summer Units 2 & 3 (approved Apr-2012)	2, SC	AP1000a	Mar-08
Vogtle Units 3 & 4 (approved Feb-2012)	2, GA	AP1000a	Mar-08
Levy County Units 1 & 2	2, FL	AP1000a	Jul-08
Fermi Unit 3 (approved Apr-2015)	1, OH	ESBWR	Sep-08
Bell Bend Nuclear Power Plant	1, PA	US EPR	Oct-08
Turkey Point Units 6 & 7	2, FL	AP1000a	Jun-09

Source: US NRC (2015e).

These changes were intended to reduce the regulatory risk of constructing new nuclear by decoupling the design and site licensing process from the operating licence, and by standardising plant designs. Plant design standardisation was a key nuclear industry concern throughout the 1990s (David and Rothwell, 1996; EPRI, 1995; NEI, 1998). Burns (2008) compares the older regulations at 10 CFR Part 50 with 10 CFR Part 52.

Design certification allows the US NRC to certify a standard design to be built at a generic site. Table 2.1 shows that, by the time of writing in 2015, the US NRC had certified more than half a dozen LWR designs and had five designs (or amendments to designs) under review. There is no longer interest in constructing any of the designs that were licensed before 2010. While the US NRC certified the System 80+ in May 1997, this reactor was not built, but the System 80+ (1,314 MW) is similar to the Korean APR1400 (1,340 MW) under construction in Korea and the United Arab Emirates (UAE). On the other hand, there is great interest in the amended AP1000 design, the AP1000a, which was approved 30 December 2011, just after the approval of the amended advanced boiling water reactor (ABWR) licence on 16 December 2011.

Table 2.4 Nuclear power plant construction and site preparation starts in the United States

Construction starts	*NRC regulation*	*State*	*Design*	*Completion expected*
TVA: Watts Bar 2	10 CFR Pt 50	TN	West–PWR	2015+
S. Nuclear: Vogtle 3 & 4	10 CFR Pt 52	GA	AP1000a	2019+
SCE&G: Summer 2 & 3	10 CFR Pt 52	SC	AP1000a	2020+

Source: US DOE (2015).

The ESP process allows a nuclear investor to license a specific site for a generic NPP, with the option of constructing a plant within 10–20 years, as well as of renewing the ESP for an additional 10–20 years. The US NRC has approved only four sites – Clinton, IL, Grand Gulf, MS, North Anna, VA, and Vogtle, GA – where twin AP1000s are under construction. Early site permits are not required, but regulatory and environmental requirements must then be addressed in the COL application.

In 1989, the US NRC introduced a new licensing procedure that would allow for the issuance of a combined construction and operating licence, so that the new nuclear owner could be assured of commercial operation by demonstrating that, at the completion of construction, the plant met initially agreed-upon criteria for operation. The first COLA was submitted for two units at the South Texas Project on 29 November 2007 (Rothwell, 2006). Since then, the nuclear utility industry has submitted more than two dozen COLAs (see US NRC, 2015a, for their locations). Table 2.3 presents only those COLAs that are still under US NRC review. The Commission has issued two COLs and five NPPs are under construction. (Compare Table 2.4 with the list of NPPs under construction in China, presented in Chapter 1, Table 1.2, which includes four AP1000s.)

While these licensing activities were in progress, the 'Waste Confidence Rule' became the 'elephant in the room' when the US Department of Energy (US DOE) stopped funding the licensing of the proposed Yucca Mountain spent nuclear fuel (SNF) repository. In November 2009, two US NRC Commissioners refused to approve an update to the Waste Confidence Rule in response to the US DOE's withdrawal of its funding. On 3 March 2010, the US DOE filed a motion to withdraw from the US NRC its licence application for the construction of Yucca Mountain. On 9 March 2010, US NRC Commissioner Dale Klein commented:

> Now that one can ask whether the nation is back to square one with regard to the back end of the fuel cycle, the NRC naturally faces the issue of waste confidence ... Part of the Commission's 'confidence' underlying the rule

> must be based on events that are beyond the NRC's control, and when those events are in flux, the Commission has to be very careful in deciding whether it can credibly say that we have 'confidence' that a repository will be open on a given date or period of time.
>
> (Klein, 2010)

On 7 August 2012, the US NRC postponed issuance of final COL approvals and licence renewal applications until it could determine whether there was confidence that used fuel at US NPPs would not now present environmental hazards.

To address this issue, the Blue Ribbon Commission on America's Nuclear Future (BRC) was chartered 'to recommend a new strategy for managing the back end of the nuclear fuel cycle' (BRC, 2012: vi). The strategy comprises eight key elements that can be grouped as follows (BRC, 2012: vii):

1 directions to the US Congress:
   - (a) to implement a 'consent-based' approach to siting future waste management facilities;
   - (b) to create a new organisation, a 'congressionally chartered federal corporation', to manage waste facilities; and
   - (c) to give this new organisation direct access to the Nuclear Waste Trust Fund;

2 directions to the US DOE:
   - (d) to renew prompt efforts to develop one or more geologic disposal facilities;
   - (e) to renew prompt efforts to develop one or more consolidated interim SNF storage facilities in which to store metric tonnes of heavy metal (MTHM) (Rothwell, 2015); and
   - (f) to renew prompt efforts to develop a waste transportation system; and

3 suggestions to US Congress:
   - (g) to support US research and development (R&D) in nuclear energy and workforce development; and
   - (h) to support US leadership in international efforts to address safety, waste management, non-proliferation and security concerns (see Rothwell, 2010, cited in BRC, 2012: 156).

To implement this strategy, six legislative changes were proposed (BRC, 2012: viii):

1 to establish a new facility siting process;
2 to authorise consolidated interim storage facilities;
3 to broaden support to jurisdictions affected by SNF transportation;
4 to establish a new waste management organisation;

5 to ensure access to dedicated funding; and
6 to promote international engagement to support safe and secure waste management.

Regarding the authorisation of consolidated storage facilities:

> The NWPA [US Nuclear Waste Policy Act of 1982] allows the government to construct one consolidated storage facility with limited capacity, but only after construction of a nuclear waste repository has been licensed ... The Act should be modified to allow for a consent-based process to site, license, and construct multiple storage facilities with adequate capacity.
>
> (BRC, 2012: viii)

To remedy this situation, Congress can vote to delete section 148(d) of the US Nuclear Waste Policy Act of 1982, as amended:

> (d) LICENSING CONDITIONS—Any license issued by the Commission for a monitored retrievable storage facility under this section shall provide that—
>
> 1 construction of such facility may not begin until the Commission has issued a license for the construction of a repository under section 115 (d) [42 USC 10135(d)];
> 2 construction of such facility or acceptance of SNF or high-level radioactive waste shall be prohibited during such time as the repository license is revoked by the Commission or construction of the repository ceases;
> 3 the quantity of SNF or high-level radioactive waste at the site of such facility at any one time may not exceed 10,000 metric tonnes of heavy metal until a repository under this Act first accepts SNF or solidified high-level radioactive waste; and
> 4 the quantity of SNF or high-level radioactive waste at the site of the facility at any one time may not exceed 15,000 metric tonnes of heavy metal [42 USC 101681].

Prompt congressional efforts to pass legislation to unlink interim storage facility development from repository development would go a long way towards restoring confidence that the US government is 'resolving the waste issue'. However, the 'waste confidence issue' was resolved in July 2014 when the US NRC found that there were no unsolvable environmental issues surrounding on-site extended interim storage of SNF at nuclear facilities; hence there was no need to revisit the licences issued under the Waste Confidence Rule, or to delay licence renewals or new licences. The US NRC outlined the purpose of the Rule as follows:

> The amendments revise 10 CFR 51.23 ... which contains the generic determination on the environmental impacts of continued storage of

> spent nuclear fuel beyond the licensed life for operation of a reactor (continued storage) ... the final rule clarifies that the generic determination applies to license renewals for independent spent fuel storage installations (ISFSI) and to reactor construction permits and early site permits.
>
> (US NRC, 2014: 1)

However, this does not allow for the consolidation of SNF into a US DOE facility (thus increasing the cost of SNF management because small facilities cannot take advantage of scale economies – Rothwell, 2015). Only congressional action and appropriations from the Nuclear Waste Trust Fund will allow this.

Note: The US Congress is the 'trustee' of the Nuclear Waste Trust Fund, but the funds become a part of the 'general fund', out of which appropriations might be made to manage nuclear waste. Therefore there is no separate 'trust fund' as such. In fact, contributions to the Fund were stopped in November 2013, when Congress cut all funding to Yucca Mountain and to the US DOE's Office of Civilian Radioactive Waste Management (OCRWM), which had been responsible for preparing a licence application for the repository at Yucca Mountain (US DOE, 2010); hence the US DOE could no longer implement the 1982 Act. Congress directed the US DOE to dismantle the OCRWM 'with prejudice' (Holt, 2015: 3), meaning that it was to be dismantled in such a way that it could never be reassembled.

2.2 US Department of Energy incentives to new nuclear generation

Since 2000, the US DOE has engaged in a series of programmes to provide incentives to new nuclear investors, including the Nuclear Power 2010 (NP2010) programme. It was envisaged that this programme would result in new NPPs operating in the United States by 2010 (Johnson, 2002: 2): 'Goals: [1] Orders for one or more new nuclear plants by 2005 [and 2] Operation of new nuclear power plants by 2010.' The US DOE funded several feasibility studies, including one for the construction of two ABWRs at the South Texas Project (STP). (See Rothwell, 2006, for a real options analysis of building two more units at the STP.) However, electric utilities did not order new NPPs until after the passage of the US Energy Policy Act of 2005.

The primary public policy rationale for such policies is to subsidise 'first-of-a-kind' (FOAK) costs to encourage investors at the margin to order new NPPs, so that more learning will lower costs, for example in establishing a supply chain, in such a way that NPPs are competitive (NEA, 2015a). In return, the US government expects the industry to offset the cost of the subsidies by generating more tax revenues and jobs.

Table 2.5 Nuclear-related provisions of US Energy Policy Act of 2005

Provision	*Title reference*	*Section reference*	*Other references*	*Responsible agencies*
(1) Production tax credits	Title XIII, 'Energy Policy Tax Incentives'	Section 1306, 'Credit for Production from Advanced Nuclear Power Facilities'	Section 45 of Title 26, 'Internal Revenue Code'	(1) Secretary of the Treasury (2) Secretary of Energy
(2) Standby support	Title VI, 'Nuclear Matters'	Section 638, 'Standby Support for Certain Nuclear Plant Delays'	Federal Credit Reform Act of 1990	Secretary of Energy
(3) Loan guarantees	Title XVII, 'Incentives for Innovative Technologies'	Section 1701, 'Definitions', to section 1704, 'Authorization of Appropriations'	Federal Credit Reform Act of 1990	Secretary of Energy

Source: Rothwell and Graber (2009).

Three provisions in the 2005 Act promote new nuclear capacity construction: production tax credits (PTCs); a standby support programme (SSP); and loan guarantees (see Table 2.5). (According to 26 USC 45(J), 'the term "advanced nuclear facility" means any nuclear facility the reactor design for which is approved after 31 December 1993, by the US NRC'; hence these incentives *do not apply to the completion of older models* licensed under the earlier regulations at 10 CFR Part 50.) The subsidies were disproportionately granted to the first half-dozen plants built – that is, those that applied for COL before 31 December 2008, as in Table 2.3. Within this group, there is a set of FOAK plants. The FOAK set of AP1000s include Sanmen Units 1 and 2 (started in 2007) and Haiyang Units 1 and 2 (started in 2008) in China, and Vogtle Units 3 and 4 (started in 2011) and Summer Units 2 and 3 (started in 2012) in the United States. The production of the FOAK units allows amortisation of the costs of engineering and licensing, and justifies the construction of dedicated manufacturing facilities.

First, the US Internal Revenue Service (IRS) issued interim guidelines for PTCs (US Treasury and IRS, 2006). The PTC is a tax credit based on a percentage of the nuclear plant's nameplate capacity. In total, there is a 6,000 MW limit – the 'nuclear MW limit' – to be allocated among qualifying advanced nuclear plants for eight years from the time of commercial operation. A twin-unit nuclear plant is considered to have two facilities and can apply separately for an allocation for each facility. There is little new about PTCs for electricity-generating plants. Section 45 of the IRS Code deals explicitly with the terms and conditions of PTCs for electric plants – particularly wind power – while section 45(J) was created under the Energy Policy Act of 2005 specifically for NPPs.

In its interim guidelines, the IRS anticipated that there would be applications for PTCs that would exceed the nuclear MW limit. Thus an important aspect of Title XIII, 'Energy Policy Tax Incentives', of the 2005 Act is how the 6,000 MW is to be allocated among those NPPs that qualify. If the qualified applications for the PTC total a nameplate capacity will be in excess of 6,000 MW, then the Secretary of Energy is responsible for allocating an equal percentage of the 6,000 MW to each applicant. All applicants in commercial production by January 2021 will receive a percentage of the 6,000 MW allocation. However, given the expected completion times of new NPPs, the nuclear MW limit is unlikely to be exceeded by 2021: only Vogtle Units 3 and 4 and Summer Units 2 and 3 are expected to be completed by then, with a combined capacity of about 4,500 MW (see Table 2.4).

The PTC is US$18 per megawatt-hour (MWh) for eight years, subject to two limits: (a) an annual limitation of $125 million per 1,000 MW of capacity; and (b) a phase-out of the PTC when electricity is sold from new nuclear at $80/MWh or higher. Both the annual limitation and the reference price of $80/MWh will be adjusted for inflation by the Secretary of Energy. For example, a price $80/MWh in 2005 US dollars would be about $100/MWh in 2013 US dollars and this range, $80–$100/MWh, provides a benchmark against which to judge the competitiveness of new nuclear.

Second, in 2007, the US DOE published a final rule on the SSP (US DOE, 2007). A new section of 10 CFR Part 52 aims to facilitate the construction and operation of ALWRs by providing 'delayed start-up risk insurance' for these projects. Standby support is limited to the first six FOAK units comprising no more than three different reactor technologies. The first two units that qualify for standby support receive substantial priorities and benefits over the remaining units. Standby support is an insurance policy against commercial operation delays resulting from the new 'one-stop' licensing process that was enacted in 1992 (10 CFR Part 52), but which has not yet been administratively exercised. The new licensing process aims to remedy major issues encountered in the old 10 CFR Part 50 licensing procedure under which NPPs required two licences: a construction licence and operating licence. The standby support is limited to covering (a) the principal and interest of the investor's debt obligations, and (b) the costs of incremental purchased power arising from a start-up affected by 'qualified delays'. The only units that will be eligible for standby support are Vogtle Units 3 and 4 and Summer Units 2 and 3 (all of which are the same technology). Some delays were encountered while building the FOAK units at Vogtle and Summer because of the design certification process, but compensation for these delays through the SSP has yet to be discussed at time of writing (see Holt, 2014: 23).

Third, while the PTC programme is intended to support new nuclear operation (by means of tax reductions) and the SSP is intended to stabilise the new nuclear licensing process (by means of financial support during unforeseen regulatory delays), the US DOE loan guarantee programme is intended to promote carbon-free emissions in electricity production from low-carbon energy technologies, including new nuclear capacity. Under this programme, the total amount is limited to congressional appropriations (which were not in place until the US Energy Independence and Security Act of 2007). The borrower must pay fees for these loan guarantees that are similar to those that international financial markets would charge for similar loan guarantees.

Title XVII of the Energy Policy Act of 2005 states that new nuclear plants are eligible for loan guarantees, although it does not specify an amount. As the US DOE (2007) has clarified, the loan guarantee programme covers up to 100% of the loan cost, with the limitation that the guaranteed loans comprise no more than 80% of the nominal construction cost. The programme provides for the repayment of principal and interest on the loan should the borrower default. In the event of a default (as with the WPPSS), the developer is required to reimburse the US Treasury for the defaulted loan after the US Attorney General recovers any value in the assets. With a maximum of 80% of the project guaranteed, equity investors must cover the remainder of the construction cost.

The Energy Policy Act of 2005 plus various appropriations Bills set the total amount of the loan guarantee programme for advanced nuclear plants at $18,500 million, to be administered by the US DOE. The owner-investors in Vogtle Units 3 and 4 were provisionally offered a loan guarantee of $8,330 million. (See US CBO, 2011, for more on loan guarantee applications for new NPPs.) After four years of negotiations, in February 2014, the US DOE awarded Vogtle co-owners Georgia Power and Oglethorpe Power a $6,500 million loan guarantee, with a loan guarantee of $1,800 million to the remaining co-owner, the Municipal Electric Authority of Georgia (MEAG).

The US DOE gave three other plants positive initial reviews: Summer Units 2 and 3 (AP1000a), with South Carolina Electric & Gas (SCE&G); Calvert Cliffs Unit 3 (a US evolutionary power reactor, or EPR), with Constellation in Maryland; and South Texas Project Units 3 and 4 (ABWRs), with NRG Energy in Texas. The Department selected Comanche Peak Units 3 and 4 (US advanced power reactors, or APWRs) of Luminant in Texas as 'a first alternate' (which selection effectively shelved the economic simplified boiling water reactor, or ESBWR, applications).

In October 2010, the US DOE offered a loan guarantee to Constellation, but Constellation rejected the offer on the grounds that the fee was too high (Wald, 2010). At time of writing, the project is therefore unlikely to go forward. This implies that the application for the other US EPR – for Bell Bend in Pennsylvania, with PPL – will not be pursued. (It is unlikely that the EPR with a digital instrumentation and control, or I&C, system will be licensed in the United States owing to US NRC requirements regarding digital I&C testing.) In 2008, PPL stated that, '[w]ithout federal loan guarantees [or other acceptable financing structures] ... PPL will not be able to secure financing for the substantial costs of building new, advanced-design nuclear energy plants' (William Spence, PPL chief operating officer, or COO, quoted in Whitten, 2008). In addition, after the Fukushima-Daiichi accident, work on STP Units 3 and 4 was halted.

Regarding the possibility of a loan guarantee for Comanche Peak Units 3 and 4 with Luminant in Texas:

> The planned $15 billion expansion of Comanche Peak ... suffered a critical funding setback in Congress this week. According to outgoing Rep. Chet Edwards [Democrat-Waco, TX], cuts in the House-passed version of the federal spending bill eliminate loan guarantees that Dallas-based Luminant said were vital to the plan's viability.
>
> (Recio, 2010)

With a cost-cutting Congress, any loan guarantee applications that did not make the first cut will be unlikely to receive a loan guarantee offer. Given delays in COL licensing, the US DOE is therefore likely only to offer loan guarantees to investors buying AP1000s.

Even with loan guarantees, the builders of new nuclear must convince Wall Street that investing in nuclear generation does not involve more risk than similar investments. In 2011, however, credit ratings agency Moody's wrote (referring to SCE&G, builder of Summer Units 2 and 3, and updating its 2007, 2008 and 2009 reports):

> Today's downgrade of SCE&G's senior unsecured and Issuer Rating to Baa2 considers the heightened risk associated with a large nuclear construction program extending through 2019 that is expected to be about 50% debt financed and will pressure future financial metrics ... Moody's rating also takes into account a credit-supportive regulatory regime.
>
> (Moody's, 2011)

While maintaining a stable A3 bond rating, regarding Georgia Power Company's construction of Vogtle Units 3 and 4, Moody's wrote:

> The cost increases and delays experienced on the project thus far have been caused by delays in obtaining initial US NRC approval for the plant's design, but also because of problems with the construction of plant modular components by Shaw Modular Solutions (now called CB&I Lake Charles Facility).
>
> (Moody's, 2013: 1)

One response to Wall Street's requirements is the emergence of smaller NPPs with lower total construction costs. According to the US DOE:

> [The] White House announced new funding to advance the development of American-made Small Modular Reactors, SMRs ... A total of $450 million will be made available to support First-of-a-Kind

engineering, design certification, and licensing for up to two SMR designs over five years, subject to congressional appropriations.

(US DOE, 2012)

Soon thereafter, the US DOE invited designers to apply for cost sharing on engineering, design certification and licensing for up to two SMR designs. Four designs were submitted by the 21 May 2012 deadline:

1 Babcock & Wilcox's mPower design;
2 NuScale Power's NuScale design (Fairfield, 2009);
3 Westinghouse's W-SMR design; and
4 Holtec's 160 MW inherently safe modular underground reactor (HI-SMUR 160).

On 20 November 2012, Babcock & Wilcox announced that it had been selected by the US DOE in the first round for cost sharing, and NuScale was selected in a second round.

In addition, a number of other countries are developing SMRs, some of which are under construction, for example in Argentina and Russia. In March 2015, the Korean Atomic Energy Research Institute (KAERI) and the Saudi Arabian King Abdullah City for Atomic and Renewable Energy (KA-CARE) signed a memorandum of understanding (MOU) to investigate the construction of KAERI's system-integrated modular advanced reactor (SMART) SMR, licensed by Korean regulators in 2012. (See Chapter 3, Sections 3.5–3.7, for estimates of SMR construction costs.)

2.3 US electric utility regulation and new nuclear power

In addition to US NRC regulation of the nuclear power industry, states also regulate (non-safety aspects of) nuclear power. To test whether state regulation has influenced investment in nuclear power capacity, this section examines how electricity regulation and deregulation might have influenced the submission of COLAs (see Table 2.3) and 'construction starts' for NPPs in the United States (see Table 2.4).

In many US states, a utilities commission oversees the tariffs charged and prudent capacity expansions of electric utilities (NARUC, 2015). The standards for determining equitable tariffs were developed in the United States in the 1920s and 1930s. Tariffs were set to cover costs and an allowed rate of return on invested capital. Most commissions did not allow a rate of return on investments that were *not* 'used and useful', for example on plants under construction or abandoned projects (Rothwell and Gomez, 2003).

Maryland allowed its utilities to charge the allowed rate of return on 'construction work in progress' (CWIP) from the inception of its commission in 1923 (see Table 2.6, column 6). By 1968, six states were using CWIP

Table 2.6 Summary of US state electricity utility regulation c. 31 December 2008

Col. 1 *Jurisdiction*	*Col. 2* *Pop/k*	*Col. 3* *MWe*	*Col. 4* *N-MW*	*Col. 5* *Dereg?*	*Col. 6* *CWIP?*	*Col. 7* *NPP?*	*Col. 8* *COL?*	*Col. 9* *Start?*
Alabama	4,780	31,400	5,012	0	1968	OK	2	0
Alaska	710	2,000	0	0	AFUDC	OK	0	0
Arizona	6,392	26,300	3,942	−1	1977	OK	0	0
Arkansas	2,916	15,300	1,835	−1	1975	OK	0	0
California	37,254	65,900	4,390	−1	AFUDC	NO	0	0
Colorado	5,029	13,000	0	0	1954	OK	0	0
Connecticut	3,574	8,000	2,103	1	AFUDC	NO	0	0
Delaware	898	3,400	0	1	1976	OK	0	0
District of Columbia	602	800	0	1	1974	OK	0	0
Florida	18,801	59,100	3,924	0	1975	OK	4	0
Georgia	**9,688**	**36,500**	**4,061**	**0**	**1972**	OK	**2**	**2**
Hawaii	1,360	2,600	0	0	AFUDC	NO	0	0
Idaho	1,568	3,800	0	0	1980	OK	0	0
Illinois	12,831	44,000	11,441	1	1961	NO	0	0
Indiana	6,484	27,900	0	0	1975	OK	0	0
Iowa	3,046	14,600	601	0	AFUDC	OK	0	0
Kansas	2,853	12,500	1,160	0	1981	NO	0	0
Kentucky	4,339	20,200	0	0	1943	NO	0	0

Table 2.6 (continued)

Col. 1 Jurisdiction	*Col. 2 Pop/k*	*Col. 3 MWe*	*Col. 4 N-MW*	*Col. 5 Dereg?*	*Col. 6 CWIP?*	*Col. 7 NPP?*	*Col. 8 COL?*	*Col. 9 Start?*
Louisiana	4,533	26,000	2,142	0	1946	OK	0	0
Maine	1,328	4,300	0	1	AFUDC	NO	0	0
Maryland	5,774	12,500	1,705	1	1923	OK	1	0
Massachusetts	6,548	13,700	685	1	AFUDC	NO	0	0
Michigan	9,884	30,300	3,953	1	1970	OK	0	0
Minnesota	5,304	14,600	1,686	0	1975	NO	0	0
Mississippi	2,967	15,800	1,251	0	1970	OK	0	0
Missouri	5,989	20,800	1,190	0	AFUDC	OK	0	0
Montana	989	5,800	0	−1	AFUDC	NO	0	0
Nebraska	1,826	7,800	1,252	0	NA	OK	0	0
Nevada	2,701	11,400	0	−1	1979	OK	0	0
New Hampshire	1,316	4,200	1,247	1	AFUDC	OK	0	0
New Jersey	8,792	18,500	4,108	1	1972	NO	0	0
New Mexico	2,059	8,000	0	−1	1969	OK	0	0
New York	19,378	39,700	5,262	1	1973	OK	0	0
North Carolina	9,535	27,600	4,958	0	1979	OK	2	0
North Dakota	673	6,000	0	0	AFUDC	OK	0	0
Ohio	11,537	33,500	2,134	1	1977	OK	1	0

(Continued)

Table 2.6 (continued)

Col. 1 *Jurisdiction*	*Col. 2* *Pop/k*	*Col. 3* *MWe*	*Col. 4* *N-MW*	*Col. 5* *Dereg?*	*Col. 6* *CWIP?*	*Col. 7* *NPP?*	*Col. 8* *COL?*	*Col. 9* *Start?*
Oklahoma	3,751	20,800	0	0	1975	OK	0	0
Oregon	3,831	14,000	0	1	AFUDC	NO	0	0
Pennsylvania	12,702	45,600	9,509	1	1972	OK	1	0
Rhode Island	1,053	1,800	0	1	AFUDC	NO	0	0
South Carolina	**4,625**	**24,000**	**6,486**	**0**	**1970**	OK	**4**	**2**
South Dakota	814	3,400	0	0	AFUDC	OK	0	0
Tennessee	**6,346**	**20,900**	**3,401**	**0**	**NA**	OK	**0**	**1**
Texas	25,146	103,000	4,927	1	1970	OK	4	0
Utah	2,764	7,400	0	0	1976	OK	0	0
Vermont	626	1,100	620	0	1971	NO	0	0
Virginia	8,001	23,800	3,513	−1	1947	OK	1	0
Washington	6,725	30,100	1,131	0	1975	OK	0	0
West Virginia	1,853	16,400	0	0	1970	NO	0	0
Wisconsin	5,687	17,700	1,583	0	1974	NO	0	0
Wyoming	564	7,600	0	0	AFUDC	OK	0	0

Sources: Pop/k = population/1,000 (US Bureau of the Census, 2011); MW = total MW in state (US EIA, 2009); N-MW = nuclear MW (US EIA, 2009); DeReg? = deregulated? (US EIA, 2010) (–1 = reversed); CWIP? = construction work in progress accounting? (Rothwell, 1985); NPP? = does state allow construction of NPPs? (Blake, 2006); 'COL?' = combined construction and operating licence? (US NRC, 2014) (some COLAs have been withdrawn); 'Start?' (from Table 2.4).

Note: States with construction are in **bold**.

accounting, while the rest used 'allowance for funds used during construction' (AFUDC) accounting. Under AFUDC, utilities are allowed to capitalise interest during construction (IDC) in a separate set of accounts for investors, but are not allowed to increase tariffs to cover those construction expenditures. As a result of large construction projects after 1968 and inflation following the oil price crisis of 1973, AFUDC regulation led to price shocks when large capitalised construction expenditures entered the rate base. To encourage electricity capacity construction and to avoid price shocks, most states switched to CWIP accounting. By 1981, two-thirds of the commissions had adopted CWIP. In those states retaining AFUDC accounting, the utility bears all of the risk of construction completion; in those with CWIP, the utility shares this risk with its customers. In return, customers in states using CWIP pay less in total because their payments during construction reduce the financing costs of the plant. Thus Wall Street requires a higher rate of return on financing for electric utilities building electricity-generating projects under AFUDC regulation or in deregulated markets than it does for those working under CWIP.

Further, possibly in reaction to the waste generated by NPPs (see Table 2.6, column 4, for nuclear-generating capacity in MW by state), some states passed regulations to conditionally prohibit their electric utilities from building NPPs (see Table 2.6, column 7, in which prohibitions are indicated by 'NO' – Blake, 2006). Following the passage of the US Nuclear Waste Policy Act of 1982, as amended, many states passed laws that tied new construction to the completion by the US DOE of tasks relating to the licensing and construction of a geologic repository. Such states include:

1 California, Connecticut, Illinois, New Jersey and Wisconsin, which require an 'approved demonstrable technology for waste disposal';
2 Kentucky, Maine and Massachusetts, which require the 'existence' of a disposal site;
3 Oregon and West Virginia, which require a 'licensed' disposal site;
4 Hawaii, Kansas, Montana, Rhode Island and Vermont, which limit nuclear power in other ways; and
5 Minnesota, which unconditionally prohibits the construction of new NPPs.

Also in the 1980s, facing the enormous costs of building pollution-controlled, coal-fired central stations or NPPs, some commissions were directed by their legislatures to begin experimenting with incentive-based systems to reduce cost overruns, for example by tying the allowed rate of return to cost targets (Che and Rothwell, 1995). This set the stage for the introduction of legislation to mandate market-based reforms.

With US experience in deregulating tariffs in industries as diverse as air transport and natural gas, and with increasing construction of natural gas combined-cycle gas turbines (CCGTs) in the 'dash for gas', beginning in the 1990s, state legislatures directed commissions in the late 1990s to create markets to set prices in the electric power industry. However, not all deregulation was well conceived or implemented: California's deregulated market was easily manipulated, forcing in-state utilities to purchase out-of-state electricity at higher prices, bankrupting Pacific Gas & Electric (PG&E), the operator of the Diablo Canyon NPP, and giving pause to the deregulation of electricity markets in other states.

By February 2003, the US Energy Information Administration (US EIA) had categorised states into four groups: (a) those in which restructuring was active; (b) those in which restructuring was delayed; (c) those in which restructuring was suspended; and (d) those in which restructuring was not active. This information is presented in Table 2.6, column 5 (as updated in US EIA, 2010, but note that Table 2.6 presents data that was relevant around the time that COLAs were required to be filed if sites were to qualify for subsidies in Table 2.5 – that is, by 31 December 2008). Market reforms, or 'retail choice with competition', were still active in those states indicated by a '1'. States that experimented with market reform, but which suspended those reforms, are indicated with a '–1'. Those states that did not implement market reforms are indicated with a '0'.

Nonetheless, according to the US Federal Energy Regulatory Commission (US FERC, 2011), four active regional electricity markets have developed:

1 in New England, including the deregulated states of Connecticut, Maine, New Hampshire and Rhode Island, and the regulated states of Massachusetts and Vermont;
2 in New York, involving only the state of New York;
3 'PJM Interconnection', originally with Pennsylvania, New Jersey and Maryland, and now including markets in the deregulated states of Delaware, District of Columbia, Illinois, Michigan and Ohio, and in some markets in the regulated states of Indiana, Kentucky, North Carolina, Virginia and West Virginia; and
4 the 'Texas Reliability Entity' (TRE), formerly known as the Electric Reliability Council of Texas (ERCOT), involving primarily the state of Texas.

Most south-eastern and western states of the United States are still rate-of-return regulated. One of the implications of rate-of-return regulation is a tendency to overcapitalise because the allowed rate of return is earned on invested capital, rather than on fuel cost mark-ups (Averch and Johnson, 1962). One of the side effects of market deregulation is undercapitalisation, because the market price is determined by the cost of the marginal fuel and there is no guarantee that the market price will cover long-term investments. For much of the time since electricity market deregulation in the mid-1990s, natural gas has been the marginal fuel. Thus firms in deregulated markets minimise the short-term risk on the difference between cost and price – that is, profit – by using natural gas (although there is no guarantee that fixed costs will be covered).

In a south-eastern state without electricity market reform, Tennessee, construction restarted on a Westinghouse PWR on the Watts Bar site, to be operated by the TVA, a corporation owned by the US government. In 1985, the TVA suspended construction of Watts Bar Unit 2. After its application to complete Watts Bar Unit 2 under the older US NRC regulations (10 CFR Part 50), in 2008 the US NRC extended the TVA's construction permit completion date to 31 March 2013 (and later extended it further, to 30 September 2016).

Table 2.7 summarises this discussion. From this summary, it is possible to conclude that the COLAs were submitted from (a) states in which there were no restrictions on NPP construction, and (b) states in which regulatory commissions used CWIP accounting or in which the TVA operates. There appears to be a bias against new nuclear power construction in states with rate-of-return regulation using AFUDC accounting and in states with deregulated electricity markets. Underlying this bias could be high Wall Street nuclear risk premiums for electric utilities in AFUDC-regulated and deregulated states.

While this awkward financial situation for new nuclear power could change if the US Congress were to legislate cuts in carbon dioxide emissions in response to the changing climate, without more loan guarantees from a budget-cutting Congress a new NPP is unlikely to be operating in any US jurisdiction with active electricity market reform or AFUDC accounting before January 2021. In addition, because of delays anticipated for NPPs not already under construction, Vogtle and Summer could receive a full eight years of PTCs. There will be four FOAK AP1000a units, with a gross capacity of 4,472 MW, in the United States and four FOAK AP1000 units, with a gross capacity of 4,460 MW (or about 8,000 MW net), in China, over which to amortise FOAK costs. (See Chapter 3, Section 3.6, for more on allocating FOAK costs.)

Table 2.7 State regulation and new nuclear power

State regulation and new nuclear power	*# of states*	*# of COLS*	*# of starts*
States with restrictions on nuclear power plant construction CA, CT, HI, IL, KS, KY, ME, MA, MN, MT, NJ, OR, RI, VT, WV, WI	16	0	0
Rate-of-return regulated states with AFUDC AK, IA, MO, ND, SD, WY	6	0	0
Rate-of-return regulated states with CWIP AL, AR, AZ, CO, FL, GA, ID, IN, LA, MS, NE, NV, NM, NC, OK, SC, TN, UT, VA, WA	20	14	5
Deregulated states DE, MI, NH, NY, MD, OH, PA, TX	8	6	0
Totals	50	20	5

Source: From Table 2.6.

Construction cost uncertainties will be resolved after a few plants are built. Nevertheless, operating cost risks will not be resolved until experience accumulates for each certified design. These uncertainties divide nuclear investor-utilities into those willing to:

1 construct under the current conditions and incentives;
2 wait until carbon fees are implemented, at some time after 2015;
3 wait until new plants come online, at some time after 2020;
4 wait until there is sufficient experience with operation by 2025; and
5 wait until after 2025.

This limits the number of electric utilities that could construct new nuclear before 2035, which is the time horizon of the US EIA's National Energy Modelling System (NEMS), used in its Annual Energy Outlook (AEO) (US EIA, 2014). (See also Section 2.4, Chapter 3, Section 3.2, and Chapter 5 for discussion of the various editions of the AEO.) For example, consider the comments by Ralph Izzo, president and chief executive officer (CEO) of the New-Jersey-based utility Public Service Enterprise Group (PSEG), which operates the Salem and Hope Creek NPPs, signalling that he falls into the third of the above categories:

> I think the biggest impediment of aggressive nuclear technology is its cost ... PSEG is waiting for the first new reactors to be licensed and built before making any decision about new nuclear plants ... The cost is not within my comfort level right now.
>
> (Ling, 2009)

Nevertheless, PSEG has submitted an application for an ESP in New Jersey (see Table 2.2). This watching and waiting has been taking place during a particularly volatile period for energy prices, as discussed in Chapter 5.

To further complicate the choice between generation technologies, the cost of natural gas now appears to be '"too cheap to avoid" in North America'. However, most studies report only the mean, or expected, or most likely, value of the cost of fossil-fired, nuclear, or renewable electricity. Also, most studies assume that the price of natural gas will continue to be low for the foreseeable future, implicitly assuming that either the natural gas supply curve will continue to shift outward with increases in demand or that the natural gas demand curve will not shift upward. These studies miss the big picture regarding the impact of the high volatility of the price of natural gas on the price of electricity. With the market price of electricity driven by natural gas prices, consumers (without access to hedging contracts) must absorb more of the risk of electricity price spikes because the electric utility industry, particularly in the United States, has invested so heavily in natural gas CCGT capacity.

While natural gas prices in the United States are now low (but high in Japan because of the closure of Japanese NPPs following the Fukushima-Daiichi accident), economics suggests that this low price will lead to increases in demand by encouraging the substitution of natural gas for more expensive energy resources. This substitution could be quick (by 2020) or slow (by 2030), but will happen within the lifetimes of the new electricity-generating capacity being constructed today.

Because of natural gas price spikes and carbon dioxide output, for example a 1,000 MW CCGT plant can produce almost 3 million metric tonnes (MT) of CO_2 per year, it is not obvious that CCGT-generated electricity will dominate new nuclear in a carbon-constrained, natural-gas-hungry world between 2020 and 2060. Because of uncertainties regarding both the cost of natural gas and nuclear power, the choice between the two depends on the decision maker's aversion to (a) natural gas price volatility and spikes, and (b) the risks of investing in new nuclear.

Simultaneously, capital markets must evaluate these uncertainties to determine which are manageable risks (which might be diversified) and which involve unknown (possibly systemic) uncertainties. Capital markets are moving toward high risk premiums for new nuclear in the range of 3–5% (Rothwell, 2006: 48; University of Chicago, 2004: 5–21). These risk premiums are likely to be higher for nuclear developers than for other electricity technology investors with similar levelised cost, *if only because of nuclear generation's high construction cost in relation to the market value of a typical nuclear electric utility*. These risk premiums reflect both a 'nuclear' effect, because the nuclear industry requires the highest level of industrial quality and security in the commercial world (similar to quality and security in the manned spacecraft industry), and a 'size' effect, which can be approximated as the ratio of total construction cost to the present value of the firm, as identified in Moody's (2011). Appendix 3A defines a risk premium as the difference between the expectation of an uncertain value and its 'certainty equivalence', such that the decision maker is indifferent between the two values, for example between the expected levelised cost and its certainty equivalent.

2.4 Public policy instruments and nuclear power's cost of capital

Various public policy instruments have been proposed to lower the cost of capital to investors in new nuclear. To determine the impact of these instruments on the cost of capital, this section discusses the results of using a cash flow model to calibrate changes in the real (constant currency) weighted average cost of capital (WACC), or **r**, with US government taxes and policy instruments.

The WACC, **r**, is defined as:

$$\mathrm{WACC} = \mathbf{r} = [\mathbf{d} \times (1 - \mathbf{tr}) \times \mathrm{dR}] + [\mathbf{e} \times (1 - \mathrm{dR})] \qquad (2.4.1)$$

where

d is the real rate of return on debt,
tr is the corporate tax rate,
dR is the debt to total capitalisation ratio, [**d**/(**d** + **e**)], and
e is the real rate of return on equity.

With baseline assumptions of straight-line depreciation, 50% debt, 50% equity and a 38% tax rate, the tax-adjusted **r** was calculated for:

1 accelerated depreciation, modified accelerated cost recovery system (MACRS);
2 investment tax credits (ITCs) of 10%;
3 PTCs of US$18/MWh during the first eight years of operation; and
4 loan guarantees at $^3/_8$% above the US Treasury bond rate for a 20-year term, with 80% debt and 20% equity.

The results of Appendix 2A are summarised here. First, as a baseline, straight-line depreciation with 50% debt, 50% equity, a 38% tax rate, a real cost of debt of 7.5% and a nominal cost of equity of 18% yields a *nominal* WACC of 12%, or a *real* cost of capital, **r**, of 10%. Because of tax effects and interaction terms, the rule of thumb that the real rate is equal to the nominal rate minus the rate of inflation is too simplistic; the real rate must be calculated more precisely, for example with a cash flow model, as summarised in Table 2A.4.

A real WACC of 10% is the baseline real cost of capital for a 'merchant', *unregulated* nuclear investor in the United States and equal to the cost of capital assumed for *all* electric utilities in the US EIA's NEMS. The US EIA describes how WACC is determined for *all* electric utility investments by the electricity capacity planning (ECP) subroutine:

> The model performs a discounted cash flow analysis of the costs of building and operating power plants over 30 years and chooses the least cost mix of options. The ECP assumes that building power plants will take place in a competitive environment rather than in a rate base or regulated environment. Each year, the assumptions and parameters for discount rates and the weighted average cost of capital (WACC) are reviewed to reflect the changing nature of the power industry and to incorporate new capital market information. For example, since the AEO2004, the US EIA has increased the equity portion of project financing and the return required on equity to reflect the greater risk associated with investments in a deregulated market. The discount rate (WACC) is a very important component because the rate reflects the riskiness of the investment and affects the mix of capacity additions … *small* changes in the weighted

average cost of capital lead to *huge* changes in capital intensive capacity additions.

(US EIA, 2013: appendix 3.C, 'Cost of capital', emphasis added)

A lower nominal rate on *equity* financing for *regulated* utilities is 15% (MIT, 2009). The consideration of taxes with straight-line depreciation yields a real cost of capital, **r**, of 8.7% – that is, a 3% decline in the nominal cost of equity results in a 1.3% decline in the real WACC. (This is not necessarily equal to the rate of return allowed by the regulator.) From a real WACC of 8.7%:

1 with MACRS, **r** declines to 8.2% (with a 10% nominal rate);
2 with an ITC of 10%, **r** declines to 7.8% (with a 9.7% nominal rate);
3 with an eight-year PTC, **r** declines to 7.5% (with a 9.3% nominal rate); and
4 with an 80% loan guarantee, **r** declines to 5.2% (with a 6.7% nominal rate).

These costs could be lower if the nuclear power investor were to take advantage of many programmes simultaneously. Therefore levelised cost will be calculated for *real* costs of capital for the following amounts (which are example costs of capital, the cost of capital being unknown for generic projects given that the actual cost of capital can be known only for an actual project on a specific date):

1 3%, sometimes known as the consensus long-run 'social cost of capital', which might be appropriate for self-regulated, state-financed, or state-owned utilities, such as the TVA;
2 5%, the 'loan guarantee' rate, appropriate for state-regulated utilities with CWIP financing with access to a loan guarantee programme;
3 7.5%, the PTC rate with loan guarantees, appropriate for state-regulated utilities with AFUDC financing;
4 10%, the rate associated with a '3% risk premium' on equity, appropriate for utilities in deregulated markets with access to loan guaranteed financing; and
5 12%, the rate associated with a '5% risk premium' on equity, appropriate for utilities in deregulated markets without access to loan guarantees or other investment subsidies.

Appendix 2A defines levelised cost, and calculates the cost of capital under various ownership and policy scenarios. Chapter 3 estimates new nuclear power's capital cost of construction and the levelised construction cost. Chapter 4 discusses new nuclear power's levelised costs and the influence of the cost of capital and risk premiums on these costs. Chapter 5 calculates the probability distributions of the levelised costs and the standard deviations of different portfolios of new nuclear, natural gas CCGTs and advanced coal.

Appendix 2A: Levelised cost and the cost of capital

Given the differences in the costs of capital and discount rates across various NPP investors, this appendix calculates costs of capital under different ownership and policy scenarios using a cash flow model based on a financial model of US NPPs underlying the cost analyses in MIT (2003, 2009) and University of Chicago (2004). This is referred to here as the 'Chicago spreadsheet' (CSS) (Taylor, 2010). This range of the costs of capital will be used in all three subsequent chapters. It begins by reviewing the definition of the levelised cost of electricity (LCOE), or, more simply, 'levelised cost' (*LC*).

Note: Some of the variable names have been changed in this appendix to be compatible with variable names used elsewhere in this book.

2A.1 Levelised cost of electricity

To better understand the LCOE from nuclear power, this section reviews the various definitions of the 'levelised cost of electricity' that have been used by the University of Chicago (2004). The international standard for defining LCOE in 2004 was that offered by the International Energy Agency and Nuclear Energy Agency (IEA and NEA, 1998), cited in University of Chicago (2004: ch. 2), and updated in IEA and NEA (2010) and IEA and NEA (2015):

$$LC = \Sigma_t[(I_t + O\&M_t + F_t) \times (1 + \mathbf{r})^{-t}] \big/ \Sigma_t[E_t(1 + \mathbf{r})^{-t}]$$
$$(t = -lt, \ldots, \mathrm{T}) \qquad (2A.1.1)$$

where

LC	is the levelised electricity generation cost (average lifetime),
I_t	are investment expenditures in year t,
$O\&M_t$	are operations and maintenance (O&M) expenditures in year t,
F_t	are fuel expenditures in year t,
E_t	are the MWh of electricity generated in year t, and
$\mathbf{r}$	is the discount rate (see Equation (2.4.1)), and
$(1 + \mathbf{r})$	is the discount factor.

The summations in Equation (2A.1.1) run from:

1 the start of construction expenditures ($t = -lt$, the construction lead time), to
2 the start of commercial operation ($t = 0$), to
3 the end of commercial operation ($t = \mathrm{T}$), the economic life of the project being equal to T years.

Because the funds for decommissioning are being accumulated from $t = 0, \ldots, T$ (although some regulators suggest including them in up-front financing), the time from T to DT, the end of site restoration, is not included in this economic analysis, although the contributed funds are included. Further, while the length of construction is not always known, plant lifetime, T, and time to decommission, DT, are usually fixed at specific lengths in financial analyses. For example, plant lifetime for an ALWR is considered to be 50–60 years (although, throughout this analysis, the plant *depreciation* life is 40 years, no matter the expected lifetime, T). After shutdown, the plant should be decontaminated, decommissioned and dismantled within 10–20 years to take advantage of plant operating personnel experience (NEA, 2015b; PNNL, 2011; Rothwell, 1991). A nuclear decommissioning trust fund is established to manage funds for the eventual decommissioning; these contributions are usually accounted for in the annual operating expenditures, even though the trust funds constitute a capital account.

If (a) all *investment* expenditures can be represented as being made before $t = 0$ – that is, all capital additions are treated as maintenance expenditures – and (b) all *other* expenditures and output are made after $t = 0$, then Equation (2A.1.1) can be rewritten as:

$$\Sigma_{t<0}[LC \times E_t \times (1+\mathbf{r})^{-t}] = \Sigma_{t>0}[I_t \times (1+\mathbf{r})^{-t}] + \Sigma_{t>0}[(O\&M_t + F_t) \times (1+\mathbf{r})^{-t}] \; (t = -lt, \ldots, \mathrm{T}) \qquad (2A.1.2)$$

These terms can be rearranged as:

$$\Sigma_{t<0}[I_t \times (1+\mathbf{r})^{-t}] = \Sigma_{t>0}[LC \times E_t - (O\&M_t + F_t) \times (1+\mathbf{r})^{-t}] \; (t = -lt, \ldots, \mathrm{T}) \qquad (2A.1.3)$$

– that is, the levelised cost, *LC*, is that cost of electricity over the life of the plant that equates discounted investment expenditures with discounted net revenues.

Levelised cost, *LC*, can be calculated in two ways: (a) using a 'top-down' approach by making appropriate simplifying assumptions to Equation (2A.1.1), or (b) using a 'cash flow' approach by estimating the value of each input in each year on the right-hand side of Equation (2A.1.1) and discounting to the present. In University of Chicago (2004), the first two chapters use a top-down approach, while the fifth chapter of that report uses a cash-flow approach to detail the tax consequences of investing in electricity-generating capacity in the United States

The remainder of this section reconciles the three levelised cost definitions with the definition of levelised cost in IEA and NEA (2015). These levelised cost methodologies represent the range of techniques used in the levelised cost literature. (Note that University of Chicago, 2004, uses chapter page numbers, so '1–1' refers to the first page of the first chapter.)

First, University of Chicago (2004: 1–4) is a 'pre-tax' LCOE and is based on a rearrangement of Equation (2A.1.1), while introducing other input variables: 'Annuitized capital cost (A), insurance [$O\&M_{IN}$], fixed O&M costs [$O\&M_f$], variable O&M costs [$O\&M_v$], and fuel costs (F).'

A is an annual annuity payment to repay the construction capital's principal and interest. The annuity payment is equal to KC times the capital recovery factor (CRF):

$$\mathrm{CRF} = \left\{\mathbf{r} \times (1+\mathbf{r})^{\mathrm{T}} / [(1+\mathbf{r})^{\mathrm{T}} - 1]\right\} \tag{2A.1.4}$$

where T is the payback period on debt, for example 30 or 40 years. In calculating CRF, **r** is equal to the 'debt and equity weighted average discount rate' (WACC).

Costs per MWh can be computed by dividing through by a constant electricity output, E (University of Chicago, 2004: 1–4):

$$E = \mathrm{MW} \times \mathrm{TT} \times CF \tag{2A.1.5}$$

where

MW is the MW capacity of a specific plant,
TT is the number of hours in a year, and
CF is the fraction of capacity at which the plant is operated during the period.

So:

$$A_{MWh} = \mathrm{CRF} \times KC/E \tag{2A.1.6}$$

where A_{MWh} is the annual payment to capital per MWh. Because $O\&M_{IN}$, $O\&M_f$ and $O\&M_v$ always appear together in University of Chicago (2004: 1–4), these O&M costs can be aggregated as $O\&M$ and fuel costs, $FUEL$, per MWh can be similarly defined:

$$O\&M_{MWh} = (O\&M_{IN} + O\&M_f + O\&M_y)/E \tag{2A.1.7}$$

$$F_{MWh} = F/E \tag{2A.1.8}$$

Costs per MWh, $O\&M_{MWh}$ and F_{MWh} are assumed constant during the operating life of the plant; hence the time subscript can be dropped. Similarly, University of Chicago (2004: 1–4) assumes that annual expenditures and annual generation are constant; thus these costs need not be written within the summation. Therefore $(1 + \mathbf{r})^{-t}$ can be divided out of the numerator and denominator, which results in an equation that is equivalent to Equation (2A.1.1):

$$LC = A_{MWh} + O\&M_{MWh} + F_{MWh} \tag{2A.1.9}$$

Second, University of Chicago (2004: 2–6) describes the levelised cost methodology used to compare US new electricity-generating costs with those outside the United States. This methodology follows Equation (2A.1.1) closely. In the first equation of University of Chicago (2004: 2–6), cash flows are assumed uniform over the operating life of the plant; hence *I*, *O&M*, *F* and *E* can be brought outside the summation signs in Equation (2A.1.1). The equation becomes (University of Chicago, 2004: 2–18):

$$LC = \left\{CC/[E \times \Sigma_t (1+\mathbf{r})^{-t}]\right\} + (O\&M/E) + F_{MWh}\ (t = 1, \ldots, \mathrm{T}) \tag{2A.1.10}$$

$$CC = CN + \Sigma_t[(CX_t - CN_t) \times (1+\mathbf{r})^{-t}]\ (t = -lt, \ldots, 0) \tag{2A.1.11}$$

where

CC is capital construction costs, a function of CX_t, $\mathbf{r}$ and lt,
CN is total contingency for all years of construction, including interest on contingency,
CX_t is the construction spending in year t,
CN_t is the total contingency associated with construction spending in year t, and
lt is lead time.

The accumulated interest, from $\Sigma_t\ (1 + \mathbf{r})^{-t}$ $(t = -lt, \ldots, 0)$, in Equation (2A.1.11) is IDC, where the IDC factor, **idc**, is a function of the cost of capital, the length of the construction lead time and the cumulative distribution of construction expenditures. In addition, Equation (2A.1.11) is discussed as follows:

> [O]vernight capital cost (less contingency costs) is the dollar amount that would be paid out if all capital expenses occurred simultaneously; no interest payments are included. [The IEA and NEA] (1998) reports contingency costs separately from overnight costs, although the U.S. definition of overnight cost includes contingency costs and owners' costs, as described in detail in Chapter 3. This data reporting difference is responsible for the separate accounting of contingency costs in the equation for capital costs above, which treats contingencies as being expended in the final year of construction.
>
> (University of Chicago, 2004: 2–17)

Third, University of Chicago (2004: 5–2) calculates levelised cost, *LC*, under the US Tax Code (which allows the performance of policy experiments with tax consequences, such as PTCs) using a (bottom-up) cash-flow approach, similar to the approach in MIT (2003). To determine the levelised cost, these cash flows are (a) escalated to then current dollars, (b) adjusted for tax effects, (c) discounted to the start of operation, and (d) deflated to 2003 US dollars.

Note: The remainder of this section was written with the help of Dr J'Tia Taylor of Argonne National Laboratory to determine the implicit equations used in the CSS.

The primary goal of University of Chicago (2004: 5–3) was to calculate the LCOE, with the report stating:

> The levelised cost of electricity, or LCOE, is defined as the constant real price of electricity over the life of the plant that compensates debt and equity investors at their required rates of return. Interest on debt accrues during the construction period and debt holders are repaid with equal annual payments [in constant dollars] over the debt term. Equity holders invest during the construction period and receive profits after tax and debt payment over the plant life. The LCOE is the electricity price that yields the . . . rate of return required by equity holders on the returns accruing to them.

So, LCOE in US$/MWh is that levelised cost, *LC*, such that the present value of *equity* investments, CXE_t (negative cash flows), during construction are equal to the present value of the positive cash flows to *equity* investors at their rate of return, **e**. This can be represented as:

$$LCOE = \{LC | [PVC(\mathbf{e}) = DCF(LC, \mathbf{e})]\} \qquad (2A.1.12)$$

where

PVC is the present value of equity investment construction expenditures,
e is the real rate of return on equity, and
DCF is the discounted cash flow during operation, as a function of *LC* and the rate of return on equity.

The discussion of Equation (2A.1.12) in the context of a discounted cash flow (DCF) model continues in the next section.

2A.2 Levelised cost in a discounted cash flow model

In a DCF model, the nominal LCOE is a constant *such that* the present value of *equity investments*, CXE_t (negative cash flows), during construction are equal to the present value of the positive cash flows to *equity investors* at the nominal equity rate of return, $\underline{\mathbf{e}}$. This is represented as (repeating Equation (2A.1.12) with nominal equity rates):

$$\underline{LCOE} = \left\{ LC \middle| [PVC(\underline{\mathbf{e}}) = DCF(LC, \underline{\mathbf{e}})] \right\} \tag{2A.2.1}$$

where $\underline{\mathbf{e}}$ is the nominal rate of return on equity (and $\mathbf{e}$ is the real rate of return on equity).

Nominal investments during construction in millions of dollars are:

$$\underline{XC}_t = [OC \times MW \times cx_t \times (1 + \mathbf{i})^{lt+t}] \ (t = 0, \ldots, -lt) \tag{2A.2.2}$$

where

- $\underline{XC}_t$ is the nominal construction funds expended during year t,
- OC is the real value of overnight construction costs (in US\$m) equal to real \$/MW,
- cx_t is the percentage expenditure in year t, and
- $\mathbf{i}$ is the appropriate rate of real *inflation* (*not escalation*), usually between 2% and 3%.

Inflation starts at time $-lt$ – that is, in the current year – and accumulates until the end of the plant's life, whereas present value calculations bring construction expenditures, revenues and expenses to the start of commercial operation – that is, lt years in the future. Because taxes and subsidies are paid in nominal currency, the impacts of taxes and subsidies must be made with nominal values and the results converted back to real values (as in Table 2A.4) if real values are required. In addition, $\underline{XD}_t$ are nominal construction expenditures financed by debt, defined as $\underline{XC}_t \times \underline{\text{dR}}$ (the ratio of nominal debt to total nominal assets) and $\underline{XE}_t$ are the nominal construction expenditures financed by equity investors, equal to $\underline{XC}_t \times (1 - \underline{\text{dR}})$, where $\underline{\text{dR}}$ is the nominal [$\underline{\text{dept}}$ / ($\underline{\text{debt}}$ + $\underline{\text{equity}}$)] ratio. In general, the nominal cost of debt, $\underline{\mathbf{d}}$, is equal to the real cost of debt, $\mathbf{d}$, plus the inflation rate, $\mathbf{i}$:

$$(1 + \underline{\mathbf{d}}) = (1 + \mathbf{d}) \times (1 + \mathbf{i}) \approx (1 + \mathbf{d} + \mathbf{i}) \tag{2A.2.3}$$

The nominal book value of investment, $\underline{BV}_t$, in each year of construction is equal to $\underline{BVD}_t$ + $\underline{BVE}_t$, where $\underline{BVD}_t$ and $\underline{BVE}_t$ are defined as:

$$\underline{BVD}_t = \underline{CXD}_t + [\underline{BVD}_{t-1} \times (1 + \underline{\mathbf{d}})] \ (t = -lt, \ldots, 0) \tag{2A.2.4}$$

and

$$\underline{BVE}_t = \underline{CXE}_t + \underline{BVE}_{t-1} \ (t = -lt, \ldots, 0) \tag{2A.2.5}$$

where interest is paid at the end of the period.

To account for IDC, the nominal book value of debt is multiplied by $(1 + \underline{\mathbf{d}})$ each year and accumulated. On the other hand, the present value, *PVC*, of *equity construction expenditures* is:

$$PVC(\underline{\mathbf{e}}) = \Sigma_t[\underline{CXE}_t \times (1+\underline{\mathbf{e}})^{-t}] \ (t = -lt, \ldots, 0) \tag{2A.2.6}$$

where construction *finishes* at time 0, and operation and sales start at the *beginning* of period 1, equal to the end of period 0.

Second, the CSS model calculates positive cash flows to investors. Nominal annual revenues, $\underline{RV}_t$ (in US\$m), during operation are defined as:

$$\underline{RV}_t = \underline{LCOE} \times E_t \times (1+\mathbf{i})^{lt+t} \ (t = 1, \ldots, \mathrm{T}) \tag{2A.2.7}$$

where E_t is defined as in Equation (2A.1.5).

Similarly, nominal annual total operating expenses, $\underline{EXP}_t$ (in US\$m, where *EXP* is equal to O&M plus fuel expenses in real current currency), are:

$$\underline{EXP}_t = EXP_t \times (1+\mathbf{i})^{lt+t} \ (t = 1, \ldots, \mathrm{T}) \tag{2A.2.8}$$

The nominal annual operating income, $\underline{OY}_t$ (in US\$m), is:

$$\underline{OY}_t = \underline{RV}_t - \underline{EXP}_t \ (t = 1, \ldots, \mathrm{T}) \tag{2A.2.9}$$

To calculate taxes on income, nominal earnings before interest and taxes, $\underline{EBIT}$, is:

$$\underline{EBIT}_t = \underline{OY}_t - \underline{DEP}_t \ (t = 1, \ldots, \mathrm{T}) \tag{2A.2.10}$$

where depreciation, $\underline{DEP}$, is calculated using either straight-line or modified accelerated cost recovery system (MACRS) algorithms.

Interest expense, $\underline{INT}$, in year *t* is:

$$\underline{INT}_t = \underline{BVD}_t \times \underline{\mathbf{d}} \ (t = 1, \ldots, \mathrm{T}) \tag{2A.2.11}$$

where $\underline{BVD}_t$ is the nominal book value of debt in year *t*.

Nominal annual taxes, $\underline{TAX}_t$, are (a) $\underline{EBIT}_t$ plus interest expenses multiplied by (b) the corporate tax rate, **tr**, minus (c) any tax credits. Here, two tax credits are considered: an ITC, with a rate of **itc**, and a PTC, with rate of **ptc**. Nominal net (after tax) income, $\underline{Y}_t$, is:

$$\underline{Y}_t = \underline{RV}_t - \underline{EXP}_t - \underline{TAX}_t \ (t = 1, \ldots, \mathrm{T}) \tag{2A.2.12}$$

To calculate residual cash flows, $\underline{CFlow}_t$, to equity investors, net income is first distributed to debt holders as an annuity, $\underline{A}$:

$$\underline{A} = \text{CRF}(\underline{\mathbf{d}}, \text{dT}) \times \underline{BVD}_0 \quad (t = 1, \ldots, \text{T}) \tag{2A.2.13}$$

where

$\underline{BVD}_0$ is the book value of debt *at the end of construction*, $t = 0$, and
dT is the payback period on debt with a default dT = T, although dT = 30 is common.

Residual cash flows are:

$$\begin{aligned}\underline{CFlow}_t &= \underline{Y}_t - \underline{A} = [\underline{RV}_t - \underline{EXP}_t - \underline{TAX}_t] - [\text{CRF}(\underline{\mathbf{d}}, \text{dT}) \times \underline{BVD}_0] \\ &= [\underline{LCOE} \times E_t \times (1 + \mathbf{i})^{lt+t}] - \underline{TX}_t \quad (t = 1, \ldots, \text{T})\end{aligned} \tag{2A.2.14}$$

where $\underline{TX}_t$ are nominal, annual total expenses, including variable expenses, interest payments and taxes.

The discounted net cash flow, DCF, as a function of LC and the equity cost of capital, is:

$$\begin{aligned}DCF[\underline{LCOE}, \underline{\mathbf{e}}] = {} & \Sigma_t[\underline{LCOE} \times E_t \times (1 + \mathbf{i})^{lt+t} - \underline{TX}_t] \\ & \times (1 + \underline{\mathbf{e}})^{-(lt+t)} \quad (t = 1, \ldots, \text{T})\end{aligned} \tag{2A.2.15}$$

Substituting Equations (2A.2.6) and (2A.2.15) into Equation (2A.2.1) yields the condition that LC must satisfy:

$$\begin{aligned}\Sigma_t[\underline{CXE}_t(1+\mathbf{e})^{lt+t}] &= \Sigma_t \underline{LCOE} \times E_t \times (1+\mathbf{i})^{lt+t} - \underline{TX}_t] \times [(1+\underline{\mathbf{e}})^{-(lt+t)}] \\ &= \underline{LCOE} \times \Sigma_t[E_t \times (1 + \mathbf{i})^{lt+t} \times (1 + \underline{\mathbf{e}})^{-(lt+t)}] \\ &\quad - \Sigma_t[\underline{TX}_t \times (1 + \underline{\mathbf{e}})^{-(lt+t)}] \quad (t = -lt, \ldots, \text{T})\end{aligned} \tag{2A.2.16}$$

Solving for $\underline{LCOE}$ gives the levelised cost that equates the present value of equity investments during construction and the present value of the cash flows to equity investors:

$$\begin{aligned}\underline{LCOE} = {} & \left\{[\Sigma_{t<0}\, \underline{CXE}_t \times (1 + \mathbf{e})^{lt+t}] - [\Sigma_{t>0} \underline{TX}_t \times (1 + \mathbf{e})^{lt+t}]\right\} \Big/ \\ & \Sigma_{t>0}[E_t \times (1 + \mathbf{i})^{lt+t} \times (1 + \underline{\mathbf{e}})^{lt+t}] \quad (t = -lt, \ldots, \text{T})\end{aligned} \tag{2A.2.17}$$

Equation (2A.2.17) is equivalent to Equation (2A.1.1) from the *viewpoint of the equity investor* concerned with inflation, taxes, subsidies and payments to debt.

2A.3 Costs of capital under various policy instruments

Using this model, the remainder of this appendix examines how four public policy instruments influence the effective real WACC, **r** (as introduced in Section 2.4): (a) accelerated depreciation, or MACRS; (b) an ITC of 10%; (c) a PTC of US$18/MWh during the first eight years of operation; and (d) a loan guarantee programme at $^{3}/_{8}$% above the US Treasury bond rate for a 20-year term, with 80% debt and 20% equity.

In MIT (2009), using 2007 US dollars, the nominal $\underline{\mathbf{r}}$ is 10%. This was adopted in the updated version of the CSS. However, to determine the real cost of capital, inflation must be calculated. In the spreadsheet, there is a general inflation rate of 3%, and real escalation rates for fuel costs (0.5%) and O&M costs (1.0%). To translate these into the general rate of inflation, the real escalation rates are set to 0% and the inflation rate is set to that rate which yields the same levelised cost (about $84/MWh), as in Table 2A.1. With real escalation rates in fuel and O&M set to 0%, the real cost of capital with MACRS, $\mathbf{r}_{MACRS}$, is 8.2% with accelerated depreciation over a 15-year depreciation period.

First, a baseline is determined by assuming a 30-year straight-line depreciation rate, 'Str8line', as in Table 2A.1. Under straight-line depreciation, where annual depreciation, $\underline{DEP}$, is constant and equal to $\Sigma\ t\ \underline{CX}_t/30$, the levelised cost increases from $84.00/MWh to $89.40/MWh. This is equivalent to raising the nominal cost of debt (after fixing the nominal cost of equity at 15%) to 9.68% under MACRS. The real cost of capital with straight-line depreciation, **r**, is about 8.7% over a 30-year depreciation period.

Table 2A.1 Changes in the real cost of capital with accelerated depreciation

Chicago Spread Sheet (CSS)	*CSS Str8line*	*CSS Str8line*	*CSS MACRS*
Inflation Rate	2.05%	2.05%	2.05%
Nominal Cost of Debt	9.7%	9.7%	8.0%
Real Cost of Debt	7.5%	7.5%	5.8%
Nominal Cost of Equity	18.0%	15.0%	15.0%
Real Cost of Equity	15.6%	12.7%	12.7%
Debt Finance	50%	50%	50%
Equity Finance	50%	50%	50%
Nominal WACC = r	12.0%	10.5%	10.0%
Real WACC = r	10.1%	8.7%	8.2%

Source: Calculations completed with CSS.

Note: In the following calculations, the plant life is 40 years, the debt term is 15 years, the construction period is 5 years, the corporate tax rate is 38%, the plant size is 1,000 MW, the capacity factor is 85% and the overnight cost of construction is $4,000/kW in 2007 US dollars, corresponding to the year in MIT (2009).

In addition, there *could be* a 3% risk premium on 'nuclear' investment, as suggested by the University of Chicago (2004: 5–21): 'Assuming that investors form consortia to spread their risks, the LCOE calculations in the present study use a risk premium of 3 percent.' Therefore the nominal rate on equity could be as high as 18%. However, this risk premium could result from the size of the project. This 'size' effect is often interpreted as a 'nuclear' effect, because of the large capital size of nuclear projects – particularly ALWRs, as discussed in Chapter 3, Appendix 3A, Section 3A.2. Increasing the cost of equity to 18% increases the real cost of capital to 10.1%.

Returning to the base case equity cost of capital of 15% and assuming straight-line depreciation, the implicit cost of capital under an ITC of 10% is calculated in Table 2A.2 (columns 1 and 2). With an ITC of 10%, the implicit real cost of capital, $\mathbf{r}_{ITC}$, is 7.8%.

Third, assuming the base case straight-line depreciation, the influence of a PTC of $18/MWh during the first eight years of operation is calculated in Table 2A.2. This PTC applies only to the first 6,000 MW of capacity, or fraction of the ALWR capacity if more than 6,000 MW are built before 31 January 2021. The implicit cost of capital associated with this PTC is $\mathbf{r}_{PTC}$ = 7.5%. This rate is a minimum: the cost of capital could be higher than 7.5%, because there could be more than 6,000 MW of new capacity, however unlikely.

Fourth, the loan guarantee programme providing funds at $^3/_8$% above the US Treasury bond rate, assumed, for example, to be 6%, is calculated for a 20-year term with 80% debt and 20% equity. Allowing early investors to borrow up to

Table 2A.2 Changes in the real cost of capital with tax credits

Chicago Spread Sheet (CSS)	*Table 2A.1 CSS Str8line*	*Col. 1 CSS itc=10%*	*Col. 2 CSS ptc=$18/MWh*
Inflation Rate	2.05%	2.05%	2.05%
Nominal Cost of Debt	9.7%	6.7%	5.9%
Real Cost of Debt	7.5%	4.8%	3.8%
Nominal Cost of Equity	15.0%	15.0%	15.0%
Real Cost of Equity	12.7%	12.7%	12.7%
Debt Finance	50%	50%	50%
Equity Finance	50%	50%	50%
Nominal WACC = r	10.5%	9.7%	9.4%
Real WACC = r	8.7%	7.8%	7.5%

Source: Calculations completed with CSS.

Table 2A.3 Changes in the real cost of capital with loan guarantee programme

Chicago Spread Sheet (CSS)	*Table 2A.1 CSS Str8line*	*Col. 1 CSS Change in dRatio*	*Col. 2 CSS Fee + Loan Guarantee*
Inflation Rate	2.05%	2.05%	2.05%
Nominal Cost of Debt	9.7%	6.0%	7.4%
Real Cost of Debt	7.5%	3.9%	5.3%
Nominal Cost of Equity	15.0%	15.0%	15.0%
Real Cost of Equity	12.7%	12.7%	12.7%
Debt Finance	50%	80%	80%
Equity Finance	50%	20%	20%
Nominal WACC = r	10.5%	9.4%	6.7%
Real WACC = r	8.7%	7.6%	5.2%

Source: Calculations completed with CSS.

80% of the total capital cost reduces the real cost of capital from 8.7% to 7.6%. Further, by allowing early investors to borrow 80% debt at 6.375%, as well as charging them a 10% fee (modelled here by raising the overnight cost 10% from $4,000/kW to $4,400/kW, which raises the effective rate on debt from 6.375% to 7.43%), the real cost of capital is 5.2%. Let $\mathbf{r}_{LGP}$ = 5.2%; as in Table 2A.3.

While US Treasury 20-year bond rates are assumed here to be 6% nominal, they have varied enormously during the last decade, as shown in Figure 2A.1. Between April 2005 and mid-2008, nominal rates floated between 4.5% and 5.5% (the top dark line), while real rates hovered between 1.5% and 2.5% (the bottom dark line), reflecting an anticipated 20-year inflation rate of around 2.5% (the middle grey line). (When initiated, the US DOE loan guarantee programme provided guarantees for funds at 0.375% above the 20-year US Treasury rate, with up to 80% debt.) The financial crisis of 2007–08 changed this picture, with nominal 20-year bond rates headed down to 2% real, as investors headed toward the safety of US treasuries – that is, loans guaranteed under the programme for interest rates of 2.375% (although no loans were made at these rates).

With the weak economic recovery since that time, the expected 20-year inflation rate has changed little from the historic 2–2.5% (although it has declined slightly, possibly as a result of the realisation of expectations that oil prices could remain low). Therefore, when nominal rates fell to less than 3% from mid-2012 to mid-2013, real rates fell below 0. Bond rates rose after mid-2013, but have been headed sporadically downwards since then. They have been barely above 0.5% real in the United States and have been below 0 for some nations' bonds, signalling the possibility of deflation in the near future, for example in Japan. Therefore, while rates on debt were higher when the loan guarantee programmes were envisioned, rates in early 2015 would be near 1% on up to 80% financing for new nuclear. However, the US DOE might have a

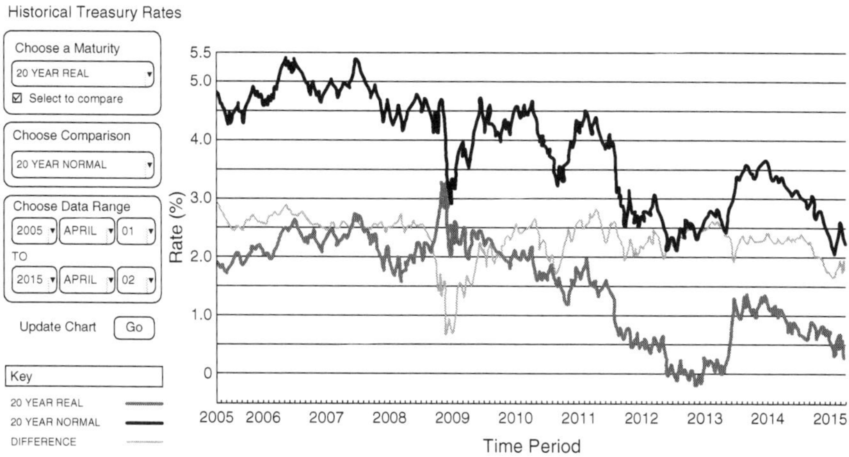

Figure 2A.1 Historical US Treasury 20-year bond rates for loan guarantee programme.

Source: US Treasury (2015).

Table 2A.4 Converting real to nominal costs of capital under US tax codes

Nominal	≈ *i*	*Real*	*Condition*	*From Table*
12.0%	1.73%	10.1%	$\underline{e}$ = 18%	2A.1
10.5%	1.66%	8.7%	$\underline{e}$ = 15%	2A.1
10.0%	1.66%	8.2%	with MACRS	2A.1
9.7%	1.76%	7.8%	with ITC	2A.2
9.4%	1.77%	7.5%	with PTC	2A.2 + 2A.3
6.7%	1.43%	5.2%	with LGP	2A.3

Source: From Table 2A.1, Table 2A.2 and Table 2A.3.

different perspective on what fees should be charged on such guarantees, meaning that such low financing for new nuclear is never assured.

The real cost of capital could be as high as 10.1% for large capital projects with straight-line depreciation (the nominal rate is 12% and Table 2A.4 shows conversions from real to nominal costs of capital under US IRS tax codes). However,

1 with a nominal cost of equity of 15%, straight-line depreciation yields $\mathbf{r}$ at 8.7% and $\underline{\mathbf{r}}$ at 10.5% nominal, as in Table 2A.1;
2 implementing accelerated depreciation yields $\mathbf{r}_{MACRS}$ of about 8.2% and $\underline{\mathbf{r}}_{MACRS}$ at 10%, as in Table 2A.1;
3 implementing an ITC of 10% yields $\mathbf{r}_{ITC}$ of about 7.8% and $\underline{\mathbf{r}}_{ITC}$ at 9.7%, as in Table 2A.2;
4 implementing an eight-year PTC yields $\mathbf{r}_{PTC}$ of about 7.5% and $\underline{\mathbf{r}}_{PTC}$ at 9.4%, as in Table 2A.2; and

5 implementing the US DOE loan guarantee programme reduces $\mathbf{r}_{LGP}$ to about 5.2% and yields $\underline{\mathbf{r}}_{LGP}$ at 6.7%, as in Table 2A.3.

These results are summarised in Table 2A.4. These costs could be lower if the ALWR investor were to be taking advantage of many programmes simultaneously. However, while there is little possibility of PTCs and SSP for the next round of nuclear new build, only a third of the nuclear new build loan guarantee funds has been committed, so it is likely that there will be new applications as soon as Vogtle Units 3 and 4 and Summer Units 2 and 3 come online near time and near budget, within nuclear utilities' 'comfort levels'.

References

Averch, H., and Johnson, L. 1962. 'Behavior of the firm under regulatory constraint', *American Economic Review*, 52(5): 1052–1069.

Blake, E. 2006. 'Where new reactors can (and can't) be built', *Nuclear News*, November: 23–25.

Blue Ribbon Commission on America's Nuclear Future, The (BRC). 2012. *Report to the Secretary of Energy*. Available online at www.energy.gov/sites/prod/files/2013/04/f0/brc_finalreport_jan2012.pdf

Burns, S. 2008. 'Looking backwards, moving forward: Licensing new reactors in the United States', *Nuclear Law Bulletin*, 81: 7–29.

Che, Y. K., and Rothwell, G. 1995. 'Performance-based pricing for nuclear power plants', *The Energy Journal*, 16(4): 57–77.

David, P., and Rothwell, G. 1996. 'Measuring standardization: An application to the American and French nuclear power industries', *European Journal of Political Economy*, 12(2): 291–308.

Electric Power Research Institute (EPRI). 1995. *Advanced Light Water Reactor Utility Requirements*, NP–6780–R1. Available online at www.epri.com/abstracts/Pages/ProductAbstract.aspx?ProductId=TR-016780-V2R8&Mode=download

Fairfield, H. 2009. 'Science illustrated: New scale for nuclear power', *The New York Times*, 1 December. Available online at http://query.nytimes.com/gst/fullpage.html?res=9405E6D7163BF932A35751C1A96F9C8B63

Holt, M. 2014. *Nuclear Energy Policy*. Congressional Research Service (CRS Report), 15 October. Available online at https://www.fas.org/sgp/crs/misc/RL33558.pdf

Holt, M. 2015. *Civilian Nuclear Waste Disposal*. Congressional Research Service (CRS Report), 24 April. Available online at http://fas.org/sgp/crs/misc/RL33461.pdf

International Energy Agency (IEA) and Nuclear Energy Agency (NEA). 1998. *Projected Costs of Generating Electricity: 1998 Update*. Paris: OECD.

International Energy Agency (IEA) and Nuclear Energy Agency (NEA). 2010. *Projected Costs of Generating Electricity: 2010 Update*. Available online at https://www.iea.org/publications/freepublications/publication/projected_costs.pdf

International Energy Agency (IEA) and Nuclear Energy Agency (NEA). 2015. *Projected Costs of Generating Electricity: 2015 Update*. Paris: OECD.

Johnson, S. 2002. 'Nuclear power 2010 program overview', Paper presented to the Nuclear Energy Research Advisory Committee, US Department of Energy, Office of Nuclear Energy, Science and Technology, 15 April. Available online at http://

energy.gov/sites/prod/files/Presentation%20-%202010%20Program%20Overview%20-%20Presentation%20to%20the%20NEAC.pdf

Klein, D. 2010. 'The challenges ahead', Remarks prepared for US NRC Regulatory Information Conference, Rockville, MD, 9 March. Available online at http://pbadupws.nrc.gov/docs/ML1006/ML100680767.pdf

Ling, K. 2009. 'Nuclear power: Can potential incentives in Climate Bill spur U.S. industry?', *Energy and Environment Daily*, 27 October. Available online at www.eenews.net/stories/83887

Massachusetts Institute of Technology (MIT). 2003. *The Future of Nuclear Power: An Interdisciplinary Study*. Cambridge, MA: MIT Press.

Massachusetts Institute of Technology (MIT). 2009. *The Future of Nuclear Power: An Interdisciplinary Study – Update*. Available online at http://web.mit.edu/nuclearpower/pdf/nuclearpower-update2009.pdf

Moody's. 2007. *New nuclear generation in the United States: Keeping options open vs. addressing an inevitable necessity*. Available online at http://saberpartners.com/press/pdf/Moody's%20New%20Nuclear%20Generation%20October%202007.pdf

Moody's. 2008. *New nuclear generating capacity: Potential credit implications for U.S. investor owned utilities*. Available online at www.ambienteparco.it/upload/UserFiles/approfondimenti/080527MoodysNewNukeGenCapacity.pdf

Moody's. 2009. *Special comment: New nuclear generation ratings pressure increasing*. Available online at www.nukefreetexas.org/downloads/Moodys_ June_2009.pdf

Moody's. 2011. *Moody's downgrades the senior unsecured rating of SCANA to Baa3 and the senior unsecured rating of South Carolina Electric and Gas to Baa2; Outlooks revised to stable*. Available online at https://www.moodys.com/research/Moodys-downgrades-the-senior-unsecured-rating-of-SCANA-to-Baa3– PR_226074

Moody's. 2013. *Georgia Power Company: Answers to frequently asked questions about the Vogtle new nuclear construction project*. Available online at http://matchbin-assets.s3.amazonaws.com/public/sites/274/assets/9O21_Moodys_report_on_Vogtle_July_11_2013.pdf

National Association of Regulatory Utility Commissioners (NARUC). 2015. *Commissions*. Available online at www.naruc.org/Commissions/

Nuclear Energy Agency (NEA). 2015a. *Nuclear New Build: Insights into Financing and Project Management*. Available online at https://www.oecd-nea.org/ndd/pubs/2015/7195-nn-build-2015.pdf

Nuclear Energy Agency (NEA). 2015b. *The Costs of Nuclear Power Plant Decommissioning in OECD–NEA Member States*. Paris: OECD.

Nuclear Energy Institute (NEI). 1998. *The U.S. Nuclear Energy Industry's Strategic Plan for Building New Nuclear Power Plants, Final Report*. Available online at http://lobby.la.psu.edu/051_Nuclear_Waste/Organizational_Statements/NEI/NEI_Strategic_Plan.pdf

Pacific Northwest National Laboratory (PNNL). 2011. *Assessment of the Adequacy of the 10 CFR 50.75(c) Minimum Decommissioning Fund Formula*. Available online at http://pbadupws.nrc.gov/docs/ML1306/ML13063A190.pdf

Recio, M. 2010. 'Comanche Peak expansion thrown in doubt', *Fort Worth Star-Telegram*, 9 December. Available online at http://nukefreetexas.org/2010/12/comanche-peak-expansion-thrown-into-doubt/

Rothwell, G. 1985. 'Electric utility power plant choice under investment regulation'. Unpublished PhD dissertation, Department of Economics, University of California, Berkeley, CA.

Rothwell, G. 1991, 'The optimal time to decommission commercial nuclear reactors', *The Energy Journal*, 12(special issue): 305–314.

Rothwell, G. 2006. 'A real options approach to evaluating new nuclear power plants', *The Energy Journal*, 27(1): 37–54.
Rothwell, G. 2010. 'Economics of reprocessing and recycling nuclear fuel', Paper presented to the Blue Ribbon Commission of America's Nuclear Future Reactor and Fuel Cycle Technology Subcommittee, Washington, DC, 30 August.
Rothwell, G. 2015. 'Scale economies in a series of generic interim SNF storage facilities', Paper presented at International Congress on Advances in Nuclear Power Plants, Nice, 3–6 May.
Rothwell, G., and Gomez, T. 2003. *Electricity Economics: Regulation and Deregulation.* Piscataway, NJ/Hoboken, NJ: IEEE Press/John Wiley & Sons.
Rothwell, G., and Graber, R. 2009. 'The role of nuclear power in climate change mitigation', in F. P. Sioshansi (ed.), *Generating Electricity in a Carbon-Constrained World*, Oxford: Elsevier, pp. 175–206.
Rothwell, G., and Williams, K. 2006. 'Is nuclear power competitive producing electricity or hydrogen?', *International Journal of Nuclear Hydrogen Production and Applications*, 1(2): 154–169.
Taylor, J'T. 2010. *Manual of LCOE Spreadsheet Model for Nuclear Power.* Lemont, IL: Nuclear Engineering Division, Argonne National Laboratory.
University of Chicago. 2004. *The Economic Future of Nuclear Power.* Available online at www.eusustel.be/public/documents_publ/links_to_docs/cost/uoc-study.pdf
US Bureau of the Census. 2011. *2010 Census data.* Available online at www.census.gov/2010census/data/
US Congressional Budget Office (US CBO). 2011. *Federal Loan Guarantees for the Construction of Nuclear Power Plants.* Available online at www.cbo.gov/doc.cfm?index=12238
US Department of Energy (US DOE). 2007. 'Loan guarantees for projects that employ innovative technologies, final rule, 10 CFR 609', *Federal Register*, 72: 60116. Available online at http://energy.gov/downloads/federal-register-loan-guarantees-projects-employ-innovative-technologies-guideline
US Department of Energy (US DOE). 2010. *Office of Civilian Radioactive Waste Management.* Available online at www.energy.gov/search/site/Office%20of%20Civilian%20Radioactive%20Waste%20Management%22?gid=31
US Department of Energy (US DOE). 2012. 'Obama Administration announces $450 million to design and commercialize U.S. small modular nuclear reactors', 22 March. Available online at http://energy.gov/articles/obama-administration-announces-450-million-design-and-commercialize-us-small-modular
US Department of Energy (US DOE). 2015. *Quarterly Nuclear Deployment Scorecard–July 2015.* Available online at http://energy.gov/ne/downloads/quarterly-nuclear-deployment-scorecard-july-2015
US Energy Information Administration (US EIA). 2009. 'U.S. electric industry generating capacity by state', in *Annual Electric Generator Report*, Form EIA-860. Available online at www.eia.gov/cneaf/electricity/epa/fig1p1.html
US Energy Information Administration (US EIA). 2010. *Status of electricity restructuring by state.* Available online at www.eia.gov/electricity/policies/restructuring/restructure_elect.html
US Energy Information Administration (US EIA). 2013. *The Electricity Market Module of the National Energy Modeling System: Model Documentation Report*, DOE-EIA-M068 (2013). Available online at www.eia.gov/forecasts/aeo/nems/documentation/electricity/pdf/m068(2013).pdf

US Energy Information Administration (US EIA). 2014. *Annual Energy Outlook 2014*, DOE/EIA–0383(2014). Available online at www.eia.gov/forecasts/aeo/pdf/0383(2014).pdf

US Federal Energy Regulatory Commission (US FERC). 2011. *Electric power markets: National overview*. Available online at www.ferc.gov/market-oversight/mkt-electric/overview.asp

US Nuclear Regulatory Commission (US NRC). 2013. *Early site permit applications for new reactors*. Available online at www.nrc.gov/reactors/new-reactors/esp.html

US Nuclear Regulatory Commission (US NRC). 2014. *Final Rule: Continued Storage of Spent Nuclear Fuel*. Available online at www.nrc.gov/reading-rm/doc-collections/commission/secys/2014/2014-0072scy.pdf

US Nuclear Regulatory Commission (US NRC). 2015a. *New reactor applications under review*. Available online at www.nrc.gov/reactors/new-reactors/col/new-reactor-map.html

US Nuclear Regulatory Commission (US NRC). 2015b. *U.S. operating commercial nuclear power reactors*. Available online at www.nrc.gov/reactors/operating/map-power-reactors.html

US Nuclear Regulatory Commission (US NRC). 2015c. *NRC to begin full certification review of APR1400*, 4 March. Available online at http://pbadupws.nrc.gov/docs/ML1506/ML15065A345.pdf

US Nuclear Regulatory Commission (US NRC). 2015d. *Design certification applications for new reactors*. Available online at www.nrc.gov/reactors/new-reactors/design-cert.html

US Nuclear Regulatory Commission (US NRC). 2015e. *Combined license applications for new reactors*. Available online at www.nrc.gov/reactors/new-reactors/col.html

US Treasury. 2015. *Resource Center: Historic yield curve chart*. Available online at www.treasury.gov/resource-center/data-chart-center/interest-rates/Pages/TextView.aspx?data=yield

US Treasury and Internal Revenue Service (IRS). 2006. *Internal Revenue Bulletin*, Bulletin No. 2006-18, 1 May. Available online at www.irs.gov/pub/irs-irbs/irb06-18.pdf

Wald, M. 2010. 'Fee dispute hinders plan for reactor', *The New York Times*, 9 October. Available online at www.nytimes.com/2010/10/10/business/energy-environment/10reactor.html?_r=0

Whitten, D. 2008. 'Utilities seek $122 billion in nuclear loan support (Update 2)', *Bloomberg*, 2 October. Available online at www.bloomberg.com/apps/news?pid=newsarchive&sid=aXjr7wWyb_tw

3 New nuclear power plant capital construction costs

3.1 Measuring nuclear power plant construction costs

Parallel to the US Department of Energy (US DOE) Nuclear Power 2010 (NP2010) programme (see Chapter 2, Section 2.2), which focused on advanced light water reactors (ALWRs), in early 2001 the US DOE's Office of Nuclear Energy, under the leadership of William Magwood IV, assembled the Generation IV (Gen IV) Roadmap Committee to (a) assess competing advanced nuclear energy systems, and (b) determine a common international framework within which member nations could share the research, development and demonstration (prototyping) of Gen IV technologies, while potentially competing in commercial markets by 2030. Member countries and organisations of the Gen IV International Forum (GIF) have included Argentina, Brazil, Canada, China, Euratom, France, Japan, Korea, Russia, South Africa, Switzerland, the United Kingdom and the United States. The early Gen IV Roadmap Committee was composed of policy committees, a cross-cutting Evaluation Methodology Group (EMG) and a number of technical working groups, each focused on a different reactor technology (water, gas, metal and other). These include the gas-cooled fast reactor (GFR), the lead-cooled fast reactor (LFR), the molten salt reactor (MSR), the super-critical water reactor (SCWR), the sodium-cooled fast reactor (SFR) and the very high temperature gas reactor (VHTR). These are extensions of the different reactor types illustrated in Chapter 1, Figure 1.2.

The EMG was tasked with developing a multi-criteria evaluation to be applied by the technical working groups to some 80 variants of nuclear energy systems for the selection of the most promising technologies. The EMG developed four sets of criteria: economic, sustainability, safety and non-proliferation. After the terrorist attacks of 11 September 2001, the last set also included 'physical protection' criteria. Deliberation reduced the five economic criteria to two:

- EC–1 – low average cost, as measured by levelised costs, *LC* (following the IEA and NEA, 1998, methodology – see Chapter 2); and
- EC–2 – low total construction cost, *KC*, measured by the overnight construction cost with contingency plus interest during construction (IDC) (EMG, 2002: 68).

While everyone agreed that levelised cost, *LC*, was the best single economic metric, some on the Roadmap Committee questioned why it was necessary to calculate construction cost, given that this information was already incorporated into levelised cost. Members of the EMG thought that, without considering the size of the construction cost, there could be selection bias against smaller reactors, which might not fare well against the scale economies of larger reactors, but might be more competitive in liberalised electricity markets. This thinking anticipated the emergence of small modular reactors (SMRs) (as discussed in Section 3.5).

Under the usual levelised cost methodology, electric utilities should be indifferent between two generating alternatives with the same levelised cost. However, holding all else equal, electric utilities are more likely to choose the generating alternative with the lowest construction cost, because utilities face constraints in financial markets. Although a new nuclear power plant (NPP) might have the lowest levelised costs among non-carbon-emitting generators, not all electric utilities can finance a US$12,000 million project, plus transmission upgrades and escalation. Without the buffer of rate-of-return regulation, in the generating station market, size matters.

The primary metric of NPP cost analysis, particularly under rate-of-return regulation, has been the levelised cost of electricity (LCOE). Here, 'levelised cost of electricity' is referred to more simply as 'levelised cost', *LC*, because LCOE connotes that nuclear power produces only electricity, whereas nuclear energy systems can also produce heat, hydrogen (Rothwell and Williams, 2006), or desalinated water (Rothwell, 2007). Microeconomic textbooks refer to *LC* as 'long-run average cost' (LRAC). Cost terms here usually refer to cost engineering definitions, to conform to the nuclear cost economics literature; thus there can be differences between these definitions and those used in microeconomics.

These two metrics, *KC* and *LC*, provide much of the economic information necessary to compare electricity-generating alternatives. However, neither of them incorporates electricity price information – that is, whether a particular technology can compete in the electric power market. The net present value (NPV) incorporates electricity price information. The NPV is equal to the present discounted value of revenues minus costs over periods of construction (for example five years), operation (for example 50 years), and decommissioning (for example ten years). In NPV analysis, the costs and benefits (primarily revenues) are discounted to the present at the decision maker's opportunity cost of capital.

Further, calculating expected construction cost, levelised cost and NPV for NPPs involves three sets of uncertainties (for which probabilities might not be known) and risks (for which there is enough experience to model the probabilities):

1 construction cost uncertainties, including those associated with overnight costs, construction lead times and total financing costs;

2 operating cost risks, including risks associated with fuel cost, operating and maintenance (O&M) costs, and plant capacity factor; and
3 electricity price risk, resulting from volatile energy prices and unknown carbon fees.

This list follows Knight's (1921) definition of 'risk', wherein the probability distribution is known, but the underlying parameters are not, for example 'known unknowns' (see the discussion of risk and return in Appendix 3A, Section 3A.3), and 'uncertainty', wherein the underlying probability is unknown, for example 'unknown unknowns'. To extend this terminology, (a) 'known knowns' are the equivalent of densities with known parameters, and (b) 'unknown knowns' are, according to Donald Rumsfeld (quoted in Reuter, 2014), 'things that you think you know that it turns out that you did not'. These are risks that turn out to be uncertainties. These definitions conform to their use in modern finance theory, discussed in Appendix 3A.

This chapter calculates levelised capital cost, *LKC*, as defined in Equation (3.1.1). Chapter 4 adds *LKC* to the other levelised costs (fuel and O&M costs) of new nuclear:

$$LKC = \mathrm{CRF}(\mathbf{r}, \mathrm{T}) \times [KC(\mathrm{MW}, OC, \mathbf{r}, lt)/E(\mathrm{MW})] \tag{3.1.1}$$

where

CRF is the capital recovery factor, defined in Chapter 2, Appendix 2A, Equation (2A.1.4),
r is the appropriate cost of capital,
T is the economic life of the facility,
KC is total capital construction costs,
MW is the size of the plant in megawatts-electric,
OC is overnight cost, including contingency (see Section 3.2),
lt is construction lead time (see Section 3.3), and
E is the annual electricity output expressed in megawatt-hours (MWh) (see Section 3.4).

Section 3.2 of this chapter estimates new nuclear total construction cost. Section 3.3 discusses anticipated construction lead times and compounding interest during construction. Section 3.4 discusses expected capacity factors. Section 3.5 introduces a 'top-down' model of SMRs. Section 3.6 discusses (a) scale economies in construction costs, and (b) how to translate 'nth-of-a-kind' (NOAK) cost estimates into 'first-of-a-kind' (FOAK) cost estimates, and vice versa. Section 3.7 discusses levelised construction costs, *LKC*, for new nuclear FOAK and NOAK plants.

3.2 Total nuclear power plant construction cost

Construction cost, *KC*, is the total amount spent on construction and testing before any electricity or revenues are generated (as defined in EMWG, 2007). Construction cost, *KC*, is equal to the overnight construction cost plus contingency and financing costs. To measure these consistently, a set of standard definitions of construction accounts, structures, equipment and personnel is required. The code of accounts (COA) used here is derived from the *Cost Estimating Guidelines for Generation IV Nuclear Energy Systems* (EMWG, 2007), developed by the Economic Modelling Working Group (EMWG) of the GIF. The model used to produce the tables in Section 3.7 is similar to that appearing in version 2 (EMWG, 2008).

The 2007 COA is based on work done in the 1980s and 1990s at the Oak Ridge National Laboratory (ORNL). For decades, the US DOE and the US national laboratories have been using cost-estimating guidelines to ensure consistent treatment of competing nuclear power and fossil-fired electric production technologies. In 1993, the ORNL issued a set of guidelines (Delene and Hudson, 1993; based on Delene, 1986, Hudson, 1987, and Delene and Hudson, 1990) to support the evaluation of liquid-metal reactors (LMRs) and high temperature gas reactors (HTGRs). In addition, the 1993 Guidelines were based on two previous sets:

- the 1987 Energy Economic Database (EEDB), developed by United Engineers and Constructors (ORNL, 1988a; US DOE 1988); and
- the 1988 Nuclear Energy Cost Database (NECDB) (US DOE, 1988).

Finally, the ORNL's 1988 report on the EEDB (ORNL, 1988b) contains a detailed description of how to calculate the LCOE for nuclear power and fossil-fired electric plants.

The International Atomic Energy Agency (IAEA) updated these guidelines (IAEA, 1986, 2000), giving an international consensus COA that differs from the original EEDB, which is in common usage in the United States. One of the primary differences is that the IAEA system does not break out labour in the cost accounts. One of the secondary differences is that the IAEA's 'Series' is not numbered the same way as is EEDB's 'Accounts', particularly for indirect costs. The IAEA numbering system is used here. In 2003, the EMWG began developing a hybrid of the original EEDB and IAEA cost accounting systems – primarily adding back labour, so that labour productivity and wages could be adjusted across GIF member countries. This became the 2007 Guidelines (EMWG, 2007). This chapter uses the latter to guide the cost estimation of new NPPs; the 2007 Guidelines (EMWG, 2007) are extended to fossil-fired alternatives in Chapter 5.

To calculate *KC*, Table 3.1 presents the cost accounts for a specific technology: the advanced boiling water reactor (ABWR), from General Electric (GE), which the US Nuclear Regulatory Commission (US NRC) certified in 1997, as in Chapter 2, Table 2.1. Several ABWRs have been built in

Table 3.1 Two construction cost estimates for ABWRs in the United States

ABWR Cost Estimates from Nuclear Energy Agency (2000) and Tennessee Valley Authority (2005)	*NEA (2000)*	*TVA (2005)*	*TVA (2005)*	*NEA (2000)*	*TVA (2005)*	*Cost increase*
Series and Title	*1999 US$/kW*	*2004 US$/kW*	*%*	*2013 US$/kW*	*2013 US$/kW*	*2013 US$/kW*
10 Capitalised pre-construction	0	0	0	0	0	0
21 Structures & improvements	293	300	11	460	403	(57)
22 Reactor equipment	366	540	20	575	726	150
23 Turbine generator equipment	183	360	13	288	484	196
24 Electrical equipment	110	150	6	173	202	29
25/26 Cooling system & miscellaneous equipment	73	70	3	115	94	(21)
20 Total direct, *DIR*	1,026	1,419	53	1,611	1,906	296
30 Capitalised indirect costs, *INDIR*	293	192	7	460	258	(202)
40 Capitalised owner's cost, *OWN*	0	240	9	0	322	322
50 Supplementary costs, *SUPP*	0	0	0	0	0	0
Base overnight cost, *BASE*	1,319	1,851	69	2,071	2,487	581
Contingency rate, C_{ON}	9%	16%	16%	9%	16%	6%
Overnight cost, *OC*	$1,440	$2,140	80%	$2,261	$2,875	$614
IDC factor (for Series 60), idc	14%	25%	25%	14%	25%	11%
Total construction cost, *KC*	$1,641	$2,680	100%	$2,577	$3,601	$1,023

Sources: NEA (2000: 99); TVA (2005: 4.2–4).

Japan – Kashiwazaki-Kariwa Units 6 and 7, Hamaka Unit 5, and Shika Unit 2; others are under construction in Japan at Ohma and Shimane, and in Chinese Taipei at Lungmen Units 1 and 2 (see Chapter 1).

Table 3.1 is based on cost data from the Nuclear Energy Agency (NEA, 2000) and the Tennessee Valley Authority (TVA, 2005). The latter considered building twin ABWRs at its Bellefonte site and produced a cost study, funded by the US DOE, for such a project. The total construction cost in constant US dollars was approximately \$10,000 million (2013 US dollars) for 2,740 MW. The construction cost for South Texas Project (STP) Units 3 and 4, a twin ABWR, was more than \$18,000 million (in mixed nominal dollars) before the STP was cancelled after the Fukushima-Daiichi accident in March 2011.

In a boiling water reactor (BWR), water, in the form of steam, circulates directly between the reactor and the turbine generator – unlike a pressurised water reactor (PWR), in which a steam generator transfers heat from the reactor to a separate circuit of steam to drive a turbine, as in Figure 3.3 (see Section 3.5). There are two water circuits in a BWR: one circulates water through the reactor to cool the reactor and moderate the reaction, and drives a turbine generator; the second circulates water through the condenser to remove heat from the reactor cooling water, and then through a cooling system, which releases the excess heat to the environment. Table 3.1 shows (where costs were converted to 2013 US dollars per kilowatt, or US\$/kW) each reference's estimated costs for building twin ABWRs. The total construction cost, *KC*, includes:

1 direct construction costs, *DIR* (Account 20), plus Account 10, which includes pre-construction costs, such as site licensing, including the environmental testing associated with the early site permit (ESP) and/or the combined construction and operating licence (COL) (assigned, in NEA, 2000, and TVA, 2005, to 'owners' costs', or Account 40);
2 indirect costs, *INDIR* (Account 30), which include engineering and administrative costs that cannot be associated with a specific cost category in Series 20, as well as capitalised indirect costs;
3 owners' costs, *OWN* (Account 40), which include expenses incurred by the owner(s) associated with the plant and plant site, but not including off-site, 'beyond the busbar', transmission costs (although some references include transmission costs in owners' costs, increasing construction costs tremendously);
4 supplemental costs, *SUPP* (Account 50), which are primarily first fuel core costs (and if first fuel core costs are levelised in the cost of fuel, as is the case here, Account 50 can be set to 0);
5 contingency, which, in the X9 Accounts (that is, those ending in '9', such as Account 29), includes contingencies on all other subaccounts in Series 20 and which is expressed here as a contingency rate, C_{ON}, for example 15% (see Appendix 3A, Section 3A.1, on cost contingency determination); and
6 IDC (Account 60), expressed as a percentage mark-up on overnight costs, **idc**, which is also known as the 'IDC factor'.

Indirect costs can be expressed as a percentage mark-up, C_{30}, on direct cost: $INDIR = DIR \times C_{30}$. To simplify notation, let $DIR^{+} = DIR(1 + C_{30})$. The indirect percentage mark-up, C_{30}, is set to 10%. This is similar to the percentage mark-up in TVA (2005), as shown in Table 3.1.

Second, the owners' costs associated with the development of the site, for example US NRC and US Environmental Protection Agency (EPA) licensing fees and site preparation expenses, are set to \$200 million plus 5% of direct costs; there are no indirect owners' costs. This creates an unknown lower bound on the competitive size of an NPP, given that each site must undergo the same regulatory scrutiny that takes a few years and costs millions of dollars. (On a discussion of what is included in other studies' definitions of investment costs, see D'haeseleer, 2013: 33–39, quoting Rothwell, 2012.)

The sum of Series 10–50 is the base overnight construction cost, *BASE*. The term 'overnight' is used to describe what the construction cost would be if money had no time value. Base overnight cost plus contingency, *CN*, equals total overnight cost, *OC*, multiplied by the contingency factor, $(1 + C_{ON})$. Some references define 'overnight costs' without contingency and some references define overnight cost with contingency, as does the US Energy Information Administration (US EIA, 2014). To make this distinction, *BASE* *excludes* contingency and *OC includes* contingency. Overnight cost, *OC*, plus Series 60 *IDC* equals total capital construction cost, *KC*. To summarise:

$$BASE = (DIR + INDIR + OWN + SUPP) \tag{3.2.1}$$

$$OC = BASE \times (1 + C_{ON}) = (DIR + INDIR + OWN + SUPP) \times (1 + C_{ON}) \tag{3.2.2}$$

$$KC = OC \times (1 + \mathbf{idc}) = (DIR + INDIR + OWN + SUPP) \times (1 + C_{ON}) \times (1 + \mathbf{idc}) \tag{3.2.3}$$

and

$$LKC = KC \times (\mathrm{CRF}/E) = [(DIR + INDIR + OWN + SUPP) \times (1+C_{ON}) \times (1+\mathbf{idc})] \times (\mathrm{CRF}/E) \tag{3.2.4}$$

Although not a part of *KC*, 'decontamination and dismantling' (D&D) costs must be set aside during operation for plant D&D later. Here, D&D funding is treated as a sinking fund. Annual contributions to a 'nuclear decommissioning trust fund' earn a rate of return, **dd**, during the life of the facility (Pasqualetti and Rothwell, 1991). This rate of return is usually restricted by decommissioning authorities to be equal to the rate of return on corporate bonds, not including electric utilities. The future value of the fund should be equal to the D&D cost of the facility. For ease of calculation, the rate of earning on the decommissioning trust fund contributions is fixed here at 3% real and contributions are made to the trust fund during the operating life of the plant. Assume that the cost of D&D is equal to 25% of the *KC*. (This is higher than in other studies: see EMWG, 2007, which asserts that 'the total constant dollar decommissioning cost should be 33% of the total direct capital cost', which would be about 20% of *KC*.)

Contributions to a nuclear decommissioning trust fund, managed by a fiducially distinct entity, are accumulated during operation, but added to the levelised construction costs. In some IAEA software programs, the cost of decommissioning is added to the cost of construction, and no return is allowed on these set-aside funds under the implicit assumption that the escalation rate is equal to the rate of return on the decommissioning funds. This greatly increases the total amount to finance by the time of commercial operation and leads to differences in levelised cost calculations when compared to non-IAEA cost estimates.

Advanced BWR construction cost estimates increased from 2000 to 2005. As shown in Table 3.1, much of the cost increase came in the form of using more realistic contingency and IDC factors – that is, resulted from the maturation of the cost estimate, as in Figure 3.2. Comparing the two estimates (NEA, 2000; TVA, 2005) in 2013 US dollars, one can conclude that:

1. the direct construction cost estimate escalated at a real, without-inflation, annual rate of 3.4%;
2. direct plus indirect construction cost estimates rose at a real escalation rate of 3.7%, indirect cost increases accounted for an additional real annual escalation rate of 0.3% (that is, the source of the cost increase cannot be attributed to increasing indirect costs);
3. the estimated contingency rate was increased from 9.2% to 15.7% (similar to the rate in US EIA, 2014, which is 15.5% = (1.10 × 1.05) – 1), which accounted for an additional real annual escalation rate of 1.2%; and
4. the estimated IDC rate increased from 14% to 25%.

In total, there was an annual *real* escalation in the overnight cost estimate of about 7% from 1999 to 2004, 50% of which increase resulted from increases in direct construction cost and 50% of which from the *maturation of the cost estimate* from 'concept screening' estimates to 'detailed estimates' (see Appendix 3A, Table 3A.1). The cost of reactor equipment increased by a real annual escalation rate of 5%. (This could have been the result of anticipated bottlenecks in reactor equipment manufacturing capacity.) *The cost of the turbine generator equipment increased at a real annual escalation rate of 11%.* (This could have been the result of a rapid increase in quantity demanded for electrical equipment made by international turbine-generator manufacturers and should not be considered to be an increase specific to nuclear construction.)

Compare the discussion here with an estimate of a 15% annual escalation rate in Du and Parsons (2009, discussed in Rothwell, 2010: 24–29):

> Using the MIT (2003) estimate of $2,000/kW in 2002 dollars, and a central estimate of $4,000/kW in 2007 dollars, our results suggest an

annual rate of increase in overnight costs of approximately 15% during this period. This represents a sizeable premium to the general rate of inflation – the 3% per annum mentioned above for the GDP deflator.

Concerning more current estimates of new NPP construction costs, there is little publicly available data on expected costs for the units in Chapter 2, Table 2.4. However, there are estimates of overnight costs for the Westinghouse advanced passive pressurised water reactors (AP1000s), because two twin AP1000s are under active construction in the United States and two twin AP1000s are being built in China (see Chapter 1, Table 1.2).

There are a few construction cost estimates available for the twin AP1000s, as follows.

1 The 'certified cost' estimate for Vogtle Units 3 and 4 is $4,418 million for a 45.7% share of 2,234 MW for Georgia Power Company (2010: 7). The overnight cost per kilowatt (including contingency, but not financing) is ($4,418m/0.457)/(2.234 GW) = $4,330/kW. Updating this from 2010 US dollars to 2013 US dollars yields $4,500/kW. (Although there has been cost escalation at Vogtle, there is a conflict over who will pay this increase; hence the amount of escalation will be unknown until the plant is completed.)
2 The South Carolina Electric & Gas (SCE&G, 2010: 3) overnight cost estimate for Summer Units 2 and 3 is ($4,270/55%)/(2.234GW) = $3,475/kW in 2007 US dollars, or $3,900/kW in 2013 US dollars.
3 The Progress Energy (2010: 52–56, 132–140, 320–321) overnight cost estimate for Levy County Units 1 and 2 is $4,800/kW in 2013 US dollars.

The average of these cost estimates is ($4,500 + $3,900 + $4,800)/3 = $4,400/kW, with a standard deviation of $460. In this chapter, the baseline for advanced nuclear construction cost is $4,400/kW in 2013 US dollars, assuming that four units have been built. (Actually, as discussed in Section 3.6, this is taken as the projected cost of the fifth AP1000 in the United States; the NOAK cost could be lower, or profits could be higher.) Of course, there is uncertainty as to what the cost might be at specific sites.

To model this uncertainty, there is a cost range for twin AP1000s in regulatory filings associated with Turkey Point Units 6 and 7 for Florida Power and Light (FPL). (See also Scroggs, 2010: 45: 'Updating the cost estimate range to 2010 dollars, adjusting for the 1,100 MW sized units a net 2.5% escalation rate, results in a cost estimate range of $3,397/kW to $4,940/kW.') Updating these to 2013 US dollars yields an approximate cost range of $3,700 to $5,200/kW in 2013 US dollars, with a mid-point of $4,450/kW. Following cost engineering guidelines, as described in Appendix 3A, if this range were expected to cover 95% of the realised overnight costs per kilowatt for Levy, the implied standard deviation would be $430/kW = ($850/1.96). The Levy cost estimate mid-point is only 1% different from the baseline here: $4,450/kW

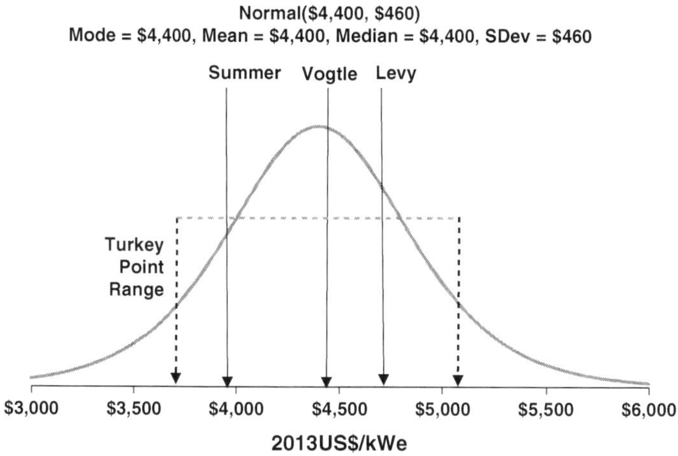

Figure 3.1 AP1000 overnight plant costs (2013 $/kW, fitted to a normal density).

Sources: Georgia Power Company (2010, 2011); Progress Energy (2010); SCE&G (2010); Scroggs (2010).

versus $4,400/kW. Figure 3.1 represents these data with a normal probability density function; Appendix 3A defines normal densities. (See D'haeseleer, 2013: 79–89, comparing many estimates of 'investment cost of new NPPs', and compare D'haeseleer, 2013: fig. 3.2, from Rothwell, 2012, which is Figure 3.1 here, and D'haeseleer, 2013: fig. 3.7, with Chapter 5, Figure 5.1 here.)

With a normal density, there is a small probability that realised overnight costs for a twin ALWR will be below $3,000/kW, or above $6,000/kW. (In Chapter 5, Section 5.2, overnight costs are modelled to fit an extreme value distribution.) Given this overnight cost estimate of $4,400/kW for twin nuclear power plants, why are other estimates higher? One difference between these estimates and those found in the press is that cost estimates here are in 2013 constant US dollars, whereas many estimates are given in as-to-be-spent (nominal) dollars – that is, costs stated in dollars of the years in which the dollars are spent. Because of inflation, which over the long run has been about 2–3% per year in North America and Western Europe, future currency is worth less than present currency; so more future currency is required to be spent than present currency. (The inflation rate does not include escalation in a particular industry; the inflation rate is used only to adjust the currency value.) For example, if (a) the power plant were $4,400/kW, and (b) the lead time were five years with a uniform expenditure rate, then the escalated cost would be $(\$4{,}400/5)[(1.03)^1 + (1.03)^2 + (1.03)^3 + (1.03)^4 + (1.03)^5] = \$4{,}812/\text{kW}$. In addition, many of these cost estimates include the cost of financing, which can add another 15–25% (discussed in Section 3.3). Finally, the financing cost can be escalated to nominal currency, which will increase the cost estimate further, as in Figure 3.2.

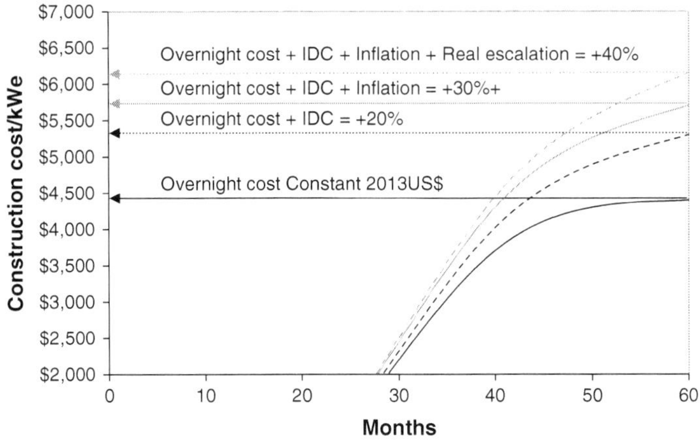

Figure 3.2 Twin AP1000 overnight costs with IDC, inflation and escalation.

Source: Adapted from Rothwell (2012).

Table 3.2 compares the overnight cost estimates here to those in the US EIA's *Annual Energy Outlook* (AEO) and those of the Massachusetts Institute of Technology (MIT, 2009). The MIT (2009) estimate was $4,000/kW in 2007 US dollars, which translates into about $4,550/kW in 2013 US dollars, which is 3.6% higher than the overnight cost estimate here. The US EIA increased its projected overnight cost estimate of 'advanced nuclear' from $3,820/kW in 2008 US dollars in the 2010 AEO (US EIA, 2010) to $5,275/kW in 2009 US dollars in the 2011 AEO (US EIA, 2011). The more recent 2012 AEO cost estimate is about $5,555/kW in 2013 US dollars (US EIA, 2012). This is 22% higher than the estimate here. Table 3.3 compares the AEO values with those in Table 3.1.

Comparing the percentage breakdown used by the US EIA with that of TVA in Table 3.1 shows that the US EIA's cost projection has much higher indirect cost (61% higher) and a much higher owners' cost (38% higher). According to the US EIA (2010: 3):

> The updated overnight capital cost estimates for coal and nuclear power plants are 25 to 37 percent above those in *AEO2010*. The higher cost estimates reflect many factors including the overall trend of rising costs of capital intensive technology in the power sector, higher global commodity prices ...

This could be the result of differences between the ABWR and the AP1000, but this large difference is unlikely to be technology-specific at this level of aggregation. Unfortunately, the US EIA provides *no references* (US EIA, 2010: ch. 12, 1–7, 'Advanced Nuclear'), so one cannot determine why indirect and

Table 3.2 US EIA *Annual Energy Outlook* assumptions for advanced nuclear

ALWR, Source: EIA, Assumptions for the . . .	*Year US$*	*Size (MW)*	*LT (y)*	C_{ON} *(%)*	*OC (US$/kW)*	*OC (2013US$/kW)*	*Variable (2013US$/MWh)*	*Fixed (2013US$/kW/y)*
AEO (1997: table 33)	1995	1,300	4	84	2,534	4,003	0.63	85
AEO (1998: table 37)	1996	1,300	5	67	2,356	3,636	0.62	85
AEO (1999: table 37)	1997	600	4	66	2,371	3,665	0.63	87
AEO (2000: table 37)	1998	600	4	27	2,390	3,788	0.65	89
AEO (2001: table 43)	1999	600	4	27	2,187	3,434	0.64	88
AEO (2002: table 38)	2000	600	4	21	2,144	3,181	0.62	85
AEO (2003: table 40)	2001	1,000	5	21	2,118	3,109	0.62	86
AEO (2004: table 38)	2002	1,000	6	16	1,928	2,899	0.65	89
AEO (2005: table 38)	2003	1,000	6	16	1,957	2,791	0.63	86
AEO (2006: table 38)	2004	1,000	6	16	2,014	2,707	0.60	83
AEO (2007: table 38)	2005	1,350	6	16	2,081	2,605	0.59	80
AEO (2008: table 38)	2006	1,350	6	16	2,475	2,961	0.57	79
AEO (2009: table 8.2)	2007	1,350	6	16	3,318	3,779	0.56	103
AEO (2010: table 8.2)	2008	1,350	6	16	3,820	4,179	0.56	101
AEO (2011: table 8.2)	2009	2,236	6	16	5,275	5,594	2.12	93
AEO (2012: table 8.2)	2010	2,236	6	16	5,335	5,494	2.10	91
AEO (2013: table 8.2)	2011	2,236	6	16	5,429	5,478	2.10	92
AEO (2014: table 8.2)	2012	2,234	6	16	5,501	5,555	2.12	94
MIT (2009: 18–22)	2007	1,000	5	16	4,000	4,550	0.48	109
Here	2013	1,000	5	15	4,400	4,400	1.03	Incl.

Source: US EIA (2014) and previous editions.

Table 3.3 US EIA assumptions for advanced nuclear

US EIA (2010) on ALWR costs Series and Title	*EIA (2010) (2010US$000s)*	*EIA (2010) (%)*	*TVA (2005) (%)*	*Adjustment*	*Adjusted EIA (2010)*
21 Structures	1,732,000	14	14	Rounded	1,700,000
22–29 Equipment	4,030,000	34	52	Rounded	4,000,000
20 Total direct cost	5,762,000	48	66	Rounded	5,700,000
30 Capitalised indirect costs	2,722,500	23	9	= to 9	1,100,000
40 Capitalised owner's cost	2,152,590	18	11	= to 11	1,300,000
Base overnight cost, *BASE*	10,637,090	89	86	Sum	8,100,000
60 Contingency, CN	1,300,000	11	14	= to 14	1,600,000
Total overnight cost, *OC*	11,937,090	100	100	Sum	9,700,000
Total overnight cost/kW, *OC*/kW	**5,339**				**4,338**

Sources: TVA (2005); US EIA (2010).

owners' costs are so high. If these costs were lower, for example if indirect and owners' costs were equal to the percentages in TVA (2005), the US EIA projected cost would be $4,338/kW in 2010 US dollars, or about $4,500/kW in 2013 US dollars, which is between the $4,400/kW estimated here and the $4,550/kW in 2013 US dollars estimated in MIT (2009), as in Table 3.2. Therefore one can reject the US EIA's estimate of new nuclear power costs as unrealistically high – so high, in fact, that the National Energy Modelling System (NEMS) has been unable to forecast the construction of any of the AP1000s. (In NEMS 'newspeak', plants under actual construction that are not forecast by the model are labelled as 'unplanned units', whereas those that are forecast by the model, but not necessarily being built, are labelled as 'planned' units.) The cost of new ALWRs should be adjusted in the NEMS to yield a more realistic forecast of new nuclear capacity in the United States.

3.3 Nuclear power plant construction lead time and financing cost

Table 3.2 presents US EIA assumptions regarding new NPP construction lead times. Construction lead time can be defined as the number of months from the date on which 'first major placing [pouring] of concrete, usually for the base mat of the reactor building, takes place' to the date on which 'the plant is first connected to the electrical grid for the supply of power' (IAEA, 2013: 8). For example, compare (a) the statement that it took 80 months to construct the single unit, Krsko, in Slovenia (IAEA, 2013: Table 8), and (b) the statement that construction on Krsko started in March 1975 and the unit was connected to the grid in November 1981 (a span of 80 months), but Krsko did not achieve commercial operation until January 1983 (making it 94 months) (IAEA, 2013: Table 14). For the purposes of calculating financing costs, construction lead time is defined here as the number of months from 'first concrete' to 'commercial operation' – that is, the period during which there is substantial IDC accumulation. Some analyses include the period between site preparation to 'first concrete' in the construction lead time, which can increase lead time greatly, but relatively little is spent during this period. (On the composition of concrete, see PCA, 2015.)

Chapter 1, Table 1.1, presented data on NPPs built during the last decade in East Asia. While these might seem foreign or not applicable outside Asia, many of the suppliers of nuclear steam supply systems (NSSSs) in Table 1.1 are attempting to build new nuclear plants around the world: Hitachi, with GE, producing the ABWR, the amended ABWR (ABWRa) and economic simplified boiling water reactor (ESBWR); and Toshiba, which owns Westinghouse, producing the AP1000 (see NEA, 2015). The average length of time was 62 months (compare to five years for MIT and six years for the US EIA in Table 3.2), with a standard deviation of nine months. (Chapter 5, Figure 5.2, presents an NPP construction lead time probability density.)

The remainder of this section discusses the relationship between construction lead time and the total project financing cost. As the lead time increases, the time value of money tied up in the project also increases, and it does so exponentially because of compounding. It is therefore important to build large capital-intensive projects, such as NPPs, on time and on budget, or total construction costs can get out of hand quickly. (With construction work in progress, or CWIP, accounting, as discussed in Chapter 2, Section 2.3, customers pay the interest on CWIP, thus lowering the final total construction cost; construction time increases thus lead to a slower increase in financing costs than under allowance for funds used during construction, or AFUDC, regulation or in deregulated markets.)

To understand the relationship between lead time and compounding *IDC*, consider capital construction expenditures, discounted to the beginning of commercial operation – that is, when revenues from the project begin to flow. Compared with Appendix 2A, Equation (2A.2.6), the 'negative' sign has been moved from the time superscript to the period, *t*:

$$IDC = \Sigma_t (cx_t \times OC) \times [(1 + \mathbf{m})^t - 1] \quad (t = lt, \ldots, 0) \tag{3.3.1}$$

where

cx_t	are construction expenditures as a percentage of OC in month t,
$\mathbf{m}$	is the monthly cost of capital during construction, $(1 + \mathbf{m}) = (1 + \mathbf{r})^{1/12}$,
-1	subtracts monthly expenditures in t, $cx_t \times OC$, from the summation,
lt	is the months of construction (from 'pouring first concrete' to operation), and
0	is the start of commercial operation with the generation of electricity and revenues.

In addition, the IDC factor, **idc**, is the percentage add-on to account for financing charges. Because IDC depends on the construction expenditure rate (how much is spent in each month), Equation (3.3.1) can be complicated, because the expenditure rate is not the same over the construction period, with smaller amounts being spent early to lay the foundation, larger amounts being spent on equipment in the middle of the project, and smaller amounts being spent at the end on instrumentation, training and fuel loading. Modelling this precisely is unwieldy in Monte Carlo simulations of levelised cost (as in Chapter 5). For probability and risk analysis, what is required is to calculate the percentage increase in the overnight cost resulting from project financing, equal to the IDC factor, as a transparent function of construction lead time and the cost of capital. (In a cash flow model, such as IEA and NEA, 2015, IDC is calculated implicitly and no IDC factor is used, but the construction period must be predetermined in complete years, for example five years, seven years, etc.) Here, periods are months, unless otherwise specified.

Equation (3.3.1) can be simplified by assuming that the construction expenditures have a uniform distribution, such that $cx_t = (1/lt)$ – that is, overnight cost divided by construction lead time, *lt*, in months. Then Equation (3.3.1) becomes (over the same summation period as in Equation (3.3.1)):

$$IDC \cong (OC/lt) \times \{\Sigma_t[(1+\mathbf{m})^t - 1]\} \ \ (t = lt, \ldots, 0) \tag{3.3.2}$$

Simplify Equation (3.3.2) by approximating the summation over the lead time as:

$$\Sigma_t(1+\mathbf{m})^t \cong [(1+\mathbf{m})^{lt} - 1]/\mathbf{m} \ \ (t = lt, \ldots, 0) \tag{3.3.3}$$

A part of this expression, $(1 + \mathbf{m})^{lt}$ can be approximated with a binomial series expansion:

$$\begin{aligned}(1+\mathbf{m})^{lt} \cong\ & 1 + [lt \times (\mathbf{m}^1/1!)] + [lt \times (lt-1) \times (\mathbf{m}^2/2!)] \\ & + [lt \times (lt-1) \times (lt-2) \times (\mathbf{m}^3/3!)] + \ldots,\end{aligned} \tag{3.3.4}$$

This can be substituted into Equation (3.3.3) and simplified (subtract 1 and divide by $\mathbf{m}$):

$$\begin{aligned}\Sigma_t(1+\mathbf{m})^t \cong\ & lt + [lt \times (lt-1) \times (\mathbf{m}/2)] + [lt \times (lt-1) \\ & \times (lt-2) \times (\mathbf{m}^2/6)]\end{aligned} \tag{3.3.5}$$

Substituting this into Equation (3.3.2) and simplifying (multiply through by OC/lt):

$$\begin{aligned}IDC \cong\ & \{[(lt-1) \times (\mathbf{m}/2)] + [(lt-1) \\ & \times (lt-2) \times (\mathbf{m}^2/6)]\} \times OC\end{aligned} \tag{3.3.6}$$

$$IDC \cong \{[(\mathbf{m}/2) \times lt] + [(\mathbf{m}^2/6) \times lt^2]\} \times OC \tag{3.3.7}$$

and

$$\mathbf{idc} \cong [(\mathbf{m}/2) \times lt] + [(\mathbf{m}^2/6) \times lt^2] \tag{3.3.8}$$

The approximation error declines as the period length decreases, for example from annual to monthly. Equation (3.3.8) can be compared to the IDC factor in Bunn *et al.* (2003). (This is given as an example of how complicated this approximation can be.) After introducing the equivalent of Equation (3.3.1), the authors model an approximation to *annual* construction expenditures with a beta-binomial distribution, where $\Gamma(n)$ is the gamma function,

n denotes lead time, k is the incremental year and p is when half of the expenditures are spent:

$$\frac{\Gamma(n)\Gamma(a+k-1)\Gamma(n+b-k)\Gamma(a+b)}{\Gamma(k)\Gamma(n+k-1)\Gamma(a+b+n-1)\Gamma(a)\Gamma(b)} \quad \text{(A.25)}$$

> where a and b are parameters that determine the shape of the distribution … We assume that $i_{\mathbf{idc}}$ is equal to the weighted cost of capital, see Table A.4. For the reference case $n = 6$ y, $i_{\mathbf{idc}} = 0.064$/y, and p is 0.65, which gives $F_{\mathbf{idc}} = 0.189$.
>
> (Bunn *et al.*, 2003: 98)

With a lead time of 72 months ('$n = 6$ y') and a monthly cost of capital, **m**, of 0.0052, the approximate IDC factor is $[(0.0052/2) \times 72] + [(0.0052^2/6) \times 72^2] = 0.187 + 0.023 = 21\%$, which is greater than the authors' value of 18.9% using annual values, but might be more realistic because interest is compounding on a monthly basis, not an annual one. On the other hand, the first-order approximation of $[(\mathbf{m}/2) \times lt] = 18.7\%$ is only 1% lower than their value and the annual approximation $[(r/2) \times lt] = [(0.064/2) \times 6] = 19.2\%$ is only 2% higher.

Given that Bunn *et al.* (2003: 98) conclude that their calculation gives 'a good fit to the distribution of costs', we might also conclude that the approximation in Equation (3.3.8) gives 'a good fit' to the IDC factor. However, Equation (3.3.8) is easier to calculate and more transparent to interpret than more complicated formulas. (It is important to use monthly data because of compounding; the approximation is much less robust with semi-annual or annual data.)

3.4 Nuclear power plant capacity factors

The capacity factor is another important component in calculating levelised fixed (capital) costs. This section decomposes the capacity factor into its components, so that each component can be specified separately, for example the number of days for a refuelling outage. Annual electricity output in year t, E_t, expressed in MWh, is defined as:

$$E_t = \text{MW} \times \text{TT} \times CF_t \quad (3.4.1)$$

where

MW is the plant's annual *net* maximum dependable output, in MW,
TT is the total time in a year – that is, 8,766 hours (a leap year being averaged over four years), and
CF_t is the capacity factor, which is the percentage of maximum output generated in year t.

The US NRC (1995) defines several capacity factors, each with a different measure of capacity. In Equation (3.4.1), let E be the NRC's 'net electrical energy generated' and MW be the 'net maximum dependable capacity'. There are many measures of NPP size:

- the nameplate rating is the size of the generator in gross megawatts electrical, MWe;
- the maximum dependable capacity (MDC) is that which can be called upon by the transmission operator, which can vary from month to month owing to changes in the temperature of the cooling water; and
- MDC net is the MDC minus the amount of electricity used to operate the plant itself (ORNL, 2001).

Further, the capacity factor can be defined over the fuel cycle rather than over a year, because fuel cycles are not necessarily one year long. For example, if the refuelling outage happens every 18 months, the capacity factor will be lower in years with refuelling and higher in years without refuelling, creating spurious volatility. The capacity factor in years without refuelling will be using fuel that was inserted during years with refuelling, so outage time should be spread over the length of the fuel cycle, not over the length of 12 months. (See analysis in Rothwell, 1990.)

Much of the analysis of NPP productivity before 1990 focused on determining factors correlated with poor performance, as measured by output (Komanoff and Roelofs, 1994). In the 1990s, authors focused on (a) comparing NPP performance internationally (Sturm, 1993, 1995; Thomas, 1990a, 1990b), and (b) trying to untangle the related effects of learning-by-doing and ageing (Krautmann and Solow, 1992; Lester and McCabe, 1993).

There are three related indicators of generating performance: productivity, availability and reliability. This section defines the functional relationships among these indicators, relying on the US NRC's 'Glossary' (US NRC, 1995).

First, 'productivity' refers to the ability of the power plant's capacity to generate electricity. Productivity is measured by the capacity factor, CF. Let:

$$CF \equiv E/(\mathrm{MW} \times \mathrm{TT}) \tag{3.4.2}$$

Although each variable could be subscripted to indicate the period, for example $CF_t = CF_{2016}$, the time subscript will not be used unless required for clarity.

Second, 'availability' measures the readiness of the power plant to generate electricity (see the discussion of 'availability' and 'unavailability' in IAEA, 1998). Availability can be measured with time or energy units. The US NRC (1995: xiv) uses time-based definitions of availability, defining the 'unit availability factor', AF, as:

$$AF \equiv (AH/\mathrm{TT}) \tag{3.4.3}$$

where AH, the 'unit available hours', are 'the total clock hours in the report period during which the unit operated on-line or was capable of such operation (Unit Reserve Shutdown Hours + Hours Generator On-Line)'. Let 'hours generator on-line' be HH, then, and the 'unit service factor', SF, be equal to (HH/TT).

In addition, there are energy-based definitions of availability. For example, the IAEA's Power Reactor Information System (PRIS) defines the 'energy availability factor' (IAEA, 2015). A similar energy-based definition of availability (Krautmann and Solow, 1992; Lester and McCabe, 1993) is the 'equivalent availability factor', EAF, defined by the Stoller Corporation (1986) as

$$EAF \equiv [(E/\mathrm{MW}) + DH]/\mathrm{TT} \tag{3.4.4}$$

where

E/MW is the mean generation in MWh per MW of capacity, and

DH are 'equivalent economic derating hours', which are hours (in which the unit was capable of full generation) lost for economic reasons, such as 'load following, fuel conservation, coast down to refueling, etc.' (Stoller Corporation, 1986: D–1, quoted in Anderson, 1987: 8, without attribution, so there were likely to be other sources of this definition).

If there are no full or partial shutdowns for *economic* reasons – that is, if DH is 0, then EAF is equal to CF in Equation (3.4.2).

Third, 'reliability' measures the certainty of power plant generation. One can define the reliability factor, RF, as:

$$RF = 1 - FR = 1 - [FH/(HH + FH)] \tag{3.4.5}$$

where

FR is the 'unit forced outage rate', and

FH is the 'forced outage hours', which are those hours during outages 'required to be initiated no later than the weekend following discovery of an off-normal condition' (US NRC, 1995: xi).

Because of this arbitrary definition – that is, a function of the relationship of the off-normal condition to a 'weekend' – FH is redefined as the total time in outages following forced, automatic scrams – that is, the rapid insertion of the reactor control rods.[1] So:

$$\mathrm{TT} \equiv HH + FH + SH \tag{3.4.6}$$

where *SH* are scheduled outage hours, primarily for maintenance and refuelling, but also include *DH*.

To summarise, *CF* measures productivity, *SF* measures availability and *RF* measures reliability. The *CF* in Equation (3.4.2) can be modified by introducing *HH*:

$$CF \equiv [E/(\mathrm{MW} \times HH)] \times (HH/\mathrm{TT}) \equiv CU \times SF \quad (3.4.7)$$

The first term, $[E/(\mathrm{MW} \times HH)]$, can be defined as the 'capacity utilisation rate', *CU*. The second term is the service factor, *SF*, equal to (HH/TT). The *CU* is a measure of how close the power plant is to its potential output when the plant is operating and the *SF* is the percentage of the time for which the power plant is running. Further, from Equation (3.4.6):

$$(\mathrm{TT} - SH) = (HH + FH) \quad (3.4.8)$$

$$HH = (\mathrm{TT} - SH) \times (1 - FR) \quad (3.4.9)$$

$$SF \equiv (HH/\mathrm{TT}) = [(\mathrm{TT} - SH)/\mathrm{TT}] \times (1 - FR) = SA \times (1 - FR) \quad (3.4.10)$$

Let $[(\mathrm{TT} - SH)/\mathrm{TT}]$ equal *SA*, the 'scheduled availability' rate. The percentage of the time for which the plant is running, *SF*, is equal to the product of the scheduled (or 'planned') availability, *SA*, and the reliability factor, $(1 - FR)$.

To estimate expected power plant capacity factors, first assume that the expected capacity utilisation rate is 100% – that is, that the plant will be running at its potential output when the plant is operating. (Capacity utilisation can be below 100% if there are regulatory restrictions, or can be greater than 100% with 'upratings' – that is, increases in designed generating capacity – and upgrading of equipment, as discussed in Davis and Wolfram, 2011.) So, if the average number of hours in the reporting period is 8,766, the capacity factor becomes:

$$CF = CU \times SF = [(8{,}766 - SH)/8{,}766] \times (1 - FR) \quad (3.4.11)$$

For example, if the refuelling period is 20 days (= 480 hours) per calendar year and the forced outage rate, *FR*, unscheduled downtime, is 5%, then the expected capacity factor is 90% [= (8,766 – 480) × (1 – 0.05)/8,766]. This corresponds to the assumption of the EMWG (2007) and is supported by capacity factors at US NPPs in the last two decades (which is discussed in Chapter 5, Section 5.2, for example in Figure 5.3).

3.5 New small modular reactors

The purpose of this section is to define SMRs as the term is used currently. In defining modular nuclear technologies, the term 'module' has many meanings. The two most common uses of 'module' in nuclear energy systems are for (a) equipment that is delivered to the site as components that can be plugged into one another and inserted into a structure with a minimum amount of labour, similar to 'plug-and-play' personal computer equipment, and (b) components and equipment of an NPP that are made under factory quality control, and delivered in a set of packages that can be assembled on-site, similar to ready-to-assemble furniture. In what follows:

- a 'module' is a piece of pre-assembled equipment, such as the 'reactor module';
- 'modular construction' involves assembling factory-produced, pre-packaged structures on-site; and
- 'on-site construction' uses site-delivered labour, machines and materials to build structures and insert modules.

The abbreviation 'SMR' has had at least three different definitions in the context of nuclear power (and refers to 'steam methane reforming' in the natural gas industry). Babcock & Wilcox (B&W) has defined SMRs as 'scalable module reactors' (NuclearStreet, 2009). The IAEA (2014b) defines SMRs as 'small and medium-sized reactors', with 'small' being below 300 MW and 'medium-sized' being below 700 MW. The US DOE (2012) defines SMRs as 'small modular reactors', even though this does not distinguish between reactor technology types. In defining one type of SMR, the small light water reactor (LWR), Figure 3.3 (an extension of Chapter 1, Figure 1.1) presents a generic power unit of a light-water SMR with five systems composed of modules with three primary inputs and three primary outputs, representing the on-site structures, System 1, into which the factory-fabricated equipment modules are inserted. (All US DOE-funded SMRs in the United States are pressurised water reactors, or PWRs.)

Figure 3.4 represents a scalable SMR with N power units. For example, if the standard equivalent SMR unit were to be 45 MW net, then:

1 Westinghouse's W-SMR, at 225 MW, could be represented as fully configured, with N = 2 (or 2 × 225 MW = 450 MW = 10 × 45 MW);
2 B&W's mPower, at 180 MW, could be represented as fully configured, with N = 2 (or 2 × 180 MW = 360 MW = 8 × 45 MW);
3 Holtec's 160 MW inherently safe modular underground reactor (HI-SMUR), at 160 MW, could be represented as fully configured, with N = 2 (or 2 × 160 MW = 320 MW ≈ 7 × 45 MW); and
4 NuScale's SMR, at 45 MW, could be represented as fully configured, with N = 12 (or 12 × 45 MW = 540 MW).

This standard unit can be used to investigate the scalability of a particular SMR – that is, how easily the SMR can be built at various sizes (Rothwell, 2011: 12–13). However, in choosing an optimal size for a specific SMR, the smaller the reactor size, the greater the cost per kilowatt (kW) of capacity (not accounting for economies of mass production).

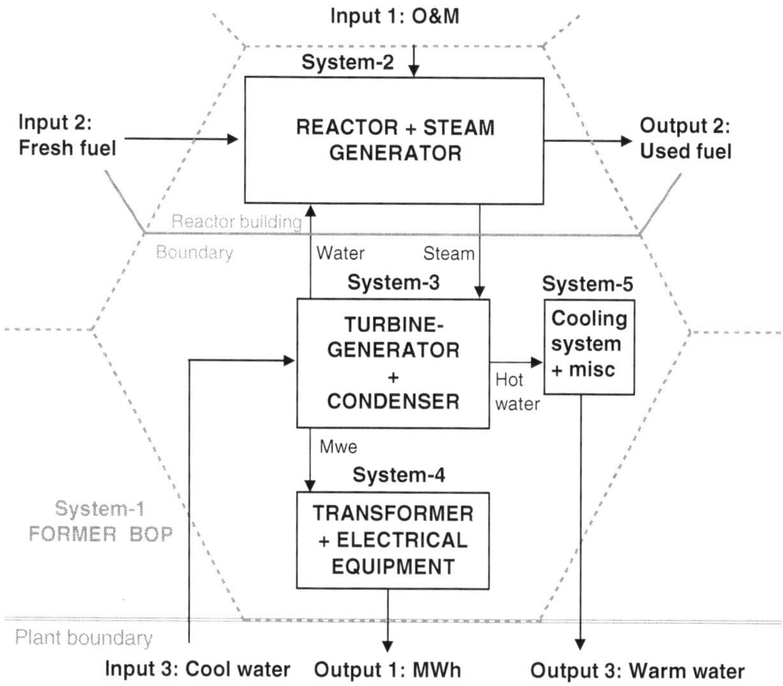

Figure 3.3 One pressurised light water reactor, 'Power Unit 1'.

Source: Author.

Note: This figure is not a schematic of a particular NPP. It is a representation of the relative magnitude of costs for structures and equipment for the SMR.

How unit costs change with reactor size are referred to as 'scale economies' and can be represented with a scale parameter, **S**, such that cost *declines* (increases) by (1 – **S**) for each *doubling* (halving) of reactor capacity. For example, if **S** = 90%, then a 500 MW reactor would be 10% more costly than a 1,000 MW reactor and a 250 MW reactor would be 23% more costly than a 1,000 MW reactor. To be more specific, a 225 MW reactor would be 27.6% more costly than a 1,117 MW reactor (from the same manufacturer, for example Westinghouse) because of scale economies in reactor design of the same technology.

While there could be scale economies in NSSS overnight cost, because larger plants take longer to build, scale economies have not been detectable in total construction cost for NPPs above 600 MW (see Rothwell, 1986; cf. Cantor and Hewlett, 1988 – particularly regarding their use of the Hausman, 1978, test of their linear estimation). There has also been found to be some correlation between construction costs and lead times, but the literature has presented no established method for sorting out how much of this was associated with

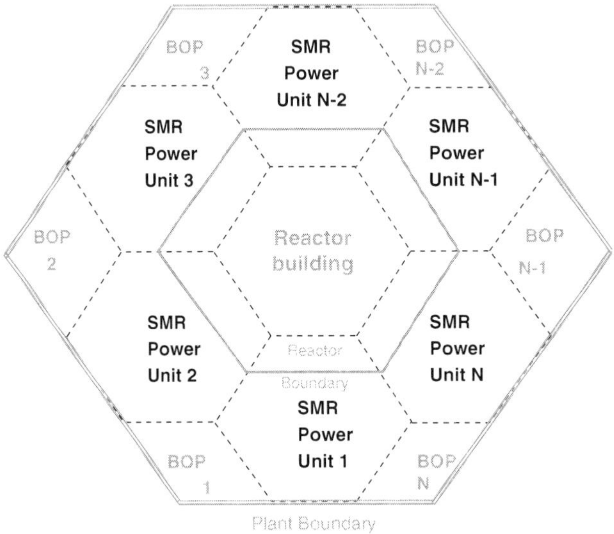

Figure 3.4 Economic representation of a scalable small light water reactor.

Source: Author.

Note: This figure is not a schematic of a particular NPP.

overnight cost escalation and how much was associated with financing costs. Historically, most regulated utilities reported total construction costs, including financing costs, in mixed nominal ('as spent') dollars. We must therefore know the specific annual cost of capital and the specific annual construction expenditure if we are to translate reported construction costs to determine the direct relationship between size and lead time, and the indirect relationship between size and lead time through financing costs. Here, this correlation is assigned to IDC, which is a function of construction lead time (see Equation (3.1.1)).

Thus the direct construction cost of a smaller reactor, DIR_{SMR}, can be related to the cost for a larger reactor, DIR_{ALWR}:

$$DIR_{\mathrm{SMR}} = DIR_{\mathrm{ALWR}} \times (\mathrm{MW}_{\mathrm{SMR}}/\mathrm{MW}_{\mathrm{ALWR}}) \times \mathbf{S}^{[(\ln \mathrm{MWSMR} - \ln \mathrm{MWALWR})/\ln 2]} \tag{3.5.1}$$

where **S** is the scaling factor, for example 90%.

For each doubling of reactor size, costs decline by 10%. If $\mathrm{MW}_{\mathrm{ALWR}}$ were 1,000 MW and $\mathrm{MW}_{\mathrm{SMR}}$ were 360 MW, then SMR costs would be 17% higher than ALWR costs per kW because of the smaller size. (See NEA, 2011, for more on this 'scaling law'.)

On the other hand, if smaller reactors enjoy economies of mass production (also known as 'serial economies', or 'series economies', **ser**) over larger

Table 3.4 Decomposition of direct construction costs (Account 20)

System	*TVA (2005)*	*Series*	*% of DIR*	*20% ×*	*BOP*
1: Structures	21%	21	C21 = 20%	20% =	4%
2: Reactor	38%	22	C22 = 40%	40% =	8%
3: Turbine generator	25%	23	C23 = 25%	25% =	5%
4: Electrical	11%	24	C24 = 10%	10% =	2%
5: Cooling & miscellaneous	5%	25+26	C25 = 5%	5% =	1%
Total direct costs, *DIR*	100%	20	100%		20%

Source: TVA (2005).

reactors, for example in improved factory quality control, SMR direct costs could be lower than given in Equation (3.5.1):

$$DIR_{\mathrm{SMR}} = DIR_{\mathrm{ALWR}} \times (\mathrm{MW_{SMR}}/\mathrm{MW_{ALWR}}) \times (1 - \mathbf{ser}) \times \mathbf{S}^{[(\ln \mathrm{MWSMR} - \ln \mathrm{MWALWR})/\ln 2]} \quad (3.5.2)$$

where **ser** is the percentage reduction in cost associated with factory production (for example if **ser** were 15%, costs would be 85% of what the costs would be with Equation (3.5.1)).

Table 3.4 gives percentages of direct cost for each system in the 20 Series (TVA, 2005) and presents a stylised version of the direct cost breakdown for new nuclear. Equipment is installed into the balance of plant, BOP, consisting of (a) reactor building(s) that would hold System 2 equipment, and (b) other structures that would hold non-reactor equipment. Series 21 (BOP equal to 20% of direct construction costs) is proportionally allocated among the systems, as direct costs are allocated in the last column in Table 3.4. Hence, here, the BOP not associated with any system, such as the administration building, is 4% of *DIR*, the reactor building accounts for 8% of *DIR* and structures of all of the other systems account for 8% of *DIR*. These proportions can be changed to explore the influence of scale effects.

In Section 3.7, construction and levelised costs of twin 180 MW SMRs are compared to the construction and levelised costs of twin 1,117 MW ALWRs (AP1000s), assuming scale economies in reactor size – that is, that the larger the SMR, the lower the cost per kW. On the other hand, transportation modes limit the size of module that can be shipped to a generic site. The stated sizes of the SMR reactor modules will vary as the designers minimise construction and levelised costs subject to manufacturing and transportation constraints.

Before discussing the projected capital costs of generating electricity with ALWRs and SMRs, Section 3.6 proposes methods for accounting for changes in cost as more units and more plants are built.

3.6 First-of-a-kind and nth-of-a-kind construction cost estimates

To understand how *KC* changes with the addition of power units at one plant site, overnight costs can be allocated to fixed capital costs, *FX*, or to variable capital costs, *VK*:

$$BASE = DIR^{+} + OWN = FX^{+} + VK^{+} \tag{3.6.1}$$

where

$^{+}$	indicates that the cost category includes indirects,
DIR^{+}	is direct construction costs plus the indirect rate on *DIR* and supplemental costs (Account 50),
FX^{+}	are fixed costs (costs that do not vary with the number of reactor units at a plant site), which include owners' costs arising from the requirement that they license the site (for example US\$200 million), and
VK^{+}	are variable capital costs, including the appropriate directs and indirects plus owners' costs.

Variable capital costs, $VK^{+}{}_{/\mathrm{kW}}$, vary with the number of power units, N, in a particular configuration:

$$BASE = FX^{+} + VK^{+}(\mathrm{N}) = FX^{+} + (VK^{+}{}_{/\mathrm{kW}} \times \mathrm{kW} \times \mathrm{N}) \tag{3.6.2}$$

where

$VK^{+}{}_{/\mathrm{kW}}$	is the variable capital cost per kW, including indirect costs,
kW	is the kilowatt size of each power unit, and
N	is the number of units in a standard plant.

Generally, $VK^{+}{}_{/\mathrm{kW}}$ declines as the power unit's generating capacity increases. To generalise Equation (3.5.1):

$$VK^{+}{}_{/\mathrm{kW}} = VK^{*} \times \mathbf{S}^{[(\ln \mathrm{MW} - \ln \mathrm{MW}^{*})/\ln 2]} \tag{3.6.3}$$

where

VK^{*}	is variable capital cost in US\$/kW for the reference power unit,
S	is the scale parameter (here, 90%),
MW	is the megawatt-electric size of the power unit being considered, and
MW*	is the reference power unit MW size, for example 1,117 MW.

To this point, the discussion has implicitly focused on FOAK costs, as assumed in the US EIA AEOs. To understand how *KC* changes with the building of plants at more than one site, the remainder of this section discusses how to transform NOAK cost estimates into FOAK cost estimates – that is, the cost for plants in a series, or 'fleet', of plants, for example after the building of 8,000 MW in ALWR FOAK plants, as assumed in EMWG (2007), with a follow-on fleet of 32,000 MW. In the case of the AP1000, the four units being built in China and the four units being built in the United States – that is, about 9,000 MW – constitute the FOAK 'family'.

However, while the EMWG (2007: 135–137) suggests that cost estimators prepare both FOAK and NOAK cost estimates, the fact is that, because of uncertainties, such as in regulation and the supply chain, cost estimators generally ignore many FOAK costs and are implicitly estimating NOAK costs, assuming that 'all goes well'. Instead, most cost estimates should be treated as NOAK estimates and the learning rates discussed next should be used to *increase* the cost estimate from the implicit NOAK estimate to the explicit FOAK estimate, so that potential investors understand what they are getting into. Promoters will instead state that they have estimated a FOAK cost and will *decrease* the cost estimate to arrive at the NOAK estimate. (Areva's cost estimate of €3,200 million for Olkiluoto Unit 3 was an optimistic NOAK estimate, not a reasonable FOAK estimate.)

To understand FOAK costs, fixed cost, FX^{+}, in Equation (3.6.2) can be decomposed into two fixed cost types, *FOAK* and FX^{*}_{i}. First, *FOAK* can be said to be a 'true First-of-a-Kind cost' (EMWG, 2007: 54), associated with the development and commercialisation of the technology:

> The total FOAK plant cost has two basic parts: (1) the standard plant cost (i.e., the types of costs that will be repeated in subsequent plants, such as site-related design and construction); and (2) the true FOAK non-recurring costs, *such as design and design certification costs.*
>
> (EMWG, 2007: 54, emphasis added)

It is possible that governments could agree to pay all 'true', non-recurring FOAK costs, because of their 'public goods' nature, as with most research and development (R&D), but here all FOAK plants share equally in compensating non-recurring FOAK costs with an amount equal to ($FOAK/N_{FOAK}$), where N_{FOAK} is the number of FOAK units, for example eight in the case of the AP1000. Second, FX^{*}_{i} are declining in 'recurring' FOAK costs for the 'i^{th}' plant arising from the finding the best procurement, manufacturing and delivery system at the time of the construction of the first set of units. FX^{*}_{i} declines to FX^{+}, by definition, when NOAK costs are achieved.

While FX^{+} costs can, in empirical fact, decline with increases in cumulative capacity, estimating this decline is speculative: while these costs can decline, this does not necessarily imply that nuclear power plant prices charged by suppliers will decline. Instead, economic profits could increase, compensating for the high start-up costs of entering the industry: profit induces reactor manufacturers to invest in this industry. In addition, a second generation of the technology could be introduced with new costs, and these costs of the next generation are known to be unknown at this time. Therefore cost decreases that might result from production beyond the assumed fleet size are ignored – that is, learning during NOAK commercialisation.

Fixed cost, FX^+, in Equation (3.6.2) can be replaced with FX^*_i, equal to (a) FOAK owners' costs, *OWN*, (b) FOAK BOP costs (Series 21), (c) FOAK reactor building costs (Series 22), (d) indirect costs (on Series 21 and 22), and (e) ($FOAK/\mathrm{N_{FOAK}}$). These costs, FX^*, decline to FX^+ during FOAK deployment.

Further, generalising $VK^+_{/\mathrm{kW}}$ in Equation (3.6.2): $VK_j^+{}_{/\mathrm{kW}}$ are costs associated with the 'j^{th}' power unit – that is, the costs of reactor units would decline at a different rate from plant costs because there are more reactors being produced than plants. Substituting FX^*_i and $VK_j^+{}_{/\mathrm{kW}}$ into Equation (3.6.2):

$$BASE_i = (FX^*_i + VK_j^+{}_{/\mathrm{kW}} \times \mathrm{kW} \times \mathrm{N}) \tag{3.6.4}$$

where plants are indexed in sequence by i and reactor units are indexed in sequence by j. When $i > \mathrm{N_{FOAK}}$, then $FX^*_i = FX^+$ and $VK_j^+{}_{/\mathrm{kW}} = VK^+{}_{/\mathrm{kW}}$. Construction costs for the 'i^{th}' plant are:

$$KC_i = (1 + \mathbf{idc}) \times (1 + C_{ON}) \times (FX^*_i + VK_j^+{}_{/\mathrm{kW}} \times \mathrm{kW} \times \mathrm{N}) \tag{3.6.5}$$

where site-specific owners' costs are assumed the same across all owner-operators.

Next, assume that FOAK costs decline because (a) $VK_j^+{}_{/\mathrm{kW}}$ changes with the cumulative number of *reactors* produced as a result of learning in procurement, manufacture and delivery systems, and (b) FX^*_i changes with the cumulative number of *plants* constructed as a result of learning in procurement, construction and construction management (on this distinction, see Koomey and Hultman, 2007). Therefore FOAK costs can be represented as:

$$VK_j^+{}_{/\mathrm{kW}} = VK^+{}_{/\mathrm{kW}} \times (1 + l_{un})^{\{[\ln(\mathrm{N} \times \mathrm{N_{FOAK}})/\ln 2] - (\ln j/\ln 2)\}} \tag{3.6.6}$$

And:

$$FX^*_i = FX^+ \times (1 + l_{pl})^{\{[\ln(\mathrm{N_{FOAK}})/\ln 2] - (\ln i/\ln 2)\}} \tag{3.6.7}$$

where

$VK^+{}_{/\mathrm{kW}}$ is the portion of costs that changes with size in the NOAK power unit cost,

l_{un} is the learning rate for power *units*, such that costs decline by *lun* with each doubling of capacity,

l_{pl} is the learning rate for power *plants*,

j is an index on units less than N_{FOAK}, and

i is an index on plants less than $N \times N_{FOAK}$, and N is the number of units at a standard plant, for example two.

NOAK costs are achieved when $j \geq N_{FOAK}$. What is an appropriate learning rate? One suggestion is that:

> A plausible range for future learning rates in the U.S. nuclear construction industry is between 3 and 10 percent. Three percent is conservative. It is consistent with a scenario involving low capacity growth, reactor orders of a variety of designs spaced widely enough apart in time that engineering and construction personnel cannot maintain continuity, some construction delays, and a construction industry that can retain internally a considerable proportion of learning benefits. A medium learning rate of 5 percent is appropriate for a scenario with more or less continuous construction, with occasional but not frequent cases of sequential units built at a single facility, a narrower range of reactor designs built by a more competitive construction industry, with delays uncommon. A 10 percent learning rate is aggressive. It would necessitate a continuous stream of orders that keep engineering teams and construction crews intact, a highly competitive construction industry, and streamlined regulation largely eliminating construction delays.
>
> (University of Chicago, 2004: 4–1)

Here, the learning rate, as reflected in changes in construction cost, is assumed to be 5%, with each doubling to $N \times N_{FOAK}$ (equal to 8,000 MW for ALWRs and 3,600 MW for SMRs), with other reductions in cost going to the nuclear suppliers as a return on their investment after building the FOAK units.

To understand changes in cost with cumulative production, consider a fleet of 450 MW SMRs consisting of (a) a set of eight fully configured FOAK plants of about 3,600 MW, and (b) a set of 32 fully configured NOAK plants of about 14,400 MW. This fleet configuration was chosen to correspond to the assumption that an SMR NOAK manufacturing facility would be able to produce the equivalent of about one 100 MW reactor steam-generation module equivalents per month, or 1,200 MW per year, or 18,000 MW (= 3,600 + 14,400) over a 15-year facility life. (With fewer throughputs, large heavy equipment manufacturers might not be interested in investing in new SMR manufacturing facilities.) (On 'learning effects and fleet effects', see D'haeseleer, 2013: 60–67.)

Finally, for completeness, declining variable costs (discussed in Chapter 4) can be expressed as a function of cumulative *operating* experience (Junginger *et al.*, 2008):

$$VC_h = VC^* \times GWY_h^{l_{vc}} \quad (3.6.8)$$

where

VC_h are variable costs of the NOAK plant in year h,
VC^* are annual (equilibrium) variable costs of the NOAK plant,
GWY_h is the cumulative number of gigawatt-years in year h of a technology's operating experience, and
l_{vc} is the experience parameter for variable costs as a function of gigawatt-years of operating experience.

For example, assuming a learning rate of 2% during operation, or a progress ratio of 0.98, l_{vc} = (log 0.98/log 2) = –0.029. If variable costs were US$10/MWh for the first NOAK plant, after 100 GWY of experience, variable costs could be about US$8.75/MWh.

In addition, an increase in the capacity factor can be expressed as a function of cumulative *operating* experience (Lako, van Heek and Rothwell, 2010):

$$CF_h = CF^* \times GWY_h^{-l_{cf}} \quad (3.6.9)$$

where

CF^* is the capacity factor for the first NOAK plant, and
l_{cf} is the experience parameter for capacity factors of a nuclear power plant.

For example, assuming a learning rate of 0.5%, or a progress ratio of 0.995, l_{cf} = (log 0.995/log 2) = –0.007. So, $-l_{cf}$ = 0.007. If NOAK CF = 90%, after 100 GWY of operating experience, CF_{100} could be about 93% per year.

3.7 New nuclear's levelised construction cost

This section presents deterministic FOAK and NOAK levelised capital cost estimates for new nuclear, combining Sections 3.1–3.6. Chapter 4 adds these *levelised capital costs* with estimates of levelised costs for fuel and O&M to calculate LC_{ALWR} and LC_{SMR}. Table 3.5 presents assumed parameters in calculating levelised capital costs for new nuclear.

1 The first set of parameters specifies the size of the unit, the plant and the number of FOAK units for each new LWR technology.
2 The second set of parameters specifies the percentage allocations of direct construction expenditures for the NOAK plant. Because these percentages are assumed the same for both technologies, the cost of the reactor is the same proportion of direct costs for both technologies (for the NOAK plants).
3 The third set of parameters specifies rates to transform direct costs into overnight costs, where a 15% contingency implies a 'detailed estimate'

for NOAK plants and a 25% contingency implies a 'preliminary estimate' for FOAK plants. (See Appendix 3A on appropriate contingencies.)

4 The fourth set of parameters specifies how costs change from the first FOAK plant to the NOAK plant and how smaller reactor costs are related through scale economies to larger reactor costs.
5 The last set of parameters is used in levelising capital costs over MWh.

Table 3.6 presents estimated total construction cost for a hypothetical FOAK–1 ALWR plant, FOAK–5 ALWR plant and NOAK ALWR plant, assuming a weighted average cost of capital (WACC), or real weighted average cost of capital, **r**, of 7.5%. Table 3.7 presents estimated total construction cost for a hypothetical FOAK–1 SMR plant, a FOAK–5 SMR plant and a NOAK SMR plant, assuming no economies of mass production. Table 3.8 presents the same set of SMR plants under the assumption that SMR designers are able to reduce costs by 10% by means of serial production (equal to 1 – **ser**). Contingency changes to reflect the appropriate stage of estimation (as presented in Table 3A.1). Non-recurring FOAK costs, assumed at US$1,000 million, including the costs of US NRC design certification, are spread equally over the first eight units.

How do SMR costs compare with ALWR costs? First, consider total construction costs:

- ALWR construction costs for 2,234 MW range from $10,300 million to $13,200 million; and
- SMR costs range from $2,000 million for a 360 MW NOAK SMR plant with compensation for mass production economy effects to $3,000 million for a 360 MW FOAK–1 SMR plant without compensation for mass production economy effects – that is, a third, to a quarter, of the cost of a dual-unit ALWR.

Second, ALWR levelised *capital* costs range from $61.65/MWh to $48.26/MWh. However, because the FOAK units are already under construction for at least the AP1000 and other ALWRs, going forward, only the NOAK estimate is relevant for comparison with SMR costs when considering competition between SMRs and ALWRs. The SMR costs range from $86.93/MWh for a FOAK–1 SMR plant without compensating for mass production economy effects to $57.84/MWh for a NOAK SMR plant with compensation for mass production economy effects.

Because the cost of capital on new construction depends on changes in the owner's debt-to-equity ratio from building a nuclear power plant, the cost of capital should be lower for SMRs than for ALWRs, given that the size of the project matters in comparison to the size of the nuclear utility. However, the cost of capital does not necessarily correct the 'size' effect in the 'nuclear' risk premium associated with the large size and capital intensity of an ALWR project. Appendix 3A models the risk premium as a function of the ratio of a

Table 3.5 Parameters for new nuclear construction cost calculations

Section	*Levelised capital cost parameters*	*ALWR*	*SMR*
(1)	Construction lead time in months, *lt*	60	40
	Unit net capacity in MWe, MW	1,117	180
	Number of units, N	2	2
	Plant net capacity in MWe, N × MW	2,234	360
	Number of FOAK units, N_{FOAK}	8	16
(2)	C21: Site improvements and structures	20%	20%
	C22: Reactor (and steam generator)	40%	40%
	C23: Turbine generator and condenser	25%	25%
	C24: Electrical equipment	10%	10%
	C25: Cooling system and miscellaneous equipment	5%	5%
(3)	Indirect rate, *INDIR*	10%	10%
	Owners cost (licensing), $200m + 5% *DIR*	$200	$200
	Owners cost (administration), all other *OWN*	5%	5%
	FOAK costs, *FX** + *VK**	$125	$125
	Contingency FOAK, $C_{ON-FOAK}$	25%	25%
	Contingency NOAK, $C_{ON-NOAK}$	15%	15%
(4)	Learning rate, l_{pl}	5%	5%
	Scale economies parameter, **S**	90%	90%
	Savings from serial economies, **ser**	NA	0%, 10%
(5)	Refuelling & scheduled outage days, *SH*	20	20
	Forced outage rate, *FR*	5%	5%
	Average capacity factor, *CF*	90%	90%
	Depreciation life, dT	40	40

Source: See discussion in text.

Table 3.6 Levelised capital costs for ALWR FOAK–1 and FOAK–5 and NOAK plants

Levelised capital cost *All values in 2013US$*	*ALWR* *r* =	*FOAK–1* *7.50%*	*FOAK–5* *7.50%*	*NOAK* *7.50%*
Net electrical capacity	MWe	2,234	2,234	2,234
Size of power unit	MWe	1,117	1,117	1,117
Number of power units, N	Number	2	2	2
Site improvements and structures, S 21	US$m	1,418	1,312	1,266
Reactor and steam generator, S 22	US$m	2,955	2,625	2,518
Turbine generator, and condenser, S 23	US$m	1,847	1,640	1,574
Transformer and electrical equipment, S 24	US$m	739	656	630
Cooling system and miscellaneous equipment, S 25+26	US$m	369	328	315
Direct costs, *DIR*	US$m	7,329	6,561	6,302
Indirect costs, *INDIR*, 10%	US$m	733	656	630
FOAK expenses	US$m	125	125	0
Owner's cost, *OWN*	US$m	566	528	515
BASE Overnight cost	US$m	8,753	7,871	7,448
Contingency	US$m	2,188	1,968	1,117

(Continued)

Table 3.6 (continued)

Levelised capital cost *All values in 2013US$*	*ALWR* *r =*	*FOAK–1* *7.50%*	*FOAK–5* *7.50%*	*NOAK* *7.50%*
Overnight cost, *OC*	US$m	10,941	9,838	8,565
Overnight cost, $/kW	US$/kW	4,893	4,400	3,830
Interest during construction factor	%	20.30	20.30	20.30
Interest during construction, *IDC*	US$m	2,224	2,000	1,741
KC, Total construction costs	US$m	13,165	11,838	10,306
KC, $/kW	US$/kW	5,888	5,294	4,609
Annual D&D contribution	US$m	43.65	39.25	34.17
Levelised capital + D&D cost	US$/MWh	61.65	55.43	48.26

Sources: Table 3.5 and Equations (3.6.5)–(3.6.7).

Table 3.7 Levelised capital costs for SMR without series economies (**ser** = 0.0%)

Levelised capital cost *All values in 2013US$*	*SMR* *r* =	*FOAK–1* *7.50%*	*FOAK–5* *7.50%*	*NOAK* *7.50%*
Net electrical capacity	MWe	360	360	360
Size of power unit	MWe	180	180	180
Number of power units, N	Number	2	2	2
Site improvements and structures, S 21	US$m	250	225	214
Reactor and steam generator, S 22	US$m	653	560	535
Turbine generator, and condenser, S 23	US$m	408	350	334
Transformer and electrical equipment, S 24	US$m	163	140	134
Cooling system and miscellaneous equipment, S 25+26	US$m	82	70	67
Direct costs, *DIR*	US$m	1,556	1,344	1,284
Indirect costs, *INDIR*, 10%	US$m	156	134	128
FOAK expenses	US$m	125	125	0
Owner's cost, *OWN*	US$m	278	267	264
BASE Overnight cost	US$m	2,115	1,871	1,677

(Continued)

Table 3.7 (continued)

Levelised capital cost *All values in 2013US$*	*SMR* *r =*	*FOAK–1* *7.50%*	*FOAK–5* *7.50%*	*NOAK* *7.50%*
Contingency	US$m	529	468	252
Overnight cost, *OC*	US$m	2,644	2,338	1,929
Overnight cost, $/kW	US$/kW	7,343	6,496	5,357
Interest during construction factor	%	13.10	13.10	13.10
Interest during construction, *IDC*	US$m	345	305	252
KC, Total construction costs	US$m	2,989	2,644	2,181
KC, $/kW	US$/kW	8,303	7,344	6,057
Annual D&D contribution	US$m	9.91	8.77	7.23
Levelised capital + D&D cost	US$/MWh	86.93	76.90	63.42

Sources: Table 3.6, with adjustments from Table 3.5.

Table 3.8 Levelised capital costs for SMR with series economies (**ser** = 0.10%)

Levelised capital cost *All values in 2013US$*	*SMR* *r* =	*FOAK–1* *7.50%*	*FOAK–5* *7.50%*	*NOAK* *7.50%*
Net electrical capacity	MWe	360	360	360
Size of power unit	MWe	180	180	180
Number of power units, N	Number	2	2	2
Site improvements and structures, S 21	US$m	225	202	193
Reactor and steam generator, S 22	US$m	588	504	482
Turbine generator, and condenser, S 23	US$m	367	315	301
Transformer and electrical equipment, S 24	US$m	147	126	120
Cooling system and miscellaneous equipment, S 25+26	US$m	73	63	60
Direct costs, *DIR*	US$m	1,401	1,210	1,156
Indirect costs, *INDIR*, 10%	US$m	140	121	116
FOAK expenses	US$m	125	125	0
Owner's cost, *OWN*	US$m	270	260	258
BASE Overnight cost	US$m	1,936	1,716	1,529

(Continued)

Table 3.8 (continued)

Levelised capital cost *All values in 2013US$*	*SMR* *r =*	*FOAK–1* *7.50%*	*FOAK–5* *7.50%*	*NOAK* *7.50%*
Contingency	US$m	484	429	229
Overnight cost, *OC*	US$m	2,420	2,145	1,759
Overnight cost, $/kW	US$/kW	6,722	5,959	4,885
Interest during construction factor	%	13.10	13.10	13.10
Interest during construction, *IDC*	US$m	316	280	230
KC, Total construction costs	US$m	2,736	2,425	1,989
KC, $/kW	US$/kW	7,600	6,737	5,524
Annual D&D contribution	US$m	9.07	8.04	6.59
Levelised capital + D&D cost	US$/MWh	79.58	70.54	57.84

Source: Table 3.6, with adjustments from Table 3.5.

plant's construction cost to the market value of the firm. If the larger plant represents half of the electric utility's value, then the smaller plant could represent a sixth to an eighth of the electric utility's value. A smaller ratio should be more satisfactory to Moody's and Standard & Poor's, as discussed in Chapter 2, Section 2.2.

Because the cost of capital is utility- and utility-type-specific, whether government-owned, privately owned and regulated, privately owned and not price-regulated, etc., costs of capital between 3% and 12% will be used in Chapter 4 to compare the construction and levelised costs of new nuclear power.

Appendix 3A: Risk, contingency and diversification in electricity generation

3A.1 Suggested contingency rates in the cost engineering literature

Traditionally, cost contingency estimation relied heavily on expert judgement based on various cost-engineering standards, whereby cost contingency is added to the cost estimate to provide a reserve for risks and uncertainties during construction. Table 3A.1 compares project stages and expected accuracy ranges recommended by the Association for the Advancement of Cost Engineering (AACE, 1997) and contingencies recommended by the Electric Power Research Institute (EPRI, 1993). Parsons (1999) makes similar comparisons of the American National Standards Institute (ANSI), the United Kingdom's Association of Cost Engineers (ACostE) and the US DOE's Office of Environmental Management. (See also D'haeseleer, 2013: 73–77, for a discussion of these issues.)

Lorance and Wendling (2001) discuss the expected accuracy ranges reproduced in Table 3A.1: 'The estimate meets the specified quality requirements if the expected accuracy ranges are achieved. This can be determined by selecting the values at the 10% and 90% points of the distribution.' With symmetric distributions, this infers that 80% of the probability is contained between the outer bounds of the accuracy ranges, $\pm X\%$.

To understand the influence of confidence intervals and accuracy ranges, consider the normal ('bell-shaped') probability distribution. The normal distribution can be described by its mean, for example the expected cost, represented mathematically as 'E(cost)', and its standard deviation (a measure of the cost estimate uncertainty), as in Figure 3A.1. The normal density is symmetric – that is, it is equally likely that the final cost will be above or below the expected cost – so the mean equals the median (half the distribution is above the median and half is below) and the mean equals the mode (the most likely cost). The normal density can be described as:

$$\mathbf{n}(\mu, \sigma) = \left(2\pi\sigma^2\right)^{-0.5} \times \exp\left\{-0.5 \times (x-\mu)^2/\sigma^2\right\} \qquad (3A.1.1)$$

Table 3A.1 Comparison of AACE and EPRI cost estimate stages

AACE end usage	*AACE expected accuracy range*	*AACE contingency*	*EPRI designation*	*EPRI contingency*
Concept screening	Low: −20% to −50%	50%	NA	NA
Level of project definition: 0–2%	High: +30% to +100%			
Feasibility study	Low: −15% to −30%	30%	Simplified estimate	30% to 50%
Level of project definition:1–5%	High: +20% to +50%			
Authorization or control	Low: −10% to −20%	20%	Preliminary estimate	15% to 30%
Level of project definition: 10–40%	High: +10% to +30%			
Control or bid/tender	Low: −5% to −15%	15%	Detailed estimate	10% to 20%
Level of project definition: 30–70%	High: +5% to +20%			
Check estimate or bid/tender	Low: −3% to −10%	5%	Finalised estimate	5% to 10%
Level of project definition: 50–100%	High: +3% to +15%			

Sources: From Rothwell (2005: table 1), reprinted with permission from AACE International, Morgantown, USA; originally from AACE (1997), updated in AACE (2011) and EPRI (1993) (the last publicly available version of EPRI's Technology Assessment Guide, later versions being proprietary, but having similar contingencies).

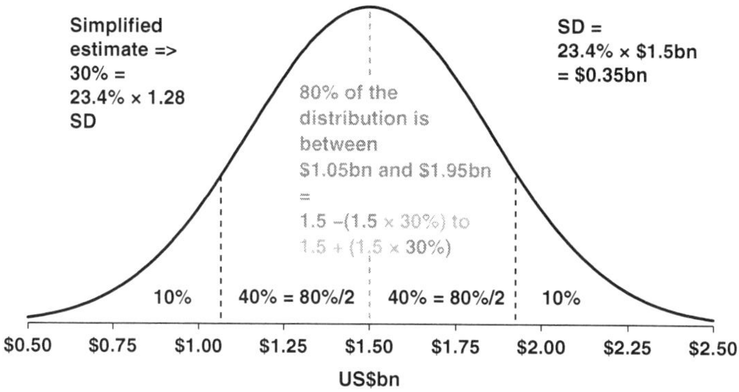

Figure 3A.1 Simplified cost estimate as a normal density.

Source: Adapted from Rothwell (2005).

Note: Normal ($1,500m, $350m); mean = $1,500m, SD = 23.4% = $350m.

where

μ is the mean, which is equal to $E(x)$ and $E(x)$ is the 'expectations' operator,
σ is the standard deviation, and
σ^2 is the variance equal to $E(x - \mu)^2$.

Figure 3A.1 shows the normal density of a cost estimate with a mean, median and mode of US$1,500 million and a standard deviation of 23.4%. Here, 10% of the distribution is below $1,050 million and 10% is above $1,950 million, yielding an 80% confidence level for an accuracy range of ±30% (= 23.4 × 1.28), where Figure 3A.2 shows the same cost estimate with a cumulative normal distribution (the solid black line).

Figure 3A.1 presents the normal density function in Equation (3A.1.1). However, the cumulative distribution of the normal density – that is, the normal distribution function, $\mathbf{N}(\mu, \sigma)$ – which is the integral of the normal density function – that is, the area under the continuous solid black line in Figure 3A.1 – is not available in 'closed form' – that is, an equation without an integral (definitions can be found in Palisade, 2015). It is:

$$\mathbf{N}(\mu, \sigma) = (2\pi\sigma^2)^{-0.5} \times \int \exp\{-0.5 \times (x - \mu)^2/\sigma^2\} \qquad (3A.1.2)$$

where the integral is from $-\infty$ to $+\infty$.

On the other hand, the normal density can be mimicked by the logistic density (used extensively in Appendix 3B):

$$\mathbf{logs}(a, b) = \exp\{(a - x)/b\}/[b \times (1 + \exp\{(a - x)/b\})^2] \qquad (3A.1.3)$$

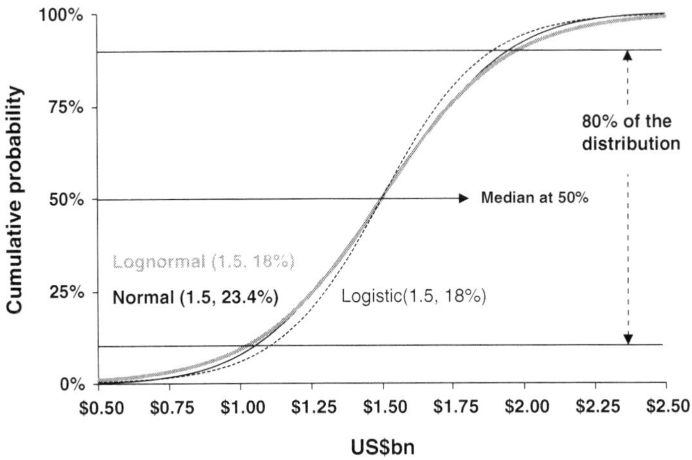

Figure 3A.2 Cost estimate with normal, lognormal and logistic distributions.

Source: Figure 3A.1 and Equation (3A.1.4).

This has a closed-form distribution (shown as a dotted line in Figure 3A.2):

$$\mathbf{LOGS}(a, b) = 1/\left[1 + \exp\{(a - x)/b\}\right] \tag{3A.1.4}$$

(See Johnson, Kotz and Balakrishnan, 1994.)

In Figure 3A.2, the logistic function (as a dotted black line) has parameters $a = 1.5$ (its mean) and $b = 0.22$, with a standard deviation equal to 0.4 ($= b \times \pi/\sqrt{3}$). The cumulative distribution from 0 (actually minus infinity) to $1,050 million is 3% and the cumulative distribution from 0 to $1,950 million is 97%: the logistic distribution has slightly fatter tails than the normal distribution – that is, there is a higher probability of observing extremely low or extremely high values with a logistic distribution than with a normal one.

If the cost estimate were normally distributed, the standard deviation would be:

$$\sigma = X/Z \tag{3A.1.5}$$

where

X is the level of accuracy, and
Z depends on the confidence level.

For example, in Table 3A.1, the level of accuracy for a 'simplified estimate' is about ±30%. If the cost estimator has an 80% confidence in *this* range of accuracy, $Z = 1.28$ – that is, 80% of the standard normal density is between the mean plus or minus 1.28 times σ. So, σ = (30%/1.28) = 23%, which is within the EPRI's suggested contingency of 15–30%. In addition, the level of accuracy for a 'preliminary estimate' is about ±20%. With the same level of confidence, Z = 1.28. So, σ = 20%/1.28 = 16%, which is within the EPRI's suggested contingency of 10–20%. The level of accuracy for a 'detailed estimate' is about ±15%. With the same level of confidence, σ = 15%/1.28 = 12%, which is within the EPRI's suggested contingency of 10–20%. Lastly, the level of accuracy for a 'finalised estimate' is about ±5%. With the same level of confidence, σ = 5%/1.28 = 4%, which is near the AACE's contingency of 5% and just below the EPRI's suggested contingency of 5–10%. *Thus one cannot reject the hypothesis that contingencies are approximately equal to the standard deviation for the normal distribution and a confidence interval of 80%* (Rothwell, 2005).

Many cost estimate accuracy ranges are non-symmetric, as shown in Table 3A.1, where the low range is less (in absolute value) than the high range. This is because (a) final costs are usually higher than those estimated, and (b) there is no probability that the final cost will be below 0 (which is a possibility with the normal distribution, however small the probability). A non-symmetric distribution is therefore more realistic for many cost estimates. One such probability distribution is the *lognormal*. Figure 3A.3 presents three lognormal densities. The lognormal density is:

$$\mathbf{logn}(\mu, \sigma) = \left\{1/[x \times (2\pi\sigma^2)^{0.5}]\right\} \times \exp\left\{-(\ln x - \mu)^2/(2\sigma^2)\right\} \tag{3A.1.6}$$

where

μ is the (natural) log of the median, and
σ^2 is the log of the median minus the log of the mode.

The mean is $\exp\{\mu + (\sigma 2/2)\}$ and the variance is $(\exp\{2\mu - \sigma^2\} \times [\exp\{\sigma^2\} - 1])$ (Johnson, Kotz and Balakrishnan, 1994). The cumulative lognormal is shown in grey in Figure 3A.2.

In Figure 3A.3, the three estimates have the same mode, but have different medians, means, variances and standard deviations, as shown in Table 3A.2. As with all standard lognormal densities, the mean is greater than the median, which is greater than the mode. Here, with the mode equal to $1,000 million ($1 billion), the variance equals [median × (median – 1)].

Setting the contingency equal to the standard deviation for a cost estimate with a lognormal density, the contingency for a 'preliminary estimate' with an 80% confidence interval of between –18% and +31% would be 18.3%, which is below the 20% contingency recommended by the AACE, but within the EPRI's suggested range of 15–30%. The contingency for a 'detailed estimate' is 13%, which is below the 15% suggested by the AACE, but within the EPRI's suggested range of 10–20%. The contingency for a 'finalised estimate' is 7%,

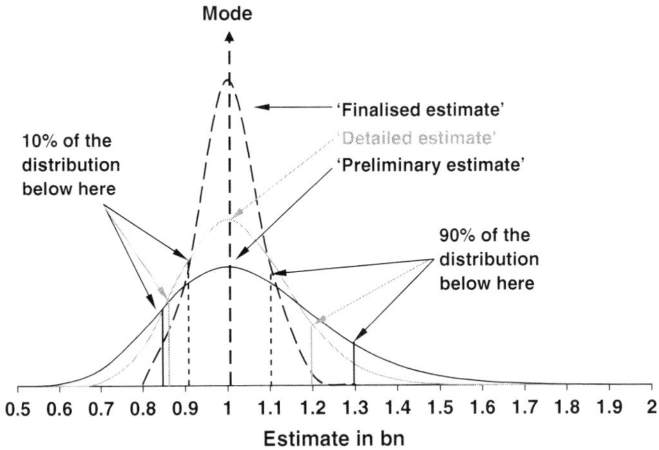

Figure 3A.3 Lognormal densities for three project stage estimates.

Source: From Rothwell (2005: fig. 2), reprinted with permission from AACE International, Morgantown, USA; originally from AACE (1997), updated in AACE (2011) and EPRI (1993).

Table 3A.2 Medians, means and standard deviations for lognormal estimates

	Mode	*Median*	*Mean*	*SD*	*80% confidence*
Preliminary estimate	1.000	1.033	1.049	18.30%	−18% to +31%
Detailed estimate	1.000	1.017	1.025	13.10%	−14% to +20%
Finalised estimate	1.000	1.005	1.008	7.00%	−8% to +10%

Sources: From Rothwell (2005: table 2), reprinted with permission from AACE International, Morgantown, USA; see Table 3A.1 and Equation (3A.1.6).

which is greater that suggested by AACE, but within the EPRI's suggested range of 5–10%. *Therefore cost estimates with lognormal distributions can also be assigned a contingency equal to their standard deviation* with an 80% confidence interval. Further, as lognormal cost estimates become more precise, the density becomes more symmetric, and the contingency approaches the values found for the symmetric normal density.

One can conclude that these guidelines suggest a 'rule of thumb': *the contingency is approximately equal to the standard deviation of the cost estimate, and vice versa – that is, that the standard deviation of a cost estimate is approximately equal to the contingency*. We can express this as:

$$C_{ON|80\%} \approx \sigma, \text{ e.g. } 13\% \qquad (3A.1.7)$$

Following this logic, for higher levels of confidence, such as 90% and 95%, assuming a normal density, the contingency would increase as follows:

$$C_{ON|90\%} \approx \sigma(1.65/1.28) = \sigma \times 1.29\text{, e.g. } 13\% \times 1.29 = 16.6\% \qquad (3A.1.8)$$

$$C_{ON|95\%} \approx \sigma(1.96/1.28) = \sigma \times 1.53\text{, e.g. } 13\% \times 1.53 = 20\% \qquad (3A.1.9)$$

3A.2 Risk aversion, risk premiums and cost contingency

The standard deviation of the cost estimate, σ, is one measure of cost estimate uncertainty. For a cost estimate with a normal density, about 68% of the probability is between plus and minus one standard deviation ($\pm\sigma$) of the mean. Determining the proper contingency for the expected cost estimate is a function of this uncertainty and the decision maker's aversion to cost uncertainty. However, the cost engineering literature neglects to mention the decision maker's risk aversion. A discussion of the economic theory of risk aversion is therefore appropriate to understand the implications of this rule of thumb to set contingency equal to the standard deviation of the cost estimate (and vice versa).

The economic theory of risk is well developed and can be applied to the problem of calculating levelised cost contingency. The theory focuses on how to determine how much compensation (that is, risk premium) a decision maker requires before accepting a risky proposition. (A more extensive discussion can be found in Copeland, Weston and Shastri, 2005, and in most finance textbooks.)

To describe how investors evaluate risk, economic analyses show how decision makers choose between risky alternatives. The microeconomic theory of demand assumes that consumers (or investors) purchase goods and services (or financial instruments) to maximise their 'well-being' or 'welfare'. (Economists refer to 'well-being' as 'utility', which derives from the philosophical movement known as utilitarianism. However, it is confusing in the context of the electric utility industry, of which nuclear power is a part, so this book uses the term 'welfare functions' rather than 'utility functions'.)

The question addressed by economists is how decision makers (individuals, firms, governments and societies) rank the different levels of wealth that might result from choosing among risky alternatives. These choices are modelled by assuming a 'welfare' function, $W(\Omega)$, where Ω represents the decision maker's net present wealth. The welfare function must be such that if $\Omega_1 > \Omega_2$, then $W(\Omega_1) > W(\Omega_2)$. However, if Ω_1 and Ω_2 were both risky, as they would be if wealth were to involve financial instruments (or electricity-generating assets), then how would decision makers compare risky outcomes? For example, how would a decision maker compare (a) a return of \$5 half the time and a return of

\$20 half the time, with an expected value of \$12.50 = (\$5 × 0.5 + \$20 × 0.5), or (b) a return of \$12.50 all the time?

To help us to make this comparison, the welfare function, $W(x)$, can be specified as a (natural) logarithmic function of wealth:

$$W(x) = \ln x \tag{3A.2.1}$$

(All welfare functions must satisfy the 'cardinality axioms': see general discussions of the 'expected utility hypothesis'.) The logarithmic function is used here because of its transparency, not because it is the best representation of decision making (see critique in Kirby, 2011).

Figure 3A.4 represents welfare as a function of wealth. If $x = 5$ half the time and $x = 20$ half the time, then the *expected welfare*, $\mathrm{E}(W)$, would be:

$$\begin{aligned} \mathrm{E}[W(x)] &= [0.5 \times W(5)] + [0.5 \times W(20)] \\ &= [0.5 \times \ln(5)] + [0.5 \times \ln(20)] \\ &= (0.5 \times 1.61) + (0.5 \times 3.00) = 2.31 \end{aligned} \tag{3A.2.2}$$

On the other hand, the *welfare of the expected wealth* $[\mathrm{E}(x) = 12.5]$ would be:

$$W[\mathrm{E}(x)] = W[(0.5 \times 5) + (0.5 \times 20)] = W \times 12.5 = 2.53 \tag{3A.2.3}$$

With logarithmic welfare function, welfare of expected wealth, a certain value, is greater than the expected welfare of uncertain wealth.

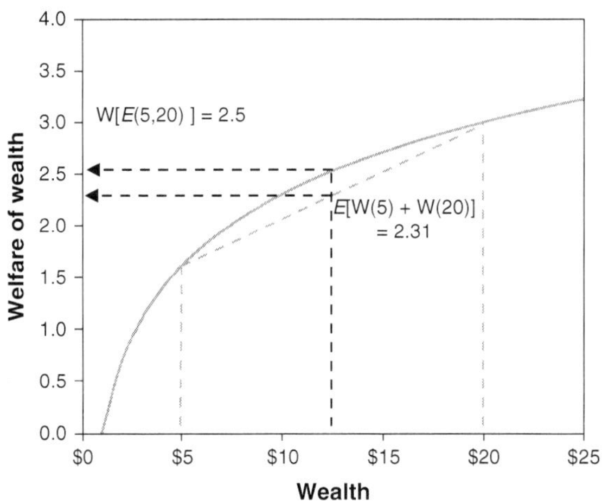

Figure 3A.4 Welfare of expected wealth versus expected welfare.

Source: Equations (3A.2.1)–(3A.2.3).

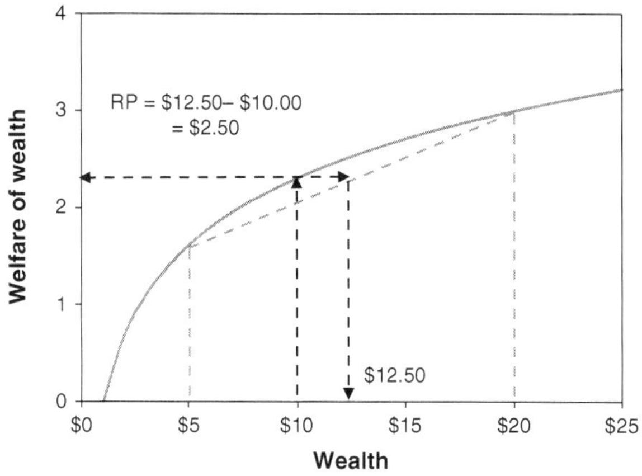

Figure 3A.5 Calculating a risk premium.

Source: Figure 3A.4 and Equation (3A.2.3).

With logarithmic welfare, the *welfare of the expected value of the certain choice is greater than the expected welfare of the uncertain choice*: $W[E(x)] > E[W(x)]$. Here, the decision maker would prefer a certain outcome (= 2.53) to a risky outcome (= 2.31), even though the certain outcome is equal to the expected value of the risky outcome.

To describe risk-averse behaviour, consider the following definitions:

- if $W[E(x)] > E[W(x)]$, then the decision maker is 'risk averse';
- if $W[E(x)] = E[W(x)]$, then the decision maker is 'risk neutral'; or
- if $W[E(x)] < E[W(x)]$, then the decision maker is 'risk preferring'.

Figure 3A.4 depicts a risk-averse decision maker, where $W[E(x)] > E[W(x)]$. A logarithmic welfare function represents a risk-averse decision maker.

The next question is what certain outcome would be equivalent to the expected risky outcome, $E[W(x)]$, such as 2.31 in our example? With a logarithmic welfare function, this would be about \$10 [log(10) = 2.31]. This is known as the 'certainty equivalent' to the risky outcome. The difference between the value of the risky outcome and its certainty equivalent is the risk premium, *RP*. In this example, *RP* is the difference between \$12.50 and \$10.00 – that is, \$2.50 – as in Figure 3A.5.

Further, the appropriate cost contingency should be a function of how a decision maker's risk aversion might change with the level of the decision maker's wealth (Arrow, 1971; Pratt, 1964). A wealthy decision maker might not be as averse to a \$1,000 gamble as a decision maker with average means.

To measure the change in risk aversion as a function of wealth, *absolute risk aversion*, ARA, is defined as:

$$\text{ARA} = -W''/W' \tag{3A.2.4}$$

where

W' is the first derivative of welfare with respect to wealth – that is, dW/dx, which is the rate at which welfare increases with wealth (the first derivative), and

W'' is the second derivative of welfare with respect to wealth, (d^2W/dx^2) – that is, how quickly welfare increases (or decreases) with wealth.

For example, with a logarithmic welfare function, $W(x) = \ln x$, then:

$$W' = dW/dx = 1/x \tag{3A.2.5}$$

$$W'' = d^2W/dx^2 = -1/x^2 \tag{3A.2.6}$$

and

$$\text{ARA} = 1/x \tag{3A.2.7}$$

With a logarithmic welfare function, ARA is an inverse function of wealth. As wealth increases, the ARA declines: $d\text{ARA}/dx < 0$. To compensate for levels of wealth, *relative risk aversion*, RRA, is defined as:

$$\text{RRA} = -x \times (W''/W') \tag{3A.2.8}$$

For example, with the logarithmic welfare function from Equation (3A.2.7):

$$\text{RRA} = x \times \text{ARA} = x(1/x) = 1 \tag{3A.2.9}$$

Therefore RRA is constant with a logarithmic welfare function; RRA does not change with wealth. In fact, Copeland and Weston (1980: 75) expected that it 'might be reasonable to expect RRA to be constant'. This is known as 'constant relative risk aversion' (CRRA). (However, this statement was deleted by the fourth edition in Copeland, Weston and Shastri, 2005: 56.)

However, decision makers' welfare functions are not necessarily logarithmic (for example they could be represented by an appropriate quadratic function, discussed in Section 3A.4). To understand the shape of welfare functions over risky outcomes, an approximation to any welfare function can be made with a Taylor series expansion of the welfare function, $W(x)$, around a randomly distributed change in wealth, $\tilde{u}$, with an expectation, $E(\tilde{u}) = \bar{u}$, and a variance, $Var(\tilde{u}) = E(\tilde{u}^2) - \bar{u}^2 = \sigma_u{}^2$. This expansion (where u_0 is the initial level of wealth) is:

$$W(u_0 + \tilde{u}) = \left\{[W(u_0)] \times \tilde{u}^0\right\} + \left\{[W'(u_0)/1!] \times \tilde{u}^1\right\} + \left\{[W''(u_0)/2!] \times \tilde{u}^2\right\} + \left\{[W'''(u_0)/3!] \times \tilde{u}^3\right\} + \ldots, \quad (3A.2.10)$$

where

W''' is the third derivative of the welfare function with respect to u_0,
'. . .' is the remainder associated with higher order moments of the probability distribution of the risky outcome.

Because the derivatives of the resulting welfare function are constant, Equation (3A.2.10) can be parameterised as $W(u_0) = d_0$, $W'(u_0)/(1!) = d_1$, $W''(u_0)/(2!) = d_2$ and $W'''(u_0)/(3!) = d_3$. So:

$$W(u_0 + \tilde{u}) = (d_0 \times \tilde{u}^0) + (d_1 \times \tilde{u}^1) + (d_2 \times \tilde{u}^2) + (d_3 \times \tilde{u}^3) + \ldots \quad (3A.2.11)$$

Taking the expectations of both sides:

$$E[W(u_0 + \tilde{u})] = d_0 + [d_1 \times E(\tilde{u})] + [d_2 \times E(\tilde{u}^2)] + [d_3 \times E(\tilde{u}^3)] + \ldots \quad (3A.2.12)$$

Therefore the expected welfare of a risky outcome is a function of (a) the welfare of initial wealth, and (b) the moments of that outcome's probability distribution. In other words, expected welfare is a function of the mean (the first moment of a distribution's characteristic function), variance (the second moment about the mean) and skewness (non-symmetry, or the third moment about the mean), ignoring the higher order moments, such as 'kurtosis' (the fourth moment about the mean, associated with 'fat tails', or 'heavy tails', with a high probability of an extreme event).

The number of moments to incorporate into the expected welfare function depends on (a) the shape of the welfare function (that is, how 'bowed' the function is), (b) the characteristics of the probability distribution of $\tilde{u}$, and (c) the accuracy of the desired approximation. If the probability distribution for $\tilde{u}$ is represented well by the normal distribution, only the first two moments of the distribution need to be considered in Equation (3A.2.12). *This is because the normal distribution is completely defined by its mean and variance* (see Equation

(3A.1.1) and Equation (3A.1.2)). Under these assumptions, the risk premium, *RP*, becomes:

$$RP = \text{ARA} \times \Phi(\sigma) \qquad (3A.2.13)$$

where

ARA is the absolute risk aversion of the decision maker, and
$\Phi(\sigma)$ is the welfare function of the standard deviation of changes in wealth, $\tilde{u}$

– that is, if the risky outcome is approximately normal, the expected welfare associated with an uncertain change in wealth is a function of its expected value and its uncertainty, as represented by the standard deviation (and higher order moments, if necessary and if known) (Copeland, Weston and Shastri, 2005: 56).

A cost estimation contingency, C_{ON} (a percentage), based on this approach to calculating risk premiums (that is, the contingency that transforms an uncertain cost estimate into a certainty equivalent cost estimate), can be defined as:

$$C_{ON} = \text{ARA} \times \Phi(\sigma) \qquad (3A.2.14)$$

where $\Phi(\sigma)$ could be equal to σ – that is, decision makers could focus on the standard deviation and ignore higher order moments, such as skewness and kurtosis. (However, under prospect theory, decision makers react differently to losses and to gains, so $\Phi(\sigma)$ would not be equal to σ: Kahneman, 2011: 278–286.) To calculate contingency, Equation (3A.2.14) must be parameterised in some form of empirical observation or experimentation, *because economic theory does not explicitly state how to parameterise it.*

To determine a reasonable value for C_{ON}, consider the implicit assumptions regarding risk aversion in standard cost-engineering guidelines, such as Table 3A.1. Economists generally assume that ARA varies with wealth, for example as in Equation (3A.2.7), but cost estimating guidelines calculate contingencies *without regard to the size of the project or the size of the firm.* The guidelines implicitly assume that ARA is a constant. This is the assumption of *constant absolute risk aversion*, CARA.

Under CARA, cost engineering estimating practices implicitly suggest that ARA = **c**, a constant across all decision-maker types. Assuming $\Phi(\sigma) = \sigma$ (that is, that the decision maker's evaluation of the standard deviation is well approximated by a second-order Taylor series expansion, such as if the distribution were approximately normal), contingency, C_{ON}, becomes:

$$C_{ON} = \mathbf{c} \times \sigma \qquad (3A.2.15)$$

– that is, the appropriate level of contingency is equal to a constant, **c**, multiplied by the standard deviation of a risky project's outcome. While economic theory does not provide a specific value for **c**, there could be an *implicit* value of **c** in cost engineering guidelines, *assuming CARA*. Interpreting the AACE and EPRI guidelines in Table 3A.1, with the normal distribution:

1 for a 'finalised estimate' with a range of $X = \pm 10\%$ (Table 3A.1) and an 80% confidence, $\sigma = 7.8\%$ – with $\mathbf{c} = 0.64$, $C_{ON} = \mathbf{c} \times \sigma = 0.64 \times 7.8\% = 5\%$; with $\mathbf{c} = 1.0$, $C_{ON} = 1.0 \times 7.8\% = 7.8\%$; and with $\mathbf{c} = 1.28$, $C_{ON} = 1.28 \times 7.8\% = 10\%$ – implying a range of 5–10% (that is, the EPRI recommendation);
2 for a 'detailed estimate' with a range of $X = \pm 20\%$ (Table 3A.1) and an 80% confidence, $\sigma = 15.6\%$, the range with $\mathbf{c} = (0.64, 1.28)$ is 10% to 20% (that is, the EPRI recommendation); and
3 for a 'preliminary estimate' with a range of $X = \pm 30\%$ (Table 3A.1) and an 80% confidence, $\sigma = 23.4\%$, the range with $\mathbf{c} = (0.64, 1.28)$ is 15% to 30% (that is, the EPRI recommendation).

So if **c** is a constant, **c** should be in the range 0.64–1.28 (with an accuracy of 80%), where $\mathbf{c} = 1$ satisfies both AACE and EPRI guidelines on contingency. A value of 0.64 implies more tolerance to risk and a value of 1.28 implies less tolerance to risk. However, these values imply an accuracy *range* of ±10% with an 80% confidence. So how does this value change with changes in the accuracy range and the level of confidence?

Assuming a normal density with 80% of the distribution between ±10%:

$$C_{ON|80\%} \approx \sigma(1.28/1.28) = \sigma(1.00), \text{ e.g. } 7.8\% \quad (3A.2.16)$$

Following this logic, for higher levels of confidence, such as 90%, 95%, 97.5%, 99%, or 99.5%, and an accuracy of ±10%, the contingency would increase as follows:

$$C_{ON|90\%} \approx \sigma(1.645/1.28) = \sigma \times 1.29, \text{ e.g. } 7.8\% \times 1.29 = 10\% \quad (3A.2.17)$$

$$C_{ON|95\%} \approx \sigma(1.960/1.28) = \sigma \times 1.53, \text{ e.g. } 7.8\% \times 1.53 = 12\% \quad (3A.2.18)$$

Table 3A.3 Risk multipliers to apply to the standard deviation of a cost estimate

σ/7.8% × *confidence*	±*10%*	*Accuracy range* ±*20%*	±*30%*
80.00%	1.0	2.0	3.0
90.00%	1.3	2.6	3.9
95.00%	1.5	3.1	4.6
97.50%	1.7	3.5	5.2
99.00%	2.0	4.0	6.0
99.50%	2.2	4.4	6.6

Source: Equations (3A.2.16)–(3A.2.21).

$$C_{ON|97.5\%} \approx \sigma(2.224/1.28) = \sigma \times 1.74, \text{ e.g. } 7.8\% \times 1.74 = 14\% \quad (3A.2.19)$$

$$C_{ON|99\%} \approx \sigma(2.576/1.28) = \sigma \times 2.01, \text{ e.g. } 7.8\% \times 2.01 = 16\% \quad (3A.2.20)$$

$$C_{ON|99.5\%} \approx \sigma(2.810/1.28) = \sigma \times 2.20, \text{ e.g. } 7.8\% \times 2.20 = 17\% \quad (3A.2.21)$$

The vector of multipliers [1.00, 1.29, 1.53, 1.74, 2.01, 2.20] can be generalised to various accuracy ranges, as in Table 3A.3.

Because it does not appear possible to determine simultaneously (a) the risk aversion constant, (b) the confidence in the cost estimate and (c) the range of accuracy, under the assumption of CARA, the cost contingency can be approximated as some multiple of the standard deviation of the (levelised) cost estimate, which can be estimated either by:

- considering the accuracy and confidence in the cost estimate based on expert judgement or traditional definitions of cost estimation completion; or
- using statistical or Monte Carlo techniques, as in Chapter 5.

This allows an easy comparison of cost contingency percentages with the probability distribution of the cost estimate *and* vice versa.

If the assumption of CARA is relaxed, the risk premium could become a function of the decision maker's change in wealth, for example represented by the (*KC*/PV) ratio (Moody's, 2011), PV being the present value without the project. The cost of capital can be modelled as a function of the ratio of the total construction cost, *KC*, to the present value of the nuclear owner-operator, PV. While the relationship between the cost of capital, **r**, and the ratio of the size of the investment to the size of the owner, (*KC*/PV), is a complex one, for example owing to tax issues, this relationship can be represented in reduced form as:

$$\mathbf{r} = \mathbf{rb} \times \exp\{\mathbf{ra}(KC/\mathrm{PV})\} \quad (3A.2.22)$$

or:

$$\ln \mathbf{r} = \ln \mathbf{rb} + [\mathbf{ra}(KC/\mathrm{PV})] \quad (3A.2.23)$$

and:

$$\mathbf{ra} = \mathrm{d} \ln \mathbf{r} / \mathrm{d}(KC/\mathrm{PV}) \quad (3A.2.24)$$

where

rb is the rate on current obligations (before construction), for example 3% real, the long-term 'social cost of capital' (as in Section 2.4 and Lévêque, 2015), and

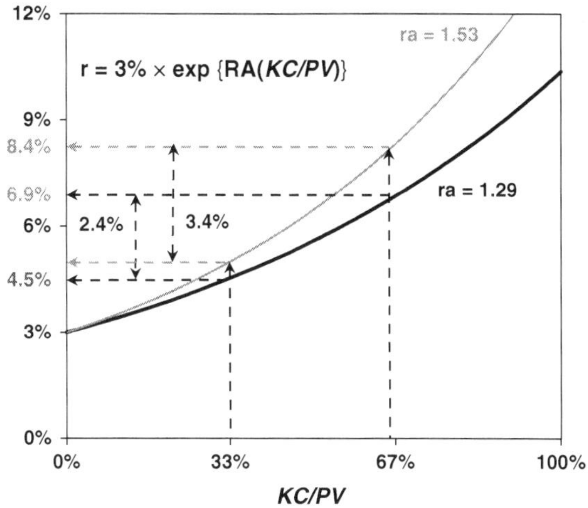

Figure 3A.6 Risk premium and the ratio of construction cost (KC) to PV.

Source: Equation (3A.2.22).

ra (a measure of risk aversion) is the proportional rate of change in **r** as a function of changes in the ratio of total capital cost of the project, *KC*, to the value of the firm, PV.

If the owner's PV is \$20,000 million, then, typically, the interest rate on debt would be higher if *KC* were \$12,000 million than if *KC* were \$4,000 million. In Equation (3A.2.22), if **ra** were 1.29 (from Equation (3A.2.17)), and if (*KC*/PV) were 33%, then **r** would be 4.5%, as in Figure 3A.6. If (*KC*/PV) were 67%, then **r** would be 6.9% – and the difference in the costs of capital for the smaller and larger investments would be 2.4%.

Further, if **ra** were 1.53 (from Equation (3A.2.18)), if investors were more risk averse and if (*KC*/PV) were 33%, then **r** would be 5%. If (*KC*/PV) were 67%, then **r** would be 8.4% – and the difference in the costs of capital for the smaller and larger investments would be 3.4%. Unfortunately, there is little empirical evidence on which to base a value for **ra**, but empirical research could be performed if a reasonable structural model could be identified and appropriate financial data could be collected.

This discussion of contingency sets a foundation for the calculation of new nuclear power capital costs, *KC*, in Chapter 3 above. However, it also leads to the question of the appropriate contingency on expected levelised costs, *LC*, assuming a certainty equivalent *KC*. On the other hand, it does not address the diversification of risk within a portfolio of assets, such as electricity-generating assets, as examined in Chapter 5. Hence the next section reviews the key insight of modern finance theory into the importance of diversification in a portfolio of assets.

3A.3 Risk and diversification

This section explores risk and return, and shows how financial markets determine risk premiums for risky investments. In well-defined capital markets, the price of risk can be calculated by correlating historic rates of return with the probability distribution of these returns. This section explores how risk can be reduced by investing in a *portfolio* of assets, following modern finance theory. (Portfolios of generating assets will be explored in Chapter 5.)

To maximise expected return for a specific level of risk, individuals can invest in a diverse set of financial instruments. (This might be different in relation to how societies invest in public assets, just as the social discount rate differs from an individual's, or a firm's, discount rate: Lévêque, 2015: 26–32.) This section discusses a portfolio of common corporate stocks selected by Dow Jones & Company, publisher of the *Wall Street Journal*. Dow Jones tracks three portfolios of common stocks: industrials, transportation and utilities. The Dow Jones Industrial Average is a portfolio of 30 common stocks of large industrial corporations headquartered in the United States.

Table 3A.4 lists the *monthly* percentage returns (from a randomly selected year) for ten companies listed in Table 3A.5, which lists the company name and the common stock symbol. Here, *nominal return* is:

$$R_t = (P_{t+1} - P_t)/P_t \tag{3A.3.1}$$

where P_t is the period-t price of the stock (with capitalised dividends). Also included in Table 3A.4 is the value-weighted (that is, weighted by the total value of each firm's equity) average return for the New York Stock Exchange (NYSE).

Investors compare average returns and risk (defined in the finance literature as the standard deviation of returns) for each stock. The average, or *expected value* of the return, $\mathrm{E}(R_t)$, is defined as:

$$\mathrm{E}(R_t) = (1/\mathrm{T}) \times \Sigma_t R_t \ (t = 1, \ldots, \mathrm{T}) \tag{3A.3.2}$$

The most common measure of variation is the *standard deviation*, $\mathrm{SD}(R_t)$, which is the square root of the *variance*, $\mathrm{Var}(R_t)$:

$$\mathrm{Var}(R_t) = [1/(\mathrm{T} - 1)] \times \Sigma_t [R_t - \mathrm{E}(R_t)]^2 \ (t = 1, \ldots, \mathrm{T}) \tag{3A.3.3}$$

Table 3A.5 lists percentage values of $\mathrm{E}(R_t)$, $\mathrm{SD}(R_t)$ and $\mathrm{Var}(R_t)$ for the ten stocks in Table 3A.4. An unbiased estimator for sample variance

Table 3A.4 Monthly returns for ten stocks in the Dow Jones Industrial Average

	NYSE	*AXP*	*BA*	*CVX*	*DIS*	*GE*	*IBM*	*KO*	*MCD*	*WMT*	*XOM*
January	5.3%	10.0%	0.6%	2.1%	4.6%	4.7%	3.5%	10.0%	0.3%	4.4%	5.7%
February	−0.1%	5.6%	−4.8%	−2.0%	1.9%	−0.6%	−8.1%	5.4%	−4.8%	11.1%	−2.5%
March	−4.4%	−8.8%	−3.1%	−7.9%	−1.9%	−3.0%	−4.5%	−8.4%	9.2%	5.9%	7.5%
April	4.3%	10.2%	0.0%	−1.6%	12.4%	11.8%	16.9%	14.1%	13.2%	0.9%	5.1%
May	7.1%	5.7%	7.1%	3.0%	0.2%	8.8%	7.9%	7.7%	−5.9%	6.2%	5.4%
June	4.4%	7.2%	0.7%	5.6%	−2.0%	7.7%	4.3%	−0.5%	−3.9%	13.4%	3.4%
July	7.6%	12.7%	10.6%	6.8%	0.9%	8.3%	17.2%	1.7%	11.3%	10.9%	4.9%
August	−3.7%	−7.2%	−6.9%	−1.2%	−5.0%	−10.8%	−3.9%	−17.1%	−11.8%	−5.3%	−4.1%
September	5.8%	5.3%	0.1%	7.3%	5.0%	9.2%	4.6%	6.7%	0.7%	3.4%	4.7%
October	−3.4%	−4.5%	−11.8%	−0.2%	2.3%	−5.1%	−7.1%	−7.2%	−5.9%	−4.4%	−4.1%
November	3.1%	1.1%	11.0%	−2.6%	15.3%	14.3%	11.4%	10.6%	8.4%	14.5%	0.0%
December	1.8%	13.4%	−7.9%	−4.0%	4.3%	−0.3%	−4.5%	6.7%	−1.5%	−1.4%	0.3%

Source: Adapted from data in Rothwell and Gomez (2003: exercise 3.1); Table 3A.5 lists abbreviations.

Table 3A.5 Annual returns to ten stocks in the Dow Jones Industrial Average

Symbol	*Corporation*	*E(R)*	*SD(R)*
NYSE	New York Stock Exchange	2.3%	4.3%
AXP	American Express	4.2%	7.5%
BA	Boeing	−0.4%	7.2%
CVX	Chevron	1.8%	4.3%
DIS	Walt Disney	3.2%	5.8%
GE	General Electric	3.8%	7.6%
IBM	IBM	3.1%	8.9%
KO	Coca Cola	2.5%	9.2%
MCD	McDonalds	0.8%	8.0%
WMT	WalMart Stores	5.0%	6.7%
XOM	ExxonMobil	2.2%	4.1%

Source: Adapted from data in Rothwell and Gomez (2003: exercise 3.1).

Table 3A.6 Correlations between ten stocks in the Dow Jones Industrial Average

	NYSE	*AXP*	*BA*	*CVX*	*DIS*	*GE*	*IBM*	*KO*	*MCD*	*WMT*	*XOM*
NYSE	100%										
AXP	**81%**	100%									
BA	73%	36%	100%								
CVX	25%	**−8%**	31%	100%							
DIS	34%	34%	36%	**−42%**	100%						
GE	**83%**	59%	80%	17%	67%	100%					
IBM	77%	50%	83%	21%	50%	**83%**	100%				
KO	73%	75%	49%	**−19%**	76%	**82%**	55%	100%			
MCD	31%	27%	52%	23%	58%	59%	66%	45%	100%		
WMT	46%	28%	73%	30%	20%	63%	40%	40%	37%	100%	
XOM	55%	33%	52%	67%	8%	55%	54%	41%	60%	34%	100%

Source: Adapted from data in Rothwell and Gomez (2003: exercise 3.1); Table 3A.5 lists abbreviations.

accounts for the degree of freedom lost in calculating the sample mean, using [1/(T − 1)], in place of (1/T). Table 3A.6 lists the correlations between these stocks.

Notice that, in Table 3A.5, the standard deviation of the returns to the stock market (for example to NYSE) is lower than most of the standard deviations of the individual stocks. This is because the variance of a portfolio depends on (a) the variances of the stocks in the portfolio, and (b) the covariances between these stocks. *Covariance* between the returns on two stocks, j and k, is:

$$\mathrm{Cov}(R_{jt}, R_{kt}) = [1/(\mathrm{T}-1)] \times \Sigma_t [R_{jt} - \mathrm{E}(R_{jt})] \times [R_{kt} - \mathrm{E}(R_{kt})] \ (t = 1, \ldots, \mathrm{T}) \quad (3A.3.4)$$

Although portfolio variance is a function of covariance between the stocks in the portfolio, it is easier to work with *correlation*, defined as:

$$\mathrm{Corr}(R_{jt}, R_{kt}) = \mathrm{Cov}(R_{jt}, R_{kt})/[\mathrm{SD}(R_{jt}) \times \mathrm{SD}(R_{kt})] \qquad (3A.3.5)$$

Positive correlation implies that the two stocks move up and down together. Negative correlation implies that the two stocks move in opposite directions. If the correlation coefficient is 1, the two stocks are perfectly positively correlated. If the correlation coefficient is 0, the two stocks are independent. If the correlation coefficient is –1, the two stocks are perfectly negatively correlated.

For example, the correlation in Table 3A.6 between GE and IBM is 83%. The stocks of these two high-tech industrial companies move together most of the time. However, between the returns on American Express and Chevron, the correlation coefficient is –8%: American Express, a financial services provider, and Chevron, a petro-chemical company, although negatively related, are almost independent.

A portfolio of assets can be constructed in the following way. (A portfolio of electricity-generating plants can be thought of in the same way, as in Chapter 5.) The *expected return of a portfolio*, where **x** is the proportion of value of the portfolio invested in one stock is:

$$\mathrm{E}(\text{Porfolio return}) = [\mathbf{x} \times \mathrm{E}(R_{jt})] + [(1 - \mathbf{x}) \times \mathrm{E}(R_{kt})] \qquad (3A.3.6)$$

The variance of a portfolio of two stocks is:

$$\begin{aligned}\mathrm{Var}(\text{Porfolio}) = {} & [\mathbf{x}^2 \times \mathrm{Var}(R_{jt})] + [(1 - \mathbf{x})^2 \times \mathrm{Var}(R_{kt})] + [2\mathbf{x} \times (1 - \mathbf{x}) \\ & \times \mathrm{Cov}(R_{jt}, R_{kt})] = [\mathbf{x}^2 \times \mathrm{Var}(R_{jt})] + [(1 - \mathbf{x})^2 \\ & \times \mathrm{Var}(R_{kt})] + [2\mathbf{x} \times (1 - \mathbf{x}) \times \mathrm{Corr}(R_{jt}, R_{kt}) \\ & \times \mathrm{SD}(R_{jt}) \times \mathrm{SD}(R_{kt})] \qquad (3A.3.7)\end{aligned}$$

For example, in an equally weighted portfolio of American Express and Chevron:

1 the expected return would be (0.5 × 4.2%) + (0.5 × 1.8%) = 3%;
2 the variance would be ($0.5^2 \times 7.5\%^2$) + ($0.5^2 \times 4.3\%^2$) + (2 × 0.5 × 0.5 × –0.08 × 7.5% × 4.3%) = 0.18%; and
3 the standard deviation would be 4.14%, which is less than the standard deviations of either of the two stocks because of the negative correlation between the two returns.

By varying the proportions of stocks in the portfolio, the investor can find an optimal combination that minimises risk for each level of expected return. This is the 'portfolio frontier'. Of course, more than two stocks should be included in a portfolio. The Dow Jones Index uses 30 stocks. The expected

Table 3A.7 Return and risk with a portfolio of American Express and Chevron

x	*0%*	*10%*	*20%*	*30%*	*40%*	*50%*	*60%*	*70%*	*80%*	*90%*	*100%*
E(Port)	1.8%	2.0%	2.3%	2.5%	2.8%	3.0%	3.3%	3.5%	3.7%	4.0%	4.2%
SD(Port)	4.3%	3.9%	3.6%	3.6%	3.8%	4.2%	4.7%	5.3%	6.0%	6.8%	7.5%

Source: Answer to Rothwell and Gomez (2003: exercise 3.2).

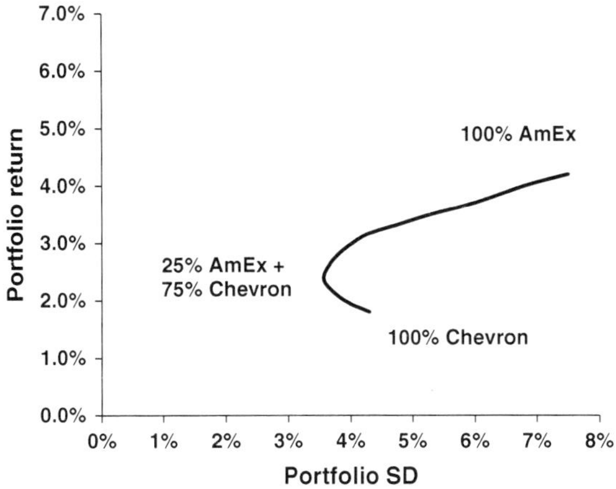

Figure 3A.7 Portfolio frontier for American Express and Chevron.

Source: Table 3A.7.

return and standard deviation for a portfolio of American Express and Chevron can be calculated at **x** = 0%, 10%, 20% , . . . , 90% and 100% from the data in Table 3A.5. Table 3A.7 presents weighted averages of the returns and standard deviations of all Chevron (**x** = 0%) to all American Express (**x** = 100%). Figure 3A.7 plots these values. This frontier represents a set of portfolios for these two assets.

With these definitions of risk aversion, the remainder of this section explores the quadratic form of the welfare function; compare with the logarithmic welfare function in Equation (3A.2.1). The parameters of this function must conform to criteria appropriate for a welfare function. This particular function will provide a method for determining which combination of risk and return an individual prefers with a particular risk–return trade-off. While this is a popularly used welfare function in the finance literature, it is more complex than the logarithmic, because the quadratic function implies a maximum, above which welfare declines even though the individual has more wealth. Therefore parameters of the quadratic function must be restricted, so that the implied maximum is not in the relevant range of interest. The quadratic welfare function is:

$$W(\tilde{u}) = a + (b \times \tilde{u}) + (c \times \tilde{u}^2) \qquad (3A.3.8)$$

The first criterion for a well-behaved welfare function is whether welfare is increasing in wealth. For a single maximum (so that welfare increases with increases in wealth), the second derivative should be less than 0. If the probability distribution of R_j is well approximated by the normal distribution, only the mean and variance of the distribution must be considered. Given the definition of variance, the second moment of the distribution of R_j, $E(R_j^2)$, is equal to $Var(R_j) + [E(R_j)]^2$; actually, $Var(R_j) = E(R_j^2) - [E(R_j)]^2$, where variance is the second moment around the mean. So:

$$\begin{aligned} E[W(R_j)] &= a + [b \times E(R_j)] + \left[c \times \left\{Var(R_j) + [E(R_j)]^2\right\}\right] \\ &= a + [b \times E(R_j)] + \left[c \times \left\{[SD(R_j)]^2 + [E(R_j)]^2\right\}\right] \qquad (3A.3.9) \end{aligned}$$

– that is, the expected welfare associated with a risky rate of return is a function of its mean and standard deviation. To satisfy these risk aversion characteristics, the values of the quadratic welfare function must be $a = 0$, $b > 0$, $c < 0$, with the additional restriction that there is no diminishing marginal welfare of wealth.

Welfare functions can be rearranged to represent an individual's indifference between levels of risk and levels of return at various levels of wealth: there are some individuals who prefer more return at a higher risk (young investors), and

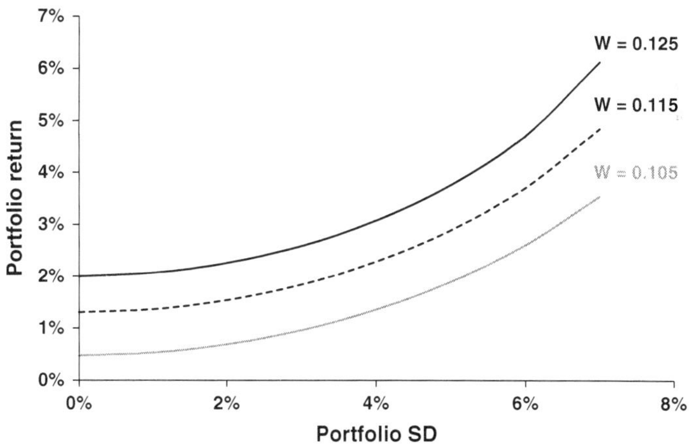

Figure 3A.8 Indifference between risk and return at three levels of welfare.

Source: Equation (3A.3.10).

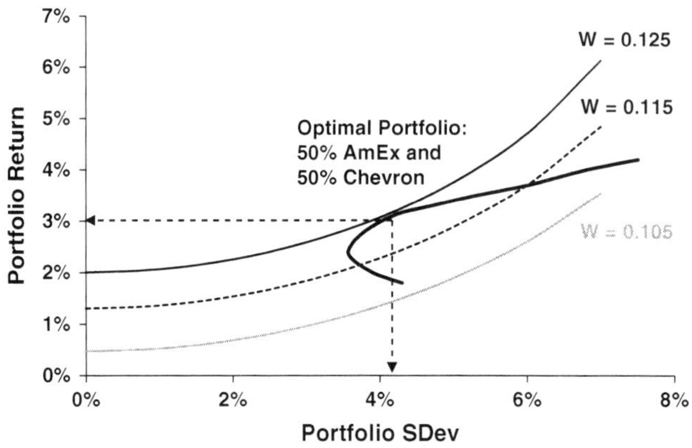

Figure 3A.9 Tangency of the indifference curves and the market line.

Source: Figures 3A.7 and 3A.8; answer to Rothwell and Gomez (2003: exercise 3.2).

others who prefer lower risk and lower returns (retired investors). For example, Equation (3A.3.10) represents one individual's indifference between portfolio risk and return at different levels of welfare (limited by wealth, **W**):

$$E(R_j) = 10\% - [(1/\mathbf{W})^2 - SD(R_j)^2]^{0.5} \tag{3A.3.10}$$

Figure 3A.8 plots Equation (3A.3.10) for $SD(R_j) = 0\%, 1\%, 2\%, \ldots, 6\%$ and 7% for **W** = 0.105, 0.115 and 0.125.

What is the highest level of welfare such that the indifference curve is just tangent to the portfolio frontier in Figure 3A.7? This is shown in Figure 3A.9. The highest level of welfare attainable (owing to wealth constraints) is a portfolio of 50% American Express and 50% Chevron. Of course, other combinations are available, but they do not maximise welfare for the individual who can be characterised by the indifference curves represented by Equation (3A.3.10) with wealth equal to 0.125. The trade-offs between levelised cost and the standard deviation of levelised costs for a portfolio of electricity-generating assets can be examined similarly, as done in Chapter 5.

3A.4 Capital asset pricing model and ordinary least squares

Economic theory does not, however, tell us what indifference curves to use or whether these are the same for customers, electric utilities, electric utility regulators, electric market investors, publicly elected decision makers, the general public, or the unborn generations who could be using these assets and managing their wastes when the rest of us are long gone.

To determine the risk premium that *financial market investors* seek on risky assets, the capital asset pricing model (CAPM) observes the following relationship:

$$E(R_j - R_f) = \beta_j \times E(R_m - R_f) \qquad (3A.4.1)$$

where

$E(R_j - R_f)$	is the expected risk premium above the risk-free interest rate for asset j,
β_j	is a measure of asset-specific risk, defined in Equation (3A.4.4),
$E(R_m - R_f)$	is the expected risk premium above the risk-free rate on a market portfolio

and, because $E(R_f) = R_f$, since the risk-free asset has no variance:

$$E(R_j) - R_f = \beta_j \times E(R_m - R_f) \qquad (3A.4.2)$$

If the investor can invest in a risk-free asset and an efficient market portfolio, the expected return on the resulting portfolio is

$$E(R_j) = R_f + \beta_j \times E(R_m - R_f) \qquad (3A.4.3)$$

The expected return, $E(R_j)$, equals R_f plus a risk premium based on (a) the riskiness of the asset, β_j, multiplied by (b) the expected risk premium on the stock market portfolio, $E(R_m - R_f)$.

For example, if R_f were to be 3% per year and $E(R_m - R_f)$ were to be 5%, then the expected return on the market portfolio (where $\beta_j = 1$) would be 8%. If $\beta_j = 1.1$, then $E(R_j) = 8.5\%$. Under the assumptions of the mean-variance approximation as with the assumption of normally distributed returns and a quadratic welfare function, the CAPM shows that:

$$\beta_j = \mathrm{Cov}(R_j, R_m)/\mathrm{Var}(R_m) \qquad (3A.4.4)$$

The risk-free asset has a $\beta = 0$ because there is no covariance between a constant, R_f, and the randomly distributed return on the market portfolio, R_m. Therefore the expected risk premium on the risk-free asset is 0. If $R_m = R_j$, then the right-hand side is equal to the left-hand side only when $\beta = 1$ – that is, the β on the market portfolio is 1. Because investors (in equilibrium) demand the expected market rate of return on the market portfolio, Equation (3A.4.4) states that the risk of the individual asset is equal to its covariance with the market rate of return normalised by the variance of the market rate of return. *Therefore the value of the asset is not simply its return (for example the difference between the price of electricity and levelised cost), but also its ability to diversify risk.* While the levelised cost is an important metric in selecting among electricity-generating investment alternatives, another important metric is how a technology diversifies a portfolio of generating assets. Chapter 5 explores this diversity in portfolios of electricity-generating assets.

The next issue to address is how to calculate β_j. This is done with a mathematical technique known as ordinary least squares (OLS) – also known as 'regression analysis' – wherein 'ordinary' refers to a restrictive set of assumptions regarding the difference, known as the 'error', between (a) the estimated value of the dependent variable, and (b) its observed value, and 'least squares' refers to the selection of parameters that minimise the sum of the squares of these differences. For example, the empirical version of Equation (3A.4.2), which considers a single equity, *j*, over time, for example one year, can be expressed as

$$E(R_t) - R_f = \alpha + \beta \times E(R_m - R_f) + \tilde{u}_t \tag{3A.4.5}$$

where the estimated value of α for each equity is expected to be 0 and $\tilde{u}$ is the 'error' term that equates the two sides of the equation.

The error term arises primarily from two problems: measurement error, for example, here, not properly capitalising dividends, stock splits, or mergers and acquisitions; and specification errors, for example omitting terms in a proposed equation such as Equation (3A.4.5), which lacks higher order moments as in Equation (3A.2.12). Considering the origin of the error term and how to address the problems associated with them are the subjects of 'econometrics'; they are usually ignored in 'regression analysis'.

Given that R_f, the 'risk-free rate', is assumed to be a known constant, Equation (3A.4.5) can be rewritten – where $y_t = E(R_t) - R_f$ and $x_t = E(R_m - R_f)$ – as:

$$y_t = \alpha + \beta \times x_t + \tilde{u}_t \tag{3A.4.6}$$

or as:

$$\tilde{u}_t = y_t - \alpha - \beta \times x_t \tag{3A.4.7}$$

Squaring both sides yields:

$$\tilde{u}_t^2 = (y_t - \alpha - \beta \times x_t)^2 \tag{3A.4.8}$$

and summing over *t*:

$$\Sigma\tilde{u}_t^2 = \Sigma[(y_t - \alpha - \beta \times x_t)^2] \tag{3A.4.9}$$

To calculate those values that minimise the sum of the squared errors, first take the derivative of the sum of squared errors with respect to α and β, and then set these two derivatives to 0, before solving for the *particular* α and β (known as estimated values a and b) that minimise this sum:

$$b = \mathrm{Cov}(y_t, x_t)/\mathrm{Var}(x_t) \quad (3A.4.10)$$

$$a = \mathrm{E}(y_t) - b \times \mathrm{E}(x_t) \quad (3A.4.11)$$

and

$$\mathrm{E}(\tilde{u}_t) = \mathrm{u_t} = y_t - a - b \times x_t \quad (3A.4.12)$$

where $\mathrm{u_t}$ is known as the 'residual', the expected value of the 'error' term.

Equation (3A.4.4) is equivalent to Equation (3A.4.10), where y_t is the equivalent of $R_j - R_f$ (the randomly distributed rate-of-return premium on equity j), and x_t is the equivalent of $R_m - R_f$ (the randomly distributed rate-of-return premium on the equity market). This is why the CAPM model variable is known as 'beta', β.

However, no assumptions have been made regarding the distribution of the uncertain dependent and independent variables. (This is why it is considered a 'mathematical' technique and not a 'statistical' one.) In general, the restrictive assumptions – that is, those that make this problem 'ordinary' and those issues most likely to be encountered in practice – are the following.

1 While the equation to be estimated can be 'non-linear', for example it may contain quadratic terms, the parameters to be estimated cannot be 'non-linear', for example one cannot estimate b in $[1/(1 - b)]$ (see, for example, the non-linear estimation in Rothwell, 1986). When this assumption is violated, no type of least squares estimator is appropriate; other techniques, such as those associated with maximum likelihood estimation (MLE), must be used.
2 The variance of $\tilde{u}_t$, $\mathrm{Var}(\tilde{u}_t)$, must be equal for all $\tilde{u}_t$ – that is, the observations must be from the same population. The violation of this assumption is known as 'hetroscedasticity'. When hetroscedasticity is present, the standard error of the estimate of β can be biased. One method of addressing this issue is using 'generalised least squares' (GLS).
3 There can be no covariance (or correlation) between the error terms: $\mathrm{E}(\tilde{u}_i, \tilde{u}_j) = 0$. The violation of this assumption is known as 'autocorrelation'. This is the primary problem associated with estimating β in the CAPM because the return for the current period could be related to the return for last period because of some underlying cause that manifested in an even earlier period. The issue of autocorrelation can be addressed with 'time-series econometrics', which is a special type of GLS.

4 There can be no covariance (or correlation) between the independent variable, x_t, and $\tilde{u}_t$. The violation of this assumption is known as 'simultaneity'. It can be corrected with techniques such as 'instrumental variables' or 'two-stage least squares' (2SLS). When this assumption is violated, as well as either assumptions (2) and/or (3), 'three-stage least squares' (3SLS) is required.

If these four restrictions are satisfied, then the variance of the error term can be estimated as:

$$\sigma^2 = (\Sigma u_t^2)/(n-2) \tag{3A.4.13}$$

where (n – 2) accounts for the two 'degrees of freedom', *df*, lost in estimating α and β. Also, the 'standard error' of the estimation is the square of the variance of the error term in Equation (3A.4.13) and the standard error of the estimate of β is $\{\sigma/\{\Sigma[x_t - E(x_t)]^2\}^{1/2}$. (The standard error can be reduced by increasing the range of the independent variable, x_t, thus increasing the size of the denominator.)

Finally, associated with all OLS estimations, although not always appropriate in comparing estimated equations, is a measure of the 'goodness of fit':

$$R^2 = 1 - \left\{(\Sigma u_t^2)/(\Sigma[y_t - E(y_t)]^2)\right\} = 1 - (RSS/TSS) \tag{3A.4.14}$$

where

RSS is the 'residual sum of squares', and
TSS is the 'total sum of squares' – that is, how much of the total sum of the squared difference (between the estimated dependent variable and the observed dependent variable) is explained by the estimated model.

Appendix 3B: An appropriate insurance premium for a nuclear power plant accident

In the United States, the Price–Anderson Nuclear Industries Indemnity Act (Price–Anderson Act, or PAA) mandates insurance for off-site damage from NPPs. (The PAA also covers US DOE contractors, subcontractors and suppliers, particularly in the nuclear weapons industry: McNett, 1989.) Dubin and Rothwell (1990) developed a model to estimate the expected congressional liability under the Act's nuclear plant accident liability limit. It is the possibility of extremely high damages, such as those at Chernobyl, that drives the US nuclear power industry to place such a high value on the Price–Anderson liability limit and nuclear industries around the world to seek protection under the 1960 Paris Convention on Nuclear Third Party Liability (NEA, 2014) or the Vienna Convention on Civil Liability for Nuclear Damage of 1963 (IAEA, 2014a). (Rothwell presented the original version of Dubin and Rothwell, 1990, at the Western Economics Association annual meeting, June 1989, in a session organised by Darwin Hall, who requested the paper to be submitted to be published in Hall, 1990.)

3B.1 Calculating US congressional liability under the Price–Anderson Act

During the last 25 years, a literature has developed on what might be the appropriate insurance premium to cover damages incurred from an NPP's off-site radioactive releases after a nuclear accident, such as that at Fukushima-Daiichi (Aoki and Rothwell, 2013). In the United States since 1957, insurance for NPP accidents has been mandated by the PAA. The PAA creates three levels of insurance: (a) privately purchased insurance held by the NPP operator, for example up to \$375 million; (b) pooled self-insurance to cover releases at other US nuclear power units up to the 'Price–Anderson liability limit' (for example now, collectively, to about \$12,000 million); and (c) potential congressional relief funds above the liability limit. However, industry liability before 1988 was capped at \$560 million in 1985 dollars, at \$6,000 million between 1988 and 2002, and at \$6,400 million after 2002 (that is, at about \$10,000 million in 2013 US dollars).

What is the expected value of this congressional liability – that is, the difference between the PAA liability limit and the expected damages? Denenberg (1973) assumed (a) an accident probability of 1/1,700, or 0.06% per reactor year, and (b) damages of \$40,000 million per accident, yielding, when multiplied, an unpaid premium of about \$24 million per reactor year (less the amount paid for private insurance).

To avoid multiplying a discrete (unknown) probability by a discrete (unknown) damage value, Dubin and Rothwell (1990) developed a method of inferring the value to US nuclear plant operators of the PAA liability limit by calibrating a probability distribution for expected losses – that is, where there was a lower probability for high losses (such as at Chernobyl) than for low losses (such as at Three Mile Island, or TMI).

Information from average insurance premiums provided evidence on expected off-site losses from \$1 million to \$160 million, the coverage provided by private insurers. (All calculations were completed in 1985 dollars, then updated to 2013 in Section 3B.4.) Information on the expected probability of a worst-case accident was used to infer the cumulative probability of the high end of the damage distribution.

Because of the range of possible off-site losses from \$1 million (the minimum level triggering the PAA and its amendments) to \$10,000 million (the maximum level considered by the US NRC in its 1985 US Senate testimony: US NRC, 1985), Dubin and Rothwell (1990) parameterised these with a logistic function and took logarithms of potential losses to reduce the domain.

They described the density and distribution functions for a *loss*, where *loss* is in millions of dollars, from an NPP accident as:

$$\mathbf{LOGS}(loss) = 1/(1 + \exp\{-[a + (b \times \ln loss)]\}) \tag{3B.1.1}$$

(where the parameters to be estimated, *a* and *b*, are implicit), which is a logistic-of-a-log function, not a log-logistic function (Dubin and Rothwell, 1990: 75). To cover (some) of these losses, in 1984 operators paid an average of \$400,000 per year for coverage of off-site damages between \$1 million and \$160 million (Brownstein, 1984). However, if there are no accidents within ten years, 70% of the premium is returned to the operators (Denenberg, 1973); hence Dubin and Rothwell (1990) assumed that expected losses amounted to 70% of the premium (or a fee of 30%), leaving \$280,000 in expected losses. The insurance companies cover all off-site damages for totals between \$1 million and \$160 million (and they cover the first \$160 million of damage for higher cost accidents). Equation (3B.1.2) describes private insurance coverage purchased by each operator:

$$\begin{aligned}\$0.28\text{m} = & \left[\int loss \times \mathbf{logs}(\ln loss) \times d\,loss\right] \\ & + \left[\mathbf{1} \times \int \mathbf{logs}(\ln loss) \times d\,loss\right]\end{aligned} \tag{3B.1.2}$$

where the first integral is from \$1 million to \$160 million and the second integral is from \$160 million to \$10,000 million. Losses above \$10,000 million are assumed to have a probability of 0.00008%, as expressed in Equation (3B.1.3):

$$0.00008\% = 1 - \mathbf{LOGS}[\ln(\$10,000)] \tag{3B.1.3}$$

These equations summarise a US NRC (1985: 293) assessment: accidents causing at least \$10,000 million in off-site property damage alone will occur with 0.00008% probability per reactor year (a 'best estimate' probability of 0.1% damages greater than \$10,000 million during 1,250 reactor years). The 'maximum damage' estimate is not a limit on damages, but a lower limit on the probability distribution of 'maximum damage'. The upper limit of \$10,000 million is only the upper limit of integration on the insurance industry's expected liability; it is not the assumed upper limit of damages from an NPP accident – that is, **logs**(*loss*) is not truncated at \$10,000 million. Values for *a* and *b* were selected such that the ratio between 0.28 and E($loss \mid 1 \leq loss \leq 160$) multiplied by the ratio between 0.00008% and {1 – **LOGS**[ln(10,000)]} was as close to 1 as possible. These values were estimated to be $a = 7.62$ and $b = 0.70$.

The model was then used to estimate the implicit unpaid premium per reactor year – that is, the premiums that operators do not pay for PAA coverage above the liability cap. The unpaid premium, *UP*, for PAA coverage per reactor year was calculated as expected losses above the liability cap less the amount of insurance coverage and industry liability, or:

$$UP = \left[\int (loss - LL) \times \mathbf{logs}(\ln loss) \times d\,loss\right] + \left[\int (loss - LL) \times \mathbf{logs}(\ln loss) \times d\,loss\right] \quad (3B.1.4)$$

where the first integral is from *LL* to \$10,000 million, *LL* is the PAA liability limit, and the second integral is from \$10,000 million to infinity.

The second term in Equation (3B.1.4) accounts for extreme losses, where there is probability mass between the 'worst-case' limit (\$10,000 million or \$500,000 million – see Section 3B.4) and the limit of the probability distribution function. Dubin and Rothwell (1990) found that the NPP operators' unpaid premium for PAA liability limits with the 1988 amendments was about \$22 million per plant per year (Wallich, 1991). (Notice that, as the liability limit approaches \$10,000 million, the unpaid premium becomes smaller; hence, when the coverage was greater than the assumed maximum damage, the unpaid premium was next to nothing.)

In response to questions from economists about the interpretation of the unpaid premium in a second-best world, Rothwell (1992: 4) addressed the economic issue of free markets versus regulation in liability insurance for NPPs:

> A more efficient solution would have been to assign full liability to those parties and let the insurance market determine the probability of an accident, its consequences, and the proper premiums for coverage. But two problems plague this market: moral hazard and small numbers. Here, moral hazard refers to changes in the insured's behavior that affect the chance of an accident once insurance has been established. If the insurer cannot accurately monitor the insured, there is no guarantee that the insured will take the same level of care expected by the insurer when determining the premium. This problem is partially solved with a deductible so that the insured is not fully insured. With a nuclear accident, the firm's financial losses and loss of reputation play the role of a deductible. For example, although there was little off-site damage, Three Mile Island's owner [General Public Utilities] sustained a substantial loss. The small-numbers problem remains because there has been little experience with these types of accidents. An insurer will never know the underlying probability of a catastrophic accident. Nor can the insurer anticipate the loss. Therefore, reasonable premiums are difficult to determine.

A similar market failure is discussed in Hofert and Wüthrich (2011: 8) in terms of the lack of a finite mean of expected NPP accident damages: 'Basically, this means that an unlimited cover against nuclear power accidents cannot be financed by a finite insurance premium … In the literature such infinite mean models are also called "extremely heavy-tailed" models.' These problems lead to market failure for NPP accident insurance, requiring some form of collective or government intervention.

After 1992, there was little published on this topic in academic journals until the late 1990s when an error ('Error 1') was identified in three similar publications by Anthony Heyes and Catherine Liston-Heyes:

- Heyes and Liston-Heyes (1998), submitted August 1996, revision accepted September 1997 and published January 1998;
- Heyes and Liston-Heyes (2000a), submitted August 1996, revision accepted June 1998 and published January 2000; and
- Heyes and Liston-Heyes (2000b).

While Heyes and Liston-Heyes (1998, 2000a, 2000b) use the same probability distribution and domain, Heyes and Liston-Heyes (1998) corrected an error in Dubin and Rothwell (1990) by adding one term to represent payments by insurers for losses above \$160 million. Heyes and Liston-Heyes (1998: 122) states, quoting Dubin and Rothwell (1990: 76), where all values are in millions of 1985 US dollars, 'Equation (1) should then be replaced by', where 'Equation (1)' is the equivalent of Equation (3B.1.2):

$$0.28 = \left[\int loss \times \mathbf{logs}(\ln loss) \times d\,loss\right] + \left[\mathbf{160} \times \int \mathbf{logs}(\ln loss) \times d\,loss\right] \qquad (3B.1.5)$$

where the first integral is from \$1 million to \$160 million and the second integral is from \$160 million to \$10,000 million.

Heyes and Liston-Heyes (1998: 123) estimated the parameters as $a = 46.933$ and $b = -3.571$, ignoring the requirement of the logistic function that b should be greater than 0, thus introducing another mistake. (Estimated parameters for a and b were not included in Heyes and Liston-Heyes, 2000a or 2000b.) With their correction, Heyes and Liston-Heyes (1998) found that the unpaid premium was closer to \$2 million per plant per year. The authors went on to use the same method to calculate the unpaid premiums of the Canadian NPP operators in Heyes and Liston-Heyes (2000a), and compared US and Canadian unpaid premiums in Heyes and Liston-Heyes (2000b).

Consequently, Radetzki and Radetzki (1997: 370) wrote that Rothwell admitted, in a 'private communication' (in May 1997), that the calculated value of the unpaid premium was closer to '\$2 million per reactor per year' than to \$22 million per reactor per year.

However, Heyes and Liston-Heyes (1998, 2000a, 2000b) failed to notice a second error: the density function associated with f(*loss*) was not correctly specified. There was a term missing from the density function – that is, (*b*/*loss*) from the logarithmic transformation. Both Dubin and Rothwell (1990) and Heyes and Liston-Heyes (1998, 2000a, 2000b) made 'Error 2'. This error also *overestimated* the unpaid liability-limit premium. At least three graduate students identified Error 2 between 2002 and 2007, as discussed in Section 3B.3: one student writing in German in Zurich; one student writing in English in Maryland; and one student writing in French in Aix-en-Provence.

By 2001, readers of this literature should have known that the maximum unpaid premium was closer to $2 million than $22 million per year. Someone could have discovered that either (a) that the maximum unpaid premium in Dubin and Rothwell (1990) and Heyes and Liston-Heyes' (1998, 2000a, 2000b) model could be lower per reactor year than anyone would imagine, or (b) that maximum damages could be greater than anyone thought possible.

3B.2 Political implications of congressional liability calculations

In 2001, when Senator Pete Domenici (Republican, NM) introduced a Bill to renew the PAA, the Nuclear-Energy Electricity Supply Assurance Act of 2001, there were two estimates of the value of the unpaid premiums provided by the PAA liability limit. The mistaken estimates in Dubin and Rothwell (1990) were ten times higher than the mistaken estimates in Heyes and Liston-Heyes (1998). During the debate that followed, opponents to extending the PAA were more likely to cite the Dubin and Rothwell (1990) calculations, or both Dubin and Rothwell (1990) and Heyes and Liston-Heyes (1998), and proponents of extending the PAA were more likely to cite Heyes and Liston-Heyes (1998), or to cite neither. (Rothwell was under contract after 31 July 2001 to the US General Accounting Office, or US GAO, to resolve the differences between Dubin and Rothwell, 1990, and Heyes and Liston-Heyes, 1998, 2000a, 2000b. The contract stated that Rothwell could not publish writings or present testimony on the PAA while under contract to the US GAO, or publish what was written for the US GAO: Rothwell, 2001.)

Even though (Denenberg's and) Dubin and Rothwell's (1990) estimates were known to be too high from 1998, they continued to be quoted by 'anti-extension' organisations and their representatives. The history of their political-economic analysis can be followed by surveying the 'anti-extentionist' politics in Friends of the Earth (2001), Public Citizen (2001), Safe Energy Communication Council[2] (2001) and Markey (2001a, 2001b). For example, said Friends of the Earth (2001: 4): 'Estimates of the value of this subsidy to nuclear power plant owners range from $3.45 million [Heyes and Liston-Heyes (1998)] to $33 million [Dubin and Rothwell (1990)] (2001 dollars) per reactor per year.' Senator Ed Markey (Democrat, MA) also stated that:

> Geoffery [*sic*] Rothwell of the CATO [*sic*] Institute has said that 'A more efficient solution would have been to assign full liability to those parties and let the insurance market determine the probability of an accident, its consequences and the proper premiums for coverage' . . . My view is that it is now time for nuclear power to grow up.
>
> (Markey, 2001b)

Thus Markey ignores the inherent market failures in insurance for low-probability, high-consequence events identified in Rothwell (1992) – and the fact that Rothwell was never associated with the Cato Institute.

Although the House of Representatives passed the PAA extension on 27 November 2001, it required many congressional sessions to pass extensions to 2017, and then to 2025, in the Energy Policy Act of 2005. About the time it was extended to 2003, Heyes (2002: 28–29) wrote:

> What is more, the latter article [Heyes and Liston-Heyes (1998)] is merely a correction of the former [Dubin and Rothwell (1990)] and is only three pages long. So really, there is only one set of estimates by academics. Dubin and Rothwell developed a very neat approach to trying to derive estimates for the amount that nuclear operators would have to pay for offsite insurance in the absence of Price-Anderson limits . . .
>
> I will let you in on a little secret: The two estimates and the methods used to generate them are, at best, unreliable and, at worst, deeply flawed. I can say that because I am one of the authors. I know squat about nuclear power. Do not get me wrong, the two papers are competent pieces of academic research and they deserved to be published in the reputable peer-reviewed academic journals in which they appeared. But the approach that they utilised is very much an experimental one, and one whose results can be highly sensitive to changes in underlying assumptions . . . One of the authors of the other study – Geoffrey Rothwell from Stanford, a notable economist who has done really excellent work in understanding the economics of nuclear power – has also noted that it is time to reexamine the Dubin and Rothwell approach.

While Heyes (2002) dismisses Dubin and Rothwell (1990) and Heyes and Liston-Heyes (1998, 2000a, 2000b) as being 'deeply flawed' (possibly anticipating unknown errors in these calculations), Heyes (2009) was much more upbeat, quoting the results of Heyes and Liston-Heyes (1998): 'Subsequent work Heyes and Liston-Heyes (1998) corrected an error in [the Dubin and Rothwell (1990)] methodology and showed the *true* figure implied by their method to be significantly lower than that number, but still substantial' (emphasis added). Nevertheless, by 2009, PAA coverage in the United States had exceeded the assumed upper limit of the integral, \$10,000 million, reducing the 'true' figure for congressional liability to one not significantly different from 0.

3B.3 Correcting congressional liability calculations in three languages

Hints of identifying Error 2 can be found in Schneider and Zweifel (2002), later published as Schneider and Zweifel (2004), which cites Zweifel and Umbricht (2002):

> In a companion study, a log-logistic density function . . . was calibrated. According to that study, an increase of liability insurance from today's

CHF 0.7B (US$ 0.47B) to CHF 4B (US$ 2.7B) would result in an increase in the price of electricity of 0.008 cents/kWh (Zweifel and Umbricht 2002, table 4.16).

However, Zweifel and Umbricht (2002), in German, was unpublished, and it was not posted on the same Internet site as its companion, Schneider and Zweifel (2004). Zweifel and Umbricht (2005) could have been the same paper as Zweifel and Umbricht (2002), and its abstract is similar to that of Umbricht and Zweifel (2004), which includes the statement: 'In addition, it presents degrees of internalization based on a correctly derived entire loss distribution function for nuclear risk.' Further, Zweifel and Umbricht (2005: n. 1) states: 'It is at this point that the formula given by Heyes and Heyes (2000a) had to be corrected because it does not contain the factor (b/x).' Also, Zweifel and Umbricht (2005: 17) states: 'Averaging over all five Swiss reactors, the marginal cost of extending coverage from CHF 0.7 bn (US$ 0.47 bn) to CHF 4 bn (US$ 2.7 bn) was estimated at 0.008 US cents/kwh [(Zweifel and Umbricht, 2002: table 4.16)].' However, their parameter estimates for a and b were not presented. The referee's report requested values for a and b for each of the countries considered – that is, Canada, Switzerland and the United States – but they were still absent in Zweifel and Umbricht (2007), which was not published. Therefore an enterprising researcher might have discovered Error 2 in Umbricht's work at some time after 2002.

Error 2 was also identified independently in two doctoral dissertations: First, Ronald Horst (2006: 83) noted that, '[u]nfortunately, [Dubin and Rothwell (1990)] and [Heyes and Liston-Heyes (1998)] omitted the term b/L in the density function'. Horst also generalised the density function by incorporating the probability of an accident (modelled with a Bernoulli density function), as well as the probability distribution of damages (modelled with a three-parameter log-logistic density).

Second, in French, Karine Fiore (2007a: ch. 2) identified Error 2 in her 2007 dissertation, which estimated parameters of $a = 170$ and $b = -17$. This work was incorporated into Fiore (2007b) and submitted for publication with estimates of $a = 1.88$ and $b = 0.97$. The referee's report on Fiore (2007b) noted that 'the log-logistic distribution requires that a and b be greater than zero; publications after [Heyes and Liston-Heyes (1998, 2000a, 2000b)] have ignored these restrictions on the parameters of this distribution'. (Both the logistic and log-logistic functions require positive parameters.) This comment was then incorporated into Fiore (2008) and resubmitted to another journal. Fiore (2008) mistakenly attributes the error to 'Dubin and alii':

> Here is the major mistake of [Dubin and Rothwell (1990); Heyes and Liston-Heyes (2000a, 2000b)]. We correct this mistake and write the new (and right) $f(x)$ as:
>
> $$f(x) = (b/x) \times [e^{-[a+b \times \ln(x)]}/(1 + e^{-[a+b \times \ln(x)]})^2]$$

> *a* and *b* are the parameters to determine. As a consequence of Dubin and alii's [*sic*] mistake, they found values of $b < 0$, which is not consistent with the log-logistic distribution curve.

Fiore (2008) should have written 'Heyes *et al.*'s'. Fiore (2008) has not been published.

Because none of these papers reference one another, it is assumed that these were three independent discoveries by three different graduate students working in three countries. Other economists around the world could have corrected Error 2 between 1990 and 1998 – even those who might have known little about nuclear power.

Had Error 2 been corrected, the anti-nuclear political-economic strategy to block the extension of the PAA might not have stayed afloat from 2001 to 2005. By the time that the new PAA limits were enacted, the total coverage had increased to over $10,000 million; thus authors who attempted to estimate the value of the 'implicit subsidy' found that it was moot. However, the damages at Chernobyl were known to be greater than $10,000 million. What should be the upper limit for the integration of the logistic cumulative distribution function, as anticipated by the insurance industry in setting the annual premium? Of course, actual damages could be higher than this limit, leading to the confusion of readers of this literature between 'the upper limit' of the integral and the highest conceivable level of NPP accident damages, for example in Equation (3B.1.4).

3B.4 Calculating an appropriate nuclear accident insurance premium

Since 2000, authors have taken notice of Dubin and Rothwell (1990) and Heyes and Liston-Heyes (1998, 2000a, 2000b) (the following is not an exhaustive list):

- articles that cite Dubin and Rothwell (1990) only (and not Heyes and Liston-Heyes, 1998, 2000a, 2000b) include Kammen and Pacca (2004);
- those that cite Heyes and Liston-Heyes (1998), (2000a), or (2000b) only (and not Dubin and Rothwell, 1990) include Faure and Hartlief (2003), Schmitt and Spaeter (2007), Mokni (2013), Huhtala and Remes (2014) and Sijm *et al.* (2014); and
- publications that cite Dubin and Rothwell (1990) and Heyes and Liston-Heyes (1998), (2000a), or (2000b) include Eeckhoudt, Schieber and Schneider (2000), Faure and Borre (2008), Faure and Fiore (2008a, 2008b, 2009), Heyes (2009), National Research Council (2010), Mondello (2011) and Lévêque (2015).

The remainder of this section provides calculations (completed by Ronald Horst) for maximum damages of $500,000 million (2013 US dollars), which could be the level of damages at Chernobyl. The United Nations Development

Programme and United Nations Children's Fund (UNDP–UNICEF, 2002) gives an estimate of damages of $148,000 million for Ukraine for the period 1986–2000; UNDP-UNICEF (2002) quotes Chernobyl Radio-ecological Centre (Ukraine, 2001), which gives an estimate of damages of $235,000 million (in 1992 US dollars) for Belarus for the period 1986–2015.

Ronald Horst has proposed the following distribution and density functions:

$$\mathbf{LOGLN}(a, b) = 1/(1 + \exp\{-[a + b \times \ln(loss)]\}) \tag{3B.4.1}$$

$$\mathbf{logln}(a, b) = (b/loss) \times \left(\exp\{-[a + b \times \ln(loss)]\}\right) / (1 + \exp\{-[a + b \times \ln(loss)]\})^2 \tag{3B.4.2}$$

Tables 3B.1 and 3B.2 present the results using Equations (3B.4.1) and (3B.4.2) with the Dubin and Rothwell (1990) model. Table 3B.1 assumes a 'maximum' damage of $10,000 million (1985 US dollars), or $19,000 million in 2013 US dollars; the resulting parameters for [*a* and *b*] are [2.61 and 1.24]. Before the 1988 PAA amendments, the model suggests that operators avoided paying premiums of about $33,000 per reactor year, and $3,000 per reactor year after 1988, with values in 1985 US dollars. These values are far smaller than those reported in Dubin and Rothwell (1990) or Heyes and Liston-Heyes (1998, 2000a, 2000b). (Rothwell, 2001, came to this conclusion by using a logistic-of-a-log function, not a log-logistic function.)

Indeed, the calculated unpaid premiums are so small that if the amounts are accurate, it may be unclear why the nuclear industry in the United States always lobbies so vigorously for PAA renewal. The answer is: because the upper limit on damages is unknown. For example, Table 3B.2 presents values for a worst-case scenario of $500,000 million in 2013 US dollars (or $260,000 million in 1985 US dollars). The recalibrated model suggests that operators avoided average premiums of about $1 million per reactor year after 1988. After correcting the functional form and greatly increasing the value of the maximum damage, the estimate of the implicit unpaid premium by nuclear power reactors in the United States is about $1 million per (light water) reactor

Table 3B.1 Liability for off-site damages with a $10,000 million (1985 US$) maximum

Worst case damage = US$10bn (in 1985 US$m dollars per reactor year)	*Parameter estimates:* a = *2.61,* b =*1.24*			
	Pre-1988	*Post-1988*	*2002*	*2003*
Expected damages > $1m	0.3367	0.3367	0.3367	0.3367
Expected insured losses	0.28	0.28	0.2847	0.2926
Expected industry liability	0.0234	0.0539	0.0435	0.036
Expected unpaid premium	0.0333	0.0028	0.0085	0.008

Source: Calculations made by Ronald Horst, based on Horst (2006).

Table 3B.2 Liability for off-site damages with a $500,000 million (2013 US$) maximum

Worst case damage = US$500bn (in 2013 US$ per reactor year)	*Parameter estimates: a = 3.41, b = 0.85*			
	Pre-1988	*Post-1998*	*2002*	*2003*
Expected damages > $1m	2.33	2.33	2.33	2.33
Expected insured losses	0.53	0.53	0.56	0.62
Expected industry liability	0.18	0.68	0.61	0.57
Expected unpaid premiums	1.61	1.12	1.16	1.14

Source: Calculations made by Ronald Horst, based on Horst (2006).

year. However, if $1 million per reactor year were to be accumulated with 100 reactors, it would take 100 years to reach $10,000 million.

Nonetheless, the model still assumes a probability (0.00008%) that the 'maximum damage' level would be exceeded (here, half a trillion dollars). This is likely to be too low. Based on the analysis presented here and the literature that has developed since the Fukushima-Daiichi accident, the appropriate insurance premium for NPP damage is assumed to be $1/MWh (Lévêque, 2015: 35, 81, 153), which would yield about $8 million per reactor per year. Had this been accumulated after Chernobyl (with all reactors in all countries contributing $1/MWh, given that 'a nuclear power plant accident in one country is an accident in all countries'), the fund could have covered much of the damage after the Fukushima-Daiichi accident and provided incentives for the global nuclear power industry to monitor itself more closely. (For a general discussion, see the review of this literature, 'Costs of nuclear accidents and liability', in D'haeseleer, 2013: 141–160, which concludes, for an NPP accident insurance premium: 'As a start, a base figure of 1€/MWh seems reasonable.') Let P_{IN} be the insurance premium per MWh – that is, $1/MWh – and let *PIN* be equal to P_{IN} (a parameter) multiplied by *E*, the annual electricity output.

Notes

1 The term 'scram' refers to the rapid insertion of neutron-absorbing control rods and materials into the reactor. The first use of the term 'scram' in printed English was in 1928, according to the *Oxford English Dictionary* (Wilton, 2011). It had been derived from either 'scramble', meaning 'get away at once', or from the German word *schramm*, the imperative of *schrammen* meaning 'to depart'. Walter Winchell (1928) first used it in an October 1928 column describing how slang changes over time. Its first use in print in the context of an emergency nuclear reactor shutdown was in 1953. However, by then, the popular mythology in the nuclear industry claimed that, during the testing of the first gas-cooled reactor (GCR) at the University of Chicago, as a safety measure, Enrico Fermi attached a single rope to the control rods above the experimental reactor. After repeated attempts at emergency hand signals, the axe man asked if Fermi would simply yell 'cut the rope', instead of using hand signals. Fermi replied that he would yell 'scram' if the reactor were to appear to be

out of control. When asked the meaning of the word 'scram', Fermi slowly replied, 'Safely cut rope, axe man!' Although by 1942, everyone should have known that 'scram' meant to get out of the area PDQ, the myth was embedded and is still found in the nuclear power literature as an acronym, instead of as a testament to Enrico Fermi's sense of humour and quick wit.

2 In 2001, the Safe Energy Communication Council included Friends of the Earth, Greenpeace, Media Access Project, Nuclear Information and Resource Service, Public Citizen, Public Media Center, Renew America, Sierra Club, Center for Ethical Production and the US Public Interest Research Group.

References

Anderson, S. 1987. 'An international comparison of the impact of safety regulation on LWR performance', Working Paper MIT-EL 87–006. Available online at http://dspace.mit.edu/bitstream/handle/1721.1/60619/EL_TR_1987_006.pdf?sequence=1

Aoki, M., and Rothwell, G. 2013. 'A comparative institutional analysis of the Fukushima nuclear disaster: Lessons and policy implications', *Energy Policy*, 53: 240–247.

Arrow, K. 1971. *Essays in the Theory of Risk-Bearing*. Amsterdam: North Holland.

Association for the Advancement of Cost Engineering (AACE). 1997. *Cost Estimate Classification System—As Applied in Engineering, Procurement, and Construction for the Process Industries*, Practice No. 18R–97 (rev'd 15 June 1998). Available online at www.costengineering.eu/Downloads/articles/AACE_CLASSIFICATION_SYSTEM.pdf

Association for the Advancement of Cost Engineering (AACE). 2011. *Construction Cost Estimating*, Professional Practice Guide No. 6. Available online at www.aacei.org/resources/ppg/#PPG6

Brownstein, B. 1984. 'The Price-Anderson Act: Is it consistent with a sound energy policy?', *Cato Policy Analysis*, 36. Available online at www.cato.org/pubs/pas/pa036es.html

Bunn, M., Fetter, S., Holdren, J., and van der Zwaan, B. 2003. *The Economics of Reprocessing vs. Direct Disposal of Spent Nuclear Fuel*. Available online at http://belfercenter.ksg.harvard.edu/publication/2089/economics_of_reprocessing_vs_direct_disposal_of_spent_nuclear_fuel.html

Cantor, R., and Hewlett, J. 1988. 'The economics of nuclear power: Further evidence on learning, economies of scale, and regulatory effects', *Resources and Energy*, 10(4): 315–335.

Copeland, T., and Weston, J. 1980. *Financial Theory and Corporate Policy*. Reading, MA: Addison-Wesley.

Copeland, T., Weston, J., and Shastri, K. 2005. *Financial Theory and Corporate Policy*, 4th edn. Reading, MA: Pearson Addison-Wesley.

D'haeseleer, W. 2013. *Synthesis on the Economics of Nuclear Energy, Final Report*. Available online at www.mech.kuleuven.be/en/tme/research/energy_environment/Pdf/ wpen2013-14.pdf

Davis, L., and Wolfram, C. 2011. 'Deregulation, consolidation, and efficiency: Evidence from U.S. nuclear power', NBER Working Paper 17341. Available online at www.nber.org/papers/w17341.pdf

Delene, J. 1986. *Cost Estimate Guidelines for Advanced Nuclear Power Technologies*. ORNL/TM–10071. Available online at http://web.ornl.gov/info/reports/1986/3445600642464.pdf

Delene, J., and Hudson, C. 1990. *Cost Estimate Guidelines for Advanced Nuclear Power Technologies*. ORNL/TM–10071/R2. Available online at www.iaea.org/inis/collection/NCLCollectionStore/_Public/21/054/21054022.pdf

Delene, J., and Hudson, C. 1993. *Cost Estimate Guidelines for Advanced Nuclear Power Technologies*. ORNL/TM–10071/R3. Available online at www.iaea.org/inis/collection/NCLCollectionStore/_Public/25/011/25011638.pdf

Denenberg, H. 1973. 'Testimony before the Atomic Safety and Licensing Board, licensing hearing for Three Mile Island Nuclear Power Plant', 93rd US Congress, Joint Committee Atomic Energy, *Possible Modification or Extension of the Price-Anderson Insurance and Indemnity Act* (31 January and 27–28 March), pp. 617–623. Available online at http://babel.hathitrust.org/cgi/pt?id=uc1.a0000097865#view=1up;seq=232

Du, Y., and Parsons, J. 2009. 'Update on the cost of nuclear power'. Center for Energy and Environmental Policy Research Working Paper 09-004. Available online at http://web.mit.edu/jparsons/www/publications/2009-004.pdf

Dubin, J., and Rothwell, G. 1990. 'Subsidy to nuclear power through the Price–Anderson liability limit', *Contemporary Policy Issues*, 8(3): 73–79.

Economic Modelling Working Group of the Gen IV International Forum (EMWG). 2007. *Cost Estimating Guidelines for Generation IV Nuclear Energy Systems*. Available online at www.gen-4.org/gif/jcms/c_40408/cost-estimating-guidelines-for-generation-iv-nuclear-energy-systems

Economic Modelling Working Group of the Gen IV International Forum (EMWG). 2008. *Generation IV Excel-based Cost Calculation of Nuclear Systems*, v. 2. Available online at www.gen-4.org/gif/jcms/c_42161/g4econs

Eeckhoudt, L., Schieber, C., and Schneider, T. 2000. 'Risk aversion and the external cost of a nuclear accident', *Journal of Environmental Management*, 58(2): 109–117.

Electric Power Research Institute (EPRI). 1993. *Technology Assessment Guide*. TR–102276–V1R7. Palo Alto, CA: EPRI.

Evaluation Methodology Group of the Gen IV Roadmap Committee (EMG). 2002. *Generation IV Roadmap: Viability and Performance Evaluation Methodology Report*. Forthcoming.

Faure, M., and Borre, T. 2008. 'Compensating nuclear damage: A comparative economic analysis of the U.S. and international liability schemes', *William and Mary Environmental Law and Policy Review*, 33(1): 219–286.

Faure, M., and Fiore, K. 2008a. 'The civil liability of European nuclear operators: Which coverage for the new 2004 Protocols? Evidence from France', *International Environmental Agreements: Politics, Law and Economics*, 8(3): 227–248.

Faure, M., and Fiore, K. 2008b. 'The coverage of the nuclear risk in Europe: Which alternative?', *Geneva Papers on Risk and Insurance: Issues and Practices*, 33(2): 288–322.

Faure, M., and Fiore, K. 2009. 'An economic analysis of the nuclear liability subsidy', *Pace Environmental Law Review*, 26(2): 419–448.

Faure, M., and Hartlief, T. 2003. *Insurance and Expanding Systematic Risks*. Paris: OECD.

Fiore, K. 2007a. 'Industrie nucléaire et gestion du risque d'accident en Europe', PhD dissertation, Faculty of Applied Economics, Université Aix Marseille III.

Fiore, K. 2007b. 'An empirical analysis of the nuclear liability limit in the OECD Conventions: A case study', Working Paper, Faculty of Applied Economics, Université Aix Marseille III.

Fiore, K. 2008. 'The nuclear liability limit in the OECD Conventions: An implicit subsidy', Maastricht Faculty of Law Working Paper. Available online at http://papers.ssrn.com/sol3/papers.cfm?abstract_id=1086290

Friends of the Earth. 2001. 'Testimony on proposed amendments to the Price–Anderson Act'. Available online at http://pbadupws.nrc.gov/docs/ML0118/ML011800137.pdf

Georgia Power Company. 2010. *Plant Vogtle Units 3 & 4, Third Semi-Annual Construction Monitoring Report*, August. Available online at www.psc.state.ga.us/factsv2/Docket.aspx?docketNumber=29849

Georgia Power Company. 2011. *Plant Vogtle Units 3 & 4, Fourth Semi-Annual Construction Monitoring Report*, 31 December. Available online at www.psc.state.ga.us/factsv2/Docket.aspx?docketNumber=29849

Hall, D. (ed.) 1990. 'Social and private costs of alternative energy technologies', *Contemporary Policy Issues*, 7(3), special issue.

Hausman, J. 1978. 'Specification tests in econometrics', *Econometrica*, 46(6): 1251–1271.

Heyes, A. 2002. 'Determining the price of Price–Anderson', *Regulation*, 25(4): 26–30.

Heyes, A. 2009. 'Is environmental regulation bad for competition? A survey', *Journal of Regulatory Economics*, 36(1): 1–28.

Heyes, A., and Liston-Heyes, C. 1998. 'Subsidy to nuclear power through Price–Anderson liability limit: Comment', *Contemporary Economic Policy*, 16(1): 122–124.

Heyes, A., and Liston-Heyes, C. 2000a. 'An empirical analysis of the Nuclear Liability Act in Canada', *Resources and Energy Economics*, 22(1): 91–101.

Heyes, A., and Liston-Heyes, C. 2000b. 'Capping environmental liability: The case of North American nuclear power', *The Geneva Papers on Risk and Insurance*, 25(2): 196–202.

Hofert, M., and Wüthrich, M. 2011. 'Statistical review of nuclear power accidents', Working Paper. Available online at http://ssrn.com/abstract=1923008

Horst, R. 2006. 'The economics of nuclear power', PhD dissertation, Department of Economics, University of Maryland, College Park, MD. Available online at http://drum.lib.umd.edu/bitstream/1903/4168/1/umi-umd-3965.pdf

Hudson, C. 1987. *Cost Estimate Guidelines for Advanced Nuclear Power Technologies*. ORNL/TM–10071/R1. Available online at www.osti.gov/scitech/servlets/purl/10176857

Huhtala, A., and Remes, P. 2014. 'Dimming hopes for nuclear power: Quantifying the social costs of perceptions of risks', Government Institute for Economic Research Working Paper. Available online at http://papers.ssrn.com/sol3/papers.cfm?abstract_id=2521439

International Atomic Energy Agency (IAEA). 1986. *Economic Evaluation of Bids for Nuclear Power Plants*. Technical Reports Series No. 269. Vienna: IAEA.

International Atomic Energy Agency (IAEA). 1998. *Evaluating and Improving Nuclear Power Plant Operating Performance*. Available online at www-pub.iaea.org/MTCD/Publications/PDF/te_1098_prn.pdf

International Atomic Energy Agency (IAEA). 2000. *Economic Evaluation of Bids for Nuclear Power Plants*. Technical Reports Series No. 396, 1999 edn. Available online at www-pub.iaea.org/MTCD/Publications/PDF/TRS396_scr.pdf

International Atomic Energy Agency (IAEA). 2013. *Nuclear Power Reactors in the World*. Reference Data Series No. 2. Available online at www-pub.iaea.org/MTCD/Publications/PDF/rds-2-34_web.pdf

International Atomic Energy Agency (IAEA). 2014a. *International conventions and legal agreements: Vienna Convention on Civil Liability for Nuclear Damage*. Available online at www.iaea.org/Publications/Documents/Conventions/liability.html

International Atomic Energy Agency (IAEA). 2014b. *Small and medium sized reactors (SMRs) development, assessment and deployment*. Available online at www.iaea.org/NuclearPower/SMR/

International Atomic Energy Agency (IAEA). 2015. *Power Reactor Information System*. Available online at www.ieae.org/pris/

International Energy Agency (IEA) and Nuclear Energy Agency (NEA). 2010. *Projected Costs of Generating Electricity, 2010 Update*. Available online at www.iea.org/publications/freepublications/publication/projected_costs.pdf

International Energy Agency (IEA) and Nuclear Energy Agency (NEA). 2015. *Projected Costs of Generating Electricity, 2015 Update*. Paris: OECD.

Johnson, N., Kotz, S., and Balakrishnan, N. 1994. *Continuous Univariate Distributions*. New York: John Wiley & Sons.

Junginger, M., Lako, P., Lensink, S., van Sark, W., and Weiss, M. (2008). *Climate Change Scientific Assessment and Policy Analysis: Technological Learning in the Energy Sector*. Bilthoven: Netherlands Environmental Assessment Agency.

Kahneman, D. 2011. *Thinking: Fast and Slow*. New York: Farra, Straus, & Giroux.

Kammen, D., and Pacca, S. 2004. 'Assessing the costs of electricity', *Annual Review of Environmental Resources*, 29(1): 301–344.

Kirby, K. 2011. 'An empirical assessment of the form of utility functions', *Journal of Experimental Psychology: Learning, Memory, and Cognition*, 37(2): 461–476.

Knight, F. 1921. *Risk, Uncertainty and Profit*. Boston, MA: Hart, Schaffner & Marx/Houghton Mifflin Co.

Komanoff, C., and Roelofs, C. 1994. 'Predicting nuclear plant capacity factors', *Public Utilities Fortnightly*, 1 December, pp. 28–31.

Koomey, J., and Hultman, N. 2007. 'A reactor-level analysis of busbar costs for US nuclear plants, 1970-2005', *Energy Policy*, 35: 5630–5642.

Krautmann, A., and Solow, J. 1992. 'Nuclear power plant performance: The post-Three Mile Island era', *Energy Economics*, 14(3): 209–216.

Lako, P., van Heek, A., and Rothwell, G. 2010. 'Learning in nuclear power', in M. Junginger, W. van Sark, and A. Faaij (eds) *Technological Learning in the Energy Sector*, Cheltenham: Edward Elgar, pp. 176–192.

Lester, R., and McCabe, M. 1993. 'The effect of industrial structure on learning by doing in nuclear power plant operation', *RAND Journal of Economics*, 24(3): 418–438.

Lévêque, F. 2015. *The Economics and Uncertainties of Nuclear Power*. Cambridge: Cambridge University Press.

Lorance, R., and Wendling, R. 2001. 'Basic techniques for analyzing and presentation of cost risk analysis', *Cost Engineering*, 43(6): 25.

Markey, E. J. 2001a. 'Let free market decide nuclear energy viability', *Roll Call*, 1 October.

Markey, E. J. 2001b. 'Statement of Rep. Edward J. Markey (D-MA), House Energy and Commerce Markup of Price–Anderson Reauthorization Legislation', 107th Congress, First Session, House of Representatives, 19 November. Available online at www.gpo.gov/fdsys/pkg/CRPT-107hrpt299/html/CRPT-107hrpt299-pt1.htm

Massachusetts Institute of Technology (MIT). 2009. *The Future of Nuclear Power: An Interdisciplinary Study – Update*. Available online at http://web.mit.edu/nuclearpower/pdf/nuclearpower-update2009.pdf

McNett, J. 1989. 'Nuclear indemnity for government contractors under the Price–Anderson Act: 1988 amendments', *Public Contract Law Journal*, 19(1): 1–13.

Mokni, S. 2013. 'L'internationalisation d'AREVA, NP', MSc thesis, Sciences de la gestion, HEC Montréal, Canada. Available online at http://biblos.hec.ca/biblio/memoires/2013NO56.PDF

Mondello, G. 2011. 'Civil liability, safety and nuclear parks: Is concentrated management better?' Working Paper. Available online at http://papers.ssrn.com/sol3/papers.cfm?abstract_id=1823455

Moody's. 2011. *Moody's downgrades the senior unsecured rating of SCANA to Baa3 and the senior unsecured rating of South Carolina Electric and Gas to Baa2; Outlooks revised to stable.* Available online at www.moodys.com/research/Moodys-downgrades-the-senior-unsecured-rating-of-SCANA-to-Baa3–PR_226074

National Research Council. 2010. *Hidden Costs of Energy: Unpriced Consequences of Energy Production and Use.* Washington, DC: The National Academy Press.

Nuclear Energy Agency (NEA). 2000. *Reduction of Capital Costs of Nuclear Power Plants.* Available online at www.oecd-nea.org/ndd/pubs/2000/2088-reduction-capital-costs.pdf

Nuclear Energy Agency (NEA). 2011. *Current Status, Technical Feasibility and Economics of Small Nuclear Reactors.* Available online at www.oecd-nea.org/ndd/reports/2011/current-status-small-reactors.pdf

Nuclear Energy Agency (NEA). 2014. *Paris Convention on Nuclear Third Party Liability.* Available online at www.oecd-nea.org/law/paris-convention.html

Nuclear Energy Agency (NEA). 2015. *Nuclear New Build: Insights into Financing and Project Management.* Available online at www.oecd-nea.org/ndd/pubs/2015/7195-nn-build-2015.pdf

NuclearStreet. 2009. 'Pictures of B&W's new mPower reactor', *Nuclear Power Industry News*, 11 June. Available online at http://nuclearstreet.com/nuclear_power_ industry_ news/b/nuclear_power_news/archive/2009/06/11/pictures-of-b-amp-w-s-new-mpower-reactor.aspx#.Vc4qCVWqpBc

Oak Ridge National Laboratory (ORNL). 1988a. *Technical Reference Book for the Energy Economic Data Base Program, EEDB-IX.* DOE/NE–0092. Oak Ridge, TN: ORNL.

Oak Ridge National Laboratory (ORNL). 1988b. *Phase IX Update (1987) Report for the Energy Economic Data Base Program, EEDB-IX.* DOE/NE–0091. Oak Ridge, TN: ORNL.

Oak Ridge National Laboratory (ORNL). 2001. *US Nuclear Power Plant Operating Cost and Experience Summaries.* NUREG/CR–6577, Supp. 1. Available online at http://pbadupws.nrc.gov/docs/ML0101/ML010120458.pdf

Palisade. 2015. *@RISK: Advanced Risk Analysis using Monte Carlo Simulation, v. 6.0.* Available online at www.palisade.com/risk/

Parsons, E. 1999. *Waste Management Project Contingency Analysis.* DOE/FETC–99/1100US. Available online at www.netl.doe.gov/publications/others/techrpts/parsons.pdf

Pasqualetti, M., and Rothwell, G. (eds) 1991. 'Nuclear decommissioning economics', *The Energy Journal*, 12, special issue.

Portland Cement Association (PCA). 2015. *Cement and concrete basic FAQs.* Available online at www.cement.org/cement-concrete-basics/faqs

Pratt, J. 1964. 'Risk aversion in the small and in the large', *Econometrica*, 32(1/2): 122–136.

Progress Energy. 2010. 'Nuclear power plant cost recovery clause, Docket 100009 before the Florida Public Service Commission, redacted direct testimony of Jeff

Lyash on behalf of Progress Energy Florida', 10 April. Available online at www.floridapsc.com/library/filings/10/03571-10/03571-10.pdf

Public Citizen. 2001. *Price Anderson Act: The billion dollar bailout for nuclear power mishaps.* Available online at www.citizen.org/documents/Price%20Anderson%20Factsheet.pdf

Radetzki, M., and Radetzki, M. 1997. 'Liability of nuclear and other industrial corporations for large scale accident damage', *Journal of Energy and Natural Resources Law*, 15(4): 366–386.

Reuter, T. 2014. 'Donald Rumsfeld's maddening confession in the unknown known', *Forbes*, 5 May. Available online at www.forbes.com/sites/timreuter/2014/05/05/donald-rumsfelds-maddening-confession-in-the-unknown-known/

Rothwell, G. 1986. 'Steam-electric scale economies and construction lead times', California Institute of Technology, Social Science Working Paper No. 627. Available online at http://s3-us-west-1.amazonaws.com/hss-prod-storage.cloud.caltech.edu/hss_working_papers/sswp627.pdf

Rothwell, G. 1990. 'Utilization and service: Decomposing nuclear reactor capacity factors', *Resources and Energy*, 12: 215–229.

Rothwell, G. 1992. 'Can nuclear power compete?' *Regulation*, Winter: 66–74.

Rothwell, G. 2001. 'Further comments on the subsidy to nuclear power through the Price–Anderson liability limit', Internal memorandum, August, US General Accounting Office, Washington, DC.

Rothwell, G. 2005. 'Cost contingency as the standard deviation of the cost estimate', *Cost Engineering*, 47(7): 22–25.

Rothwell, G. 2007. 'IAEA's DEEP in Carlsbad: Co-producing energy and water in Southern California', *International Journal of Nuclear Desalination*, 2(3): 265–279.

Rothwell, G. 2010. 'New U.S. nuclear generation: 2010–2030', Stanford Institute for Economic Policy Research (SIEPR) Discussion Paper No. 09-025. Available online at http://siepr.stanford.edu/system/files/shared/pubs/papers/Rothwell-Nuclear-RFF_June2010.pdf

Rothwell, G. 2011. *The Economics of Future Nuclear Power: Update of the University of Chicago's The Economic Future of Nuclear Power*, 17 March. Chicago, IL: Energy Policy Institute at Chicago, Harris School of Public Policy, University of Chicago. (It has been deleted from the Harris School website, but is discussed online at http://csis.org/event/small-modular-reactors-key-future-nuclear-power-generation-us)

Rothwell, G. 2012. 'Small modular reactors: Costs, waste and safety benefits', National Energy Policy Institute (NEPI) Working Paper. Available online at www.uxc.com/smr/Library%5CGeneral/2012%20-%20NEPI%20Working%20Paper-SMRs%20Costs,%20Waste%20and%20Safety%20Benefits.pdf

Rothwell, G., and Gomez, T. 2003. *Electricity Economics: Regulation and Deregulation.* Piscataway, NJ/Hoboken, NJ: IEEE Press/John Wiley & Sons.

Rothwell, G., and Williams, K. 2006. 'Is nuclear power competitive producing electricity or hydrogen?' *International Journal of Nuclear Hydrogen Production and Applications*, 1(2): 154–169.

Safe Energy Communication Council. 2001. *Fact sheet: The Price–Anderson Act.* Available online at www.nirs.org/reactorwatch/paa/priceandersonsubsidyseccfctsht.pdf

Schmitt, A., and Spaeter, S. 2007. 'Risque nucléaire civil et responsabilité optimale de l'exploitant', *Revue Économique*, 58(6): 1331–1352.

Schneider, Y., and Zweifel, P. 2002. 'How much internalization of nuclear risk through liability insurance?', Socioeconomic Institute Working Paper No. 0211. Available online at www.soi.uzh.ch/research/wp/2002/wp0211.pdf

Schneider, Y., and Zweifel, P. 2004. 'How much internalization of nuclear risk through liability insurance?', *Journal of Risk and Uncertainty*, 29(3): 219–240.

Scroggs, S. 2010. 'Testimony & exhibits of Steven D. Scroggs, before the Florida Public Service Commission, Docket No. 100009-EI, Florida Power & Light Company, 3 May 2010, in re: Nuclear Power Plant Cost Recovery for the years ending December 2010 and 2011'. Available online at www.psc.state.fl.us/library/FILINGS/11/05744-11/05744-11.pdf

Sijm, J., Lehmann, P., Chewpreecha, U., Gawel, E., Mercure, J.-F., Pollitt, H., and Strunz, S. 2014. 'EU climate and energy policy beyond 2020: Are additional targets and instruments for renewables economically reasonable?', Helmholtz Centre for Environmental Research (UFZ) Discussion Paper No. 3/2014. Available online at www.researchgate.net/profile/Jos_Sijm/publications

South Carolina Electric & Gas Company (SCE&G). 2010. *Quarterly Report to the South Carolina Office of Regulatory Staff, Pursuant to Public Service Commission Order No. 2009–104(A)*, 30 September. Available online at http://dms.psc.sc.gov/pdf/matters/54C244B7-9C28-8971-DB3654C3EE6B1161.pdf

Stoller Corporation. 1986. *Nuclear Unit Operating Experience: 1983–1984 Update*, EPRI NP–4368. Palo Alto, CA: EPRI.

Sturm, R. 1993. 'Nuclear power in Eastern Europe: Learning or forgetting curves?', *Energy Economics*, 15(3): 183–189.

Sturm, R. 1995. 'Why does nuclear power performance differ across Europe?', *European Economic Review*, 39(6): 1197–1214.

Tennessee Valley Authority (TVA). 2005. *ABWR Cost/Schedule/COL Project at TVA's Bellefonte Site*. US DOE Contract DE–AI07–04ID14620. Available online at www.nei.org/corporatesite/media/filefolder/tva_abwr_feasibility_study_2005.pdf

Thomas, S. 1990a. 'COMECON nuclear power plant performance: A comparison with the USA and Japan', *Energy Policy*, 18(6): 506–524.

Thomas, S. 1990b. 'Operating performance of nuclear reactors in the non-communist world', *Energy Policy*, 18(10): 888–912.

Ukraine. 2001. *Fifteen Years of the Chernobyl Disaster: The Experience of Overcoming: The National Report of Ukraine*. Kyiv: Chernobyl Radioecological Center of the Ministry of Emergencies of Ukraine.

Umbricht, R., and Zweifel, P. 2004. *The Cost of Additional Nuclear Liability Coverage: Final Report to the Swiss Energy Agency*. Available online at www.research-projects.uzh.ch/p4914.htm

United Nations Development Programme (UNDP) and United Nations Children's Fund (UNICEF). 2002. *The Human Consequences of the Chernobyl Nuclear Accident: A Strategy for Recovery*. Available online at www.un.org/ha/chernobyl/docs/report.pdf

University of Chicago. 2004. *The Economic Future of Nuclear Power*. Available online at www.eusustel.be/public/documents_publ/links_to_docs/cost/uoc-study.pdf

US Department of Energy (US DOE). 1988. *Nuclear Energy Cost Data Base: A Reference Data Base for Nuclear and Coal-Fired Power Plant Power Generation Cost Analysis*. DOE/NE–0095. Available online at https://inis.iaea.org/search/search.aspx?orig_q=RN:20013280

US Department of Energy (US DOE). 2012. 'Obama administration announces $450 million to design and commercialize U.S. small modular nuclear reactors', *Energy.gov*, 22 March. Available online at http://energy.gov/articles/obama-administration-announces-450-million-design-and-commercialize-us-small-modular

US Energy Information Administration (US EIA). 2010. *Updated Capital Cost Estimates for Electricity Generation Plants*. Available online at www.eia.gov/oiaf/beck_plantcosts/pdf/updatedplantcosts.pdf

US Energy Information Administration (US EIA). 2011. *Annual Energy Outlook 2011*. DOE/EIA–0383(2011). Available online at www.eia.gov/forecasts/aeo/pdf/0383(2011).pdf

US Energy Information Administration (US EIA). 2012. *Annual Energy Outlook 2012*. DOE/EIA–0383(2012). Available online at www.eia.gov/forecasts/aeo/pdf/0383(2012).pdf

US Energy Information Administration (US EIA). 2014. *Assumptions to the Annual Energy Outlook 2014*. DOE/EIA–0554(2014). Available online at www.eia.gov/forecasts/aeo/assumptions/

US Nuclear Regulatory Commission (US NRC). 1985. 'Statement of the U.S. Nuclear Regulatory Commission concerning Price–Anderson', Reauthorization of the Price–Anderson Act, Hearings before the Subcommittee on Nuclear Regulation of the Committee on Environment and Public Works, U.S. Senate, 99th Congress, 1st Session, 22–23 October, pp. 255–310. Available online at https://archive.org/stream/reauthorizatione00unit/reauthorizatione00unit_djvu.txt

US Nuclear Regulatory Commission (US NRC). 1995. *Licensed Operating Reactors: Status Summary Report, Data as of 12–31–94*. NUREG–0020. Available online at www.iaea.org/inis/collection/NCLCollectionStore/_Public/26/060/26060116.pdf

Wallich, P. 1991. 'No accounting for disaster', *Scientific American*, 265(5): 134.

Wilton, D. 2011. '1928 words in the OED', *Wordorigins*, 30 August. Available online at www.wordorigins.org/index.php/site/comments/1928_words/

Winchell, W. 1928. 'Your Broadway and mine', *The New York Graphic*, 4 October.

Zweifel, P., and Umbricht, R. 2002. 'Verbesserte Duckung des Nuklearrisikos – zu welchen Bedingungen [Extended coverage of nuclear risk – on what conditions?]', Forschungsprogramm Energiewirtschafliche Grundlagen, Bundesamt für Energie, Socioeconomic Institute of the University of Zurich, Switzerland.

Zweifel, P., and Umbricht, R. 2005. 'Degrees of internalization of nuclear risk: An international comparison', Socioeconomic Institute of the University of Zurich Working Paper, September.

Zweifel, P., and Umbricht, R. 2007. 'Degrees of internalization of nuclear risk: An international comparison', Socioeconomic Institute of the University of Zurich Working Paper, April.

4 New light water reactor operating and levelised costs

This chapter presents the levelised cost of electricity (LCOE) for new nuclear power. Section 4.1 redefines levelised cost, assuming that the costs are constant in each year of plant operation. Section 4.2 calculates nuclear fuel costs and probability distributions. Section 4.3 calculates operations and maintenance (O&M) costs and probability distributions. Section 4.4 presents first-of-a-kind (FOAK) and nth-of-a-kind (NOAK) deterministic levelised cost estimates for new nuclear by combining the results of Chapter 3 with Sections 4.2–4.3. Appendix 4A discusses used nuclear fuel recycling, extending the discussion in Section 4.2. To determine levelised costs, this chapter uses a range of costs of capital between 3% and 12% (as discussed in Chapter 2, Section 2.4). Chapter 5 calculates, simulates and compares probability distributions of levelised costs of new nuclear, combined-cycle natural gas turbines and pollution-controlled coal.

4.1 New nuclear power's total construction and levelised costs

Extending the microeconomics definition of total cost (Berndt and Woods, 1975), Equation (4.1.1) defines total annual cost at a nuclear power plant (NPP):

$$TC_{ik} = (\mathrm{CRF} \times KC_{ik}) + F_{ik}(P_F) + (P_L \times L_{ik}) + M_{ik} \tag{4.1.1}$$

where

CRF is from Chapter 2, Appendix 2A, Equation (2A.1.4),

i indicates the serial number of the plant, for example if the series has eight units, then $i = 1$–8,

k indicates the technology, for example advanced light water reactor (ALWR), small modular reactor (SMR), etc.,

F_{ik} is the annual fuel expense, in US$m,

P_F is the price of fuel inputs (including waste management),

P_L is average annual (burdened) salary of an employee,

L_{ik} is the number of employees at the facility, and
M_{ik} represents miscellaneous, non-labour $O\&M_{ik}$ expenses, in US$m (which also includes insurance premiums, *PIN*, for off-site damages of NPP accidents, as discussed in Chapter 3, Appendix 3B).

Because the *technology* is fixed during the life of the plant, total construction cost, *KC*, and levelised capital cost, *LKC*, are fixed at the time of construction completion (capital additions, for example refurbishments, upgrades and uprates, are levelised and added to $O\&M_{ik}$ costs, following industry practice). Real prices remain unchanged. Unless otherwise specified, all monetary values are in 2013 US dollars. In this context, and dropping the subscripts:

$$LC = [(\mathrm{CRF} \times KC) + F(P_F) + O\&M]/E \tag{4.1.2}$$

where

$F(P_F)$ is the annual fuel payment, including used fuel management and disposal,
$O\&M$ is the annual O&M payment, including *PIN*, and
E is the levelised annual energy output.

Further, given the importance of variable and fixed cost uncertainties in power generation, on top of fuel price uncertainties in the minds of electric utilities, investors and the public, this chapter shows how to model these uncertainties based on the means and variances of historic data for nuclear fuel and O&M costs. Chapter 5 models capital cost uncertainties, and extends the probabilistic analysis to natural gas and coal-fired power plant costs.

To keep the analysis simple and transparent, only probability densities for *primary inputs* with closed-form cumulative distributions are used (for example no densities or distributions involving integrals, such as the gamma function, as in Chapter 3, Section 3.3). For *inputs*, these include:

1 the uniform, where the mean is equal to the average of the minimum and maximum values;
2 the exponential density and distribution in Equations (4.1.3) and (4.1.4); and
3 the extreme value density and distribution in Equations (4.1.5) and (4.1.6).

These distributions also have the advantage of excluding negative values in simulation, given that most prices and quantities are positive.

For *intermediate inputs or outputs*, these include (a) the normal (see Chapter 3, Appendix 3A, Equation (3A.1.1)), and (b) the lognormal (see Chapter 3, Appendix 3A, Equation (3A.1.6)). This is because, when random inputs are *added together*, the *output* tends toward a normal distribution, and when random inputs are *multiplied together*, the *output* tends toward a lognormal distribution. Further, the normal and uniform densities are symmetric. On the other hand, the lognormal, the extreme value and the exponential densities are non-symmetric, and are better for mimicking skewed distributions with long right-hand side tails, such as those of fuel prices.

The exponential density and distribution are:

$$\textbf{expo}(b) = [\exp\{(-x/b)\}]/b \tag{4.1.3}$$

$$\textbf{EXPO}(b) = 1 - \exp\{(-x/b)\} \tag{4.1.4}$$

where b and x are greater than 0, and b is equal to the mean and the standard deviation.

The extreme value density and distribution are:

$$\textbf{maxv}(a, b) = (1/b) \times ab \times \exp\{(-ab)\} \tag{4.1.5}$$

$$\textbf{MAXV}(a, b) = \exp\{-ab\} \tag{4.1.6}$$

where

ab is equal to $\exp\{-[(x - a)/b]\}$,
a is equal to the mode, and
b is equal to the standard deviation divided by $(\pi/\sqrt{6})$ (≈ 1.283).

(See Johnson, Kotz and Balakrishnan, 1994.) The direction of the skewness in the extreme value distribution can be reversed, such that it has an extreme minimum value. This is designated as **minv**(a, b) and **MINV**(a, b). This analysis uses a spreadsheet add-in program, @RISK, to determine the most appropriate densities to represent random variables and their probabilities.

4.2 New nuclear fuel costs

Low enriched uranium (LEU) fuel accounting is complex if done precisely – that is, by considering lead and lag times of each fuel bundle from the first fuel core through to the last fuel core, including irradiated fuel management. Here, as in most cost analyses, the assumption is that fuel is paid for in a uniform stream over the life of the plant, without regard to the changing nature of a reactor's set of irradiated fuel. (This assumption can lead to slight differences between cost models regarding the value of the unused U-235 in the last fuel core.) This is similar to the assumption of leasing fuel from a third party at a per megawatt-hour (MWh) fee and is the logic of charging NPPs US$1/MWh for long-term irradiated fuel disposal, which is accumulated in the US Federal Budget General Fund under the Nuclear Waste Trust Fund account (see Chapter 2, Section 2.1). (This fee is no longer being collected because of the lack of progress in licensing a geologic repository.) However, unlike fossil-fired plants, for which fuel is expensed, nuclear fuel is depreciated as a capital investment. (On 'fuel-cycle costs', see D'haeseleer, 2013: 95–110, citing Rothwell, 2010.)

Following Bunn *et al.* (2003: 102), and dropping time subscripts:

$$F = \{[FC/(24 \times \mathrm{B} \times \mathrm{eff})] + WASTE\} \times E \tag{4.2.1}$$

where

FC	is the cost of nuclear fuel in US dollars per kilogram of uranium (US$/kgU),
24	is the number of thermal MWh in a thermal megawatt-day,
B	is the burnup rate measured in thermal megawatt-days per kgU,
eff	is the thermal efficiency of converting MW-thermal into MW-electric,
$WASTE$	is the interim storage cost per MWh (costs to manage used fuel from Rothwell, 2015) plus geologic disposal costs (set equal to US $1/MWh real – that is, implicitly increasing with inflation, unlike contributions to the Nuclear Waste Trust Fund).

FC can be calculated with Equation (4.2.2), in which all prices are given in 2013 US$/kg of product (and fractional losses during processing less than 1% are ignored):

$$FC = [NU \times P_{\mathrm{UF6}}(1 + \mathbf{r})^{\mathrm{lt_U}}] + [SWU \times P_{\mathrm{SWU}}(1 + \mathbf{r})^{\mathrm{lt_S}}] + [P_{\mathrm{FAB}}(1 + \mathbf{r})^{\mathrm{lt_F}}] \tag{4.2.2}$$

where

NU	is the ratio of natural uranium input to enriched uranium output,
P_{UF6}	is the price of natural uranium input *plus its conversion to* UF_6,
$\mathrm{lt_U}$	is the carrying time from uranium purchase to reactor loading, for example 1.0 years,
SWU	is the number of separative work units required in enrichment,
P_{SWU}	is the price of enriching uranium hexafluoride, UF_6,
$\mathrm{lt_S}$	is the carrying time from conversion to reactor loading, for example 0.5 years,
P_{FAB}	is the price of fabricating UO_2 fuel from enriched UF_6, and
$\mathrm{lt_F}$	is the carrying time from fabrication to reactor loading, for example 0.25 years (90 days).

In Equation (4.2.2), each price is discounted to the loading of the fuel into the reactor. (There is a small error – less than 0.16%, or about $4 – introduced in calculating the total cost of LEU fuel by assuming that UF_6 conversion incurs a carrying charge starting at the time of uranium purchase, rather than between the times of payment for uranium and the payment for enrichment services.) In Equation (4.2.2), *NU* is the natural uranium input for 1 kgU of enriched uranium product:

$$NU = (X_{PE} - X_{TE})/(X_{FE} - X_{TE}) \tag{4.2.3}$$

where

- X_{FE} is the percentage of U-235 (assay) in initial feed natural uranium – that is, about 0.711%,
- X_{PE} is the percentage of U-235 in the enriched uranium product, for example 4.0%, and
- X_{TE} is the optimal percentage of U-235 in the tails, for example 0.35% (see Chapter 1, Figure 1.4).

The optimal tails assay can be approximated by an exponential function of the ratio of P_{SWU} and P_{UF6} for enrichments with feed assays of 0.711%. Equation (4.2.4) was estimated with ordinary least squares (OLS) with data from numerical optimisation with a fixed product assay (here, 4.5%) and is not applicable to other product assays – that is, it must be estimated for each product assay (X_{TE} is an endogenous variable and must be calculated with an optimisation routine). In Equation (4.2.2), *SWU* is the number of separative work units (SWUs) required in enrichment, as given in Equation (4.2.5):

$$X_{TE} = \exp\{-6.085 + 0.468 \times [\ln(P_{SWU}/P_{UF6})] - 0.074 \times [\ln(P_{SWU}/P_{UF6})]^2\} \tag{4.2.4}$$

$$SWU = [V(X_{PE}) - V(X_{TE})] - NU[V(X_{FE}) - V(X_{TE})] \tag{4.2.5}$$

$$V(X_i) = (2X_i - 1) \times \ln[X_i/(1 - X_i)] \tag{4.2.6}$$

where

- i is feed assay, *FE*, product assay, *PE*, or tail assay, *TE*, and
- $V(X_i)$ is known as the 'value function', with $0 < X < 1$ – that is, $V(X_{FE})$, $V(X_{PE})$ and $V(X_{TE})$.

Before discussing the cost of nuclear fuel per MWh, first consider the distributions of uranium and SWU prices based on data from Chapter 1, Figure 1.6. Figures 4.1 and 4.2 present histograms and proposed densities of annual observations (converted from monthly averages) from 1970 to 2014 for uranium prices and SWU prices, respectively, as in references for Chapter 1, Figure 1.6. In Figure 4.1, the origin, $0, has been shifted to the right, to

Table 4.1 Parameters for new nuclear fuel cost calculations

Levelised fuel cost parameters	*ALWR value*	*SMR value*
Price of uranium + Conversion to UF_6, US$/kg	$110	$110
Uranium enrichment, %	4.50%	4.95%
Price per separative work unit, US$/kg	$120	$120
Optimal tails assay, %	0.24%	0.24%
Feed assay, %	0.71%	0.71%
NU (natural U input to kgU output)	8.99	9.94
Value function (feed assay)	4.87	4.87
Value function (tails assay)	6.01	6.01
Value function (product assay)	2.78	2.66
SWU/kg	7.06	8.03
Fuel fabrication price, US$/kg	$300	$350
Burnup: GWd/MTU	50	40
Efficiency of MWth to MWe	33%	30%
Burnup × Efficiency × 24, MWh/kgU	**396**	**288**
Fuel cost/kg	**$2,366**	**$2,663**

Source: Values are from Rothwell *et al.* (2014: table 1).

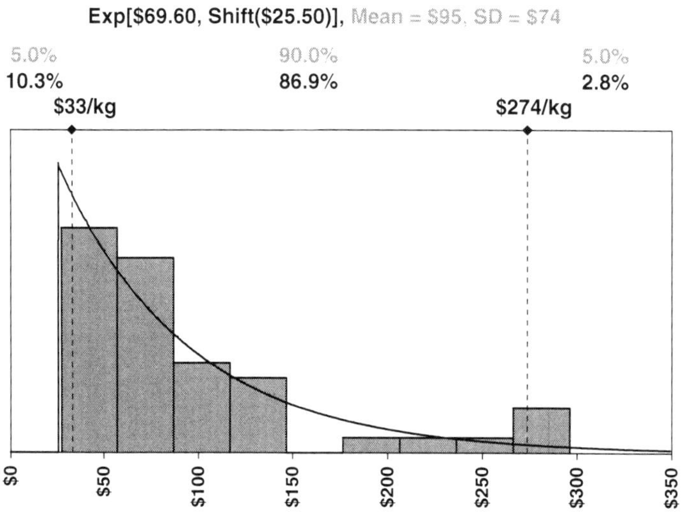

Figure 4.1 Natural uranium 2013 US$/kg U0308 prices, fitted to an exponential density.

Source: Annualised data presented in Chapter 1, Figure 1.6.

$25.50/kgU – that is, with such a distribution, the minimum simulated price per kilogram cannot be less than $25.50/kgU. On the other hand, there is a 2.8% probability that the price could be above $274/kgU. The mean in this distribution is $95/kgU. The mean uranium price has been about $100/kgU

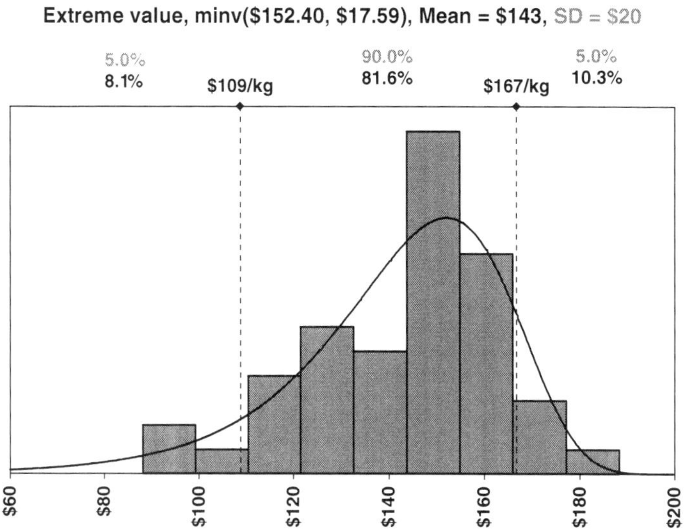

Figure 4.2 Separative work units 2013 US$/kg prices, fitted to an extreme value minimum density.

Source: Annualised data from Chapter 1, Figure 1.6.

(in 2013 US dollars) since the US government began buying it from private producers in 1948. Spikes in spot uranium prices were not as pronounced for long-term contract prices (IAEA and NEA, 2012: 114). Simulated values of the uranium price per kilogram are constrained to be in the range US$25.50–400/kgU.

In contrast, the SWU price has been stable (at least until the closure of the diffusion plants and the lifting of restrictions on Russian producers, allowing them to enter international markets). The SWU price can be modelled with an extreme (minimum) value distribution with a mean of $143 and a standard deviation of $20. However, as discussed in Chapter 1, the SWU price has declined recently and could decline further (Rothwell, 2009). Using this estimated extreme value distribution with a higher-than-expected SWU price could increase the simulated value of new nuclear's levelised cost, *biasing cost comparisons in favour of fossil fuels*. Simulated values of the SWU price per kilogram are constrained to be in the range US$30–300/kg, where $30/kg is approximately equal to the lowest estimated price in Rothwell (2009) – that is, for huge depreciated centrifuge facilities.

Table 4.1 specifies the baseline parameters for new nuclear fuel. The carrying charge times are fixed at $[lt_U, lt_S, lt_F] = [1.0, 0.5, 0.25]$, as much as a result of index sequencing as to accurately discount uranium fuel expenditures to the time of insertion into a reactor. Further, because of the historic stability and little impact on the price of LEU, the price to convert U_3O_8 to UF_6, P_C, is set to $10/kg, and P_{FAB}, the price to reconvert the UF_6 to UO_2 and to fabricate the UO_2 into LEU fuel, is set to \$300/kg in 2013 US dollars from the analysis in Rothwell (2010). The levelised deterministic cost of ALWR fuel is about \$6.60/MWh. In Table 4.4, the \$1/MWh for used fuel disposal and the \$0.53/MWh for ALWR interim storage (that is, \$208/kgU from Rothwell, 2015) are added to the levelised cost calculations. With fees, fuel costs with waste fees for ALWRs are about \$8/MWh. Using the fitted densities in Figures 4.1 and 4.2, and the information from Table 4.1, the cost of nuclear fuel can be simulated. Figure 4.3 presents such a simulation for ALWR fuel. Because of the skewness of the distribution resulting from the extreme values of uranium and SWU prices, the deterministic value of \$8/MWh is less than the mean of the simulation.

Next, consider the levelised fuel cost for SMRs. There are two primary differences between ALWR and SMR fuel (shown in Table 4.1):

1 SMR fuel is enriched to just below 5% (for example 4.95%), so the enrichment is slightly higher for SMRs than for ALWRs, requiring more SWUs; and
2 the burnup (B, in thermal gigawatt-days per tonne of uranium, or GWd/tU) is lower, for example 40 GWd/tU, compared to 50 GWd/tU, or higher, for ALWRs (Pannier and Skoda, 2014: 87) on mPower.

In addition, the efficiency, eff, in converting thermal gigawatts into electrical gigawatts is lower for SMRs, for example around 30%, compared to

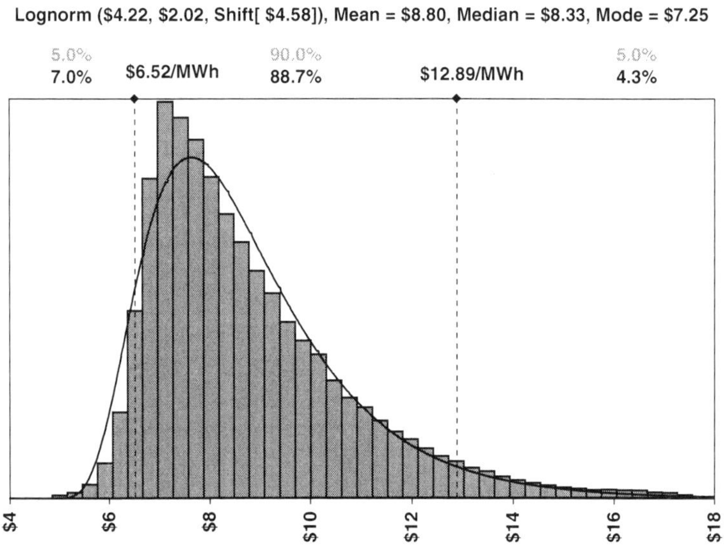

Figure 4.3 Simulated ALWR fuel cost in 2013 US\$/MWh, fitted to a lognormal density.

Source: Equations (4.2.1) and (4.2.2); Table 4.1; Figures 4.1 and 4.2.

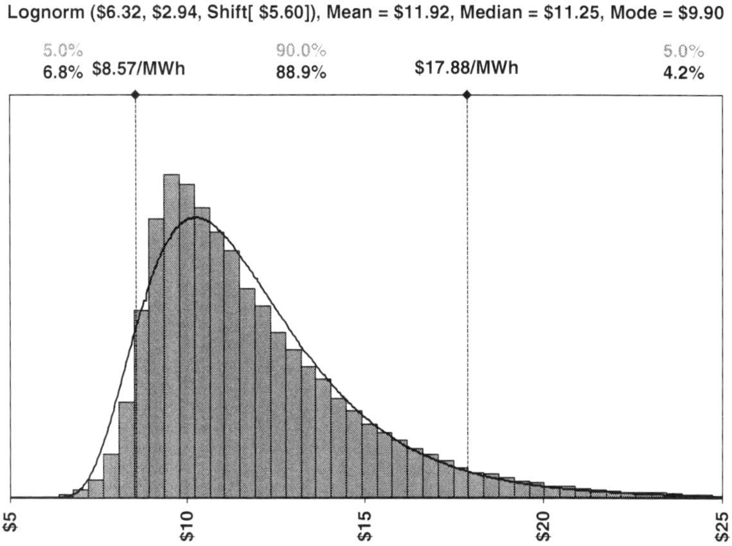

Figure 4.4 Simulated SMR fuel cost in 2013 US$/MWh, fitted to a lognormal density.

Source: Equations (4.2.1) and (4.2.2); Table 4.1; Figures 4.1 and 4.2.

around 33% for ALWRs (see Table 1.2). Therefore the SMR uses more uranium and SWU than ALWRs per MWh. In addition, the fuel fabrication cost is likely to be higher than ALWR fuel, because there are likely to be fewer licensed suppliers. If ALWR fuel fabrication is $300/kg, P_{FAB} for SMR fuel is likely to be at least $350/kg. These calculations assume that there are no scale economies in fuel fabrication or changes from FOAK to NOAK fuel costs. *With fees* (including $0.72/MWh for interim storage after removal from the reactor and disposal in a repository of $1/MWh), fuel costs for SMRs are about $12.00/MWh. With higher enrichment levels required in smaller reactors, and the lack of experience and potential competition in SMR fuel markets, smaller reactor fuel per kilogram of uranium will be more costly than larger reactor fuel.

Again, the cost of SMR fuel can be simulated. Figure 4.4 presents this simulation. The deterministic value of about $11.98/MWh (see Section 4.4, Table 4.5) is similar to the mean of $11.92/MWh in the simulated probability density.

4.3 Nuclear power plant operations and maintenance costs

Little is available in the public domain regarding the O&M costs of the currently operating light water reactors (LWRs) (Rothwell, 2006: 42; NEA, 2015a).

Unfortunately, the best data on NPP O&M costs are proprietary. These data are collected by EUCG (formerly known as the Electric Utility Cost Group) and are available on a 'give-to-get' basis among members. As Peltier (2009) explains:

> [C]omparable performance data were used to populate the EUCG's Nuclear Integrated Information Database (NIID) ... Today's NIID includes plant and unit performance and cost data, operating and outage cost data, capital cost investments, staffing information, and more. The database ... is the most comprehensive source of nuclear plant data in the world.

Without access to these data, the following model is proposed, wherein labour, *L*, and miscellaneous, *M*, costs are often grouped together in nuclear facility costs as O&M costs where:

$$O\&M = (P_L \times L) + M + PIN \tag{4.3.1}$$

Labour costs, $P_L \times L$, are the product of the number of plant employees and the average employee wages and benefits. Miscellaneous costs, *M*, include maintenance materials, supplies, operating fees, property taxes and insurance (not including a premium, *PIN*, for accidental off-site NPP damages, which is added separately).

To estimate appropriate values for Equation (4.3.1), first consider NPP employment under US Nuclear Regulatory Commission (NRC) regulation. The Idaho National Laboratory (INL) offers an example of 'nuclear plant employment impact regression analysis', in which:

> Using classical economic production models, we let
>
> $$L = a \times MW^b \tag{1}$$
>
> where
>
> *L* is the direct employment at the plant,
> *MW* is the plant capacity in megawatts, and
> *a* and *b* are coefficients to be estimated
>
> Taking logarithms of 0 [*sic*], we have
>
> $$\ln(L) = \ln(a) + [b \times \ln(MW)] \tag{2}$$
>
> which was used as the linear model for a linear regression fit with all direct employment and capacity data from the NEI studies [NEI, 2003, 2004a,

> 2004b, 2004c] and the Dominion constructability report [Dominion Energy *et al.*, 2004]. The regression fit is done using data from Table B–1 below ... a regression fit of 0 [*sic*] was performed to get a fit to the values for ln(*a*) and *b*, ... From two-variable linear model theory [Johnston, 1984: 38–41], this estimate actually is the mean of the logarithm of the direct employment level.
>
> (INL, 2004: B-2–B-4)

Table 4.2 presents the INL's data, with parameters converted from the Greek to *a* and *b*, and variable names changed to be compatible with the variable names used in Chapters 3 and 4 (see discussion of OLS in Chapter 3, Appendix 3A, Section 3A.4).

The INL's estimated equation is:

$$\ln(L) = -1.423 + [1.134 \times \ln(MW)],\ \mathrm{R}^2 = 0.86 \qquad (4.3.2)$$

where the standard error, defined in Chapter 3, Appendix 3A, Equation (3A.4.13), on the constant is 1.269, the standard error on the coefficient associated with [ln(MW)] is 0.174 and the standard error of the residual (or 'estimate') is 0.1887. (See Chapter 3, Appendix 3A, Equation (3A.4.14), for the definition of R^2.)

In fact, there are many 'classical' economic models. (The model discussed in INL, 2004: B-2–B-4, is not a 'production' model, given that the size of the plant does not produce the size of the labour force; this is a case in which the dependent and independent variables are simultaneously determined.) Using the log-log form implies that the minimum number of employees is less than 1 [exp(−1.423) = 0.24], for example one employee working almost two hours per day, as in Figure 4.5.

While the coefficient on *b* is significant, the significance on the coefficient *a* is non-existent. Further, because this OLS estimation mixes observations from operating plants with estimates for proposed nuclear technologies, the error terms cannot have the same variance – that is, they are 'hetroscedastic'; hence the standard errors in Equation (4.3.2) are biased. Therefore the OLS results in Equation (4.3.2) are not useful for estimating the minimum staffing level – that is, for SMRs – as is done in INL (2004).

While the log-log regression equation is inappropriate because the estimated regression line passes through the origin (or is not significantly different from 0), what other equations might be more appropriate? Johnston (1984: 64–74) discusses a half-dozen models, as follows (ignoring the observation subscripts on the variables).

Linear model

$$y_i = \alpha + \beta \times x_i + \varepsilon_i \qquad (4.3.3)$$

Table 4.2 Nuclear power plant direct labour and capacity

Plant name	*Source*	*MW*	*Labour*	*Equation (4.3.2) Labour*	*Equation (4.3.11) Labour*	*Equation (4.3.12) Labour*
Oyster Creek	NEI (2004b)	637	451	364	407	446
AP1000	Dominion (2004)	1,150	698	712	650	697
ESBWR	Dominion (2004)	1,340	700	847	773	822
ABWR	Dominion (2004)	1,371	701	869	795	845
ACR-700	Dominion (2004)	1,406	761	894	820	871
North Anna 1 & 2	Dominion (2004)	1,842	1,106	1,215	1,221	1,272
Millstone 1, 2 & 3	NEI 2003)	2,020	1,464	1,349	1,437	1,485
Indian Point 1 & 2	NEI (2004c)	1,978	1,683	1,317	1,383	1,432
Diablo Canyon 1 & 2	NEI (2004a)	2,200	1,707	1,486	1,693	1,737

Source: INL (2004: table B–1).

Log-log model

$$\ln(y_i) = \alpha + \beta \times \ln(x_i) + \varepsilon_i \quad (4.3.4)$$

Semi-log model

$$\ln(y_i) = \alpha + \beta \times x_i + \varepsilon_i \quad (4.3.5)$$

Reciprocal model

$$y_i = \alpha + \beta \times (1/x_i) + \varepsilon_i \quad (4.3.6)$$

Log-reciprocal model

$$\ln(y_i) = \alpha - \beta \times (1/x_i) + \varepsilon_i \quad (4.3.7)$$

Quadratic model

$$y_i = \alpha + \beta \times x_i + \gamma \times x_i^2 + \varepsilon_i \quad (4.3.8)$$

Equation (4.3.3) is the standard linear model, which is a good place to start and compare with plots of all of the dependent variables that might be related to any of the independent variables. For example, if the data appear to have a quadratic relationship (see Equation (4.3.8)), this can be seen by plotting the standard linear model, but the goodness-of-fit measures will all show that there is no (linear) relationship, leading to the mistaken conclusion that there is no relationship between the dependent and independent variables. The relationship could be non-linear.

Equation (4.3.4) is appropriate where the estimation of an elasticity is sought because b can be interpreted directly as an estimate of the elasticity, equal to [d ln (y_i)/d $\ln(x_i)$], the elasticity is the percentage change in the dependent variable divided by the percentage change in the independent variable. Equation (4.3.5) implies that the intercept is greater than 0 and there is a constant proportional rate of change in the dependent variable per unit change in the independent variable. Equation (4.3.6) is useful where there is a positive asymptote equal to a. Equation (4.3.7) implies that the regression line passes through the origin, but achieves an asymptote at $\exp\{a\}$. Finally, Equation (4.3.8) is similar to the quadratic welfare function in Chapter 3, Appendix 3A, Equation (3A.3.8).

A more appropriate functional form than the 'log-log' model should therefore be used, because the intercept is not at the origin, the 'semi-log' model better represents the data (as shown in Figure 4.5) and is more robust to the deletion of observations on *proposed* nuclear plants, including the advanced Canadian deuterium uranium (CANDU) reactor (ACR700):

$$\ln(L) = a + b\,(MW/1{,}000) \quad (4.3.9)$$

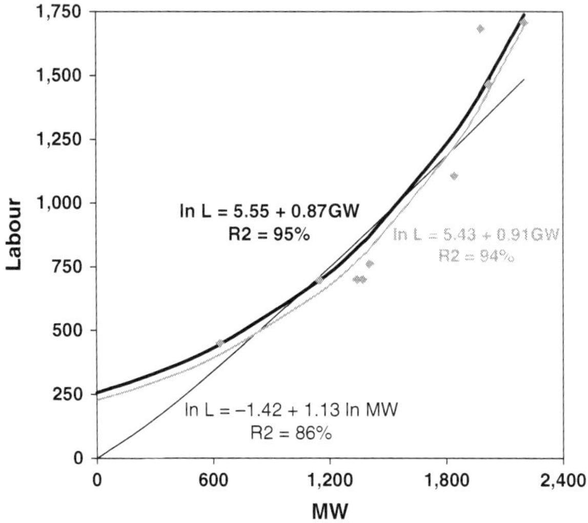

Figure 4.5 Labour at NPPs.

Source: Table 4.2; Equations (4.3.2), (4.3.11) and (4.3.12).

or

$$L = e^{a} \times e^{b \times GW} \tag{4.3.10}$$

Equation (4.3.9) can be estimated with the same data as used in Equation (4.3.2). The OLS estimates are:

$$\ln(L) = 5.427 + 0.913 \times GW,\ R^2 = 0.94 \tag{4.3.11}$$

where the standard error on the constant is 0.134, the standard error on the coefficient associated with *GW* is 0.083 and the standard error of the residual is 0.117 using all observations in Table 4.2, and:

$$\ln(L) = 5.547 + 0.870 \times GW,\ R^2 = 0.95 \tag{4.3.12}$$

where the standard error on the constant is 0.181, the standard error on the coefficient associated with *GW* is 0.099 and the standard error of the residual is 0.124 using only observations on operating plants in Table 4.2.

Table 4.3 presents the OLS calculation of the estimated parameters *a* and *b* in Equation (4.3.12). The standard error is reduced by about a third from that in Equation (4.3.2). In the semi-log form, the estimated constant, exp[*a*], is the

Table 4.3 Ordinary least squares calculation of Equation (4.3.12)

Y *LN L*	*X* *GW*	*[Y – E(Y)]*	*[X – E(X)]*	*[Y – E(Y)]* × *[X – E(X)]*	*[X – E(X)]* × *[X – E(X)]*
6.1115	0.6370	−0.9445	−1.0984	1.0374	1.2065
7.0085	1.8420	−0.0474	0.1066	−0.0051	0.0114
7.2889	2.0200	0.2330	0.2846	0.0663	0.0810
7.4283	1.9780	0.3724	0.2426	0.0903	0.0589
7.4425	2.2000	0.3865	0.4646	0.1796	0.2159
7.0559	**1.7354**		**Sums =**	0.2737	0.3147
= E(Y)	**= E(X)**			**b =**	**0.870**
a =	**E(Y) – [b × E(X)] =**		**7.0559 – (0.87 × 1.7354) =**		**5.547**

Source: Table 4.2; Chapter 3, Appendix 3A, Equations (3A.4.10) and (3A.4.11).

minimum number of employees (exp{5.547} = 257) from Equation (4.3.12), and the estimated slope, exp[*b*], is the growth rate in employees with each gigawatt increase in size (Johnston, 1984: 66). The Nuclear Energy Agency (NEA, 2015a) offers more labour data collected by the Nuclear Energy Institute (NEI). The estimated number of employees changes little with the addition of these observations.

Labour is calculated for *two* 1,117 MW ALWRs, $L = 2 \times 257 \times 2.643 =$ 1,356. Assuming that the burdened labour rate, including benefits, P_L, is $80,000 per employee per year, labour costs at twin ALWRs are:

$$P_L \times L_{\mathrm{ALWR}} = \$80,000 \times 1,356 = \$109\mathrm{m/year} \qquad (4.3.13)$$

Next, consider O&M expenses – that is, miscellaneous expenses, *M*, minus labour costs and *PIN*. Following the US Energy Information Administration (EIA) on O&M expenses:

> [A]pproximately 67 percent of the total reported O&M costs are labour related, and the remaining 33 percent are for expenditures on maintenance materials and supplies. It has been estimated that for a typical 1,000-megawatt plant, about 47 percent of the staff performs maintenance and support activities. Power plant operators comprise about 16 percent, and security workers about 17 percent of the total on-site staff. Most of the remaining 20 percent perform various administrative and managerial activities. Thus, the reported O&M costs consist mainly of labor expenses, with the largest single component representing maintenance activities.
>
> (US EIA, 1995: 3)

Following Equation (4.3.12), a 1,000 MW plant would employ about 612 people, of whom about 250 (or 41%) would represent security and administrative personnel, which is similar to the minimum staffing level in Equation (4.3.12). However, the US EIA (1995: 4) includes a caveat with its O&M data:

> After the accident at Three Mile Island [TMI], insurance costs became significant. Additionally, NRC regulatory fees . . . are not included in the O&M data. In total, it has been estimated that the reported O&M costs understate the actual costs by up to 30 percent.

Because no increase in labour requirements is suggested, non-labour expenses are increased by 30% to cover post-TMI insurance costs and regulatory fees. Therefore non-labour expenses are about 65% of labour expenses, rather than 50% = 66%/33%. Let this percentage mark-up be **om**; then:

$$M_{\mathrm{A}} = \mathbf{om} \times (P_L \times L_{\mathrm{ALWR}}) = 0.65 \times (\$109/\mathrm{year}) = \$71\mathrm{m/year} \tag{4.3.14}$$

where $(P_L \times L_{\mathrm{ALWR}})$ is given in Equation (4.3.13). Substituting M_{A} into Equation (4.3.1):

$$\begin{aligned} O\&M_{\mathrm{A}} - PIN_{\mathrm{A}} &= (P_L \times L_{\mathrm{ALWR}}) + M_{\mathrm{ALWR}} \\ &= \$109\mathrm{m} + \$71\mathrm{m} = \$180\mathrm{m/year} \end{aligned} \tag{4.3.15}$$

One can compare these estimates of the number of employees and O&M costs with those in NEA (2015a). Payments for damage insurance, *PIN*, set equal to \$1/MWh are added (Table 4.4):

$$PIN_{\mathrm{A}} = E_{\mathrm{A}} \times P_{\mathrm{IN\text{-}A}} \tag{4.3.16}$$

where

E_{A} is the expected electricity output from an ALWR (see Chapter 3, Equation (3.4.1)), and

$P_{\mathrm{IN\text{-}A}}$ is the insurance premium per MWh for potential losses from an ALWR accident.

Estimates of labour, *L*, and miscellaneous, *M*, costs for a SMR are similarly calculated. Labour is calculated for one (fully configured) 360 MW SMR, $L = 257 \times 1.480 = 351$. Equation (4.3.12) implies that the staffing level for a 360 MW SMR would be about 350. Although not linear, this implies a base of 250 employees, with about 50 extra employees for a 180 MW SMR. Assuming that the burdened labour rate, including benefits, P_L, is \$80,000 per employee per year:

$$P_L \times L_S = P_L \times e^{5.55} \times e^{0.87GW} = \$80,000 \times 351 = \$28m/year \tag{4.3.17}$$

Let the percentage mark-up, **om**, be 0.65, as in Equation (4.3.14); then M_{SMR} is about \$18m/year and:

$$O\&M_S - PIN_S = (1 + \mathbf{om}) \times (P_L \times L_S) = 1.65 \times \$28m = \$46m/year \tag{4.3.18}$$

Payments for off-site damage insurance, PIN_S, set equal to \$1/MWh, are added (see Tables 4.5 and 4.6), where premium payments per MWh for SMRs could be less than premium payments per MWh for ALWRs, but are assumed to be the same until SMRs are operating.

The expected value for the number of employees can be modelled with Equation (4.3.12), assuming a normal density for the error term with a mean of 0 and a standard deviation of 0.1243, the standard error of the estimate.

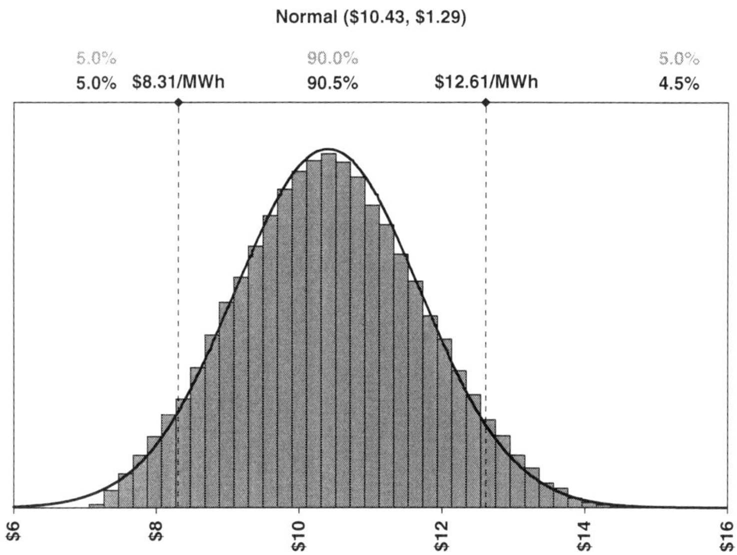

Figure 4.6 Simulated ALWR O&M cost in 2013 US\$/MWh, fitted to a normal density.

Source: Equations (4.3.13) and (4.3.14).

Note: **om** = [0.55, 0.75].

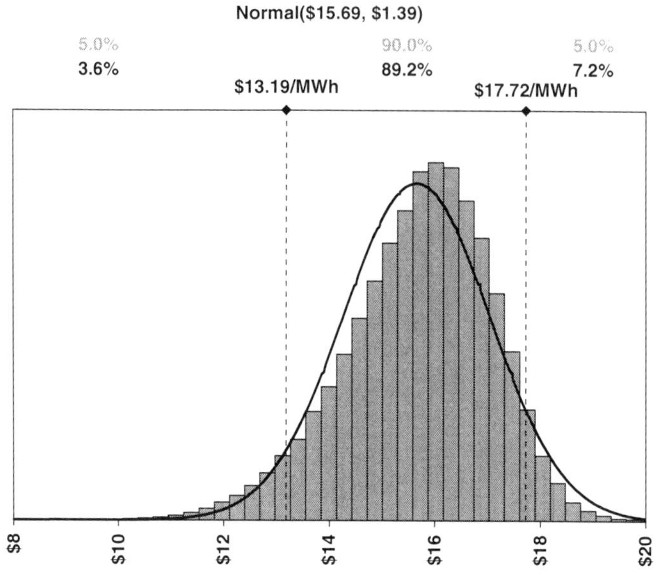

Figure 4.7 Simulated SMR O&M cost in 2013 US$/MWh, fitted to a normal density.

Source: Equations (4.3.17) and (4.3.18).

Note: **om** = [0.55, 0.75].

This standard deviation can be interpreted as approximately 12% because the logarithm of labour is the dependent variable. Most (95%) of the outcomes should be ±25% of the value calculated with Equation (4.3.12). Further, the mark-up on labour to calculate O&M is modelled with a uniform distribution with a maximum of 75% and a minimum of 55%, with a median value of 65%, as assumed in Table 4.4.

Figure 4.6 represents the product of the simulation of Equation (4.3.12), a normal distribution, and the simulation of the mark-up on labour, a uniform distribution for ALWR costs (compare with O&M costs in IEA and NEA, 2015: table 3.11). In simulation, 90.5% of the values were between $8.31/MWh and $12.61/MWh, fitted to a normal density with a mean of $10.43 and a standard deviation of $1.29. Similarly, Figure 4.7 represents an SMR O&M cost simulation in which 89.2% of the values were between $13.19/MWh and $17.72/MWh, with a fitted normal with a mean of $15.69 and a standard deviation of $1.39.

After discussing the deterministic estimates of *LC* for ALWRs and SMRs in the next section, the probability analysis will be extended to total levelised costs in Chapter 5.

4.4 Advanced light water reactor and small modular reactor levelised costs

Table 4.4 continues the levelised cost calculation in Chapter 3, Table 3.6, with a cost of capital of 7.5% and the assumptions from Chapter 3, Table 3.5. The levelised costs of an ALWR are estimated to be between \$67/MWh for a NOAK plant and \$81/MWh for a FOAK plant (including premiums per MWh for off-site accidental damage insurance, P_{IN}, included in Tables 4.4–4.6). Given the construction of four AP1000s in China, the AP1000s in the United States could produce power at a cost between \$67/MWh and \$74/MWh (FOAK–5) based on an overnight cost of \$4,400/kW. Therefore the ALWR appears to be competitive. (Compare with conclusions regarding LCOE in D'haeseleer, 2013: 113–114.)

Table 4.5 continues the levelised cost calculation in Chapter 3, Table 3.8, with a cost of capital of 7.5% and the assumptions in Chapter 3, Table 3.5. At a cost of capital of 7.5%, the levelised cost of a SMR is estimated to be \$87/MWh for a NOAK plant, and between \$100/MWh and \$111/MWh for the first eight SMR nuclear power plants (twin units) from one manufacturer. This also assumes that the manufacturer is able to reduce direct costs by 10% compared to an ALWR of the same size because of serial production.

Table 4.6 calculates the levelised cost calculation with a cost of capital of 5% and the assumptions in Chapter 3, Table 3.5. At a cost of capital of 5%, the levelised cost of a SMR is estimated to be \$70/MWh for a NOAK plant, and between \$80/MWh and \$88/MWh for the first eight SMR NPPs from one manufacturer. At a cost of capital of 7.5%, SMR levelised costs might not be competitive. However, at a cost of capital of 5%, SMR levelised costs are likely to be competitive (Rothwell and Ganda, 2014). This would support arguments for an extension of the US DOE loan guarantee programme (as discussed in Chapter 2) for SMRs (but cf. NEA, 2015b: 35).

Figure 4.8 presents estimates for ALWR and SMR levelised costs for weighted average costs of capital (WACC) of 3%, 5%, 7.5%, 10% and 12%. Focusing on NOAK costs, the SMR is competitive with the ALWR if SMRs are able to get financing at costs of capital 2.5–3% lower than the financing available to ALWRs. This could be the result of lower total construction cost compared to the present value of the nuclear investor, as portrayed in Chapter 3, Appendix 3A, Figure 3A.6. This difference in the cost of capital will depend on Wall Street's 'nuclear risk premium' on smaller reactors.

Further, to understand how the levelised cost changes with the cost of capital, consider the derivative of Equation (4.1.2), with respect to **r**:

$$\begin{aligned} \mathrm{d}LC/\mathrm{d}\mathbf{r} = \{&[\mathrm{d}\,\mathrm{k}(\mathbf{r}, \mathrm{T})/\mathrm{d}\mathbf{r} \times KC(OC, \mathbf{r}, LT)] \\ &+ [\mathrm{k}(\mathbf{r}, \mathrm{T}) \times \mathrm{d}KC(OC, \mathbf{r}, LT)/\mathrm{d}\mathbf{r}]\}/\mathrm{E} \qquad (4.4.1) \end{aligned}$$

Table 4.4 Levelised cost for ALWR generation

Levelised cost *All values in 2013US$*	*ALWR* *r =*	*FOAK-1* *7.50%*	*FOAK-5* *7.50%*	*NOAK* *7.50%*
Net electrical capacity	MWe	2,234	2,234	2,234
Size of power unit	MWe	1,117	1,117	1,117
Fuel cost	$/kg	2,366	2,366	2,366
Fuel cost per MWh	$/MWh	6.63	6.63	6.63
Interim storage	$/MWh	0.53	0.53	0.53
Long-term disposal	$/MWh	1	1	1
Number of employees	Number	1,517	1,404	1,354
Labour costs	$m	121	112	109
Miscellaneous costs	$m	80	74	71
Levelised capital cost + D&D cost	$/MWh	61.65	55.43	48.26
Levelised O&M costs with P_{IN}	$/MWh	11.45	10.60	10.23
Levelised fuel cost + Waste fees	$/MWh	8.16	8.16	8.16
LC, Levelised cost	$/MWh	81.26	74.19	66.65

Sources: Chapter 3, Table 3.6; Equations (4.3.12) and (4.3.15); Chapter 3, Appendix 3B; Rothwell (2010).

Note: Continued from Chapter 3, Table 3.6.

Table 4.5 Levelised cost for SMR generation

Levelised cost *All values in 2013US$*	*SMR* *r =*	*FOAK-1* *7.50%*	*FOAK-5* *7.50%*	*NOAK* *7.50%*
Net electrical capacity	MWe	360	360	360
Size of power unit	MWe	180	180	180
Fuel cost	$/kg	2,663	2,663	2,663
Fuel cost per MWh	$/MWh	10.26	10.26	10.26
Interim storage	$/MWh	0.72	0.72	0.72
Long-term disposal	$/MWh	1	1	1
Number of employees	Number	409	368	350
Labour costs	$m	32.698	29.413	28.012
Miscellaneous costs	$m	23.254	21.118	20.208
Levelised capital cost + D&D cost	$/MWh	79.58	70.54	57.84
Levelised O&M costs with P_{IN}	$/MWh	19.67	17.77	16.96
Levelised fuel cost + Waste fees	$/MWh	11.98	11.98	11.98
LC, Levelised cost	$/MWh	111.23	100.29	86.78

Sources: Chapter 3, Table 3.8; Equations (4.3.12) and (4.3.18); Chapter 3, Appendix 3B; Rothwell (2010).

Note: Continued from Chapter 3, Table 3.8.

Table 4.6 Levelised cost for SMR generation (with a cost of capital of 5%)

Levelised cost *All values in 2013US$*	*SMR* *r =*	*FOAK-1* *5%*	*FOAK-5* *5%*	*NOAK* *5%*
Net electrical capacity	MWe	360	360	360
Size of power unit	MWe	180	180	180
Fuel cost	$/kg	2,577	2,577	2,577
Fuel cost per MWh	$/MWh	9.93	9.93	9.93
Interim storage	$/MWh	0.72	0.72	0.72
Long-term disposal	$/MWh	1	1	1
Number of employees	Number	409	368	350
Labour costs	$m	32.698	29.413	28.012
Miscellaneous costs	$m	23.254	21.118	20.208
Levelised capital cost + D&D cost	$/MWh	56.91	50.45	41.36
Levelised O&M costs with P_{IN}	$/MWh	19.67	17.77	16.96
Levelised fuel cost + Waste fees	$/MWh	11.65	11.65	11.65
LC, Levelised cost	$/MWh	88.23	79.87	69.97

Sources: Chapter 3, Table 3.8; Equations (4.3.12) and (4.3.18); Chapter 3, Appendix 3B; Rothwell (2010).

noting that P_F, F_k, P_L, L_k and M_k in Equation (4.1.1), and implicitly in Equation (4.1.2), are not functions of **r**, hence do not appear in d LC/d **r**. (While $F(FC(\mathbf{r}))$ is a function of **r**, it varies so little compared to (d KC/d **r**) that its derivative can be ignored.)

Equation (4.4.1) can be approximated numerically by calculating LC for a range of **r** values (as in Figure 4.8) and regressing LC on **r**, using the following functional form, the *semi-log model*, as in Equation (4.3.5):

$$\ln(LC) = a + (b \times \mathbf{r}) \tag{4.4.2}$$

with OLS regression parameter estimates and estimated standard errors:

$$\ln(LC) = 3.498 + (8.693 \times \mathbf{r}),\ \mathrm{R}^2 = 0.99 \tag{4.4.3}$$

where the standard error on the constant is 0.025, the standard error on the coefficient associated with **r** is 0.217 and the standard error of the residual is 0.046. The derivative of LC with respect to **r** then becomes $(1/LC) \times (\mathrm{d}\,LC/\mathrm{d}\,\mathbf{r}) = 8.693$ at the mean – that is, b is equal to the proportional rate of change in LC for a unit percentage change in **r**, or with *each unit percentage increase in the cost of capital, the levelised cost increases by almost 9%.* A 3% increase in the WACC increases LC by about 26%.

Finally, to understand how the levelised cost changes with overnight costs, the cost of capital can be set at specific values and the overnight cost can be

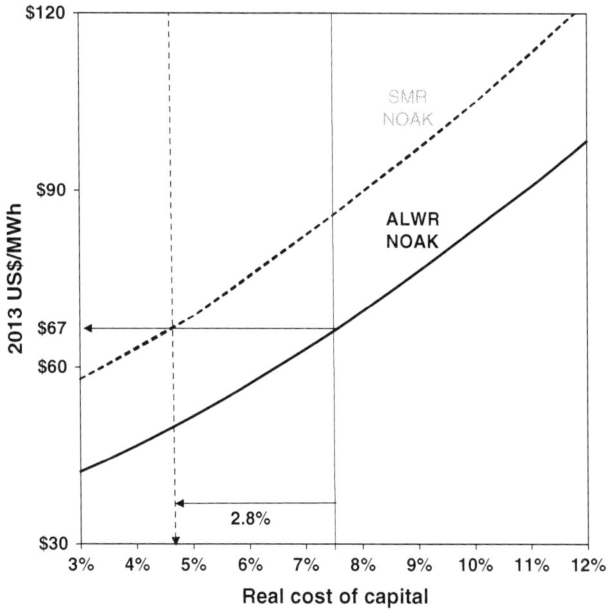

Figure 4.8 Advanced LWR and SMR levelised cost and the real cost of capital.

Source: Tables 4.4 and 4.6, with costs of capital of 3–12%.

varied to calculate different values of *LC*. The relationship between *LC* and *OC* (per MW) can be represented as:

$$LC = a + b \times (OC/\text{MW}) \tag{4.4.4}$$

This relationship can be estimated with data generated with the model by varying **r** holding *OC* constant (see Rothwell, 2011: 27–28). For example, setting (*OC*/1,000) to \$4/MW, the following estimation of Equation (4.4.4) explains 99% of the variance in the estimated levelised costs:

$$\begin{aligned} LC = &\{\exp[3.12 + (0.008/\mathbf{r}) - (1.174 \times \mathbf{r})]\} \\ &+ \{\exp[1.87 - (0.011/\mathbf{r}) + (10.27 \times \mathbf{r})]\} \times (OC/\text{MW}) \end{aligned} \tag{4.4.5}$$

For example, setting *OC* to \$4/MW (for simplicity, see the last column in Chapter 3, Table 3.6, for an overnight cost estimate of a NOAK ALWR and compare with the levelised cost of ALWRs at **r** = 10% (or 0.10) in Chapter 5, Figure 5.5):

$$\begin{aligned} \$87/\text{MWh} = &\exp\{3.12 + (0.008/0.1) - (1.174 \times 0.1)\} \\ &+ [\exp\{1.87 - (0.011/0.1) + (10.27 \times 0.1)\}] \times \$4 \end{aligned} \tag{4.4.6}$$

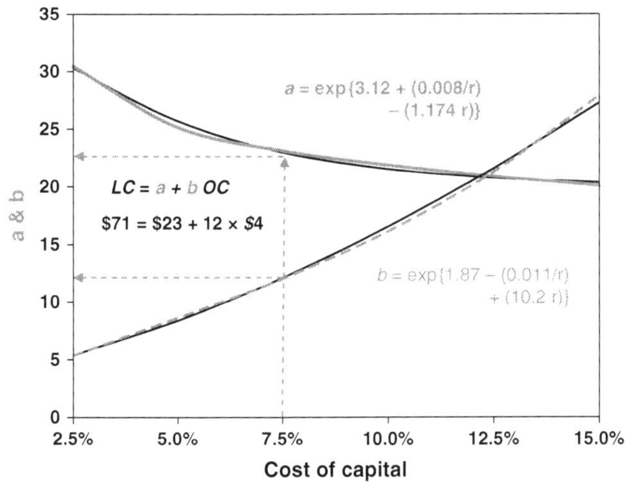

Figure 4.9 Advanced LWR levelised cost as a function of overnight cost and the cost of capital.

Source: Equation (4.4.6).

As shown in Figure 4.9, (a) as the cost of capital rises, *a* declines as a proportion of levelised cost (that is, that part of *LC* not associated with *OC*, such as fuel and O&M costs, represented by the black line declining from 30 to 20), and (b) *b* rises steeply with the cost of capital (and rises faster than *a* falls).

As quoted above, the US EIA (2013: appendix 3.C, 'Cost of capital') observes, 'small changes in the weighted average cost of capital lead to huge changes in capital intensive capacity additions'. If one wants to limit the viability of new nuclear, all one needs to do is enumerate nuclear power's uncertainties, implying large risk premiums and high costs of capital.

The next chapter compares nuclear power's uncertainties with those of carbon-based electricity-generating alternatives. It shows that nuclear power adds diversification to a portfolio of generating technologies, increasing its value to the electric utility, the investor and the public.

Appendix 4A: Expected cost of recycling used uranium oxide fuel

This appendix presents a cost model of LWR uranium oxide (UOX) reprocessing. It extends the cost model of low-enriched UOX fuel, LEU (discussed in Section 4.2) by developing a microeconomics model of LEU reprocessing using plutonium-uranium extraction (PUREX) technology. The extracted plutonium can be mixed with UOX and fabricated into fuel rods as a substitute for LEU fuel rods. (A cost comparison of these two alternatives can be found in Rothwell *et al.*, 2014, MIT, 2011, and NEA, 2013, compare the cost of these fuel cycles with ones that involve fast reactors.)

Note: This appendix is presented at the limit of what can be done with the type of cost modelling presented in this book. This is because information on the cost of reprocessing used nuclear fuel is proprietary (for example the cost of reprocessing at European and Japanese facilities), classified (for example the cost of reprocessing at retired US government facilities), or classified *and* not well documented (for example at Russian and Chinese facilities). Therefore the number of observations on relevant costs is minimal. Thus this appendix shows how microeconomic and cost-engineering logic can be applied to situations in which there is very little empirical information.

4A.1 Updating capital costs for UOX reprocessing facilities

Haire (2003) estimated nuclear fuel reprocessing costs for eight types of nuclear fuel – that is, light water enriched uranium; light water mixed oxide (MOX); light water thorium; heavy water MOX; heavy water thorium; fast breeder MOX; fast MOX with thorium; and fast with thorium:

> The objective of this work was to estimate the costs of reprocessing eight types of nuclear fuel. Costs are estimated for plants dedicated to the reprocessing of a single fuel type at an annual average throughput rate of 1,500 metric tons of heavy metal (MTHM/year). The constituents of capital and operating costs are given.
>
> (Haire, 2003: 3)

Haire's capital costs are based on estimates of nuclear fuel reprocessing costs from design studies with early 1980s health and safety standards. None of the plants were built and/or operated, for example the Allied-General Nuclear Services Plant in Barnwell, SC, was built, but never operated. Further, most of Haire's observations are from designs for commercial plants using PUREX technology with expected capacities of 1,500 MTHM per year. Haire is able to assess scale economies by incorporating cost estimates for prototype projects, thus mixing estimates at different stages of technology development and for different technologies. Spencer, Guillermo and Collins (2003) extend Haire (2003), as does the Idaho National Laboratory (INL, 2008), which summarises this literature thus:

> Haire recommended an optimal size for a reprocessing plant of ~2,500 MT/yr. Spencer, *et al.* extended Haire's work to include several additional plant designs, supporting the development of a scaling curve, showing the difference in plant cost versus design throughput. This curve is provided in Figure F1–6. While the bottom of the curve is a ~7,000 MT/yr, they noted very little unit cost difference between 2,000 and 10,000 MT/yr. A throughput of 7,000 MTHM/yr may require 4 to 7 solvent extraction lines. Data for capacities beyond 10,000 MT/yr are questionable or suggest

Table 4A.1 Reprocessing facility capital cost at a 3% cost of capital

Account	*Reprocessing facility size (1,500 MTHM)* *Account name*	*2013US$m*	*Haire %*
10 Subtotal	Capitalised pre-construction costs	0	
21	Structures & improvements (civil)	1,690	26
22	Nuclear-grade process equipment	975	15
23	Conventional process equipment	2,600	40
26	Miscellaneous plant equipment	1,235	19
20 Subtotal	Capitalised direct cost	6,500	100
30 Subtotal	Capitalised indirect costs	6,500	
BASE =	Base cost with no contingencies	13,000	
CN	Contingency (15$)	1,950	
OC	Total overnight cost	14,950	
IDC	Interest during construction	1,432	
***KC* =**	**Total capitalised cost**	**16,382**	

Source: Updated from Haire (2003).

> a capacity point where multiple plant locations become the only practical siting means, thus the unit cost increases.
>
> (INL, 2008: F1–8)

Based on this literature, reprocessing cost estimates can be made by adapting the Generation IV (Gen IV) Excel-based Cost Calculation of Nuclear Systems of the Economic Modelling Working Group (EMWG, 2008). Overnight construction cost for a new PUREX facility is estimated with information on two operating facilities in France (UP2–800 and UP–3) and one in the United Kingdom (THORP). The INL (2008: F–14, table F1–1) presents data (in 2005 US dollars) used in its statistical analysis. Those values (updated to 2013 US dollars) are US$8,300 million for UP–3 (completed in 1990 with an actual throughput of approximately 800 MTHM/year, or an equivalent of $10.4m/MTHM at this capacity), $6,880 million for THORP (completed in 1994 with an *actual* throughput of approximately 600 MTHM/year, or $11.4m/MTHM of capacity), and $9,800 million for UP2–800 (completed in 1994 with an actual throughput of approximately 900 MTHM per year, or $10.9m/MTHM of capacity).

The mean capital cost has been $11m/MTHM of capacity, with a standard deviation of $0.5m/MTHM. Here, the capacity cost of treating 1 tonne of used UOX per year is $11 million. *The capacity factor is already incorporated into these estimates and is not used in the levelised capital cost calculation.* A reprocessing facility with an annual *actual* throughput of 1,500 MTHM per year would cost approximately $16,400 million (2013 US dollars). Table 4A.1 shows interest during construction (IDC) calculated at a cost of capital of 3% over six years of construction. (Rothwell *et al.*, 2014, discuss the appropriate cost of capital.)

4A.2 Light water reactor UOX reprocessing operating and levelised cost

Table 4A.2 follows Haire's (2003) methodology to determine reprocessing facility operating costs: 'equipment replacement' (here, Account 77) is 'five percent of initial equipment cost per year' and 'equipment replacement' is

Table 4A.2 Reprocessing facility operating costs for 1,500 MTHM/year

Account	*Operations cost account name*	*2013US$m*	*Haire %*
71+72	On-site base staffing cost (71: Non-management; 72: Management)	575	23
74	Consumables including utilities	550	22
77	Capital replacements/upgrades (levelised) [using % above]	325	13
78a	Insurance premiums & taxes	350	14
78d	Other general & administrative (G&A)	700	28
O&M	**Total O&M annual cost**	**2,500**	**100**

Source: Updated from Haire (2003).

Note: Capital upgrades and replacements are 5% of direct capital costs in Haire (2003).

Table 4A.3 Reprocessing levelised cost at 3% cost of capital

Levelised cost	*Units*	*2013US$*
Facility capacity	MTHM/yr	1,500
Overnight cost	$m	14,950
Plant construction cost	$m	16,382
Discount rate for amortisation (life = 20)	%	3.00
Fixed charge rate for amortisation	%	6.72
Specific capital cost ($m/MTHM)	$m	10,921
IDC as % of overnight cost	%	9.58
Annual and levelised cost Cost components	**per year (US$m)**	**per unit (US$/kgHM)**
Capital	1,100	730
O&M (Production)	2,500	1,650
D&D fund	185	120
Total and RC ($/kgHM)	**3,785**	**2,500**

Sources: Adapted from Haire (2003).

equal to 13% of operating costs (Haire, 2003: table 4). Assuming that these are both referring to the same cost category, the total annual O&M operating budget for 1,500 MTHM would be about $2,500 million.

Table 4A.3 calculates the levelised cost, assuming that the cost of decommissioning is set to 33% of the total construction cost, with a sinking fund that accumulates annual contributions, and earns a real rate of return of 3%. (The cost of decommissioning is higher than for decommissioning an LWR because there are more structures and equipment to decontaminate, hence there would be more waste to manage, and because the decontamination and dismantlement would involve FOAK costs.) The levelised cost is $2,500 per kilogram of heavy metal (kgHM). (This is higher than estimates in the literature that usually rely on incumbent cost estimates, such as those of Areva at La Hague.) On the other hand, compare with Bunn *et al.*'s (2003: 29) estimate of the costs at Rokkasho for (a) a reprocessing plant, (b) a MOX fuel fabrication plant (Section 4A.3), and (c) a waste vitrification plant: 'Total costs including these other costs are expected to be dramatically higher still, at over $4100/kgHM—though it is not entirely clear which components of the reprocessing-recycling-waste disposal program are included in that huge total ... '

These levelised costs are higher than in Haire (2003), INL (2008), MIT (2011) and Spencer, Guillermo and Collins (2003) primarily because the actual capacity factors of reprocessing facilities have been lower than expected. However, these estimates might help to explain why the cost of Rokkasho (INL, 2008: F1–29) have increased dramatically from the original cost estimates. Experience at Rokkasho signals that the costs of reprocessing could be higher than previously anticipated (although Rokkasho's remote location and the technical problems with its vitrification system could be other factors in its high cost). The US General Accounting Office (US GAO, 2013) reviews the cost increases at Savannah River. (For an update, see ORNL, 2015.)

To determine the cost of using MOX, the next section estimates MOX fuel fabrication costs from data on operating facilities.

4A.3 Mixed oxide fuel fabrication cost

The fabrication of MOX fuel for LWRs is similar to the fabrication of LEU fuel for LWRs. According to the INL (2008: D1–24):

> The steps involved in the fabrication of MOX fuel are basically the same as those for LEU fuel assembly production except that most of the front and middle steps must be enclosed in glove boxes to protect the workers and public from exposure to radiotoxic plutonium compounds.

Table 4A.4 displays commercial MOX fabricators. The French group Areva now owns half of the world's MOX fuel fabrication capacity.

Table 4A.4 Annual MOX production capacity for LWR fuel

	Firms	*Location*	*Open*	*To close*	*Planned MTHM*	*Operating MTHM*	*Retired MTHM*	*Total MTHM*	*CF*
BE	Belgonuclearie	Dessel	1973	2006			35	35	88%
FR	COGEMA (Areva)-CFCa	Cadarache	1990	2003			30	30	88%
FR	MELOX (Areva)	Marcoule	1995	2027		195		195	88%
IN	Adv. FFF: Department of Atomic Energy	Tarapur	1993	?		50		50	77%
JP	Federation of Electric Power Companies	Rokkasho	?	?	130			130	77%
UK	BNFL (Sellafield MOX Plant, SMP)	Sellafield	2005	2016		120		120	45%
UK	BNFL (MOX Demonstration Plant)	Sellafield	1993	2000			8	8	45%
US	DOE/NNSA (SRS-MFFF)	Aiken, SC	?	?	70			70	59%
	Total capacity				**200**	**365**	**73**	**638**	

Sources: Based on IAEA (2002: 6), WISE (2014), and see Table 4A.5.

Table 4A.5 MOX fuel fabrication cost estimates (2002 US$)

Country	*Location*	*MTHM per year*	*Capacity factor*[a]	*CF* × *MT/yr*	*KC*	*Labour*	*Sources*
Belgium	Dessel	35	NA	NA	NA	250	(1)
Japan	Rokkasho	130	76.9%	100	$1,160	NA	(2)
UK	Sellafield	120	44.7%	54	$750	930	(3), (4)
US	Aiken, SC	70	58.9%	41	$550	NA	(3)

Sources: (1) Bergmans and van Steenberge (2006: A–31); (2) FEPC (2007); (3) construction cost from Bunn *et al.* (2003); (4) labour from DTZ Pieda Consulting (2005: 22).

Notes: [a]Capacity factors were determined by comparing stated cumulative output with nominal capacity or stated production goals over the life of the plant. The Rokkasho was expected to have a MOX fabrication capacity in the region of 100 MTHM/yr; Sellafield had contracts to produce 1,700 MOX assemblies over its lifetime, from 2005 to 2016; at 120 MTHM/yr, the potential lifetime capacity is 3,800 assemblies – ie a capacity factor of 447%; Savannah River is being built to dispose of 34MT of plutonium, implying a lifetime capacity factor of 59%.

There are three nuclear fuel fabrication cost components:

- total capital construction cost, KC_{MOX};
- labour, L_{MOX}; and
- hardware costs, HW_{MOX}.

(The cost of energy in MOX fuel fabrication is negligible.) The capital construction cost is modelled as a function of nominal capacity ($SIZE_{\mathrm{MOX}}$ measured in metric tonnes per year). The model is tested by comparing its estimated capital costs with the announced construction costs for MOX plants at Sellafield in the United Kingdom, Rokkasho in Japan and the Savannah River site in the United States.

Table 4A.5 gives limited data on international commercial MOX plants for which employee, capacity factor, or construction cost data are publicly available. Unlike LEU fuel fabrication facilities, most of the MOX plant owners are subject to some form of government scrutiny, for example the Savannah River site is under the supervision of the US government and the Sellafield MOX plant is under the supervision of the UK government.

The construction cost of a MOX fuel fabrication plant is based on data in Table 4A.5. Capital costs are assumed to be a function of the operating size, equal to the nominal capacity times the capacity factor. Capacity factors in Table 4A.5 were determined by examining reports of actual or anticipated throughput. Table 4A.5 presents estimated KC_{MOX} for three MOX plants:

1. the Japanese Rokkasho MOX fuel fabrication plant cost was estimated to be $1,160 million;
2. the British Nuclear Fuel Ltd (BNFL) Sellafield MOX (fuel fabrication) plant (SMP) at $750 million; and
3. the US Department of Energy (US DOE) plant at the Savannah River site (SRS) at $550 million.

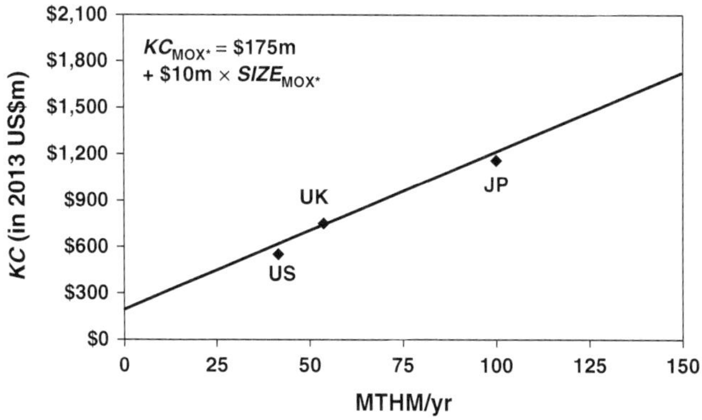

Figure 4A.1 KC_{MOX} as a function of tU/year, capacity factor adjusted.

Source: Equation (4A.3.1).

Note: MOX* is the expected capacity – that is, nominal (nameplate) adjusted by the expected capacity factor.

(Costs have increased substantially since 2002 and adjustments are made next.) Figure 4A.1 presents these data (for which capacity has been adjusted by the anticipated capacity factor).

To summarise the information in these data, an equation is proposed for KC_{MOX} and estimated with OLS with one degree of freedom (Figure 4A.1):

$$KC_{MOX*} \approx \$173m + (\$9.96m \times SIZE_{MOX*}) \qquad (4A.3.1)$$

where $SIZE_{MOX*}$ is adjusted by the anticipated operating capacity factor.

However, investment costs at Savannah River increased to at least $1,200 million (INL, 2008: D1–28). Without updated information on the cost of Rokkasho, it is not possible to determine appropriate updated values for *both* parameters in Equation (4A.3.1). (The cost estimate has not changed since Rokkasho was announced, although the dollar-to-yen rate has changed.) Therefore, assume that (a) the constant in Equation (4A.3.1) has doubled to $350 million (fixed costs, including the cost of licensing a MOX plant), and (b) *plant size is not adjusted by the capacity factor* (because $1,200 million is not adjusted for the anticipated capacity factor). Solving so that the KC_{MOX} of Savannah River is $1,200 million:

$$KC_{MOX} \approx \$350m + (\$12.14m \times SIZE_{MOX}) \qquad (4A.3.2)$$

as shown in Figure 4A.2. If Equation (4A.3.2) holds generally, then the Rokkasho MOX fuel fabrication plant could cost almost $2,000 million (about ¥200,000 million in 2013 yen).

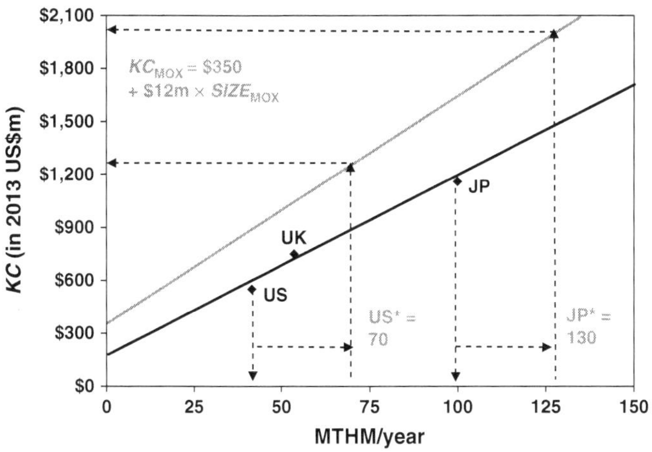

Figure 4A.2 KC_{MOX} as a function of MTHM/year, updated.

Source: Equation (4A.3.2).

The next step is to determine hardware and labour costs per kilogram of fuel. Hardware costs for LEU from Rothwell (2010) and MOX fuel are assumed equal. Labour costs are estimated from publicly available data on staff sizes at MOX plants, and average annual incomes and benefits are set equal to $80,000. (While cost data at these plants is not publicly available, there are other sources for the number of employees, including regulatory reports and local newspaper articles.) Table 4A.5 presents the location of the plant, its annual capacity in tU, the number of employees and the source of the employee data. Figure 4A.3 is a plot of these data – represented by dashes (–), accompanied by the International Atomic Energy Agency (IAEA) country abbreviation – which compares MOX fuel fabrication plant employees with LEU fuel fabrication employees from Rothwell (2010).

There are only two observations on the number of employees (L_{MOX}) and capacity ($SIZE_{MOX}$):

1 250 employees at the Belgium Dessel plant of 35 MTHM/year (Bergmans and van Steenberge, 2006: A–31, which is the same source for the number of employees at the LEU fuel fabrication facility in Belgium); and
2 approximately 930 employees at the Sellafield plant of 120 MTHM/year in the United Kingdom.

The nominal labour-to-capacity ratio at the two plants is similar – that is, (250/35 = 7.1) and (930/120 = 7.8). While a statistical test cannot be performed with two observations, it is difficult to reject constant returns to

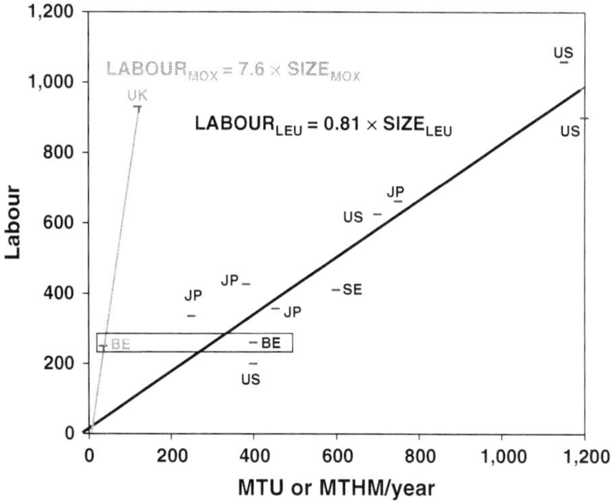

Figure 4A.3 Number of fuel fabrication employees as a function of size in output/year.

Sources: Table 4A.5; Belgian (BE) data from Bergmans and van Steenberge (2006: A–31); LEU fuel fabrication data from Rothwell (2010).

scale in labour. Therefore labour requirements at MOX fuel fabrication facilities should be reasonably well approximated as:

$$L_{\text{MOX}} \approx [(250 + 930)/(35 + 120)] \times SIZE_{\text{MOX}}$$
$$= 7.6 \times SIZE_{\text{MOX}} \qquad (4A.3.3)$$

The coefficient on $SIZE_{\text{MOX}}$ is *almost an order of magnitude larger* for MOX plants than for LEU plants. (At the two Belgian facilities, the LEU plant has a capital-to-labour ratio of 1.5 tU/employee and the MOX plant has a ratio of 0.14 MTHM/employee.) Assuming the same wage rate, labour costs are much higher for MOX fuel fabrication facilities than for LEU facilities. This is likely to be the result of increases in the costs of maintaining specialised equipment (such as glove boxes), and hiring health and safety technicians, maintenance technicians and security personnel.

Two other types of variable cost for MOX fuel fabrication must be identified and estimated. One set of variable costs depends on the level of output at the plant; another set is related to the total capital investment cost, KC_{MOX}. Following Judkins and Olsen (1979), these costs include:

1.1 general and administrative expenses, equal to \$10/kgHM in 2013 US dollars;
1.2 direct and indirect materials and supplies, updated to \$7/kgHM in 2013 US dollars;

Table 4A.6 Annual fixed and variable costs for MOX fuel fabrication

Plant capacity	*MTU/yr*	*35*	*70*	*100*	*120*	*200*
New entrant's *KC*	\$m	775	1,200	1,564	1,807	2,778
Incumbent's *KC**	\$m	280	560	800	960	1,600
Annual fixed expenses in 2013US\$						
Annual capital charge	\$m	98.59	152.64	198.98	229.87	353.43
Incumbent's capital charge	\$m	35.62	71.25	101.78	122.14	203.56
D&D cost in 2005US\$	\$m	258	400	521	602	926
Incumbent D&D cost	\$m	93	187	267	320	533
Annual D&D charge	\$m	11.97	18.53	24.16	27.91	42.91
Incumbent D&D charge	\$m	4.33	8.65	12.36	14.83	24.72
Annual variable expenses in 2013US\$						
PWR hardware (H)	\$m	0.79	1.58	2.25	2.70	4.50
BWR hardware (H)	\$m	2.54	5.08	7.25	8.70	14.50
Staff size – Labour (*L*)	Labour	266	532	760	912	1520
Annual labour bill	\$m	21.28	42.56	60.80	72.96	121.60
Supplies and G&A	\$m	0.61	1.21	1.73	2.07	3.46
Property taxes and insurance	\$m	23.25	35.99	46.92	54.20	83.34
Equipment replacement	\$m	7.75	12.00	15.64	18.07	27.78

Sources: Table 4A.5, calculated with cost model in Rothwell (2010).

Note: KC*, the incumbent's construction cost, is the cost of adding capacity – i.e. these costs do not include the costs of design, licensing and testing.

2.1 property taxes and property insurance, equal to 3% of the KC_{MOX} per year; and

2.2 an equipment replacement charge, equal to 1% of the KC_{MOX} per year.

Because taxes, insurance and equipment replacement are proportional to *KC*, these are added to the capital cost per kilogram of uranium or heavy metal. Variable costs (1.1) and (1.2) are scaled from the ratio of KC_{LEU} to KC_{MOX} from Rothwell (2010). In addition, calculations in Tables 4A.6 and 4A.7 are made with the following assumptions:

1 the capacity factor is set at 100% (because the operating capacity factor has already been incorporated into the size of the facility);
2 KC_{MOX} ('Investment') follows Equation (4A.3.2);
3 for comparability with Judkins and Olsen (1979), a cost of capital of 3% real is used to calculate costs in Table 4A.6;
4 the number of employees ('Staff size') follows Equation (4A.3.3);
5 capacities are set at 35, 70, 100, 120 and 200 MTHM per year; and
6 incumbent capital costs follow Equation (4A.3.2), with the constant set equal to 0 – that is, design, licensing and testing costs are assumed to have been amortised.

Hence new capacity additions are much less expensive than new entrant capacity.

Table 4A.7 Levelised costs for new entrant and incumbent MOX fuel fabrication

Levelised (average) cost, LAC	*MTU/yr*	*35*	*70*	*100*	*120*	*200*
Capital cost	$/kg	2,817	2,181	1,990	1,916	1,767
Labour cost	$/kg	608	608	608	608	608
Other operating costs	$/kg	903	703	643	620	573
Materials (BWR hardware)	$/kg	73	73	73	73	73
Materials (PWR hardware)	$/kg	23	23	23	23	23
D&D/kg	$/kg	342	265	242	233	215
Incumbent capital + D&D cost	$/kg	1,141	1,141	1,141	1,141	1,141
Entrant's LWR LAC (w/o hardware)	$/kg	4,670	3,756	3,482	3,376	3,163
Entrant's PWR LAC (w/hardware)	$/kg	4,692	3,779	3,505	3,398	3,185
Entrant's BWR LAC (w/hardware)	$/kg	4,742	3,829	3,555	3,448	3,235
Incumbent LWR LAC (w/o hardware)	$/kg	2,652	2,452	2,392	2,369	2,322
Incumbent PWR LAC (w/hardware)	$/kg	2,675	2,475	2,415	2,391	2,345
Incumbent BWR LAC (w/hardware)	$/kg	2,725	2,525	2,465	2,441	2,395

Source: Table 4A.6.

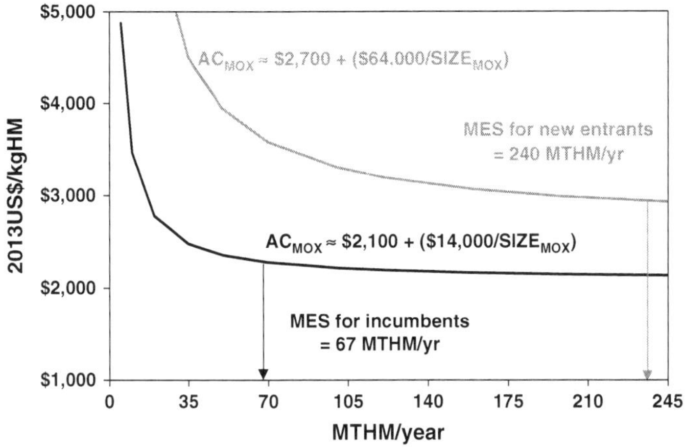

Figure 4A.4 Cost of MOX nuclear fuel fabrication for new entrants and incumbents.

Source: Table 4A.7.

Figure 4A.4 presents the entrant and incumbent's postulated average cost curves based on information in Tables 4A.6 and 4A.7. New entrants face high entry costs and increasing returns to scale, with a minimum efficient scale (MES) of (64,000/[10% × 2,670]) = 240 MTHM/year – that is, larger than any existing or planned facility. The MES for incumbents (14,000/[10% × 2,080]) = 67 MTHM/year – that is, about the same size as the Savannah River site. It is the costs of designing, licensing and testing that increase the MES of new MOX plants. Simultaneously, increasing these costs also increases commercial entry barriers, thus increasing non-proliferation protection – that is, if this process is not commercial, then it is being done for non-commercial reasons.

4A.4 Expected 'twice through' costs

Based on Rothwell *et al.* (2014), there appear to be four key cost drivers in considering the competitiveness of MOX with LEU: (a) the price of uranium; (b) the price of UOX reprocessing; (c) the price of MOX fuel fabrication (usually built with reprocessing facilities); and (d) the cost of spent MOX geologic disposal.

The relationship between $P_U{}^*$ (the breakeven price of uranium) and RC (the levelised cost of used UOX reprocessing, such that MOX fuel is competitive with once-through LEU) can be expressed as:

$$P_U{}^* = (0.244 \times RC) - \$57 \tag{4A.4.1}$$

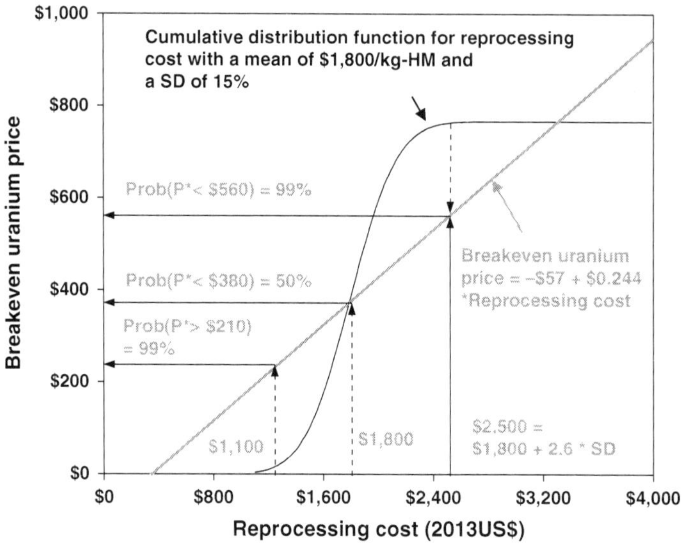

Figure 4A.5 Breakeven price of reprocessing as a function of the price of uranium.

Source: Updated from Rothwell and Wood (2011).

where the cost of reprocessing, *RC*, is uncertain, with a mean of $\underline{RC}$ and a standard deviation of σ_{RC}.

A cost estimate with a contingency of 15% can be shown to be equivalent to an expected cost with a standard deviation of 15%, or $270/kgHM (from Chapter 3, Appendix 3A, Section 3A.1). Assuming that this distribution is normal, 97% of the time, the realised *RC* should be between $1,260/kgHM and $2,340/kgHM, and 99% of the time, *RC* should be between $1,100/kgHM and $2,500/kgHM.

The cumulative probability distribution is plotted in Figure 4A.5, such that, 50% of the time, *RC* will be below $1,800/kgHM. At a reprocessing cost of $1,800/kgHM, the breakeven uranium price is $380/kgU, which is similar to the estimate of $360/kgU in Bunn *et al.* (2003), in which the reprocessing cost was estimated to be $1,000/kgHM. Here, there is a 99% probability that uranium prices would need to be between $210/kgU and $560/kgU for MOX to compete with UOX.

The probability that uranium prices will be this high is not 0, but *RC*, the cost of reprocessing, could be higher than $1,800/kgHM. For example, if the cost of reprocessing were as high as $2,500/kgHM, which is 2.6 standard deviations above the expected value of $1,800/kgHM, the breakeven uranium price would be as high as $560/kgU. Recent estimates put a limit price of '$1,230/kgU with a 95% confidence interval of [$1030/kgU, $1430/kgU]' as a function of the cost of uranium recovery from seawater (Schneider, Sachde and Lindner, 2012; Linder and Schneider, 2015).

Regarding used nuclear fuel management policy in the United States, this appendix supports the recommendations of the Blue Ribbon Commission on America's Nuclear Future (BRC, 2012): focus nuclear fuel cycle research and development (R&D) funds on reducing the cost and cost uncertainty of LWR used fuel reprocessing (because reprocessing is so expensive), and pursue this option while planning a repository (because there is time to do so and the US government is obligated to do so – that is, to build a geologic repository).

References

Bergmans, A., and Van Steenberge, A. 2006. *CARL Country Report – Belgium: Appendices*. Available online at http://uahost.uantwerpen.be/carlresearch/docs/20060313114231GGUR.pdf

Berndt, E., and Woods, D. 1975. 'Technology, prices, and the derived demand for energy', *Review of Economics and Statistics*, 57(3): 376–384.

Blue Ribbon Commission on America's Nuclear Future, The (BRC). 2012. *Report to the Secretary of Energy*. Available online at www.energy.gov/sites/prod/files/2013/04/f0/brc_finalreport_jan2012.pdf

Bunn, M., Fetter, S., Holdren, J., and van der Zwaan, B. 2003. *The Economics of Reprocessing vs. Direct Disposal of Spent Nuclear Fuel*. Available online at http://belfercenter.ksg.harvard.edu/publication/2089/economics_of_reprocessing_vs_direct_disposal_of_spent_nuclear_fuel.html

D'haeseleer, W. 2013. *Synthesis on the Economics of Nuclear Energy, Final Report*. Available online at www.mech.kuleuven.be/en/tme/research/energy_environment/Pdf/ wpen2013-14.pdf

Dominion Energy, Inc., Bechtel Power Corporation, TLG, Inc., and MPR Associates. 2004. *Study of Construction Technologies and Schedules, O&M Staffing and Cost, Decommissioning Costs and Funding Requirements for Advanced Reactor Designs, Volume 1, under Contract DE-AT01–020NE23476*, 27 May. Available online at http://pbadupws.nrc.gov/docs/ML1018/ML101820632.pdf

DTZ Pieda Consulting. 2005. *Furness and West Cumbria Housing Market Renewal Prospectus, Technical Appendices*. Available online at www.barrowbc.gov.uk/EasySiteWeb/GatewayLink.aspx?alId=2066

Economic Modelling Working Group of the Gen IV International Forum (EMWG). 2008. *Generation IV Excel-based Cost Calculation of Nuclear Systems*, v. 2. Available online at www.gen-4.org/gif/jcms/c_42161/g4econs

Federation of Electric Power Companies (FEPC). 2007. 'A domestic fuel cycle contributes to energy security', Press release, 11 September. Available online at www.fepc.or.jp/english/library/electricity_eview_japan/__icsFiles/afieldfile/2008/09/11/2007l.pdf

Haire, M. 2003. *Nuclear Fuel Reprocessing Costs*. Available online at http://csmb.ornl.gov/~webworks/cppr/y2001/pres/116757.pdf

International Atomic Energy Agency (IAEA). 2002. *Environmental Aspects Based on Operational Performance of Nuclear Fuel Fabrication Facilities*, IAEA-TECDOC–1306. Available online at www-pub.iaea.org/MTCD/publications/PDF/te_1306_web.pdf

International Atomic Energy Agency (IAEA) and Nuclear Energy Agency (NEA). 2012. *Uranium 2011: Resources, Production and Demand (Red Book)*. Available online at www.oecd-nea.org/ndd/pubs/2012/7059-uranium-2011.pdf

International Energy Agency (IEA) and Nuclear Energy Agency (NEA). 2010. *Projected Costs of Generating Electricity: 2010 Edition*. Available online at www.iea.org/publications/freepublications/publication/projected_costs.pdf

International Energy Agency (IEA) and Nuclear Energy Agency (NEA). 2015. *Projected Costs of Generating Electricity: 2015 Update*. Paris: OECD. Available online at www.oecd-nea.org/ndd/egc/2015/

Idaho National Laboratory (INL). 2004. *U.S. Job Creation Due to Nuclear Power Resurgence in the United States*, INL/EXT–04–02384. Available online at www5vip.inl.gov/technicalpublications/Documents/3772069.pdf

Idaho National Laboratory (INL). 2008. *Advanced Fuel Cycle Cost Basis*, INL/EXT–07–12107. Available online at www5vip.inl.gov/technicalpublications/Documents/3915965.pdf

Johnson, N., Kotz, S., and Balakrishnan, N. 1994. *Continuous Univariate Distributions*. New York: John Wiley & Sons.

Johnston, J. 1984. *Econometric Methods*. New York: McGraw-Hill.

Judkins, R., and Olsen, A. 1979. *Estimation of Costs for Fabrication of Pressurized-Water Reactor Fuel*, ORNL/TM–6501. Available online at https://inis.iaea.org/search/search.aspx?orig_q=RN:10452758

Lévêque, F. 2015. *The Economics and Uncertainties of Nuclear Power*. Cambridge: Cambridge University Press.

Linder, H., and Schneider, S. 2015. 'Review of the cost estimates for uranium recovery from seawater', *Energy Economics*, 49: 9–22.

Massachusetts Institute of Technology (MIT). 2011. *The Future of the Nuclear Fuel Cycle: An Interdisciplinary Study*. Available online at https://mitei.mit.edu/system/files/The_Nuclear_Fuel_Cycle-all.pdf

Nuclear Energy Agency (NEA). 2013. *The Economics of the Back End of the Nuclear Fuel Cycle*. Paris: OECD. Available online at www.oecd-nea.org/ndd/pubs/2013/7061-ebenfc.pdf

Nuclear Energy Agency (NEA). 2015a. *Guidance Document for Measuring Employment in Electricity Generation: Methodology and Implementation in the Nuclear Power Sector*. Paris: OECD.

Nuclear Energy Agency (NEA). 2015b. *Nuclear New Build: Insights into Financing and Project Management*. Paris: OECD. Available online at www.oecd-nea.org/ndd/pubs/2015/7195-nn-build-2015.pdf

Nuclear Energy Institute (NEI). 2003. *Economic Benefits of Millstone Power Station: An Economic Impact Study by the Nuclear Energy Institute*. Available online at www.nei.org/corporatesite/media/filefolder/economic_benefits_millstone.pdf

Nuclear Energy Institute (NEI). 2004a. *Economic Benefits of Diablo Canyon Power Plant: An Economic Impact Study*. Available online at www.pge.com/includes/docs/pdfs/shared/edusafety/systemworks/dcpp/PGE_Economic_Impact_Report_Final.pdf

Nuclear Energy Institute (NEI). 2004b. *Economic Benefits of Oyster Creek*. Washington, DC: NEI.

Nuclear Energy Institute (NEI). 2004c. *Economic Benefits of Indian Point Energy Center: An Economic Impact Study by the Nuclear Energy Institute*. Available online at http://large.stanford.edu/courses/2013/ph241/perret1/docs/economic_benefits_indian_point.pdf

Oak Ridge National Laboratory (ORNL). 2015. *Final Report of the Plutonium Disposition Red Team*. Oak Ridge, TN: ORNL.

Pannier, C., and Skoda, R. 2014. 'Comparison of small modular reactor and large nuclear reactor fuel cost', *Energy and Power Engineering*, 6: 82–94.

Peltier, R. 2009. 'Benchmarking nuclear power plant operating costs', *POWER*, 1 November.

Rothwell, G. 2006. 'A real options approach to evaluating new nuclear power plants', *The Energy Journal*, 27(1): 37–54.

Rothwell, G. 2009. 'Market power in uranium enrichment', *Science & Global Security*, 17(2–3): 132–154.

Rothwell, G. 2010. 'International nuclear fuel fabrication supply: Are fabrication services assured?' *Energy Economics*, 32(3): 538–544.

Rothwell, G. 2011. *The Economics of Future Nuclear Power: Update of the University of Chicago's The Economic Future of Nuclear Power*. Energy Policy Institute at Chicago, Harris School of Public Policy, University of Chicago, Chicago, IL. (It has been deleted from the Harris School website, but is discussed online at http://csis.org/event/small-modular-reactors-key-future-nuclear-power-generation-us)

Rothwell, G. 2015. 'Scale economies in a series of generic interim SNF storage facilities', Paper presented at International Congress on Advances in Nuclear Power Plants, Nice, 3–6 May.

Rothwell, G., and Ganda, F. 2014. 'Electricity generating portfolios with small modular reactors', Working Paper. Available online at www.energy.gov/sites/prod/files/2014/06/f16/Electricity%20Generating%20Portfolios%20with%20SMRs.pdf

Rothwell, G., and Wood, T. 2011. 'The option value of spent nuclear fuel retrievability', IAEA Working Paper.

Rothwell, G., Wood, T., Daly, D., and Weimer, M. 2014. 'Sustainability of light water reactor fuel cycles', *Energy Policy*, 72(S1): S16–S23.

Schneider, E., Sachde, D., and Lindner, H. 2012. 'Life cycle cost and energy balance of uranium recovered by a braid adsorbent system', Paper presented at the American Chemical Society's 244th National Meeting, 21 August, Philadelphia, PA.

Spencer, B., Guillermo, D., and Collins, E. 2003. *Effect of Scale on Capital Costs of Nuclear Fuel Reprocessing*. Available online at http://web.ornl.gov/~webworks/cppr/y2001/pres/117445.pdf

US Energy Information Administration (US EIA). 1995. *An Analysis of Nuclear Plant Operating Costs: A 1995 Update*, SR/OIAF/95–01. Washington, DC: US DOE.

US Energy Information Administration (US EIA). 2013. *The Electricity Market Module of the National Energy Modeling System: Model Documentation Report*, Doc. No. DOE-EIA-M068(2013). Available online at www.eia.gov/forecasts/aeo/nems/documentation/electricity/pdf/m068(2013).pdf

US General Accounting Office (US GAO). 2013. *Department of Energy: Concerns with Major Construction Projects at the Office of Environmental Management and NNSA*, GAO 13–484T. Available online at www.gao.gov/products/GAO-13-484T

World Information Service on Energy (WISE). 2014. 'Mixed oxide (MOX) fuel fabrication', *WISE Uranium Project*. Available online at www.wise-uranium.org/efac.html#FUELFABLWMOX

5 Levelised cost and cost risk for portfolios of generating assets

5.1 Levelised costs for electricity-generating alternatives

This chapter generalises the levelised cost calculations in Chapters 3 and 4 by providing a methodology for:

1 calculating the levelised cost of generating electricity with combined-cycle gas turbines (CCGTs), burning natural gas, and coal-fired power plants with sulphur scrubbers;
2 simulating probability distributions of levelised cost for nuclear power plants (NPPs) and for fossil-fired plants; and
3 simulating the levelised costs and standard deviations of portfolios composed of new nuclear and fossil-fired plants.

This is done with Equation (5.1.1), combining Chapter 3, Equations (3.1.1) and (3.4.1), with Chapter 4, Equation (4.1.2):

$$
\begin{aligned}
LC_{kt} = &\{[\mathrm{CRF}(\mathbf{r}) \times KC(OC_k, \mathbf{r}, lt_k)] \\
&+ F_k(P_{kt}) + O\&M_k\}/\{\mathrm{MW}_k \times \mathrm{TT} \times CF_k\}
\end{aligned}
\tag{5.1.1}
$$

where

k is advanced light water reactor (ALWR), CCGT, or 'scrubbed coal new' (COAL) technology, and
t is the period of the levelised cost estimate.

(Small modular reactors, or SMRs, will not be considered in this chapter because their cost has been modelled as a function of the cost of the ALWR; hence their cost probability distributions are not independent. For an analysis of SMRs similar to that in this chapter, see Rothwell and Ganda, 2014.) A majority of the cost information for generating electricity with CCGT and

COAL comes from the US Energy Information Administration (US EIA) *Annual Energy Outlook* (AEO) assumptions for the National Energy Modelling System (NEMS) (US EIA, 2013). (Using these data ensures compatibility with US Department of Energy, or US DOE, studies that are required to use NEMS for their forecasts.)

However, the NEMS assumptions do not include fuel prices. Therefore any forecasting model based on NEMS data without access to the NEMS model itself (maintained by a US EIA contractor) must also forecast fuel prices. This forecasting is done here with information from Chapter 4 and the US EIA's State Energy Data System (SEDS) (US EIA, 2014c). With these data, probability densities are estimated to represent uncertain fuel prices in levelised cost calculations.

Throughout this chapter, energy price data are derived from prices in the state of Texas. This is because Texas is a self-contained electricity market, formerly known as the Electricity Reliability Council of Texas (ERCOT) and now known as the Texas Reliability Entity (TRE). The TRE is the largest electricity market in the United States and is almost as large as that of the United Kingdom (Chapter 2, Table 2.6, shows each state's megawatt, or MW, capacity), in which about half of the electricity is generated with natural gas, a third is generated with coal, a tenth is generated by two NPPs – Comanche Peak and the South Texas Project (STP) – and about 7% is generated by wind.

Texas provides a complete energy economy with crude oil extraction and refining, natural gas aggregation and liquefaction, and a hydrogen highway between Houston and Lake Charles, LA, as well as electricity generation. Texan energy markets are some of the most competitive and integrated markets in the world. Thus Texas markets provide a natural laboratory in which to examine energy price relationships (with national data, these relationships are dampened by aggregating state-level data). However, *using Texas prices downwardly biases levelised electricity cost estimates in favour of fossil fuels* – primarily natural gas (because the natural gas transportation costs and pipeline bottlenecks are so low within Texas, unlike, for example, California and New York).

To understand the probability distributions of potential levelised costs from electricity generators, Section 5.2 (a) determines the key variables that drive new nuclear's levelised cost by calculating the elasticities of cost with respect to each input, (b) fits these key cost drivers with probability densities, and (c) simulates the probability distributions of ALWR levelised cost. Sections 5.3 and 5.4 present probabilistic models of the levelised costs of generating electricity using natural gas in CCGTs and coal with sulphur scrubbing, respectively. Section 5.5 compares the cumulative probability distributions of ALWRs, CCGTs and COAL electricity costs, and examines the portfolio effects of combining new nuclear power with fossil-fired power plants. Section 5.6 summarises the chapter and offers some conclusions.

This work extends that of Roques, Newbery and Nuttall (2006), and Roques *et al.* (2006), which focuses on fuel and electricity price uncertainties with uniform densities. Roques, Newbery and Nuttall (2006: n. 13) rely on the following conclusion:

> Awerbuch and Berger (2003) take into account operation and maintenance (O&M) cost uncertainties and construction cost uncertainties on top of fuel cost uncertainties, but show that this does not alter their findings significantly as compared to the case in which they only consider fuel cost risk.

However, Awerbuch and Berger (2003: 57) state:

> [W]e used financial proxies to derive estimates for all but the fuel-price risk. We had no access to historic project data covering O&M costs. In the case of construction period costs and risks, public data is also difficult to find.

In this way, they emphasise the importance of extending their work to consider the uncertainties facing electricity generators. Therefore, given the importance of variable and fixed cost uncertainties in power generation, on top of fuel price uncertainties in the minds of electric utilities, investors and the public, this chapter shows how to model these uncertainties based on the means and variances in historic data, and how to simulate levelised costs of generating portfolios. (Note, however, that the chapter does not incorporate covariances among the variables, which are difficult to identify.) This chapter relies on a spreadsheet add-in program, @RISK, to determine the most appropriate densities to represent random variables associated with levelised cost calculations to simulate probabilities with Monte Carlo techniques.

5.2 New nuclear levelised cost probability distributions

The levelised capital cost estimates in Chapter 3 are *expected values* for total construction cost and will not be known until plants are completed. The levelised cost estimates in Chapter 4 are expected values for operating costs, which will not be known until plants have been operating. To understand the probability distributions of the costs of new nuclear, this section first determines which variables are most influential in the cost-estimating equations, then suggests probability density functions for these variables. With these densities, the levelised cost of new nuclear is simulated and the standard deviations of the cost estimates are calculated.

While it is possible to calculate the standard deviation of the cost estimate using the equations in Chapters 3 and 4, it is easier to create a mathematical model and to use readily available software to simulate the distribution for levelised costs, as in Rothwell (2006). To determine which variables most influence the levelised cost, the elasticity of levelised cost with respect to each variable can be calculated (see the discussion of elasticity associated with Equation (4.3.4) in Chapter 4, Section 4.3). An easy way in which to calculate these elasticities is to perturb the base case values, such as those values in Chapter 3, Table 3.6, and Chapter 4, Table 4.4, by increasing each by 10%, for example noting the percentage change in levelised cost and then dividing the percentage change by 10%.

For example, if an increase of 10% in overnight cost, *OC*, induces an increase of 7% in levelised cost, *LC*, the elasticity would be equal to 0.7 (= 7% / 10%). (The elasticity is less than 1.0 because levelised overnight cost is less than levelised total cost.) Further, while levelised cost is important in comparing electricity-generating alternatives, after the plant is built and plant investment is sunk, variable costs (fuel and O&M) determine the operating profitability of the plant. Also, the cost of capital, **r**, is a parameter, *not a random variable*; hence the influence of **r** is conducted with sensitivity analysis, not with probability analysis, as in Chapter 4, Section 4.4. (The theme of Chapter 3, Appendix 3A, was one of trying to endogenise the cost of capital as a function of project and firm size.)

The *variables* that drive new nuclear plant costs (ALWRs) are (in approximate order of the value of their elasticity):

1 the overnight cost, *OC* (see Chapter 3, Section 3.2);
2 the construction lead time, *lt* (see Chapter 3, Section 3.3);
3 the capacity factor, *CF* (see Chapter 3, Section 3.4);
4 the number of employees, *L* (see Chapter 4, Section 4.3);
5 the percentage mark-up on labour costs, used to calculate **om** (see Chapter 4, Section 4.3);
6 the price of UF_6, P_{UF6} (equal to the price of U_3O_8 plus conversion to UF_6) (see Chapter 4, Section 4.2); and
7 the price of enrichment services, P_{SWU} (see Chapter 4, Section 4.2).

Given that the last four cost drivers were discussed in the previous chapter, the first three will be discussed here.

First, Chapter 3 proposed that *overnight* construction cost estimates for 'first-of-a-kind', or FOAK, units could have a normal density with a mean (expected value) of US$4,400/kW and a standard deviation of $460/kW. However, it is unlikely that overnight cost is symmetric, as in Chapter 3, Figure 3.1. Therefore, an extreme value distribution is used, **maxv**($4,400, $360), with the standard deviation equal to $460 = ($360 × 1.28), as in Figure 5.1. (Note that these overnight costs are for units still within the FOAK set – that is, the fifth unit in a set of eight – so 'nth-of-their-kind', or NOAK, plant costs could be lower; *therefore these overnight costs might bias the analysis in this chapter in favour of non-nuclear units.*) Simulated values are constrained to be between $3,500/kW and $8,000/kW. Values are constrained in simulation because there is a chance with many thousands of iterations that a simulated observation will be an unreasonable outlier, which makes it is difficult to interpret the resulting density

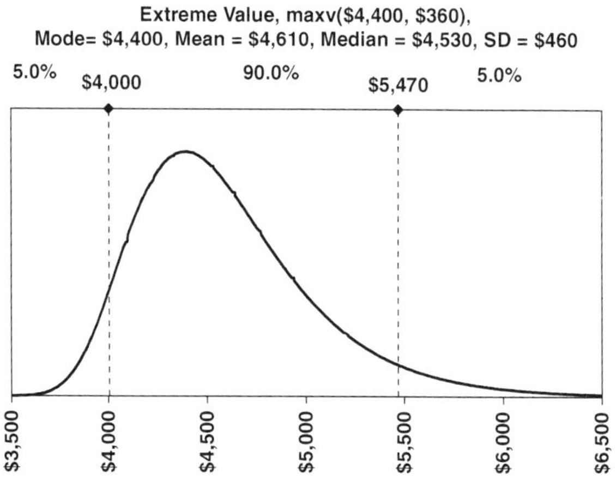

Figure 5.1 Advanced LWR overnight plant costs, 2013 US$/kW, fitted to an extreme value density.

Source: Chapter 3, Figure 3.1, adjusted with Chapter 4, Equation (4.1.5).

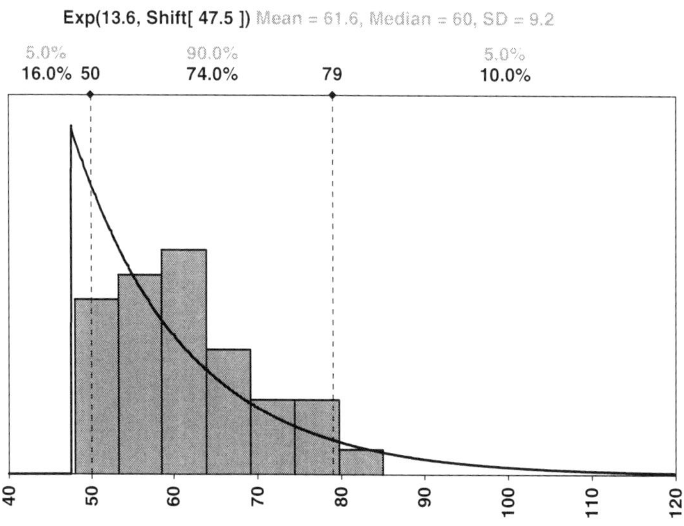

Figure 5.2 Advanced LWR construction lead time in months, fitted to exponential density.

Source: Chapter 1, Table 1.1, last column.

function; therefore minimum and maximum plausible values are imposed on the simulation.

Second, data on construction lead time, *lt*, come from Chapter 1, Table 1.1, and are discussed in Chapter 3, Section 3.3. Figure 5.2 presents a proposed probability density for construction lead times, as defined in Chapter 3, Section 3.3, with an exponential distribution. See Chapter 4, Equation (4.1.3), with **expo**(11.8, shift(47.5)), in which the 'shift' parameter moves the minimum to 47.5 months, yielding a mean of 59 months (= 47.5 + 11.8) and the standard deviation is equal to 11.8 months. Of the observations (in grey), 90% are between 50 and 79 months. (In the probability density figures, grey indicates input data and black indicates output densities; this is also true of statistics, such as means and standard deviations.) Under the proposed distribution, 74% of the outcomes are predicted to be between 50 and 79 months, with 19% of the expected outcomes to be less than 50 months and 7% of them to be over 79 months. Four units in Chapter 1, Table 1.1, required more than 72 months to construct; this does not include site preparation. This skews the distribution toward higher-than-expected lead times. Given that there is no upper bound constraint on the simulated values of lt with an exponential distribution, simulated values of lt_{ALWR} are constrained to between 47.5 months and 120 months in simulation.

Third, the model uses expectations regarding scheduled outage times (in days, for example 20 days per year) and forced outage rates (such as 5%), as in Chapter 3, Equation (3.4.11). However, these data are much harder to obtain than the data on capacity factors, which are available for the US nuclear power fleet in US EIA (2014b). (Rothwell, 1990, analysed outage times and forced outage rates based on data from the monthly US NRC NUREG–0020, with daily output data on accompanying diskettes, for example US NRC, 1995. These data were available on a 'need to know' basis from January 1979 to December 2001, after which time daily data were no longer collected for 'security reasons' after the terrorist attacks of 11 September 2001.) Figure 5.3 presents average plant capacity factors for the period 1987–2012 from information on US nuclear fleet performance from the US EIA, and models these data with an extreme value distribution, **minv**(89.6%, 2%), in which 89% is the mean and the standard deviation is equal to 3% = (2.5% × 1.28). Of the observed values, 90% are between 78% and 92%. Simulated values are constrained to [60%, 99%].

Chapter 3, Table 3.5, presented parameters in calculating levelised capital costs for ALWRs. Chapter 3, Table 3.6, and Chapter 4, Table 4.4, presented expected (deterministic) levelised costs for ALWRs. At a cost of capital of 7.5%, the levelised cost of a NOAK ALWR is estimated to be about $67/MWh. At a weighted average cost of capital (WACC) of 5%, levelised costs are about 22% less. At a WACC of 10%, levelised costs are about 26% more. This shows the importance of the cost of capital in determining the competitiveness of ALWRs, and hence the importance of understanding uncertainties in ALWR construction and operating costs, if the cost of capital is related to these uncertainties, for example through risk premiums.

Monte Carlo simulations were performed using these parameters and density functions with the software program @RISK for various costs of capital (Palisade, 2015). Figure 5.4 presents the resulting simulated levelised cost of electricity (LCOE) for ALWRs at a cost of capital of 7.5%, fitted to a lognormal density, wherein LC_{ALWR} values for levelised cost were constrained to be

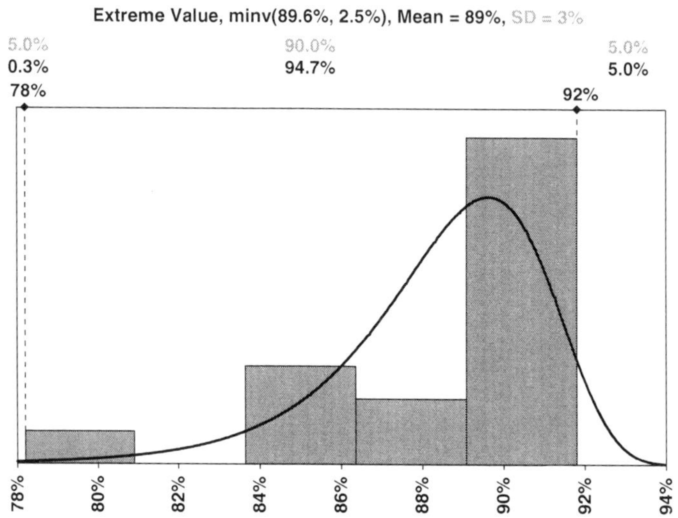

Figure 5.3 US NPP capacity factors, fitted to an extreme value density.

Source: US EIA (2014d).

Note: Annual averages for the US fleet of light water NPPs.

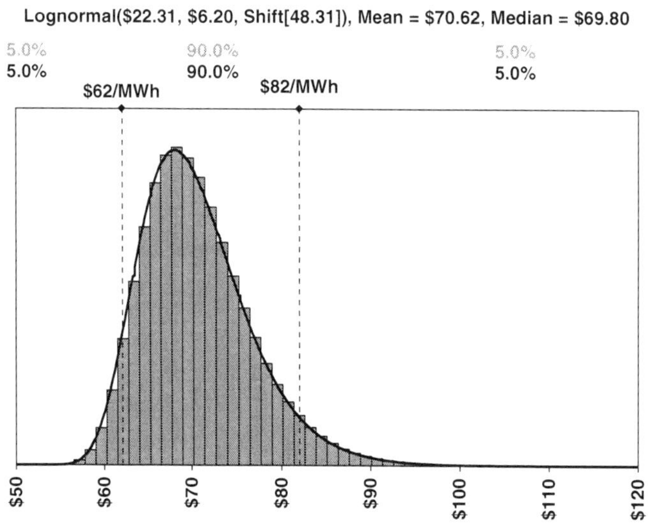

Figure 5.4 Advanced LWR levelised cost, simulated, fitted to a lognormal density (**r** = 7.5%).

Source: Simulated values with data from Chapter 4, Figures 4.1–4.3, and Figures 5.1–5.3.

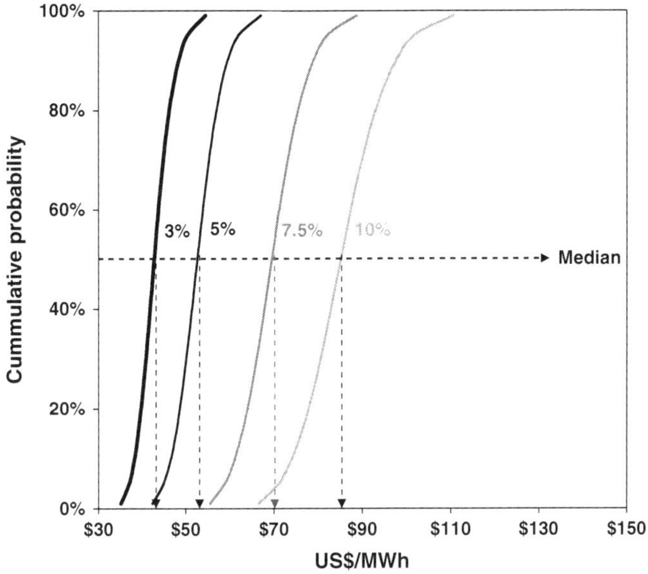

Figure 5.5 Advanced LWR levelised cost, simulated cumulative distributions.

Source: Simulations similar to those in Figure 5.4 with different costs of capital.

below \$300/MWh. With this density, the simulated levelised costs of ALWRs, LC_{ALWR}, cannot be below \$48.31/MWh, with a mean of \$70.62/MWh (= \$48.31/MWh + \$22.31/MWh), which is \$0.10/MWh less than the deterministic mean. Figure 5.5 examines the impact of changes in the cost of capital on the cumulative cost distributions at 3%, 5%, 7.5% and 10%.

In the next sections, these cumulative cost distributions are compared with those of natural gas CCGTs and coal-fired power plants.

5.3 Uncertain natural-gas-fired combined-cycle gas turbine levelised electricity cost

This section models the LCOE for fossil-fired power plants based on US EIA generating cost assumptions and US EIA price data. Two issues must be discussed before assessing fossil-fired electricity generation: (a) the price and cost of a tonne of carbon dioxide (CO_2); and (b) the capacity factor of fossil-fired generating units. (Although there are many other pollutants from fossil-fired electricity-generating plants, as well as NPPs, there is no consensus on which externalities to internalize. Instead, to make the analysis transparent, only some of these costs are included in this probability analysis. Readers are encouraged to extend this list, as long as the benefits are also included, such as energy security benefits.)

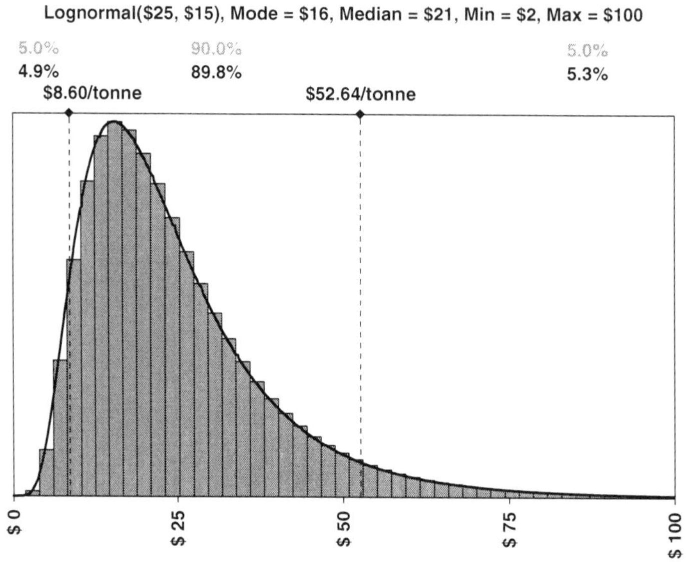

Figure 5.6 Cost of CO_2 in US$/tonne, simulated with lognormal density.

Source: Mean from MIT (2009), fitted to a lognormal density with SD = $15.

First, the Massachusetts Institute of Technology (MIT, 2009) assumed a CO_2 fee of $25 per metric tonne of CO_2 (tCO_2), as in most energy-economic analyses during the past decade (owing to early empirical experience with 'cap-and-trade' markets). However, the 'social cost' of CO_2 (as opposed to the price of CO_2) is unknown. The question is what is the appropriate cost probability density and standard deviation?

Here, it is modelled with a wide (and skewed) probability distribution: **lognormal**($25, $15). Figure 5.6 presents this density: 90% of the time, the price of (or damages from) tCO_2, P_{CO2}, could be between $8.60/$tCO_2$ and $52.64/$tCO_2$, with 99% of the realisations above $5.90/$tCO_2$ and 99% of the realisations below $77.88/$tCO_2$ (in 500,000 iterations). This distribution of the price of CO_2 is similar to that in Nordhaus (2011).

Second, while capacity factors for NPPs are easy to find and interpret (because most US nuclear plants are operated as base load, are approximately the same size and are of approximately the same vintage), this is not the case for natural gas and coal plants. In the US EIA database, there are no capacity factors specifically for CCGTs and there are no capacity factors specifically for old or new coal plants. However, capacity factors for all coal plants (big and small, old and new) are available from the US EIA. Figure 5.7 presents these capacity factors fitted to an extreme value function. These are used in the simulation of both coal and natural gas capacity factors.

Third, Table 5.1 presents costs from the US EIA's AEO assumptions 1995–2014 (for example US EIA, 2014a) and MIT (2009). The first column

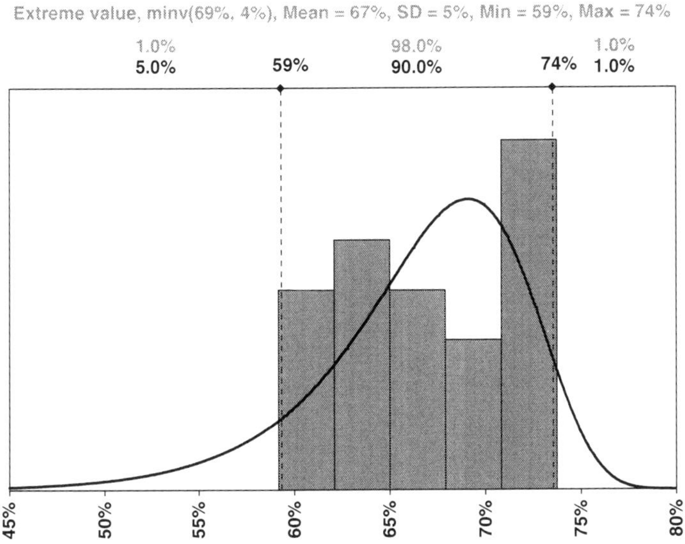

Figure 5.7 US fossil-fired plant capacity factors, fitted to an extreme value density.

Source: US EIA (2014e) and earlier equivalents.

gives the reference point at which US EIA data can be found. The cost data are given in real US dollars of the year indicated, which is usually two years before the publication date of the AEO. Since 1995, the US EIA has used 400 MW as the standard size of an advanced gas/oil CCGT. However, MIT (2009) uses a 1,000 MW CCGT as standard, to be compatible with the size of a single nuclear power unit (as in Chapter 3, Section 3.2) and a coal plant (as in Section 5.4) in its analysis. The lead time, *lt*, of a CCGT plant has 'declined' over time, becoming more compatible with the International Atomic Energy Agency (IAEA) standard of defining the construction period starting with the pouring of first concrete – that is, the earlier estimates of lead time included permitting and site preparation time, whereas later estimates, such as MIT (2009), include only actual construction time during which the bulk of the overnight cost, *OC*, is being financed.

Overnight costs for the CCGT are listed in real US dollars per kilowatt-electric (US$/kW) in the fifth column of Table 5.1 and converted to real 2013 US dollars in the sixth column. Variable (O&M) costs per kilowatt-hour (kWh) have been converted to 2013 US dollars per megawatt-hour (US $/MWh). Fixed (O&M) costs per kilowatt have been converted to 2013 US dollars per kilowatt (US$/kW). Note that, between the AEOs of 1995 and 1996, between those of 1997, 1998 and 1999, and between those of 2002 and 2003, some O&M costs were shifted from fixed to variable costs. The definitions of variable and fixed O&M have been stable since the AEO of 2003. The last column in Table 5.1 gives the heat rate in British thermal units

Table 5.1 US EIA AEO assumptions for NEMS, CCGT, in 2013 US$

CCGT, Source EIA, Assumptions for the …	*Year US$*	*Size (MW)*	*LT (y)*	*OC (US $/kW)*	*OC (2013US $/kW)*	*Variable (2013US $/MWh)*	*Fixed (2013US$/ kW/y)*	*Heat rate (BTU/ kWh)*
AEO (1995: table 29)	1987	400	4	476	853	4.66	48.38	7,369
AEO (1996: 54)	1987	400	4	332	595	0.72	48.38	7,300
AEO (1997: table 33)	1995	400	4	620	979	0.79	42.65	6,985
AEO (1998: table 37)	1996	400	3	572	883	3.09	21.30	6,985
AEO (1999: table 37)	1997	400	3	575	889	0.79	21.99	6,985
AEO (2000: table 37)	1998	400	3	576	912	0.81	22.55	6,985
AEO (2001: table 43)	1999	400	3	576	904	0.80	22.17	6,927
AEO (2002: table 38)	2000	400	3	590	875	0.77	21.45	6,870
AEO (2003: table 40)	2001	400	3	608	893	3.00	15.01	7,000
AEO (2004: table 38)	2002	400	3	615	924	3.11	15.55	6,928
AEO (2005: table 38)	2003	400	3	558	797	2.52	14.76	6,732
AEO (2006: table 38)	2004	400	3	575	772	2.45	14.31	6,732
AEO (2007: table 38)	2005	400	3	594	743	2.35	13.78	6,717
AEO (2008: table 38)	2006	400	3	706	845	2.33	13.61	6,752
AEO (2009: table 8.2)	2007	400	3	947	1,079	2.28	13.33	6,752
AEO (2010: table 8.2)	2008	400	3	968	1,059	2.23	13.09	6,752
AEO (2011: table 8.2)	2009	400	3	917	972	3.26	15.31	6,333
AEO (2012: table 8.2)	2010	400	3	1,003	1,055	3.27	15.37	6,430
AEO (2013: table 8.2)	2011	400	3	1,006	1,037	3.31	15.55	6,333
AEO (2014: table 8.2)	2012	400	3	1,021	1,031	3.30	15.52	6,333
MIT (2009: 18–22)	2007	1,000	2	850	968	0.47	26.20	6,800

Source: US EIA (2014b) and previous editions.

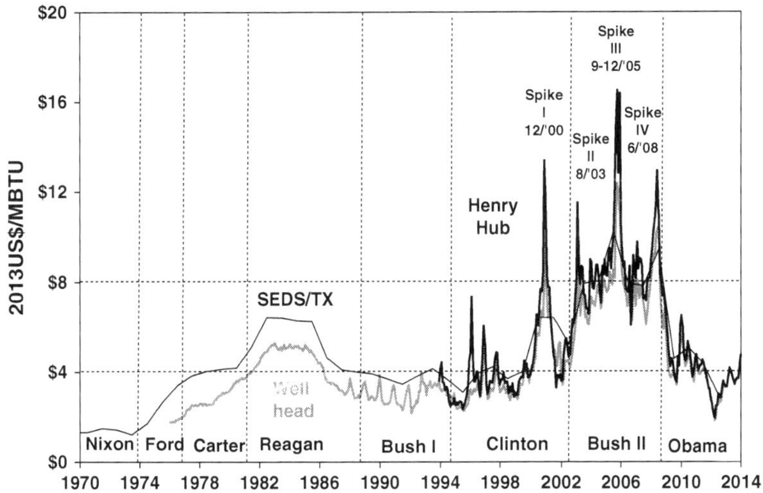

Figure 5.8 Natural gas prices, 2013 US$/MBTU, 1970–2014.

Sources: US EIA (2014c, 2015a); Federal Reserve Bank of St. Louis (2014).

(BTUs) per kWh representing the average heat rate as of the last complete year of data.

Fourth, to forecast fuel prices, Figure 5.8 presents three natural gas price series:

1 interpolated monthly Texas natural gas prices (from annual data) *for electric utilities* from 1970 to 2012 from the US EIA's SEDS for Texas;
2 the monthly US natural gas 'wellhead price' from 1977 to 2014; and
3 monthly 'Henry Hub' spot-market prices in Louisiana from 1994 to 2014.

Figure 5.8 shows the natural gas market experienced at least four price spikes in the last decade-and-a-half. (Prices to electric utilities are higher than wellhead and Henry Hub prices because of transmission charges.) Williams (2015) presents more recent natural gas price data. Figure 5.9 presents a histogram and fitted probability density for the SEDS/TX prices in Figure 5.8. The data and the density show a skewed distribution with a mode of $3.69 per million BTUs (MBTU), a median of $4.34/MBTU and a mean of $4.70/MBTU, with a standard deviation of $2.11/MBTU. (For a geometric Brownian motion, or GBM, model of fossil-fuel prices, similar to the GBM model of uranium prices in Rothwell *et al.*, 2014, see Hogue, 2012: 55–56.)

Table 5.2 presents *deterministic* levelised cost estimates for CCGT natural gas for different levels of the cost of capital with deterministic capacity factors, CF_{CCGT}, of 89% (equal to those for ALWRs), a mean natural gas price,

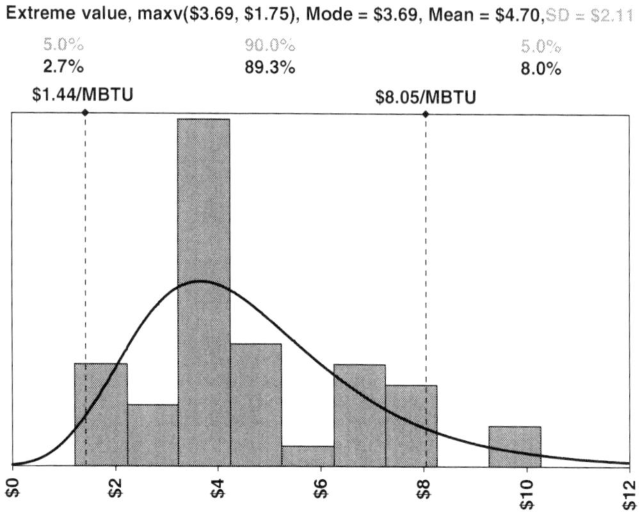

Figure 5.9 Histogram of natural gas prices at Henry Hub, 1990–2013.

Source: Data in Figure 5.8.

P_{CCGT}, of \$4.71/MBTU, and EIA values from Table 5.1 for OC_{CCGT}, lt_{CCGT} and $\mathrm{MW}_{\mathrm{CCGT}}$. However, $O\&M_k$ and F_k in Equation (5.1.1) must be defined:

$$OM_{\mathrm{CCGT/MWh}} = VOM_{\mathrm{CCGT}} + [(1{,}000 \times FOM_{\mathrm{CCGT}})/(CF_{\mathrm{CCGT}} \times 8{,}766)] \tag{5.3.1}$$

where

VOM_{CCGT} is variable O&M from Table 5.1, and
FOM_{CCGT} is fixed O&M from Table 5.1,

and

$$F_{\mathrm{CCGT/MWh}} = [(P_{\mathrm{NGAS}} \times \mathrm{HR}_{\mathrm{CCGT}})/1{,}000] + (P_{\mathrm{CO2}} \times \mathrm{CO}_{2\mathrm{CCGT}}) \tag{5.3.2}$$

where

F_{CCGT} is the total natural gas expense,
$F_{\mathrm{CCGT/MWh}}$ is the cost of natural gas per MWh,
P_{NGAS} is the price of natural gas,
$\mathrm{HR}_{\mathrm{CCGT}}$ is the heat rate (in BTU/kWh) for CCGTs from Table 5.1,

Table 5.2 Levelised cost for new natural gas generation, 2013 US$

Combined-cycle gas turbine (CCGT) levelised cost *All values in 2013 dollars*	*r* =	*(1)* *CCGT* *3.00%*	*(2)* *CCGT* *5.00%*	*(3)* *CCGT* *7.50%*	*(4)* *CCGT* *10.00%*	*MIT* *CCGT* *7.80%*
Net electrical capacity	MWe	400	400	400	400	1,000
Average capacity factor	%	89	89	89	89	85
Total overnight cost	$/kw	1,037	1,037	1,037	1,037	968
Interest during construction factor	%	4.40	7.50	11.30	15.20	7.55
KC per kW with IDC	$/kw	1,083	1,114	1,154	1,195	968
Fuel price ($/GJ = 0.948 × $/MBTU)	$/MBTU	4.71	4.71	4.71	4.71	4.71
CO_2 price ($/tonne)	$/tonne	25.00	25.00	25.00	25.00	25.00
CO_2 per MWh	t/MWh	0.361	0.361	0.361	0.361	0.361
Heat rate	BTU/kWh	6,333	6,333	6,333	6,333	6,800
Variable O&M	$/MWh	3.31	3.31	3.31	3.31	0.47
Fixed O&M	$/kW	15.55	15.55	15.55	15.55	26.20
Levelised capital cost	$/MWh	6.04	8.37	11.81	15.75	10.66
Levelised O&M cost	$/MWh	5.31	5.31	5.31	5.31	3.99
Levelised fuel	$/MWh	29.80	29.80	29.80	29.80	32.00
Levelised fuel waste fee	$/MWh	8.41	8.41	8.41	8.41	9.03
Levelised cost without waste fee	**$/MWh**	**41.15**	**43.48**	**46.92**	**50.86**	**46.65**
Levelised cost with waste fee	**$/MWh**	**49.56**	**51.89**	**55.33**	**59.27**	**55.68**

Source: Table 5.1; Equations (5.1.1), (5.3.1) and (5.3.2).

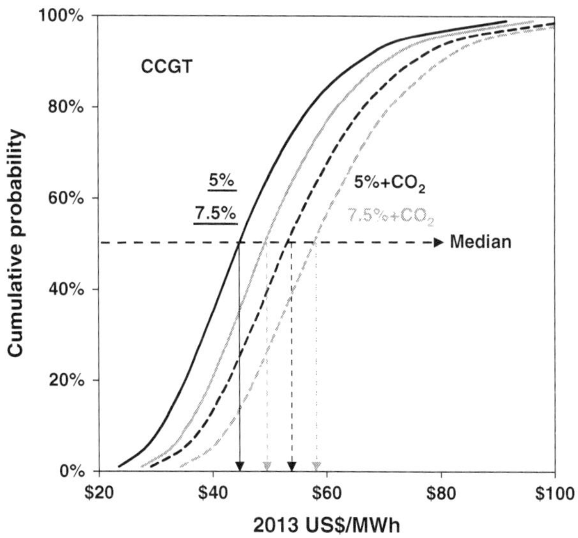

Figure 5.10 Levelised cost of CCGT, simulated cumulative distributions (**r** = 5%, 7.5%).

Sources: Table 5.2; Figures 5.6 and 5.9.

P_{CO2} is the price of tCO_2 ($F_{CCGT/MWh}$ is calculated with and without the price of CO_2), and

CO_{2CCGT} is the tonnage of CO_2 produced by the CCGT unit per MWh, known as the 'carbon intensity factor'.

The table presents the calculation of levelised cost for natural-gas-fired electricity assuming costs of capital of 3%, 5%, 7.5% and 10% compared with MIT (2009), updated to 2013 US dollars with the *same price of natural gas as in the rest of the table.* (Entries with probability densities are in italic.) For natural gas CCGT, Figure 5.10 presents the cumulative probability distributions for Monte Carlo simulations both with and without a $25/tCO_2$ fee at real costs of capital of 5% and 7.5%. Because of the high number of price spikes in the natural gas price data, the cumulative (extreme value) distributions for LC_{CCGT} have long tails.

5.4 Uncertain coal-fired levelised electricity costs

Table 5.3 presents costs from the US EIA's assumptions to the AEO (for example US EIA, 2014b) and MIT (2009) regarding coal-fired electricity generation. The discussion of Table 5.1 in the previous section presents these definitions. As with Table 5.1, there appear to be discontinuities in the EIA data owing to changes in technology definitions, for example 'pulverised coal'

Table 5.3 US EIA AEO assumptions for NEMS, coal, in 2013 US$

CCGT, Source EIA, Assumptions for the ...	*Year US$*	*Size (MW)*	*LT (y)*	*OC (US$/kW)*	*OC (2013US$/kW)*	*Variable (2013US$/MWh)*	*Fixed (2013US$/kW/y)*	*Heat rate (BTU/kWh)*
AEO (1995: table 29)	1987	400	4	1,213	2,173	7.70	61.28	9,649
AEO (1996: 54)	1987	400	4	1,190	2,132	3.40	61.28	9,961
AEO (1997: table 33)	1995	400	4	1,430	2,259	3.79	54.03	9,961
AEO (1998: table 37)	1996	400	4	1,079	1,665	5.02	34.72	9,585
AEO (1999: table 37)	1997	400	4	1,093	1,689	5.15	35.60	9,585
AEO (2000: table 37)	1998	400	4	1,030	1,632	5.28	36.50	9,585
AEO (2001: table 43)	1999	400	4	1,092	1,715	5.18	35.87	9,419
AEO (2002: table 38)	2000	400	4	1,119	1,661	5.01	34.73	9,386
AEO (2003: table 40)	2001	600	4	1,155	1,695	4.51	36.01	9,000
AEO (2004: table 38)	2002	600	4	1,167	1,755	4.66	37.31	9,000
AEO (2005: table 38)	2003	600	4	1,213	1,731	5.79	34.75	8,844
AEO (2006: table 38)	2004	600	4	1,249	1,678	5.62	33.70	8,844
AEO (2007: table 38)	2005	600	4	1,290	1,615	5.41	32.43	8,844
AEO (2008: table 38)	2006	600	4	1,534	1,835	5.33	32.05	9,200
AEO (2009: table 8.2)	2007	600	4	2,058	2,344	5.23	31.36	9,200
AEO (2010: table 8.2)	2008	600	4	2,223	2,433	5.13	30.80	9,200
AEO (2011: table 8.2)	2009	1,300	4	2,809	2,979	4.45	31.08	8,740
AEO (2012: table 8.2)	2010	1,300	4	2,844	2,991	4.47	31.20	8,800
AEO (2013: table 8.2)	2011	1,300	4	2,883	2,969	4.52	31.56	8,740
AEO (2014: table 8.2)	2012	1,300	4	2,925	2,955	4.52	31.49	8,740
MIT (2009: 18–22)	2007	1,000	4	2,300	2,620	4.07	58.09	8,870

Source: US EIA (2014b) and previous editions.

Table 5.4 Real levelised cost for new coal-fired generation, in 2013 US$

Coal with scrubbers (COAL) levelised cost *All values in 2013US$*	*r* =	*(1)* *COAL* *3.0%*	*(2)* *COAL* *5.0%*	*(3)* *COAL* *7.5%*	*(4)* *COAL* *10.0%*	*MIT* *COAL* *7.8%*
Net electrical capacity	MWe	1,300	1,300	1,300	1,300	1,000
Average capacity factor	%	89	89	89	89	85
Total overnight cost	$/kw	2,969	2,969	2,969	2,969	2,223
Interest during construction factor	%	6.0	10.2	15.5	21.0	16.2
KC per kW with IDC	$/kw	3,148	3,271	3,430	3,593	2,583
KC, Total capital investment cost	$m	4,092	4,252	4,459	4,671	2,583
Fuel price ($/GJ = 0.948 × $/MBTU)	$/M BTU	2.18	2.18	2.18	2.18	2.18
CO_2 price ($/tonne)	$/tonne	25.00	25.00	25.00	25.00	25.00
CO_2 per MWh	t/MWh	0.839	0.839	0.839	0.839	0.839
Heat rate	BTU/kWh	8,740	8,740	8,740	8,740	8,870
Variable O&M	$/MWh	4.52	4.52	4.52	4.52	4.07
Fixed O&M	$/kW	31.56	31.56	31.56	31.56	58.09
Levelised capital cost	$/MWh	17.55	24.57	35.10	47.36	27.04
Levelised O&M cost	$/MWh	8.59	8.59	8.59	8.59	11.86
Levelised fuel	$/MWh	19.07	19.07	19.07	19.07	19.35
Levelised fuel waste fee	$/MWh	20.67	20.67	20.67	20.67	20.98
Levelised cost without waste fee	**$/MWh**	**45.20**	**52.22**	**62.75**	**75.01**	**58.25**
Levelised cost with waste fee	**$/MWh**	**65.87**	**72.89**	**83.42**	**95.68**	**79.23**

Source: Table 5.3; Equations (5.1.1), (5.4.1) and (5.4.2).

versus 'advanced coal' versus 'scrubbed coal new', which is referred to as 'COAL'. Data from the assumptions for the 2013 AEO are used to forecast values in Table 5.4.

Figure 5.11 presents two price series:

1 Texas annual average coal prices from 1970 to 2012 (for which monthly data were interpolated from annual data – that is, a weighted average of the two consecutive years' values as a function of the month); and
2 the monthly average price of sub-bituminous coal in the United States from the US EIA.

Because the interpolated Texas prices closely follow the US average monthly price from 1990 to 2010, US monthly coal prices were used in the simulations of the LCOE from coal-fired power plants. Figure 5.12 presents a histogram of these US monthly prices in Figure 5.11. (State-level coal price data can also be derived from US EIA, 2007, but doing so is laborious.)

Table 5.4 presents *deterministic* levelised cost estimates for coal-fired electricity, COAL, for different levels of the cost of capital with deterministic capacity factors, CF_{COAL}, of 89% (equal to those for ALWRs), a mean coal gas price, P_{COAL}, of \$2.18/MBTU, and EIA values from Table 5.3 for OC_{COAL}, lt_{COAL} and $\mathrm{MW}_{\mathrm{COAL}}$. Further, $O\&M_{\mathrm{COAL/MWh}}$ and $F_{\mathrm{COAL/MWh}}$ are calculated as in Equations (5.3.1) and (5.3.2). $F_{\mathrm{COAL/MWh}}$ is calculated with and without the price of CO_2:

$$O\&M_{\mathrm{COAL/MWh}} = VOM_{\mathrm{COAL}} + [(1,000 \times FOM_{\mathrm{COAL}})/(CF_{\mathrm{COAL}} \times 8,766)] \quad (5.4.1)$$

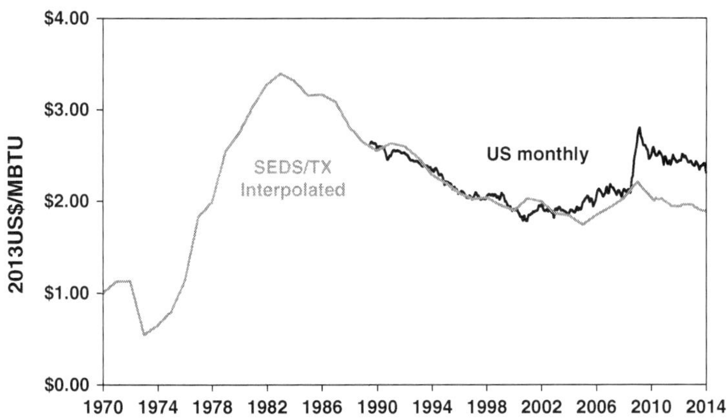

Figure 5.11 Interpolated Texas and US coal prices, 2013 US\$/MBTU, 1970–2014.

Sources: US EIA (2014c, 2015b).

Note: The divergence between Texas and average US prices of coal could be due to changes in transportation costs; see http://www.eia.gov/todayinenergy/detail.cfm?id=8830.

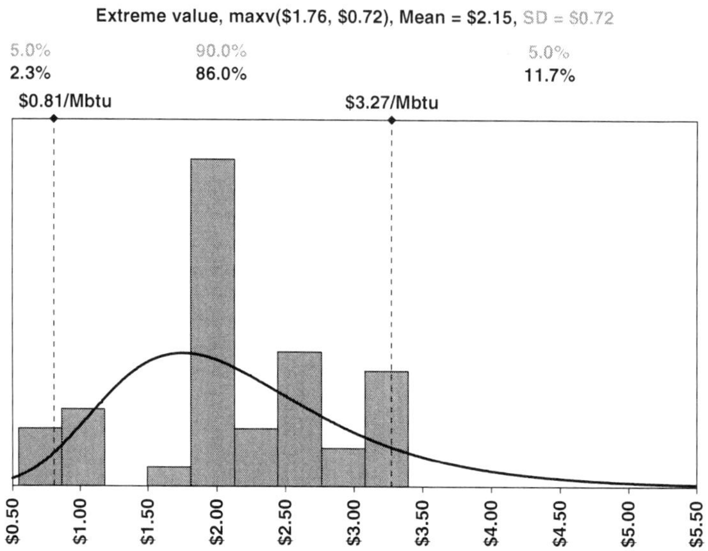

Figure 5.12 Texas electric utility coal prices, fitted to an extreme value density.

Source: Data from Figure 5.11.

$$F_{\mathrm{COAL/MWh}} = [(P_{\mathrm{COAL}} \times \mathrm{HR}_{\mathrm{COAL}})/1,000] + (P_{\mathrm{CO2}} \times \mathrm{CO}_{2\mathrm{COAL}}) \tag{5.4.2}$$

where the variables and parameters are similarly defined as in Equations (5.3.1) and (5.3.2).

Table 5.4 presents the calculation of levelised cost for coal-fired electricity assuming costs of capital of 3%, 5%, 7.5% and 10%, compared with MIT (2009), updated to 2013 US dollars with the *same price of coal as in the rest of the table*. For COAL, Figure 5.13 presents the cumulative probability distributions for Monte Carlo simulations without and with a $25/tCO_2$ fee at real costs of capital of 5% and 7.5%. Unlike the cumulative distributions for LC_{CCGT}, the levelised cost of COAL is more influenced by the uncertainty associated with the price of CO_2.

These levelised cost probability distributions are compared in Figure 5.14 for ALWR, CCGT and COAL units for a cost of capital of 5% for ALWRs, and 7.5% with and without the price of CO_2 for all technologies. At a cost of capital of 5%, ALWRs are competitive with CCGTs. At a cost of capital of 7.5% and with a price for CO_2, ALWRs at 7.5% can be competitive with CCGTs when the price of natural gas approaches its historic highs. Advanced LWRs are cheaper than COAL including the price of CO_2 at a cost of capital of 7.5%.

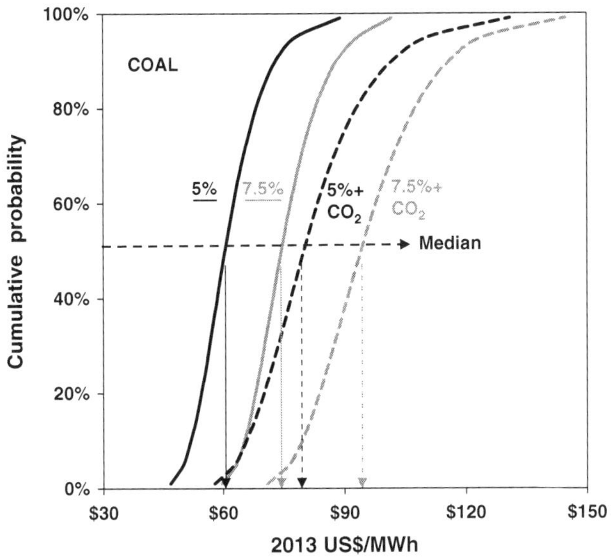

Figure 5.13 Coal levelised cost, simulated cumulative distributions (**r** = 5%, 7.5%).

Sources: Table 5.4; Figures 5.6 and 5.12.

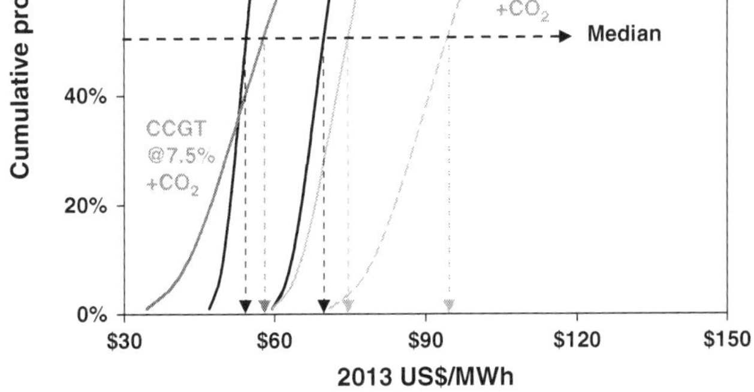

Figure 5.14 Levelised cost distributions without and with a CO_2 fee.

Sources: Figures 5.5, 5.10 and 5.13.

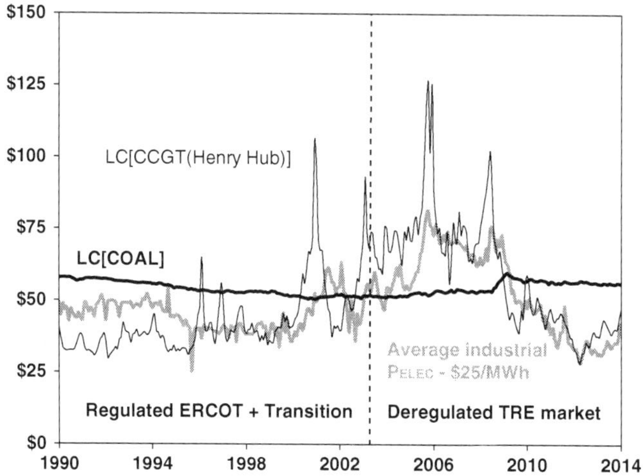

Figure 5.15 Electricity prices in ERCOT/TRE, 1990–2014.

Source: US EIA (2015c).

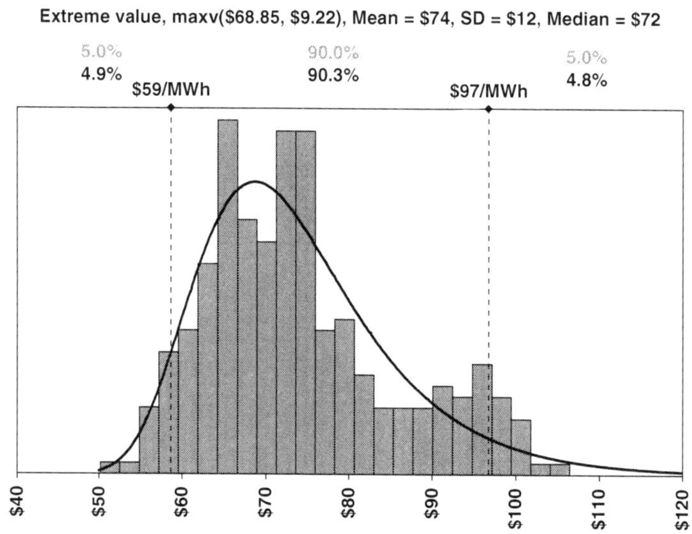

Figure 5.16 Probability density of electricity prices in Texas ERCOT/TRE, 1990–2014.

Source: Data from Figure 5.15.

Because the next section requires an average electricity price, Figure 5.15 presents the average industrial price of electricity, as well as (a) the levelised cost of generating electricity from natural gas using a CCGT (as in Section 5.3), and

(b) the levelised cost of sulphur-scrubbed, coal-fired, steam-turbine electricity (as in Figure 5.11) in Texas between 1991 and 2014, minus industrial transmission and distribution charges, in 2013 US dollars. After electricity market deregulation in Texas, electricity prices closely followed the levelised costs of generating electricity with natural gas. There were four natural gas price spikes (shown in Figure 5.8) after 2000, leading to two electricity price spikes near Spike III (September–December 2005) and Spike IV (June 2008).

In determining whether an electricity generator is competitive, this chapter uses the price of electricity from Texas as a proxy for the market price of electricity (not directly, but as a guideline to determine whether a technology or portfolio of technologies can compete). Figure 5.16 presents the average industrial price of electricity in Texas between 1991 and 2014 with a mean of \$74.17/MWh and a standard deviation of \$11.83/MWh. (This mean is used in Section 5.5 to evaluate the competitive feasibility of portfolios of generating assets.)

5.5 Probabilistic analysis of portfolios of electricity-generating assets

While the simulations in Figure 5.14 are interesting, without an explicit understanding of who is choosing among these technologies and how these decision makers value the trade-off between levelised cost and the standard deviation of levelised cost, there is no obvious choice, because no technology stochastically dominates the others (when the fuel price and the cost of CO_2 volatilities are taken into account). In earlier times (and still in some US states), the choice of which technology to build was determined through the interaction of the electric utility regulator (representing the ratepayers) and the power plant owner-operators, who enjoyed a monopoly in electricity provision in their regulated territory. More recently, in half of the United States, some sort of electricity market is guiding the choice of electricity-generation technology, as discussed in Chapter 2.

What is absent is the basic tenet of modern finance theory – that is, that diversification reduces risk for each level of return. Here, a diversification of generating assets could reduce levelised cost risk at each value of levelised cost. However, transferring the accepted wisdom from financial markets to electricity markets is not straightforward. In financial markets, stocks, bonds and derivatives can be purchased in small chunks and mixed to form an optimal portfolio for each investor, as in Chapter 3, Appendix 3A. Real estate can be included through investments in real estate investment trusts and gold can be included in the form of investments in gold mining corporations. Hence an optimal portfolio need not contain anything 'real', as in real property. On the other hand, electricity-generating assets are real and bulky. For example, the standard size of a CCGT *unit* is about 400 MW, the standard size of a coal power *unit* with modern air pollution equipment is about 600 MW and an ALWR *unit* is about 1,200 MW.

Also, because of regulatory restrictions by the US Securities and Exchange Commission (SEC), the US Federal Energy Regulatory Commission (FERC), the US Environmental Protection Agency (EPA), the US Nuclear Regulatory Commission (NRC), state and local water and transportation commissions, and local property owners with stakes to drive into any electricity-generating project, owner-operators find it difficult to manage these bulky assets to produce both (a) output, and (b) revenues to pay bankers and investors, and to provide for capacity growth. In addition, because of the necessity of providing 'uninterruptable' electric power, the generating portfolio must meet demand (load) at all times, for example during heatwaves and polar vortexes.

A rule of thumb is that no single generating asset should be larger than 10% of the connected transmission grid; therefore one needs either (a) a minimum system size composed of natural-gas-fired units of 4,000 MW (if no single unit is greater than 400 MW or 10% of the grid size), or (b) a minimum system size composed of natural-gas-fired or coal-fired units and/or ALWRs of 12,000 MW (if no single unit is greater than 1,200 MW). Of course, smaller systems could be built at higher delivered power prices. However, because of the integer divisibility of the 12,000 MW systems with 400 MW units, 600 MW units and 1,200 MW units, a system of 12,000 MW is considered here to be the minimum standard system (maximum dependable electricity-generating capacity) for adding ALWRs. From the third column of Chapter 2, Table 2.6, 11 states have less than 6,000 MW of capacity, 25 states have capacities between 6,000 MW and 24,000 MW, and 15 states have capacities between 24,000 MW and 103,000 MW (Texas).

5.5.1 Portfolio of fossil-fired electricity-generating assets

Given that generating assets are discrete, the portfolio's levelised cost and variance will be equal to a weighted sum of the underlying assets' levelised costs, variances and correlations (see Chapter 3, Appendix 3A, Equations (3A.3.6) and (3A.3.7)). Table 5.5 presents the results of simulating portfolios of 12,000 MW with CCGT and COAL units. These results are plotted in Figure 5.17. (Figures 5.17, 5.18 and 5.19 follow the same logic as in Chapter 3, Appendix 3A, Figure 3A.7; Tables 5.5, 5.6 and 5.7 follow the same logic as in Chapter 3, Appendix 3A, Table 3A.7.)

The minimum standard deviation is achieved with a portfolio of half coal-fired units and half natural-gas-fired units (see Figure 5.17), but this combination is too expensive – that is, greater than $74/MWh. Because of the low correlation between natural gas and coal prices, combining coal-fired units with natural-gas-fired units lowers the variance of the LCOE. (Natural gas and coal prices are positively correlated at 35% for data in Figures 5.9 and 5.12; natural gas and uranium prices are barely correlated at 4%; and coal and uranium prices are negatively correlated at –20%. In the simulations, LC_{CCGT} and LC_{COAL} are correlated at positive 30%, but LC_{ALWR} is uncorrelated with either LC_{CCGT} or LC_{COAL}.) Some portfolios (in grey in Table 5.5) yield

Table 5.5 Portfolios of natural gas and coal-fired units

TOTAL	*12,000*	*12,000*	*12,000*	*12,000*	*12,000*	*12,000*	*12,000*	*12,000*	*12,000*	*12,000*	*12,000*
CCGT	*12,000*	*10,800*	*9,600*	*8,400*	*7,200*	*6,000*	*4,800*	*3,600*	*2,400*	*1,200*	*0*
COAL	*0*	*1,200*	*2,400*	*3,600*	*4,800*	*6,000*	*7,200*	*8,400*	*9,600*	*10,800*	*12,000*
LC+1SD	**$75**	$78	$81	$84	$87	$91	$95	$99	$103	$108	$112
LC+2SD	**$90**	$92	$94	$97	$100	$103	$107	$112	$117	$122	$127
LC+3SD	**$105.6**	$106.3	$108	$109	$112	$116	$120	$125	$130	$137	$143
LC+4SD	$121	**$120**	$121	$122	$125	$128	$132	$138	$144	$151	$159
LC+5SD	$136	$135	**$134**	$135	$137	$140	$145	$151	$158	$166	$174

Source: Author.

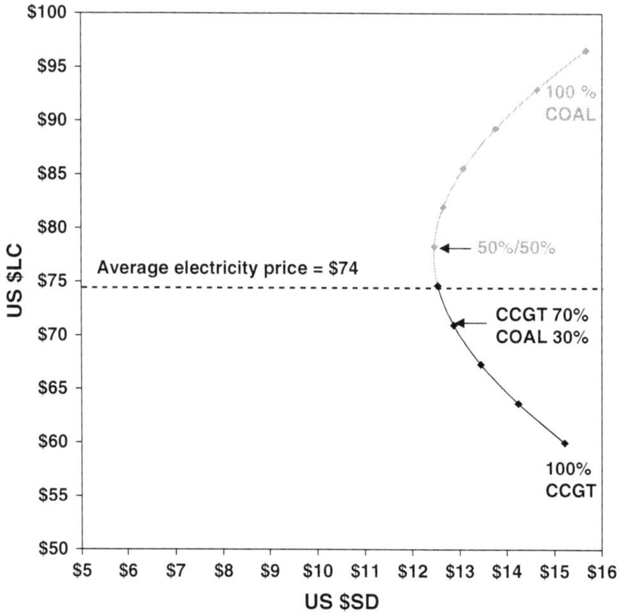

Figure 5.17 Portfolios of natural gas and coal-fired generating assets.

Source: Table 5.5.

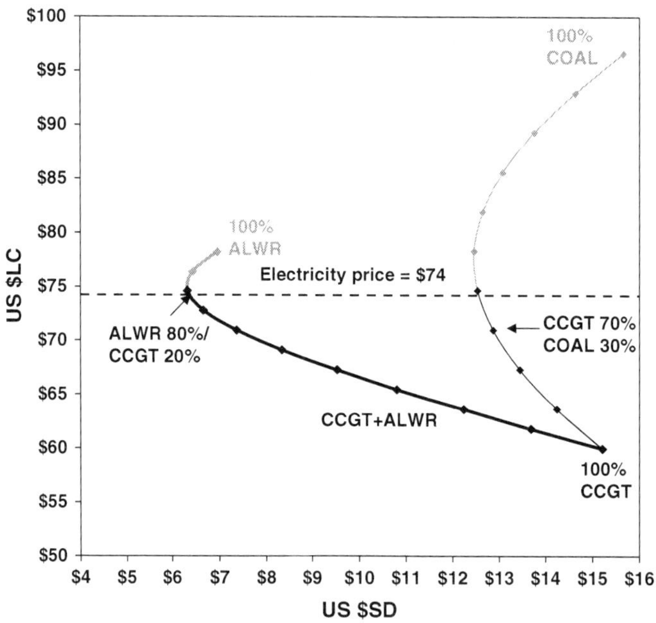

Figure 5.18 Portfolios of ALWR and natural gas generating assets.

Source: Table 5.6.

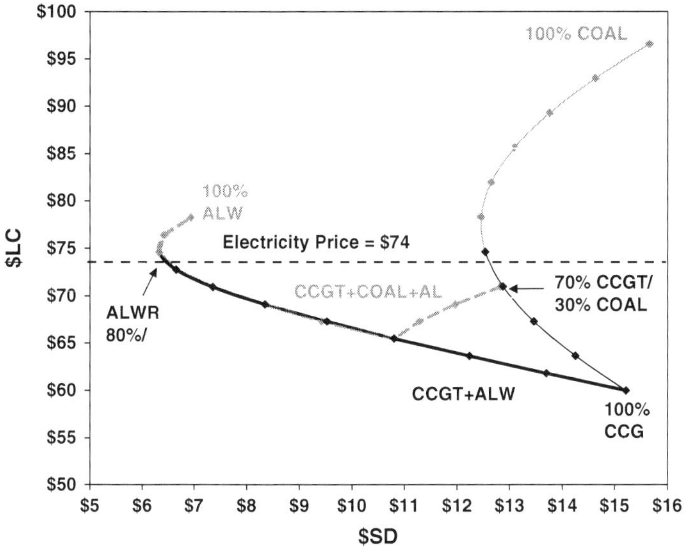

Figure 5.19 Portfolios of natural gas, coal-fired and ALWR generating assets.

Source: Table 5.7.

levelised costs above $74/MWh and are therefore inadvisable. (Although the price of electricity is itself a randomly distributed variable, the average electricity price should not be considered a 'solid line', but more a 'guideline'.)

Table 5.5 presents sums of levelised cost, *LC*, plus various multiples of the simulated standard deviation, SD, where the multipliers are from Chapter 3, Appendix 3A, Table 3A.3. Holding the risk aversion parameter to 1, the multipliers increase with the requirement of higher levels of confidence (80–99%) in the cost estimate and with larger accuracy ranges (that is, with less well-developed cost estimates). Values in bold are the minimum values in each row. For example, the lowest levelised cost, *LC*, is $60 with an all-CCGT system, but the system that yields the lowest standard deviation is one with half CCGT and half coal. The lowest *LC* plus between one and three standard deviations points towards all-CCGT systems. The multipliers from Chapter 3, Appendix 3A, Table 3A.3 increase as risk aversion increases, as the confidence in the cost estimate increases and as the accuracy range becomes more precise. However, as multipliers increase, the 'no regrets' strategy appears to be a system with some coal, given that coal capacity stabilises the levelised cost volatility associated with natural gas prices, as in Figure 5.15. Again, the primary problem is that we do not know how customers, electric utilities and financial institutions evaluate the trade-off between cost and cost risk. We can conclude, however, that systems that rely on too much coal

Table 5.6 Portfolios of CCGTs and ALWRs

TOTAL	*12,000*	*12,000*	*12,000*	*12,000*	*12,000*	*12,000*	*12,000*	*12,000*	*12,000*	*12,000*	*12,000*
CCGT	*12,000*	*10,800*	*9,600*	*8,400*	*7,200*	*6,000*	*4,800*	*3,600*	*2,400*	*1,200*	*0*
ALWR	*0*	*1,200*	*2,400*	*3,600*	*4,800*	*6,000*	*7,200*	*8,400*	*9,600*	*10,800*	*12,000*
LC+1SD	$75	$75	$74	$74.0	$73.7	$73.52	**$73.50**	$73.73	$74.3	$75	$77
LC+2SD	$90	$88	$87	$85	$83	$82	$81	**$80.0**	$80.1	$81	$83
LC+3SD	$106	$102	$99	$96	$93	$90	$88	$86.3	**$86.0**	$87	$89
LC+4SD	$121	$116	$111	$106	$102	$98	$95	$93	**$92**	$93	$95
LC+5SD	$136	$130	$123	$117	$112	$106	$102	$99	**$98**	$99	$102

Source: Author.

Table 5.7 Portfolios of fossil-fired units and ALWRs

TOTAL	*12,000*	*12,000*	*12,000*	*12,000*	*12,000*	*12,000*	*12,000*	*12,000*	*12,000*	*12,000*	*12,000*
COAL	*3,600*	*2,400*	*1,200*	*0*	*0*	*0*	*0*	*0*	*0*	*0*	*0*
CCGT	*8,400*	*8,400*	*8,400*	*8,400*	*7,200*	*6,000*	*4,800*	*3,600*	*2,400*	*1,200*	*0*
ALWR	*0*	*1,200*	*2,400*	*3,600*	*4,800*	*6,000*	*7,200*	*8,400*	*9,600*	*10,800*	*12,000*
LC+1SD	$84	$80	$77	$74.0	$73.7	$73.52	**$73.50**	$73.73	$74.3	$75	$77
LC+2SD	$97	$92	$88	$85	$83	$82	$81	**$80.0**	$80.1	$81	$83
LC+3SD	$109	$104	$99	$96	$93	$90	$88	$86.3	**$86.0**	$87	$89
LC+4SD	$122	$116	$111	$106	$102	$98	$95	$93	**$92**	$93	$95
LC+5SD	$135	$128	$122	$117	$112	$106	$102	$99	**$98**	$99	$102

Source: Author.

are both expensive and risky, given that we do not know the cost associated with CO_2.

5.5.2 Adding advanced light water reactors to a portfolio of fossil-fired electricity-generating assets

Table 5.6 adds ALWR plants of 1,200 MW to a portfolio of only CCGTs. The standard deviation of the portfolio decreases with the addition of ALWRs, as shown in Figure 5.18. However, a 100% ALWR system appears to increase cost risk (note that although the total construction capital cost risk has been incorporated into the overnight cost contingency, there are still risks associated with construction lead time, etc.). In fact, too much nuclear is too expensive (the last three columns in Table 5.6 showing that systems with more than 60% nuclear capacity do not take advantage of the diversity of natural gas). On the other hand, a portfolio of 20–40% CCGTs appears to have the lowest risk-adjusted levelised cost. As the importance of cost risk increases, a portfolio of 20% CCGTs with 80% ALWRs appears to yield the lowest cost risk. Because of the lack of correlation between ALWRs and fossil-fired units, adding ALWRs decreases the cost riskiness of the portfolio (although the portfolios' levelised costs are higher).

Table 5.7 adds ALWRs to a portfolio of 70% CCGTs and 30% coal capacity: first replacing coal capacity, then replacing CCGTs, as in Figure 5.19. There is a dramatic reduction in *both* the levelised cost and the standard deviation of levelised cost with the replacement of coal units with ALWRs. Once coal is replaced, ALWRs can still reduce cost risk by replacing CCGTs, following the same path as in Figure 5.18. What Table 5.7 shows is that when the price of CO_2 is considered, coal-fired power plants are both expensive and risky going forward.

This analysis would suggest that the cost-risk-minimising path for minimising CO_2 emissions while maintaining competitive electricity prices in an electricity system of 12,000 MW would be, first, to replace coal units (that have not already been replaced with natural gas units) with nuclear units, then to continue to replace natural gas units with nuclear power units, until a trade-off is achieved between the long-run stability of nuclear power costs and the short-run cheapness of natural gas – that is, to replace CCGTs with nuclear units as the price of natural gas rises, for example in the United States to equilibrium international natural gas prices and the imposition of the social costs of CO_2.

5.6 Summary and conclusions

This book has extended the LCOE literature by showing that there is no single levelised cost for any technology, but a probability distribution of levelised costs, which is a function of underlying randomly distributed cost drivers and assumed parameters. It has modelled these probability distributions for ALWRs, SMRs, CCGTs and coal-fired steam-electric units with advanced pollution control equipment. To limit complexity, this analysis has restricted the class of probability densities to those that have closed-form distribution functions for inputs, and to those in the 'normal family' for intermediate and final outputs. After empirically estimating these probability densities, it has simulated levelised costs of portfolios of base-load generating assets.

The book began by introducing the nuclear power industry in a historical and country-by-country context. It defined nuclear energy systems as combinations of (a) heat-producing nuclear reactors with various moderators and coolants, coupled with various heat-to-electricity conversion technologies, and (b) nuclear fuel cycles using natural uranium, enriched uranium, and uranium oxide mixed with recycled plutonium oxide (as discussed in Chapter 4, Appendix 4A). The uranium market was described at length, providing price data that were used in Chapter 4 to model the probability distributions of fuel costs for ALWRs and SMRs using exponential, extreme value and lognormal density functions.

Chapter 2 placed these nuclear energy systems in their regulatory context, including safety regulators, financial regulators, tariff regulators, market regulators, and national, regional and local environmental regulators. Each regulator introduces uncertainty into the process of generating and selling electricity. These risks and uncertainties have driven up the cost of capital for new nuclear power, as discussed in Chapter 3, Appendix 3A (on risk premiums) and Appendix 3B (on insurance premiums), leading to failures to secure financing for all low-carbon, high-capital-intensity electricity generators, including solar, wind and nuclear energy systems, in nations with competitive procurement and competitive electricity markets. Only where there is active government involvement aiming to overcome the short-term interests of financiers do low-carbon, high-capital electricity generators operate. Chapter 2, Appendix 2A, investigated the impact of government incentive programmes on the cost of capital facing large (relative to the financial size of the owner-operator) NPPs.

Chapter 3 began to quantify the total capital construction costs for these large nuclear generators. The average capital cost of a nuclear generating station is a function of several uncertain variables: the overnight cost (particularly for FOAK units with underdeveloped component supply chains), modelled in Chapter 5 with a maximum extreme value density of data from regulatory proceedings in the United States; the construction lead time (particularly for FOAK units with inexperienced contractors), modelled in Chapter 5 with an exponential density of data from East Asia; and after-commercial-operation capacity factors, modelled with a minimum extreme value density with data from currently operating NPPs.

Chapter 3, Appendix 3A, discussed the normal and lognormal distributions, and showed how they could be used to model contingency of the overnight cost of new nuclear as a function of the maturity of the cost estimate, the expected accuracy of the estimate, the confidence of the decision maker that the final cost would be within this accuracy range and the risk aversion of the decision maker towards the confidence in the accuracy range at a given stage of cost estimation. In general, for both normal and lognormal cost estimate distributions, overnight cost contingency can be modelled as a function of the standard deviation of its cost estimate, ignoring higher order moments, such as skewness and kurtosis.

This result was applied in Chapter 5 to estimate possible contingencies for the distribution of the levelised cost estimate for new nuclear, CCGTs and pollution-controlled coal-fired power plants. Chapter 3, Appendix 3A, also introduced modern finance theory and the importance of diversification in a portfolio of assets, as shown in the capital asset pricing model (CAPM), with parameters estimated with ordinary least squares (OLS). Chapter 3, Appendix 3B, used a logistic model to estimate a reasonable insurance premium for off-site potential losses from an NPP accident, such as those at Three Mile Island (TMI) in March 1979, Chernobyl in April 1986 and Fukushima-Daiichi in March 2011.

This insurance premium entered into the calculation of variable costs for fuel and O&M in Chapter 4. That chapter discussed the differences between the cost of fuel and O&M for ALWRs and SMRs. Using OLS techniques introduced in Chapter 3, Appendix 3A, with a semi-logarithmic model and a normally distributed error term, labour at the two types of plants was estimated and simulated. Operations and maintenance costs were assumed to be a multiplicative function of labour expenses. Simulated O&M costs were approximately normal. The chapter concluded with a discussion of the deterministic LCOE for NPPs and the importance of the cost of capital in calculated levelised costs: For each unit percentage increase in the WACC, the levelised cost increases by about 9%. Chapter 5 compared these levelised costs with those of natural gas and coal-fired power plants.

Although there are other probability densities and distributions with which to model prices and quantities, and those chosen here could bias the results, the strategy was to be as transparent as possible, so that readers could reproduce the method and change the assumptions. As stated at the outset, this analysis is meant to be illustrative rather than demonstrative. There is no 'true' levelised cost, or risk-adjusted levelised cost; rather, there are cost distributions, and conclusions depend on the decision makers' aversions to different types of risk, including input cost risk, price risk, construction completion risk, climate change risk, etc. Following Popper's *Logic of Scientific Discovery* (1959), this analysis has not been written to prove anything, but to help readers to critically review electricity-generation cost estimates – and particularly to question myopic point estimates.

In a portfolio of fossil-fired assets, Chapter 5 found that the diversity in the combination of half natural gas and half coal assets minimises the standard deviation of levelised cost. (However, this did not yield the lowest risk-adjusted levelised cost.) This result is a function of two facts: (a) that the LCOE for natural gas (with or without carbon prices) is less than the cost of coal; and (b) that the price of natural gas is not highly correlated with the price of coal, hence coal helps to stabilise the LCOE during price spikes in the cost of natural gas and bottlenecks in natural gas transmission.

Further, because there is little cost covariance between fossil-fired generators and NPPs, adding nuclear reduces the standard deviation of the levelised cost of a fossil portfolio and, as risk aversion increases, the role of new nuclear in generation portfolios becomes more valuable. To reduce the unknowns associated with carbon emissions and to reduce the volatility of electricity prices, electric utilities (and their investors and financiers) should consider adding new nuclear power to their unnaturally gas-heavy (CH_4 and CO_2) generating assets, as shown in Section 5.5.

Finally, the analysis showed that the cost-risk-reducing path for minimising electricity cost risk and CO_2 emissions, while maintaining competitive electricity prices in a medium-sized electricity system, would be, first, to replace coal units with nuclear units, then to replace natural gas units with nuclear units as the price of natural gas rises. Future research will consider portfolios with renewable assets. However, the problem inherent to adding renewables to the mix is their output variability and 'must-run' status; hence a much more complex electricity dispatch model would be required than that implied here. (On the problem of modelling variable renewables, see NEA, 2012, and IEA and NEA, 2015.)

Encouraging NPP construction to achieve clean emissions standards should therefore focus on reducing the cost of capital and the risks of building new nuclear. This would reduce the capital cost of nuclear power, as discussed in Chapter 3, making nuclear power more competitive. Reducing the cost of construction and the variability in construction lead time is the responsibility of the builder ('on time and on budget'), the component supplier (to deliver well-designed, well-built and well-documented inputs), the owner (by diversifying generating assets), the operator (with high safety and reliability), the national government (for example by creating programmes to overcome capital market failures) and investors (who must become familiar with new nuclear technology). With these forces aligned, in the next two decades, the world could rapidly reduce greenhouse gas emissions.

To reiterate, the primary conclusions of this analysis are as follows.

- Point estimates of the LCOE are not credible; only cost distributions are reasonable.
- The history of the nuclear power industry has been influenced by a tension between the peaceful and non-peaceful uses of nuclear technology; hence non-proliferation must always be kept in mind when choosing among nuclear energy systems.
- The electricity market regime influences the choice of generating technology and the level of carbon emissions; *no* NPPs are being built by non-subsidised merchant investors.
- The costs of capital vary greatly across regulatory regimes; regulatory uncertainty always increases the WACC.

- Most cost estimates, while claiming to be estimated for FOAK plants, should be considered NOAK estimates; learning rates should increase these NOAK estimates to FOAK estimates – not the reverse.
- Appropriate contingencies for overnight costs are a function of the uncertainty of the cost estimate, as measured by its maturity, its accuracy range, the confidence of the decision makers that the actual cost will be in that range and the risk aversion of those decision makers.
- The cost of new ALWRs should be adjusted in the US EIA's NEMS model to yield a more realistic forecast of new nuclear capacity in the United States.
- In the nuclear power industry, size matters: the size of the plant in the transmission grid; the size of the investment to be financed; the size of the owner-operator; and the size of the order books of the component suppliers.
- A 1% (100 basis points) increase in the cost of capital increases the levelised cost of new nuclear by almost 10%.
- An accident at one NPP influences the fixed and variable costs, and capacity factors, at all NPPs; safety culture increases reliability, and reliability increases profitability – that is, a safe plant can be a profitable plant.
- Because of regulatory requirements, an NPP of any size requires approximately 250 people to provide security, quality assurance, health physics, emergency preparedness, engineering, instrumentation and control maintenance, government and public relations, and administration.
- The cost of used nuclear fuel reprocessing for incumbents is vastly different from the cost for new entrants, and is very much dependent on the capacity factor of the reprocessing facility.
- The cost competitiveness of mixed oxide (MOX) fuels requires prices of uranium that are at least as high as they have ever been in the spot market.
- Electricity-generating portfolio risk diminishes with diversity as a function of the negative correlation between the cash flows of a portfolio's assets.
- Nuclear power plant cash flows have little correlation with fossil-fuel plant cash flows; hence they add diversity to carbon-based and non-carbon-based electricity systems.
- To reduce the unknowns associated with carbon emissions and to reduce the volatility of electricity prices, electric utilities should consider adding new nuclear power to their generating portfolios.

In closing, this book has shown that estimates of the cost of generating electricity are best represented by probability distributions, not deterministic point estimates, or ranges of them. It has presented this approach in a systematic manner so that readers, particularly managers, investors and decision makers, can evaluate risky choices regarding electricity asset portfolios as climate changes become apparent. To paraphrase President Kennedy's address to the 18th General Assembly of the United Nations on 20 September 1963: today's electricity capacity providers have the power to create the best portfolios of generators in the history of the world *and* to make them sustainable for all future generations.

References

Awerbuch, S., and Berger, M. 2003. 'Applying portfolio theory to EU electricity planning and policy-making', IEA/EET Working Paper EET/2003/03. Available online at www.awerbuch.com/shimonpages/shimondocs/iea-portfolio.pdf

Federal Reserve Bank of St. Louis. 2014. *FRED Economic Data: Natural Gas Price, Henry Hub, LA.* Available online at http://research.stlouisfed.org/fred2/series/GASPRICE/downloaddata?cid=98

Hogue, M. 2012. 'A review of the costs of nuclear power generation', Bureau of Economic and Business Research Working Paper. Available online at http://bebr.business.utah.edu/sites/bebr/Documents/studies/Nuclear_Report_Final_Web_7Mar2012.pdf

International Energy Agency (IEA) and Nuclear Energy Agency (NEA). 2015. *Projected Costs of Generating Electricity: 2015 Update.* Paris: OECD.

Massachusetts Institute of Technology (MIT). 2009. *The Future of Nuclear Power: An Interdisciplinary Study – Update.* Available online at http://web.mit.edu/nuclearpower/pdf/nuclearpower-update2009.pdf

Nordhaus, W. D. 2011. 'Estimates of the social cost of carbon: Background and results from the RICE-2011 model', Cowles Foundation Discussion Paper No. 1826. Available online at www.econ.yale.edu/~nordhaus/homepage/documents/CFDP1826.pdf

Nuclear Energy Agency (NEA). 2012. *Nuclear Energy and Renewables: System Effects in Low-Carbon Electricity Systems.* Available online at www.oecd-nea.org/ndd/pubs/2012/7056-system-effects.pdf

Palisade. 2015. *@RISK: Advanced Risk Analysis using Monte Carlo Simulation*, v. 6.0. Available online at www.palisade.com/risk/

Popper, K. 1959. *Logic of Scientific Discovery.* London: Routledge.

Roques, F., Newbery, D., and Nuttall, W. 2006. 'Fuel mix diversification in liberalised electricity markets: A mean-variance portfolio theory approach', European University Institute Working Paper EUI RSCAS 2006/33. Available online at www.eprg.group.cam.ac.uk/wp-content/uploads/2014/01/eprg0626.pdf

Roques, F., Newbery, D., Nuttall, W. D., de Neufville, R., and Connors, S. 2006. 'Nuclear power a hedge against uncertain gas and carbon prices?', *Energy Journal*, 27 (4): 1–24.

Rothwell, G. 1990. 'Utilization and service: Decomposing nuclear reactor capacity factors', *Resources and Energy*, 12: 215–229.

Rothwell, G. 2006. 'A real options approach to evaluating new nuclear power plants', *Energy Journal*, 27(1): 37–54.

Rothwell, G., and Ganda, F. 2014. 'Electricity generating portfolios with small modular reactors', Working Paper. Available online at www.energy.gov/sites/prod/files/2014/06/f16/Electricity%20Generating%20Portfolios%20with%20SMRs.pdf

Rothwell, G., Wood, T., Daly, D., and Weimer, M. 2014. 'Sustainability of light water reactor fuel cycles', *Energy Policy*, 72(S1): S16–S23.

US Energy Information Administration (US EIA). 2007. *Form FERC–423: Monthly cost and quality of fuels for electric plants data, 1972–2007*. Available online at www.eia.gov/cneaf/electricity/page/ferc423.html

US Energy Information Administration (US EIA). 2013. *The Electricity Market Module of the National Energy Modeling System: Model Documentation Report*, DOE-EIA-M068 (2013). Available online at www.eia.gov/forecasts/aeo/nems/documentation/electricity/pdf/m068(2013).pdf

US Energy Information Administration (US EIA). 2014a. *Annual Energy Outlook 2014*, DOE/EIA–0383(2014). Available online at www.eia.gov/forecasts/aeo/

US Energy Information Administration (US EIA). 2014b. *Assumptions to the Annual Energy Outlook 2014*, DOE/EIA–0554(2014). Available online at www.eia.gov/forecasts/aeo/assumptions/

US Energy Information Administration (US EIA). 2014c. *State Energy Data System (SEDS): 2013 Updates by Energy Source*. Available online at www.eia.gov/state/seds/seds-data-fuel.cfm?sid=US

US Energy Information Administration (US EIA). 2014d. *U.S. nuclear generation and generating capacity*. Available online at www.eia.gov/nuclear/generation/index.html

US Energy Information Administration (US EIA). 2014e. *Capacity factors for utility scale generators primarily using fossil fuels*. Available online at www.eia.gov/electricity/monthly/epm_table_grapher.cfm?t=epmt_6_07_a

US Energy Information Administration (US EIA). 2015a. *Monthly U.S. natural gas wellhead price*. Available online at www.eia.gov/dnav/ng/hist/n9190us3m.htm

US Energy Information Administration (US EIA). 2015b. *Electric Power Monthly*. Available online at www.eia.gov/electricity/monthly/pdf/epm.pdf

US Energy Information Administration (US EIA). 2015c. *Electricity: Detailed state data*. Available online at www.eia.gov/electricity/data/state/

US Nuclear Regulatory Commission (US NRC). 1995. *Licensed Operating Reactors: Status Summary Report, Data as of 12–31–94*, NUREG–0020. Available online at www.iaea.org/inis/collection/NCLCollectionStore/_Public/26/060/26060116.pdf

Williams, J. 2015. *Natural gas spot prices: Henry hub*. Available online at http://www.wtrg.com/daily/oilandgasspot.html

Index

Note: Tables are indicated in bold; figures are in italic. All acts of legislation listed are U.S.